Beyond the
Border War

New Perspectives on Southern Africa's
Late-Cold War Conflicts

Beyond the
Border War

New Perspectives on Southern Africa's
Late-Cold War Conflicts

Edited by
Gary Baines & Peter Vale

© 2008 University of South Africa

First edition, first impression

ISBN 978-1-86888-456-8

Published by Unisa Press
University of South Africa
P O Box 392, 0003 UNISA

Book Designer: Thea Venter
Editor: Gail Malcomson
Typesetting: Karen Graphics
Printer: Interpak

Contents

List of figures

Notes on contributors

Gary Baines is Associate Professor in the History Department, Rhodes University, Grahamstown, South Africa. He holds a Masters degree from Rhodes University and a PhD from the University of Cape Town. He has published a monograph and numerous articles on the history of Port Elizabeth. His research interests in South African history and culture include film, photography, literature and music. This project is a result of a particular interest in the representations of war and veterans.

Karen Batley is a graduate of the universities of Cape Town, Pretoria and Unisa. She was Associate Professor in the Department of English at Unisa, and is now an independent editor and freelance publisher. She has published a collection of soldiers' writing on the Border/Angolan War and has lectured and written regularly on this material.

Heike Becker is Associate Professor of Anthropology at the University of the Western Cape. Formerly a researcher and lecturer at the University of Namibia, she is the author of *Namibian Women's Movement 1980 to 1992: From Anti-colonial Resistance to Reconstruction* and an associate editor of *Women Writing Africa: The Southern Region.* Her work on gender in Namibian culture and history has appeared in, among others, the *Journal of Southern African Studies* and *History & Anthropology.* She currently works on memory and remembrance in northern Namibia, and on transformations of public culture and public anthropology in southern Africa.

Daniel Conway BA (HONS) Exeter, MSc (Bristol), PhD (Rhodes) is a Lecturer in Politics at Loughborough University. His research on gender and war resistance in apartheid South Africa was developed while he was an Economic and Social Research Council (ESRC) Post-Doctoral Fellow in the Department of Politics, University of Bristol.

Dylan Craig was awarded his MA in Historical Studies by the University of Cape Town. He taught at Rhodes University and the University of Cape Town in 2003 and 2004, and is currently pursuing his PhD in International Relations at the School of International Service of American University in Washington, D.C. His primary research interests are African military history, warfare as a socio-political process, and the emerging security hegemony in Africa after the Cold War.

Edgar J. Dosman was educated at the universities of Saskatchewan, Munich, Oxford and Harvard where he received a PhD in Government. Currently Senior Research Fellow and Professor in the Department of Political Science at York University in Toronto, he was the founding Executive Director of FOCAL (Canadian Foundation of the Americas) in 1990. A frequent writer and commentator on international affairs, he is currently completing a book on Cuba and the War in Angola, 1975–1991.

Michael Drewett is a senior lecturer in the Department of Sociology at Rhodes University. He teaches courses in gender and popular culture at undergraduate and postgraduate level. He has recently completed his PhD on the censorship of popular music in South Africa in the 1980s. He has written various locally and internationally published articles on South African popular music and popular culture more generally, including popular culture and the military in South Africa during the apartheid era. He has recently produced a documentary dealing with an instance of South African music censorship for the Danish Film Institute and Freemuse.

Sasha Gear is a senior researcher at the Centre for the Study of Violence and Reconciliation (CSVR) in Johannesburg. As part of the CSVR's Violence and Transition Project she conducted some of the first post-1994, in-depth research with former soldiers from across apartheid-era South Africa's political divides, seeking to understand their situations and experiences in the context of transition. While her current focus is sexual violence in South African men's prisons, she retains a keen interest in ex-combatant issues.

Robert Gordon has taught and worked in many parts of the world including Papua New Guinea, South Africa and Lesotho, but keeps on returning to Namibia, his birthplace. He is the author or editor of some ten books including *The Bushman Myth*, *Picturing Bushmen*, *Law and Order in the New Guinea Highlands* and *Tarzan Was an Eco-Tourist* (forthcoming).

Justine Hunter is Project Manager of the Public Dialogue Centre at the Namibia Institute for Democracy (NID) in Windhoek. She holds a Masters degree in Political Science, History and Anthropology from Rheinische-Friedrich Wilhelm University, Bonn, Germany and a PhD in Political Science from Albert-Ludwigs-University, Freiburg i.Br., Germany. Her PhD thesis on *The Politics of Memory and Forgetting in Independent Namibia: Dealing with Gross Human Rights Abuses Committed During the Era of Armed Liberation Struggle, 1966–1989* is to be published (in German). Her other publications include *Who Should Own the Land? Analyses and Views on Land Reform and the Land Question in Namibia and southern Africa* (Windhoek: NID, 2004).

Wendy Morris holds a Masters degree in Visual Arts from Unisa and is currently a PhD candidate in Visual Arts at the Catholic University of Leuven, Belgium. She works in the medium of drawn film and has produced three short works which investigate how episodes in the Belgian past are remembered.

Mathilde Rogez is a former student of the École Normale Supérieure (ENS Ulm, Paris), where she set up a seminar on postcolonial literatures three years ago. She is writing her PhD on the notion of frontier in Mark Behr and J. M. Coetzee's fiction. She currently holds the position of Research Fellow at the University of Paris X-Nanterre.

Monica Popescu is Assistant Professor of English at McGill University, Montreal. Her research focuses on contemporary South African literature and postcolonial theory, especially at the intersection with post-communist studies. She has published articles on cultural translation in South Africa, liminality and hybridity, gender and nationalism, as well as a book entitled *The Politics of Violence in Post-communist Films*.

Henriette Roos is Professor and Head of the Department of Afrikaans at Unisa. Her fields of interest include Narrative Fiction in Afrikaans, Dutch and English South African Literature. Some of her most recent publications include essays on the Afrikaans author Karel Schoeman, the representation of Islam in South African literature, and Afrikaans Literary Prose of the Twentieth Century. She has also contributed items on 'Border' literature to popular magazines.

Christopher Saunders is Professor in the Historical Studies Department, University of Cape Town (UCT). Educated at Oxford, he has taught at UCT since 1970, and written on a wide range of topics in the history of southern Africa. One of his recent interests is the way in which Namibia moved towards independence from the 1970s to 1990.

Peter Vale is the Nelson Mandela Chair of Politics at Rhodes University. Previously, he was Senior Professor in the School of Government at the University of Western Cape. At the same institution he served as Vice-Rector and Deputy Vice-Chancellor for Academic Affairs (1998–2001), as Professor of Southern African Studies (1990–1998), and as sometime Professor of Social Theory. He has published over 200 academic pieces. His most recent book *Security and Politics in South Africa: The Regional Dimension* was published in 2003 by UCT Press. Vale, who is an elected Member of the Academy of Sciences of South Africa, was the recipient of the International Medal of the University of Utrecht in 2004.

Elaine Windrich is a research scholar in African Studies at Stanford University. Her field of specialisation is the politics of southern Africa. She has written several books on Zimbabwe, including *The Rhodesian Problem* (Routledge, 1975), *Britain and the Politics of Rhodesian Independence* (Croom Helm, 1978) and *The Mass Media in the Struggle for Zimbabwe* (Mambo Press, 1981); as well as *The Cold War Guerrilla: Jonas Savimbi, the US Media and the Angolan War* (Greenwood Publishers, 1992) and the chapter on Angola in *Africa's Media Image* edited by Beverly Hawk (Praeger, 1992). She has taught at Stanford and several other universities in the US and was an adviser on Africa for the Labour Party and a consultant on the media for the Zimbabwe government in the early 1980s.

Glossary of terms, abreviations and acronyms

AK47	Russian-designed and manufactured assault rifle
ANC	African National Congress
APLA	Azanian People's Liberation Army, the PAC's armed wing
BWSM	Breaking the Wall of Silence Movement, a Namibian NGO that publicises the detainee issue
Casevac	Casualty evacuation
Casspir	An acronym of SAP (South African Police) and CSIR (Council for Scientific and Industrial Research) who collaborated to develop this armoured personnel carrier that is able to withstand mine blasts
CCB	Civil Co-operation Bureau
CCN	Council of Churches in Namibia
CEO	chief executive officer
CIA	Central Intelligence Agency (of the US)
CO	conscientious objector
COIN	counterinsurgency
Cuca	a small shop found in Namibian homesteads named after a Portuguese-Angolan beer
Cut line	a cleared strip or DMZ (see below) that served as a boundary between Namibia and Angola
DRC	Dutch Reformed Church
DRPs	Demobilisation, Re-integration Programmes
DSM	Diagnostic Statistical Manual, the US medical fraternity's bible
DMZ	Demilitarised zone where all peoples are treated as the enemy
EEC	End Conscription Campaign
EKD	Evangelische Kirche Deutschlands (Evangelical Church of Germany)
EU	European Union
FAPLA	Popular Armed Forces for the Liberation of Angola – armed forces of the MPLA (see below) government in Angola
Flossie	C130 Hercules transport aircraft
G5/G6	artillery cannon manufactured by Denel to combat the Russian-built Stalin organ

ICRC	International Committee of the Red Cross
INF	Inter-mediate range Nuclear Force
Koevoet	Afrikaans for 'crowbar'. Official name for the unit was the South West African Police Counter-insurgency (SWAPOLCOIN)
LAC	Legal Assistance Centre, a Namibian NGO
LWF	Lutheran World Foundation
MI	Military Intelligence
MiG	Russian-built Mikojam and Gurevich fighter-interceptor aircraft
MK	Umkhonto we Sizwe ('Spear of the Nation'), the ANC's armed wing
MOTH	The Memorable Order of the Tin Hats, an ex-servicemen's association
MNR	Mozambique National Resistance, front organisation established by the Smith regime and later sponsored by South Africa
MPLA	Popular Movement for the Liberation of Angola
NGK	Nederduitse Gereformeerde Kerk (Dutch Reformed Church)
NIS	National Intelligence Service
NP	National Party, the ruling party in South Africa from 1948 to 1994
NSHR	National Society for Human Rights, a Namibian NGO
NSMS	National Security Management System, the network that exercised executive control of South Africa during the Presidency of P.W. Botha
NCO	Non-Commissioned Officer
NGO	non-governmental organisation
PAC	Pan Africanist Congress
Panga	a large, heavy, very sharp, sword-like weapon
PCC	Political Consultative Council, a Namibian pressure group
PCN	Parents' Committee of Namibia, a Namibian pressure group
PLAN	People's Liberation Army of Namibia, SWAPO's armed wing
POWs	prisoners of war
PTSD	post-traumatic stress disorder
R1/4	South African 7,62 mm calibre rifle modelled on the Belgian FN
Ratel	Afrikaans for 'badger'. A personnel carrier fitted with a 20 mm or 90 mm weapon
Recces	members of the SADF's reconnaissance or special forces
RENAMO	an alternative acronym for MNR
RPG	Russian-designed shoulder-mounted rocket launcher that fires armour-piercing 85 mm rounds
SAAF	South African Air Force
SABC	South African Broadcasting Corporation
SADF	South African Defence Force
SANDF	South African National Defence Force

SAP	South African Police
SCF	Southern Cross Fund
SWA	South West Africa, now called Namibia
SWAPO	South West Africa People's Organization
SWAPOL	South West African Police
SWATF	South West African Territory Force
TRC	Truth and Reconciliation Commission of South Africa
UDF	United Democratic Front
UDI	Unilateral Declaration of Independence
UK	United Kingdom
UN	United Nations
UNITA	National Union for the Total Independence of Angola
UNMD	United Nations Mission on Detainees
UNSC	United Nations Security Council
UNTAG	United Nations Transitional Assistance Group
US	United States of America
USAF	United States Air Force
WCC	World Council of Churches

Preface

More than anything, providence explains why my name appears on the cover of this timely collection. My friend and co-editor, Gary Baines, conceived of the entire project and he has done all the work – he canvassed the chapters, he corresponded with the contributors, he negotiated with the publisher, and he has edited each contribution – he has also done much more besides. So, this Preface begins as it will end, with thanks to Gary Baines.

On the night the Berlin Wall came down I was in Lusaka, Zambia; with my German hosts – the three of us each a child of the Cold War – we talked until the early hours about a better world that would surely follow. However, as I write these words, land-mines in Angola and Mozambique continue to take the lives and limbs of children born long after that long night of talk. And as we look out at the challenges associated with life in southern Africa in this, the early Twenty-First Century, we might ask this counter-factual question: how many of the young men and women who lost their lives as the idea of a Cold War rode rough-shod over the region's people and pastures could have contributed to their solution?

Understanding the Cold War, let alone its legacy – in southern Africa and elsewhere – is a dynamic intellectual process. Because it so obviously overlaps the formal disciplinary boundaries of Politics, of International Relations and of History, Cold War Studies – as many now call it – is richly inter-disciplinary. But the chapters in this book suggest how Cold War Studies is endlessly augmented by other academic disciplines, too: Anthropology, Cultural Studies, Literature, Psychology and many more.

Although each of the contributing writers has chosen a particular disciplinary lens as a point of analytical entry, the collection reflects the 'present' in which all the writers and those who will read this book live. Differently put, our individual and collective understanding of the Cold War and southern Africa cannot be separated from the time, space and place we currently occupy. Of course, this is Benedetti Croce's great formulation of the historian's craft but, with every passing day, readers and writers know that this is the delight – not the damnation – of the luxurious Humanities.

This book does not mark the end of efforts by Southern Africans to explain and understand the Cold War – both Early and Late – and their region. It is the beginning of another long conversation; because this is so, readers will quickly discover that these writers have more – no, much more – to say on this topic.

xviii

But, for now, and for bringing readers and writers to the ideas between these immediate covers, our thanks go to the extraordinary efforts of Gary Baines.

Peter Vale, FRSSAf, MASSAf
NELSON MANDELA PROFESSOR OF POLITICS
Rhodes University

Acknowledgements

While not wishing to engage in mutual back slapping, I wish to thank Peter Vale who gave his unqualified support to the project and helped me to bring it to completion. In particular, he prodded me to make the tough decisions that editors are called upon to make in finalising the contents of such collected volumes. I would also like to thank the contributors to this book for their commitment to the project and their patience during the process of turning a vague proposal into a publication.

I wish to express my appreciation to the Unisa Press team: Sharon Boshoff, Gail Malcomson and Thea Venter in enabling me to realise this project in such an efficient manner.

I wish to thank Justine Hunter and Dudley Baines for providing the photographs that were used to create the images to illustrate the cover. My thanks, too, to the Rhodes University Graphic Services Unit for the map.

Every effort has been made by the contributors to trace the copyright owners of images and song lyrics referenced in this book. Most of these are acknowledged in the text. But in a few instances it has not been possible to ascertain or trace the owners. Where such ownership can be established, the publishers are prepared to make good this omission in future editions of this volume.

Gary Baines

Chapter 1

Introduction: Challenging the Boundaries, Breaking the Silences

Gary Baines

More than 15 years have passed since South Africa withdrew its armed forces from Angola and agreed to a negotiated settlement based on United Nations Security Council (UNSC) Resolution 435 for Namibia, the Cold War ended, and the liberation movements suspended the armed struggle against the apartheid regime. This chain of events brought an end to the late Cold War conflicts in southern Africa that had caused widespread death and destruction and ruptured the region's stability. Yet scant attention has been paid to the convergence of these events and how they contributed to the political transition in South Africa.[1] Especially neglected has been the bearing of events in the region on the country's domestic changes and vice versa. For instance, the Report of the Truth and Reconciliation Commission (TRC) devoted a single chapter of its seven-volume report to events beyond South Africa's borders.[2] Researchers have been commissioned by the TRC and the legal teams involved in investigating these events, but scholars have not followed their lead in any systematic way whatsoever. The records of the apartheid regime have not readily yielded their secrets to scholars in part because its functionaries destroyed large volumes of top secret files, but also because gaining access to the military archives involves a lengthy procedure of declassification. Yet, ironically, it is access to records from the United States of America (US) and Cuba that has afforded a better understanding of why and how South Africa's white minority regime waged war in the context of the changing dynamics of the Cold War.[3] This volume takes such work as a point of departure for examining the place of these conflicts in public consciousness and cultural memory.

The editors and the contributors bring their own particular concerns to the project. Certain contributors employ fairly conventional historical approaches to the military, political, ideological and diplomatic aspects of the region's wars from the vantage point of post-apartheid retrospection. A few combine such approaches with discourse and/or textual analysis. Some approach the subject using the tools of cultural and literary studies so as to explore how the wars were represented in, *inter alia*, literature, music, visual media and art exhibits. Others again place their work within the burgeoning field of memory studies that has developed in relation to war and other traumatic events and ask how the war has been remembered by participants, as well as by the general public. And still others situate their work within the paradigm of victimology studies and explore how ex-soldiers have adapted to civilian life during the political transition in South Africa. Notwithstanding the variety of approaches employed by contributors to this volume, the chapters assembled here evince an interest in certain common themes, especially with regard to borders/frontiers and secrets/silences. This is not as a result of the editors attempting to impose an artificial unity on the volume's contents. Rather, the attention paid to these issues suggests both current pre-occupations and new directions which the study of South Africa's late Cold War conflicts is likely to follow.

Challenging the boundaries

Realist security discourse imagines a world in which territorially bounded nation states appear to be the only natural political units. The concept of a 'bounded state' is premised on the realist understanding of national sovereignty that privileges the state as the primary actor in politics and recognises the right of such states to exert authority within a specific geographical space by force or aggression, if necessary. As Charles Tilly's famous dictum has it: 'States make war, and war makes the state.[4] Apartheid South Africa can be described as a 'bounded state' in that it sought to fix and rigorously enforce boundaries between 'insiders' and 'outsiders'.[5] These fault lines were not necessarily defined in racial and ethnic terms. Violence was not directed indiscriminately against all members of an 'out-group' (as in fascist states) but mainly against political opponents.[6] My co-editor, Peter Vale, holds that realist security discourse informs the prevalent understanding of South Africa's role in the region. His critique of this paradigm demonstrates that sovereignty in southern Africa is not entirely stable.[7] This is not to say that post-colonial southern Africa is merely a geographical expression or a balkanised entity. Rather, it is to suggest that the configuration of the region's states is contingent and that the region's borders are more incidental than real.[8] Vale's critique should not be construed as lamenting the loss of national sovereignty in an era of accelerating globalisation (as the opening of frontiers in favour of the rich and the powerful is now called). For he advocates the diminution of the power of the state run by a ruling elite in order to facilitate a people- rather than a state-centred solution to the region's structural developmental problems. In other words, Vale prioritises human above state security in a region which historically has had relatively fluid frontiers.

The boundaries of present-day South Africa were established by the 1910 Act of Union. The Union of South Africa was the first in a community of unequal states in the region.[9] The Act made provision for South Africa to incorporate neighbouring states in a greater South Africa.

The Union Defence Force's occupation of German South West Africa in 1914 in accordance with the wishes of the Western Allies resulted in South Africa administering South West Africa (SWA) as a mandate on behalf of the League of Nations. The mandate system was the brainchild of General Jan Smuts, South Africa's first international statesman and later Prime Minister. Smuts harboured imperialist ambitions and sought to incorporate southern Rhodesia into the Union, but was foiled by the white Rhodesians' misgivings about South Africa's intentions. Attempts by Smuts and successive South African premiers to incorporate the British protectorates of Basutoland, Bechuanaland and Swaziland into the Union floundered in the face of imperial objections and the rising tide of African nationalism. Suspicions of South Africa's quest for regional hegemony intensified after the country became a republic outside of the British Commonwealth in 1961. The apartheid state's arbitrary demarcation of boundaries so as to create nominally-sovereign polities ('homelands' or Bantustans) for African ethnic groups suggests that there was nothing sacrosanct about the borders of southern Africa as far as the architects of grand apartheid were concerned. SWA continued to be administered as South Africa's 'fifth province' after the United Nations terminated its mandate in 1966. Apart from introducing 'homelands' in SWA, the apartheid state sought to retain control of the Walvis Bay enclave and to promote the secession of the Caprivi Strip. According to the apartheid apologist/ publicist, Eschel Rhoodie, SWA was the last frontier in Africa.[10]

From behind its corrugated iron curtain, South Africa sought to safeguard its borders against what it viewed as the 'total onslaught': the threat of African nationalism aided and abetted by Soviet communism. The assignment of South African Police (SAP) forces to help shore up Ian Smith's minority regime in Rhodesia was short lived and did little to forestall black majority rule in South Africa's northern neighbour. Nor did pre-emptive actions in the Portuguese colonies of Angola and Mozambique prevent the transfer of power to liberation movements in these countries. Meanwhile, Namibia became a testing ground for the deployment of first SAP, and then from 1973, South African Defence Force (SADF) units. The apartheid regime actually waged war on many fronts, especially against states in the region that supported the liberation movements. Apart from conducting cross-border raids, periodical incursions into neighbouring states, and even extensive military campaigns on foreign soil, the state sought to prevent the infiltration of its borders – in both directions – by Umkhonto we Sizwe (MK) and Azanian People's Liberation Army (APLA) recruits to the frontline states and cadres returning to the home front. Despite planting devices such as landmines and patrolling the infiltration routes, South Africa's borders proved too extensive and too porous to monitor effectively. The permeability of its borders, no less than South Africa's destabilisation of the region, served as indicators of the existence of open frontiers where political authority was still contested.

Makeshift borders were especially evident in northern Namibia and Angola. Both the SADF and its enemies created borders where none had existed previously. The SADF initially occupied a region north of an imaginary line through Namibia that demarcated the southern perimeter of the 'operational area'. Then they cleared and patrolled a strip of land between the Kunene and Okavango rivers known as the 'cut line' which was declared a demilitarised or free-fire zone. This meant that anyone crossing the 'cut line' could be fired upon without warning. Following its withdrawal from southern Angola in 1979, the SADF continued supporting and supplying its proxy, the National Union for the Total Independence of Angola (UNITA). Aware of the SADF's air superiority, the Popular Armed Forces for the Liberation of Angola (FAPLA) and its Cuban allies constructed the defensive Namibé-Lubango-Menongue line approximately 250 kilometres north of the Namibian border.[11] The Cubans did not venture southwards until the situation changed in 1988 when they deployed mobile air-defence systems and MiG-23 fighter planes in support of their augmented ground forces.[12] The Cuban challenge to the SADF's air superiority broke the deadlock on the battlefield in southern Angola and forced the SADF troops to beat a hasty retreat to the Namibian border. In short, the balance of power and the battle lines in Angola were contingent upon access to sophisticated technology and weaponry, as well as the air cover provided for the respective armies.

South Africa's white minority was obsessed with security largely because the apartheid state not only identified communism as the major threat to its national interests, but also created a host of enemies by defining itself in contradistinction to 'the outside world'. In the face of South Africa's increasing isolation, the county's pariah status contributed to paranoia and a siege mentality. In Chapter Two, Vale shows how security discourse and the regional conflicts were framed by the binaries of the Cold War. However, South Africa's alignment with the West in the Cold War did not necessarily mean that it shared the same interests and values as its allies. In Chapter Three, Monica Popescu exposes the paradox that Afrikaner Nationalist ideology actually mirrored that of the Soviet Communist state – the very state declared 'public enemy number one' – in certain respects. Cold War ideology first inspired, and then legitimised, apartheid's security establishment. It also affected social organisation and shaped cultural forms. Popescu's reading of Mark Behr's *The Smell of Apples* ably inserts the crumbling apartheid edifice within the context of the dismantling of the Soviet Union and the collapse of communism.

In Chapter Four, Dylan Craig shows how the South African government subsidised the film industry and employed propaganda to reinforce ideological conformity. The government also sought to discredit its opponents by spreading disinformation. State functionaries such as bureaucrats, censors, policemen, and military personnel were tasked with keeping everyone and everything in check. So late-apartheid South Africa remained a relatively closed society. Although he does not employ the term 'bounded state', Craig's description of South Africa as a 'garrison society' at odds with the 'outside world' and at war with itself amounts to a state preoccupied with security. SADF troops were deployed in the townships in the mid-1980s to bolster the SAP presence and keep a lid on the insurrection. In terms of two successive declarations of a State of Emergency by the government, Casspirs patrolled the streets of townships that anti-apartheid forces were committed to making 'ungovernable'. The security forces were thus tasked to 'defend the suburbs from the townships',[13] or in Archbishop Desmond Tutu's words, to erect 'the border in our midst'.[14] The borders had shifted from a faraway operational area in northern Namibia/Angola to the soldiers' own back yards. In his short story 'Sappeur Fiza and the Cow' in *Forces' Favourites*, James Whyte has his protagonist remark:

> In those days they weren't sending soldiers into the townships. In those
> days the border was pretty much the border of the country. Now the border
> goes all over the place. Sometimes straight through families, which is, I
> suppose what civil war is all about.[15]

The country was torn apart in a cycle of revolutionary violence and state repression. In this climate, there developed, as Daniel Conway shows in Chapter Five, an increasing resistance to conscription and the ever-increasing demands of national service amongst school-leavers as well as to the ongoing camps for 'Dad's Army'. The End Conscription Campaign (ECC) articulated this disenchantment and questioned the necessity of the sacrifices that a cohort of young white men had to make to uphold the apartheid system. As a corollary, Michael Drewett reveals in Chapter Six how popular cultural forms were produced which subverted hegemonic political discourse, including the meaning of the border in public consciousness. This was exemplified by an ECC poster with a map of sites of conflagration in the country that asked rhetorically: 'Where's the Border Now?'[16] The border was clearly an unstable, fluid frontier and not necessarily a permanent fixture.

The term 'border' is polysemic; it has acquired a host of both literal and figurative meanings, and it has accumulated a host of connotations when used in association with the wars in southern Africa between the 1960s and 1980s. It has been used to describe natural or topographical features such as rivers, as well as man-made (colonial-cum-national) boundaries. It has also been used in a spatial sense to describe the so-called 'operational area' that straddled the Namibian and Angolan frontiers. Places on the border could be pinpointed by mapping co-ordinates during military operations, but landmarks could not be specified in communications to the home front. Conversely, messages aired on the radio request programme *Forces Favourites* had to make do with vague phrases such as 'somewhere on the border' so as to conceal the whereabouts of the soldier for whom the message was intended. In fact, such was the secretive nature of the war that those who sent such requests were not permitted to know the exact location of SADF soldiers serving on the border.

Metaphorically, the term 'border' evoked various shades of meaning that are evident in literary and popular cultural representations, some of which are teased out by contributors to this volume. Conway's 'border of credibility' suggests that the apartheid state's version of events stretched the truth to breaking point. The credibility gap was self evident not only to informed observers, but also to the SADF soldiers on the ground. For instance, as a conscript who fought in Angola in 1988, Clive Holt was well aware of the discrepancies between official statements about the war in Angola and what he witnessed first hand.[17] While some chose to believe the official li(n)e that the war in Angola ended in a stalemate and that the withdrawal from that country and Namibia was strategic, others were understandably sceptical of SADF statements and press releases. In a moment of dramatic irony in Behr's *The Smell of Apples*, SADF troops in Angola listen with incredulity to broadcasts of statements by a government spokesperson who denies the presence of South African soldiers in that country.[18] If the regime's version of reality was a web of disinformation and deliberate lies, then the soldiers' perceptions of reality were also compromised by their involvement in the fighting. Mathilde Rogez's phrase 'borderline cases' can be equated with rather cruder army terms like *bosbefok* (literally 'bush-fucked') or *bossies* that denote being out of touch with reality. These terms suggest the trope of liminality, of the permeable borderline between madness and sanity that has precedents in the literature of earlier wars.[19] While there is no evidence to show that the South African writers whom Rogez treats in Chapter Seven consciously borrowed from such works, the literature of the Border War certainly does have resonances with that of other wars, especially the one in Vietnam.[20]

All of the above meanings – and many more – of the term 'border' are apparent in the literature of the Border War surveyed by Henriette Roos in Chapter Eight. She introduces the Afrikaans term *grens* (border or frontier) which probably has acquired an even greater accretion of meanings than its English counterparts. This much is evident in the crop of fictional Afrikaans writings called *grensliteratuur* that appeared in the 1970s and 1980s wherein the frontier between the real and the imaginary was frequently traversed. Roos reveals that the fixation with the Border War was neither confined to this period nor to Afrikaans literature. As with certain authors, some artists who had no personal connection with the Border War were obviously affected by it and appropriated some of its themes. In Chapter Nine, Wendy Morris' discussion of the art exhibit titled *Memórias Íntimas Marcas* (Memory Intimacy Traces) shows how its features are transformed by artists who explore – or play with – the frontiers of memory and forgetting. Equally revealing are Morris' own self-reflective memories of growing up in apartheid South Africa where the cultural mythology of the border was taken for granted.

The notion of the 'myth of the border' employed by Conway takes its cue from the pioneering work of social anthropologist Roland Barthes who holds that a myth is 'a discourse which is ahistorical that communicates the past in a pure, unambiguous and simple fashion'.[21] This usage distinguishes it from the commonsensical understanding of a deliberate invention. Equally usefully, the literary historian Samuel Hynes defines myth 'not [as] a falsification of reality but an imagined version of it, the story that has evolved and has come to be accepted as true'.[22] Also, John Hellmann notes that 'a myth is the construction in narrative, or story, of a collective memory. That memory involves acts of forgetting and fantasy as much as of preserving'. He adds that reference is made to the core story – articulated through a succession of specific variations upon a theme – expressing the dominant ideology of the nation-state.[23] In the case of apartheid South Africa, the 'myth of the border' served to provide inspiration for the fight against the tide of communism and African nationalism threatening to engulf white society. This amounted to invoking the spirit of the pioneer who was responsible for establishing a semblance of order on the frontiers of 'civilized' society which, as Rogez shows, is precisely the theme that J. M. Coetzee explores in *Dusklands* (and *Waiting for the Barbarians*). But whereas frontier mythology is remote, the contemporaneous US experience of Vietnam resonated with the South African troops.[24] Images of this analogous war mediated by films, comic stories and books, enabled soldiers to re-imagine and mythicise the Border War in relation to the cultural memory of the Vietnam War.[25]

The term 'Border War' encodes white South African points of view although it was not actually employed by South African government spokespersons. Still, its usage in the mainstream media and public discourse implied widespread acceptance of government rhetoric that the SADF was shielding citizens from a military threat posed by the enemy forces massing on the borders. Initially, most SADF conscripts accepted that it was their duty to defend the country's borders even though these were extended as far as the Zambezi River or Angola. That is not to suggest that there were no misgivings about the legality of the SADF's action amongst its own troops. In Tony Eprile's *The Persistence of Memory*, when the protagonist-narrator is deployed to the 'operational area', he observes: 'Thus begins my first day of defending our sacred borders – though the border really belongs to someone else.'[26] Apart from questioning why they were being deployed on foreign soil, SADF soldiers occasionally had misgivings about transgressing national borders and entering the unfamiliar/unknown. In Chapter Ten, Karen Batley equates the Angolan border with the 'thin red line' to convey the idea that it was not simply a physical boundary, but represented a point of no return into the metaphorical 'heart of darkness'. The invocation of this trope might well be archetypal as Batley suggests. It might also suggest a familiarity with Joseph Conrad's well-known story of Marlowe's journey on the Congo River into the African hinterland. But it is more likely that the cultural memory of the soldiers was influenced by Francis Ford Coppola's updated version of the journey into the heart of darkness depicted in his film *Apocalypse Now* (1979). The cultural mythology of the frontier was transposed from one war zone to another.

In the extant literature, various terms are used to describe the conflicts in Southern African between the 1960s and late 1980s. None of these terms is neutral, neither are the differences merely a matter of semantics. In fact, they are socially, historically and ideologically constructed.

In his best-selling works, military correspondent Willem Steenkamp uses the phrase 'Border War' loosely to describe both the low-key counter-insurgency conflict waged against the South West Africa People's Organization (SWAPO) by the SADF and the South West African Territory Force (SWATF), as well as the conventional fighting when SADF forces invaded and occupied regions of Angola and engaged in large-scale battles with FAPLA and its Cuban allies.[27] The equally popular work of war correspondent Helmut-Romer Heitman describes the latter phase of this conflict in the late 1980s as the 'Angolan War'.[28] Both labels still enjoy currency and are sometimes used interchangeably in military and veteran circles, although the term 'Bush War' is occasionally preferred.[29] On the other hand, the term 'Border War' has been studiously avoided by academics and commentators critical of the policies of the apartheid state and the militarisation of South African society.[30] Some texts focus attention on South Africa's 'destabilisation' of the sub-continent during the 1980s when Reagan's policy of 'constructive engagement' 'was virtually an American *carte blanche* for the South African government to lay its neighbours to waste'.[31] While recognising that the conventional, guerrilla and street wars were part of a single struggle, this volume focuses on the large-scale and lengthy war waged in Namibia/Angola. Given these caveats, the editors have allowed contributors their own terminology. Therefore, certain contributors writing about or from the perspective of (white) South African soldiers or citizens tend to employ the term 'Border War'. Other contributors, when writing about the armed struggle on Namibian soil or about the perspective of SWAPO members or supporters, have chosen to write of the 'War of (National) Liberation'. I have used the term 'Border War' without qualification, but this should neither be construed as an endorsement of the needless war waged in the name of apartheid and anti-communism by the apartheid state, nor as an attempt to rehabilitate a phrase simply for the sake of being politically incorrect. Rather, its use is to encourage readers to problematise the phrase and engage with new perspectives on southern Africa's late Cold War conflicts.

Breaking the silences

It is with good reason that Vale has expressed concern regarding the silences in the historiography of South Africa's role in the Cold War.[32] With equal concern, Popescu has noted the 'Cold War silences' in the disciplines of literary criticism and cultural studies.[33] But does scholarly 'silence' necessarily mean that the subject is out of bounds to society at large? Is it taboo, like a shameful family secret, that South Africans have been loath to acknowledge, even privately? Has the country's quest for reconciliation meant that society has placed a premium on former adversaries forgiving and forgetting the past at the cost of full disclosure? Has the peaceful political transition invalidated the memory of the war prosecuted by the apartheid regime as far as former SADF conscripts are concerned? There are those who believe that the Border War is best forgotten as the country focuses on building a new future. But the memories of ex-combatants, and the legacy of an often brutal conflict, cannot simply be wished away. Soldiers' stories need to be told for the sake of individual healing and the wellbeing of society. So it is significant that ex-combatants should have recently begun to tell their stories as a way of negotiating the meaning of the Border War in post-apartheid South Africa. Academics are only beginning to catch on and to probe these developments.

Elaine Windrich and Edgar Dosman are both keenly aware that access to previously closed archives is necessary in order to make good some of the gaps in the diplomatic and military history of southern Africa. Their contributions address Cold War silences and controversies. In Chapter 11, Windrich deconstructs the image of Jonas Savimbi by interrogating UNITA and South Africa's (often conflicting) communiqués and propaganda. As it became increasingly dependent on the SADF, UNITA sacrificed any autonomy it might have had and served only to minimise the loss of white conscripts in the regional conflict. It was precisely when the body count reached critical mass as a result of Cuba's intervention that the SADF cut its losses and withdrew from Angola and, subsequently, from Namibia. Certain commentators have dismissed claims that the SADF was defeated at Cuito Cuanavale as Cuban propaganda insisting that the battle ended in stalemate and that the SADF staged a 'tactical withdrawal'.[34] Moreover, former SADF generals have maintained that they were under pressure from the Department of Foreign Affairs to allow the Cubans to find a face-saving way of withdrawing from the conflict.[35] In Chapter 12, Dosman presents a far more nuanced version of these events. He gives credit to the SADF's military accomplishments on the battlefield where it is due, but is equally honest in recognising its failings when its commanders made strategic and tactical blunders. Dosman's access to Cuban sources enables him to reveal how they planned and executed their military operations. Rather than portraying the Popular Movement for the Liberation of Angola (MPLA) government and FAPLA troops as surrogates of Cuba, Dosman teases out some of the tensions that existed between the Angolans, Cubans and Russians. In challenging the orthodoxy of the military history of the sub-continent, Dosman supports Piero Gleijeses' contention that intervention in Angola proved to be South Africa's, and not Cuba's, Vietnam![36]

The SADF learned the (mistaken) lesson of Vietnam from the US forces, namely that unrestricted media coverage of war could be demoralising and self-defeating.[37] Accordingly, censorship was used to restrict the South African public's access to information about the Border War. For instance, there was a 'black out' of coverage by local media of Operation Savannah in 1975 during which SADF forces advanced within 120 kilometres of the Angolan capital, Luanda.[38] That local media were kept in the dark whilst the story was broken by their international counterparts occasioned acute embarrassment for the former. Subsequently, the SADF attempted to win over the local media by inviting carefully vetted (photo)journalists and military correspondents to accompany units in the field. Fact-finding trips to the 'operational area' were also arranged for members of parliament, dignitaries and celebrities. These public relations exercises clearly convinced the correspondents who duly reported that the SADF's prowess and superior training ensured victory (provided that it was linked to a political settlement). Thus the mainstream media – the Afrikaans and English press, as well as the South African Broadcasting Corporation (SABC) that monopolised radio and television broadcasts (the latter from 1976) – lent their support to the 'boys on the border'. Propaganda and disinformation was also employed by the apartheid state in the battle for the hearts and minds of its citizens, including the conscripts.

However, the Nationalist Party (NP) government and the SADF did not take the soldiers or their families into their confidence. The authorities disclosed information about military matters only on a need to know basis. They repeatedly refused to disclose the truth about the number and nature of South Africa's (often self-inflicted) casualties.[39] Stories released to and published by the media were often contrived versions of what had actually caused the deaths of servicemen.[40] This was compounded by the SADF's reluctance to disclose the circumstances of soldiers' deaths to their next of kin.[41] Even the troops themselves were seldom informed about the strategic objectives of military operations in which they were involved. For instance, troops were not briefed beforehand when they were bound for Angola, and officers were instructed not to divulge the enemy's logistical and numerical superiority to their own troops at the battle of Cuito Cuanavale.[42] Clandestine operations carried out by the SADF's elite reconnaissance forces are not the only ones that deserve the appellation the 'Silent War'.[43] For the undeclared war was generally conducted amidst considerable secrecy and wild rumours.

Secrets can reveal much about society and governance as 'they are more about a kind of information than a kind of concealment'.[44] SADF national servicemen were sworn to secrecy in terms of the Defence Act and had to sign declarations not to divulge information pertaining to military operations.[45] This bound veterans of the Border War to refrain from telling their stories even to friends and family (although they undoubtedly swapped stories with one another and shared their memories of their experiences). For some ex-SADF soldiers the camaraderie of cyberspace has largely replaced bonding/drinking sessions in pubs and reunions of veterans' associations. In fact, the reach and scope of the informal networks (often via email listservs or websites hosted outside of the country) serve as a kind of virtual veteran's association. These veterans who served in the SADF, belonged to a specific unit, or performed border duty, have established a network of sites to exchange memories and, in some cases, provide platforms for advice on matters like post-traumatic stress disorder (PTSD).[46] They constitute 'cyber-communities' in which hyperlinks, multiple postings, and cross-citation facilitate communication between individuals who hold similar views. Certain Web authors and their readers share membership of a 'virtual' community and provide social support for one another.

Why should former SADF national servicemen have gravitated to the Internet in order to share their stories? Do they see themselves as contesting their invisibility in post-apartheid South

Africa occasioned by their forgotten war and what Sasha Gear in Chapter 14 calls the 'silence of stigmatized knowledge'? Have SADF veterans ventured into the apparently neutral terrain of cyberspace to tell stories that might be deemed 'politically incorrect' in the 'new' South Africa. Jodi Dean argues that there is no longer a 'consensus reality' according to which contested questions of fact can be resolved. She suggests that, instead, there are multiple contending realities which keep contested issues from being decided. In other words, Dean reckons that there has been dissolution of the boundary between the margins and the mainstream. [47] This implies that groups sidelined in the realm of *realpolitik* are able to challenge the consensus established by hegemonic groups. However, Michael Barkun believes that while the boundary has become more permeable it still exists and that virtual communities remain on the fringes of the power brokering of interest groups and political elites.[48] Veterans have created Internet sites that mostly disclaim political affiliations, although a few advertise their (invariably right-wing) political orientations and reminisce nostalgically about their time in the army. They have arguably found the (cyber)space to express their grievances and reclaim their memories in the public domain.

The apartheid regime's officially imposed amnesia led some ex-soldiers to find alternative forms of remembering such as writing fiction. A few veterans with literary pretensions told their stories in thinly disguised, fictional autobiographical works, especially short stories, through the medium of Afrikaans. But the protagonists in this *grensliteratuur* were very often misfits, outcasts and even anti-heroes.[49] More popular were novels by Al Venter and Peter Essex, which related far-fetched stories of machismo heroes and their beautiful, dutiful women taming the hostile African continent.[50] Equally popular were stories that appeared in magazines such as *Huisgenoot* and *Scope*, photocomix such as *Grensvegter*,[51] and films such as *Kaptein Caprivi* and *Boetie Gaan Border Toe*,[52] which celebrated the actions of adventurous and fun-loving heroes whose military training made them more than a match for their adversaries. However, such glamorisation of the *troopie's* life was a far cry from reality when Non-Commissioned Officers (NCOs) took perverse pleasure in *rondfok* (literally, fucking the troops around) during drills and training exercises, and when boredom verging on stupor was induced by repetitive routines and a 'hurry up and wait' mentality. Border duty might have offered the adrenalin rush of combat and the inducement of 'danger pay' but, as Rob Gordon points out in Chapter 13, the SADF troops' sense of adventure evaporated as soon as operations resulted in a mounting death toll. The SADF troops left the 'operational area' with little to show for their efforts but Pro Patria medals and commemorative tee-shirts.

No official recognition was given to the sacrifices of South African soldiers until a memorial was unveiled at Fort Klapperkop in 1979. Erected on a hill outside of Pretoria (now Tshwane) to honour of all those who had lost their lives in defence of the Republic of South Africa,[53] its elevated site has not prevented the memorial from becoming invisible and neglected. It is viewed as neither a site of remembrance, nor a place of mourning for friends and families of the deceased. Indeed, the Fort Klapperkop memorial is hardly known to ex-servicemen's organisations, let alone the general public. Thus a forum for veterans of the Border War has sought to have the names of those killed fighting for their country included in the roll of honour compiled for the Sikhumbuto memorial wall in Freedom Park being erected as an act of symbolic reparation for those who died in the struggle for liberation from white minority rule. The veterans also objected to the fact that the memorial wall is to include the names of Cuban soldiers who died in Angola fighting the SADF. At the time of writing, their request for 'fair treatment' had been rejected by Wally Serote, the CEO of the Freedom Park Trust, on the grounds that the SADF soldiers were fighting to preserve apartheid and not freedom and humanity.[54] This snub was regarded by former conscripts as further testimony that their neglect by the NP government would continue under the African National Congress (ANC) government.

SADF veterans' acute sense of betrayal was partly attributable to the outcome of the war and negotiated settlement that, undoubtedly, devalued their memories. The silence imposed by the apartheid state was compounded by the veterans' own wish to forget. Official invisibility intensified individual amnesia. Under such circumstances, veterans tended to repress their traumatic memories so as not to admit recollections too painful to recall. The marginalisation of ex-combatants can be seen not only in difficulties faced by veterans of notorious SADF units such as 32 Battalion,[55] but also in society's failure to acknowledge the hardships that 'regular' soldiers who were not necessarily involved in heinous acts faced in coming to terms with their experiences. Soldiers were seldom afforded any opportunity to come to terms with their frequently traumatic and life-transforming experiences. One account relates how soldiers involved in some of the fiercest fighting in Angola in 1988 were rounded up before the *uitklaar* (demobilisation) parade and given a pep talk by their commanding officer, offered a perfunctory prayer by the military chaplain, and a superficial collective counselling session by a clinical psychologist.[56] There was no debriefing whatsoever and the soldiers were sent home to resume their lives in civvy street. There was little or no treatment for those with the symptoms of PTSD. SADF veterans of the Border War are unlikely to heal their psychological wounds until such time as they receive therapy. This is not to insist that healing is assured or that closure is attainable for 'questions remain about what constitutes . . . a suitable trauma history, and what sentiments can be expressed in the national public sphere'.[57]

If the old order was not inclined to admit the distresses of its foot soldiers, then at least the TRC acknowledged the existence of the problem. However, SADF conscripts were wary and suspicious of the TRC despite its assurance that the testimonies given during its hearings were 'neither an attempt to look for perpetrators, nor a process that will lead to the awarding of victim status'.[58] Karen Whitty explains their reluctance to testify in the following terms: 'Bound by a sense of honour to their fellow troops, and the patriarchy still espoused by white South

Africa, few men have come forward and spoken about their experiences, however barbaric and mundane, in South Africa's border wars.'[59]

Some reported that the lack of public knowledge about the war created suspicion of their stories, while others were summarily dismissed as sympathy seekers or outright liars by former SADF generals and their apologists.[60] Thus ex-soldiers felt betrayed when the very authorities that they were convinced would protect them and provide security left them in the lurch. If trauma involves a betrayal of trust and the abuse of relations of power,[61] then it is not surprising that many veterans embraced silence and victimhood. Consequently, the TRC 'left the experiences of "ordinary" soldiers largely invisible – not merely forgotten but "wished away"' as a report of the Centre for the Study of Violence and Reconciliation (CSVR) avers.[62]

For their part, the former SADF generals sought to exculpate themselves of any wrongdoing before the TRC. They remained steadfastly convinced that the TRC was biased against the SADF and predisposed to finding it guilty of ignoring the rules of engagement in South Africa's conflicts. The generals showed their true political stripes (stars?) when they refused to testify before the TRC and feigned ignorance of war crimes sanctioned by the government.[63] They displayed a singular lack of willingness to take responsibility for their acts of commission and omission. The TRC deplored the intransigence of the SADF hierarchy and its reticence to supply documents or acknowledge its responsibility for flaunting the international community's rules for the conduct of war. It opined that this attitude hindered the healing of the nation's traumas. However, the intransigence of the SADF was emulated by the leadership of the ANC's armed wing. MK also failed to make full disclosure before the TRC, arguing that it should not be held accountable for atrocities committed while waging a legitimate armed struggle.

In its concern about the casualties of war, the TRC Report acknowledged the need to 'raise public awareness about the reality and effects of post-traumatic stress disorder' and to encourage former conscripts and soldiers who participated in the conflict 'to share their pain and reflect on their experiences'.[64] Apart from proposing projects aimed at rehabilitating and rebuilding the lives of ex-combatants, the TRC envisaged that they could possibly be 'help[ed] to tell and write their stories'.[65] Some have begun to do so although not necessarily as a result of the TRC's suggestion. Rather, they obviously believe that the time is right for a re-evaluation of their roles in South Africa's past conflicts and that recounting their experiences will effectively valorise their yearning for acknowledgment of the sacrifices they made for their country. Conversely, they wish to rid themselves of the shame of being regarded as vanquished soldiers. And they have also sought reaffirmation of their place in post-apartheid society by belatedly recasting themselves as victims rather than oppressors.

Such sentiments are apparent in a number of publications in English penned by former SADF conscripts who relate stories about aspects of military service. It would appear that the passage of time for reflection has given soldier–authors the space to make sense of their experiences and construct narratives thereof. Certain of these works were written in a cathartic vein and might be described as 'confessional' texts.[66] The (sometimes) reluctant soldiers often admit complicity in upholding the apartheid system not on account of ideological convictions or patriotism, but rather because they believed that they had little choice in the matter.[67] The most popular text has proved to be a collection of reminiscences published under the inappropriate title *An Unpopular War*.[68] The stories are told with a blend of honesty and self-delusion, candour and scepticism, and self-deprecating humour. Many of these stories are suffused in nostalgia for the 'good old days' while, contrarily, evincing a modicum of guilt about the role narrators played as perpetrators of violence and terror. But the overwhelming impression is that these ex-soldiers see themselves as having simply performed their duties as national servicemen.

A few personal accounts of the Border War by former army career officers express few qualms about their actions such as killing 'terrorists' or leading armed sorties into South Africa's neighbouring states.[69] The memoirs of retired SADF generals are noticeably devoid of self-recrimination. For instance, the chief of the army and then the SADF between 1985 and 1990, Jannie Geldenhuys, published *A General's Story*[70] that was no *mea culpa*. Geldenhuys insisted on his own professional integrity and defended the impartiality of the SADF, maintaining that its function had not been to support a particular political party, but rather to ensure the security of all the citizens of the state. Magnus Malan's more recently published memoir is also an evasive and self-serving justification of his role in the SADF and of the military in creating the requisite stability to enable the transfer of power.[71] In fact, Malan was not merely a professional soldier who served the government of the day, but accepted an appointment as a cabinet minister thereby becoming a representative of the very white minority government that was actively supported by the security establishment. It might be true that the SADF under the leadership of General George Meiring effectively prevented the right wing from sabotaging the negotiated settlement and desisted from staging a military coup. But as a *quid pro quo* the newly installed ANC refrained from prosecuting apartheid-era politicians and generals. Instead, middle-ranking securocrats were targeted and, consequently, believed themselves to have been subjected to a witch-hunt. When the generals closed ranks so as to look after their own interests they ignored the plight of the foot soldiers who felt betrayed by their political masters.[72]

Certain ex-combatants in the ranks of the liberation movements feel equally betrayed by the post-apartheid state. Groups comprising ex-combatants or veterans of the liberation movements also attest to being sidelined during the scramble for power and patronage in the new dispensation. They regard their treatment by the authorities as discriminatory in that it has favoured ex-

SADF members rather than freedom fighters. And within the newly integrated South African National Defence Force (SANDF), there have been tensions between former MK and APLA cadres, as well as between returned exiles and 'stay-at-homes'.[73] According to Thula Bopela and Daluxolo Luthuli in their co-authored *Umkhonto we Sizwe*,[74] ethnic divisions were rampant in the ranks of MK and are still exploited in post-apartheid South Africa. These manifestations of anomie and high levels of alienation amongst male ex-combatants have been confirmed by studies produced by the CSVR. Indeed, a main finding of one such report was that: 'Former combatants nowadays tend to receive public attention only in relation to real or imaginary security threats',[75] a point confirmed by the attention paid to the violence that accompanied the recent strike by security employees.[76] When ex-combatants make the headlines as ruthless criminals or family killers then the public sits up and takes notice. Otherwise they are forgotten and silenced.

Perhaps in part because of the silence surrounding the Border War, and because it remains for most of the South African public 'far away' (according to an ex-*Koevoet* member who testified before the TRC), the hearings on the atrocities committed in Angola and Namibia do not seem to have attracted as much attention as similar acts committed at home. Unlike the TRC's treatment of South Africa's domestic matters there were no victim hearings whatsoever for human rights violations outside of the country. The TRC Report stated that: 'South Africa's occupation of South West Africa would merit a separate truth commission of its own.'[77] The same might be said of the SADF's actions in Angola. However, Christopher Saunders notes in Chapter 15 that the Report amounted to little more than a survey of South Africa's acts of aggression against neighbouring states based largely on the perpetrator's own incomplete records. The TRC had neither the co-operation of these governments nor the resources to conduct an in-depth investigation into human rights abuses and war crimes committed in these territories.

As is the case with ex-combatants,[78] Namibia's civilian population has been neglected by the SWAPO government since independence. In some cases they risked an enormous amount in order to support People's Liberation Army of Namibia (PLAN, the armed wing of SWAPO) cadres. In Chapter 16, Heike Becker illustrates how their stories have been marginalised in the Namibian narrative of the liberation struggle which is entirely dominated by the stories of SWAPO leaders. Notwithstanding the erection of a giant bronze statue of a PLAN soldier in Heroes' Acre, Windhoek in 2002 (modelled on its namesake in Harare),[79] national history has effectively ignored civilians and rank and file soldiers. Whereas SWAPO leaders have been lionised, Becker shows that attempts by writers to insert civilians into the founding history of the Namibian nation have all but been ignored.[80] Their stories have been sidelined in the triumphalist narrative of the War of National Liberation and their ongoing plight suggests the inequities of apartheid have not been overcome in post-war Namibia.

SWAPO rejected a proposal that Namibia hold a fact-finding commission to uncover the country's violent past as contrary to the spirit of reconciliation. One consequence of this, as Justine Hunter shows in Chapter 17, has been the refusal of SWAPO to own up to the abuses and atrocities committed in its name, especially the mistreatment, torture and even execution of detainees in military camps established in neighbouring states during the war. Hunter rightly observes that unless this 'wall of silence' is addressed in a transparent fashion, it will continue to bedevil the political process in post-war Namibia. Hunter also alludes to the recent discovery of unmarked mass graves of SWAPO cadres who were killed in the last months of the war. The public outcry caused by this incident was compounded by the disavowals of former SADF generals to knowledge of or responsibility for the massacres on their watch. In fact, it was a matter of public record, for revelations about the incident had been made in at least one publication about the final days of the war.[81] The media coverage reflected the ongoing public interest in the 'unfinished business' of the Border War.

While this volume has been in preparation, a number of issues have served as reminders that the legacy of the Border War is still very much part of the landscape of post-apartheid southern Africa. I have referred to the SWAPO detainees and mass graves issues in Namibia. There has also been a vibrant public discourse on matters relating to ex-combatants in that country.[82] In South Africa, the Freedom Park memorial wall controversy has been the subject of media attention and even occasioned the mobilisation of civil society groups. And the book *An Unpopular War* remains on the bestseller lists.[83] The popularity of this collection might simply suggest nostalgia for the old order or might equally hint at a deep-seated desire to come to terms with the past. Whatever the case, there can be no doubting the public interest in these matters. Contributors to this volume have placed the subject of the Border War squarely back on the academic agenda in a way that is commensurate with this public interest in the 'unfinished business' of the Border War. They have challenged the boundaries and broken the silences, even tackled some taboos. It is the editors' sincere hope that readers of this volume will consequently be able to move beyond the Border War and understand something of its place in the public imaginary.

Notes to Chapter One

1   Even a major project such as the multi-volumed South African Democracy Education Trust (SADET) entitled *The Road to Democracy in South Africa* focuses primarily on the national liberation struggle within the country rather than on the regional and global dimensions of the conflict. Exceptions to this tendency include C. Alden, *Apartheid's Last Stand: The Rise and Fall of the South African Security State* (Basingstoke: Macmillan, 1996) and A. Guelke, *Rethinking the Rise and Fall of Apartheid* (Basingstoke: Palgrave Macmillan, 2005).

2   *Truth and Reconciliation Commission of South Africa (TRC) Report*, Vol. 2 (Cape Town: TRC, 1998), ch. 2 'The State Outside South Africa Between 1960 and 1990'.

3   Pioneered by P. Gleijeses, *Conflicting Missions: Havana, Washington, Pretoria* (Chapel Hill: University of North Carolina Press, 2002 and Alberton: Galago, 2003). See also his more recent article 'Moscow's Proxy? Cuba and Africa 1975–1988', *Journal of Cold War Studies*, 8, 2 (Spring 2006), 3–51.

4   C. Tilly, *Coercion, Capital and European States, AD 990–1992* (Oxford: Blackwell, 1993). The maxim is a paraphrase of the title of ch. 3: 'Wars make states, and vice versa'.

5   This analogy is borrowed from physics/electromagnetism. It is also based on my interpretation of the notion of racial modernism in B. Bozzoli, *Theatres of Struggle and the End of Apartheid* (Athens: Ohio University Press, 2004). The 'bounded state' has parallels with the 'bunker state' of S. M. Davis, *Apartheid's Rebels: Inside South Africa's Hidden War* (Craighall: Ad. Donker, 1987), 160–4 and the 'garrison state' of P. Frankel, *Pretoria's Praetorians: Civil-military Relations in South Africa* (Cambridge: Cambridge University Press, 1984), 29–70.

6   H. Adam and K. Adam, 'The Politics of Memory in Divided Societies', in *After the TRC: Reflections on Truth and Reconciliation in South Africa*, ed. W. James and L. van de Vijver (Cape Town: David Philip, 2000), 46.

7   P. Vale, *Security and Politics in South Africa: The Regional Dimension* (Boulder, Co.: Lynne Rienner Publishers, 2003), 53.

8   Ibid. 2, 52.

9   Ibid. 29, 50.

10   E. Rhoodie, *South West: The Last Frontier in Africa* (Johannesburg: Voortrekkerpers, 1967). See critique in D. Haarhoff, *The Wild South-West: Frontier Myths and Metaphors Set in Namibia* (Johannesburg: Witwatersrand University Press, 1991)

11   Gleijeses, 'Moscow's Proxy?' 25. See also Dosman's chapter in this volume.

12   Gleijeses, 'Moscow's Proxy?' 40.

13   R. Jürgens, *The Many Houses of Exile* (Weltevredenpark: Covos Day, 2000), 177.

14   *TRC Report, Vol. 4, Institutional and Special Hearings* (Cape Town: TRC, 1998), 220.

15   *Forces' Favourites* (Johannesburg: Taurus, 1986), 70–1.

16   Reproduced in Catholic Institute of International Relations, *Out of Step: War Resistance in South Africa* (London: CIIR, 1989), 93.

17   C. Holt, in *At Thy Call We Shall Not Falter* (Cape Town: Zebra Press, 2005), uncritically reproduces the official SADF statistics for losses of men and materiál in Angola in 1988 when it is widely recognised that these figures seldom included the losses sustained by the SADF's surrogates such as UNITA, mercenaries attached to units like 32 Battalion or black Namibians conscripted to the SWATF or SWAPOL. However, he is aware of the discrepancies between official statements about the war in Angola and what he saw with his own eyes.

18   M. Behr, *The Smell of Apples* (London: Abacus, 1995), 82–3.

19   For example, the fairly conventional combat story of the capture of Guadalcanal by US marines in *The Thin Red Line* by James Jones was adapted into a film by Terrence Malick that explored the boundaries between binaries such as good/evil, life/death and madness/sanity. See Rose Lucas, 'Theatres of Extremity: Permeable Subjectivity in *The Thin Red Line*', Paper presented to Frontlines: Gender, Identity and War Conference, Monash University, Melbourne, 12–13 July 2002.

20   G. Baines, 'South Africa's Vietnam? Literary History and Cultural Memory of the Border War', *South African Historical Journal*, 49 (Nov. 2003), 171–92.

21   R. Barthes, *Mythologies: Selected Writings Translated From the French by Annette Lavers* (New York: Hill and Wang, 1972).

22   S. Hynes, *A War Imagined: The First World War in English Culture* (New York: Collier Books, 1990) ix–x.

23   J. Hellmann, *American Myth and the Legacy of Vietnam* (New York: Columbia University Press, 1986).

24   S. Roberts, 'The Invisible Enemy: South African Border War Narratives', in *Readings in the Post/colonial Literatures in English* (Atlanta: Rodopi, 1993), 89–98

25   Baines, 'South Africa's Vietnam?' 173.

26   T. Eprile, *The Persistence of Memory* (Cape Town: Double Storey, 2004), 104.

27   Willem Steenkamp, the long-serving military reporter for *The Cape Times* and member of the SADF citizen force, had ready access to high-ranking SADF personnel which gave his works *Borderstrike! South Africa into Angola* (Durban: Butterworths, 1983) and *South Africa's Border War 1966–1989* (Gibraltar: Ashanti, 1989) an official imprimatur. The latter had a first print run of 25 000 copies which sold out in three months and a further 17 000 were reprinted. Sales of 500 are considered good for works of non-fiction in South Africa. See P. Moorcraft, 'Ashanti Rising', *Southern African Review of Books*, 3, 6, Issue 16 (Aug/Oct. 1990), 7.

28   H-R. Heitman was a correspondent for *Jane's Weekly* and also a member of the SADF citizen force. His lavishly illustrated work *War in Angola: The Final South African Phase* (Gibraltar: Ashanti, 1990) sold 9 000 copies. Moorcraft, 'Ashanti Rising', 7.

29   See, for instance, the website 'The South African Bush War 1966–1989'. http://www.geocities.com/sabushwar. This term was originally used in connection with the Zimbabwean war of independence by former soldiers who fought for Rhodesia's UDI government. This is also known as the 'Rhodesian War' or the 'Second Chimurenga', depending on which side the soldier–author fought.

30   There is a considerable body of writing on this theme. This includes R. Leonard, *South Africa at War: White Power and the Crisis in southern Africa* (Craighall: Ad. Donker, 1983); J. Cock and L. Nathan, eds., *War and Society: The Militarisation of South Africa* (Cape Town and Johannesburg: David Philip, 1989); P. Frankel, *Pretoria's Praetorians: Civil-Military Relations in South Africa* (Cambridge: Cambridge University Press, 1984); J. Frederickse, *South Africa: A Different Kind of War* (Johannesburg: Ravan Press, 1986); G. Cawthra, *Brutal Force: The Apartheid War Machine* (London: IDAF, 1986); K. Grundy, *The Militarisation of South African Politics* (Oxford: Oxford University Press, 1988).

31   Destabilisation included clandestine operations by SADF units and apartheid state security agents (such as the CCB) against its designated enemies in the frontline states. See, for instance, V. Brittain, *Hidden Lives, Hidden Deaths: South Africa's Crippling of a Continent* (London: Faber and Faber, 1988); J. Hanlon, *Beggar Your Neighbours: Apartheid Power in southern Africa* (London: James Currey, 1986); P. Johnson and D. Martin, eds., *Destructive Engagement: southern Africa at War* (Harare: Zimbabwe Publishing House, 1986). The quote is from Guelke, *Rethinking the Rise and Fall of Apartheid*, 140.

32   P. Vale, 'Pivot, Puppet or Periphery: The Cold War and South Africa', Paper delivered at the International Studies Association Conference, Portland, Oregon, Feb–March, 2003.

33   See Popescu's chapter in this volume.

34   See, for instance, R. Allport, 'The Battle of Cuito Cuanavale: Cuba's Mythical Victory'. http://www.rhodesia.nl/cuito.htm

35   H. Hamann, *Days of the Generals* (Cape Town: Zebra Press, 2001), 95.

36   Gleijeses, 'Moscow's Proxy?' 3–51.

37   G. N. Addison, 'Censorship of the Press in South Africa during the Angolan War: A Case Study of News Manipulation and Suppression', MA thesis, Rhodes University, 1980. The myth perpetuated by the US military was that media, especially television, coverage of the Vietnam War caused the tide of public opinion to turn against the intervention and that this, in turn, caused the politicians to scale down and eventually withdraw US forces thus effectively losing the war. For a critique of this perception, see D.

Hallin, *The Uncensored War: The Media and Vietnam* (Berkeley, Ca.: University of California Press, 1986).

38 R. Hallett, 'The South African Intervention in Angola 1975–76', *African Affairs*, 77 (July 1978), 347–68.

39 With good reason, the SADF has been called 'the world's most accident-prone army' by Eprile, *The Persistence of Memory*, 171.

40 J. H. Thompson, *An Unpopular War: Voices of South African National Servicemen* (Cape Town: Zebra Press, 2006), 149.

41 Steenkamp, *South Africa's Border War*, 29.

42 Holt, *At Thy Call*, 122, 137; Behr, *The Smell of Apples*, 82.

43 P. Stiff, *The Silent War: South African Recce Operations 1969–1994* (Alberton: Galago, 1999).

44 G. Minkley and M. Legassick, '"Not Telling": Secrets, Lies and History', *History and Theory*, 39, 4 (Dec. 2000), 8.

45 Section 118(4) of the Defence Act of 1967 rendered it an offence for a person to disclose any secret or confidential information relating to the defence of the country which came to his/her knowledge by reason of his membership of the SADF or employment in the public service. See K. Satchwell, 'The Power to Defend: An Analysis of Various Aspects of the Defence Act', in Cook and Nathan, *War in Society*, 48.

46 See, for instance, Army Talk at http://moo.sun.ac.za/mailman/listinfo/armytalk/ which hosted a chat line utilised mainly by ex- Citizen Force SADF members (i.e. conscripts). But it is likely that such sites are also accessed by military buffs, as well as veterans of South Africa's and other recent wars. These sites are obviously male domains. Recently, this site seems to have been shut down or relocated, and its mailing list discontinued.

47 J. Dean, *Aliens in America: Conspiracy Cultures from Outer space to Cyberspace* (Ithaca, NY: Cornell University Press), 1998, 8–9.

48 M. Barkun, *A Culture of Conspiracy: Apocalyptic Visions in Contemporary America* (Berkeley, Ca: University of California Press), 2003, 185–6.

49 H. van Coller, 'Border/Frontier Literature', in *Space and boundaries in literature: Proceedings of the 12th Congress of the International Comparative Literature Association*, ed. R. Bauer, D. Fokkema and M. de Graat (Munich: Ludicium, 1990), 254–9.

50 This includes titles such as A. J. Venter, *Soldier of Fortune* (London: W. H. Allen, 1980) and P. Essex, *The Exile* (London: Collins, 1984). See D. Maugham-Brown, 'Images of War: Popular Fiction in English and the War on South Africa's Border', *The English Academy Review*, 4 (1987), 53–66.

51 Photocomix like the *Grensvegter* series which featured intrepid heroes in uniform single-handedly winning the war, not unlike a Rambo-type figure, were widely known by the colloquial Afrikaans name *poesboeke*. This literally means 'cunt books' and is an oblique reference to the fact that the picture frames were filled with an array of pin-up women, most of whom were bikini-clad and occasionally topless but never naked. *Poesboeke* were essentially a poor substitute for pornography in apartheid South Africa. See http://www.allatsea.co.za/army/pboek.htm.

52 See K. Tomaselli and K. Carlean, *Boetie Gaan Border Toe*. http://www.und.ac.za/und/ccms/publications/articles/boetie.htm; D. Craig, 'The Viewer as Conscript: Dynamic Struggles for Ideological Supremacy in South African Border War Film, 1971–1988', MA thesis, University of Cape Town, 2003, and 'Screening the Border War, 1971–88', *Kleio*, 36 (2004), 28–46.

53 *Paratus* Special Supplement, July 1979 v. 30. no. 7.

54 *Pretoria News*, 17 January 2007 ('Include us, say ex-SADF members').

55 In the particular case of 32 Battalion, these difficulties include deprivation, an uncertain future as a refugee community shuttled from camp to camp within some of the most desolate areas of the country, unsympathetic treatment by the ANC government, and easy prey to mercenary recruiters. A brief summary

of their conditions can be found at http://www.mg.co.za/articlePage.aspx?articleid=198866&area=/insight/insightnational/.

56 B. Fowler, *Grensvegter? South African Army Psychologist* (Halifax: Sentinel Projects, 1996), 123–7 outlines the SADF's 'model' debriefing session. Holt, *At Thy Call*, 116–20 reproduces it and at 122 relates how it worked in practice.

57 L. Meskell, 'Trauma Culture: Remembering and Forgetting in the New South Africa', in D. Bell, ed., *Memory, Trauma and World Politics* (Basingstoke: Palgrave Macmillan, 2006), 164.

58 *TRC Report*, v. 4, 221.

59 K. Whitty, Review of Clive Holt, *At Thy Call We Did Not Falter*, http://www.iafrica.com/pls/procs/SEARCH.ARCHIVE?p_content_id=474801&p_site_id=2 (posted 22 August 2005).

60 For instance, the testimony of conscript Kevin Hall has been carefully scrutinised and rebutted by H. Hamann, *Days of the Generals* (Cape Town: Zebra Press, 2001), 221–3 and M. Malan, *My Lewe saam met die SA Weermag* (Pretoria: Protea Boekhuis, 2006), 474–6.

61 J. Edkins, *Trauma and the Memory of Politics* (Cambridge: Cambridge University Press, 2003), 4.

62 S. Gear, *Wishing Us Away: Challenges Facing Ex-combatants in the 'New' South Africa* (Johannesburg: CSVR, 2002), http://www.wits.ac.za/csvr/papers/papvtp8e.htm (accessed 14 June 2006).

63 A clique of former SADF generals did make a submission to the TRC. It was co-ordinated by General Dirk Marais, former Deputy Chief of the Army, under the title: 'The Military in a Political Arena: The SADF and the TRC'. See Hamann, *Days of the Generals*, 130.

64 *TRC Report*, Vol. 4, 221.

65 Ibid. 242.

66 Most obviously Holt, *At Thy Call We Did Not Falter*. Others include the short stories collected in Barry Fowler, ed., *Pro Patria.* (Halifax: Sentinel Projects, 1995); Anthony Feinstein, *In Conflict* (Windhoek: New Namibia Books, 1998); and Rick Andrew, *Buried in the Sky* (Johannesburg: Penguin, 2001).

67 White male conscripts faced difficult options: answer the call-up and spend two years or more (if camps are included) in uniform, object on conscientious or religious grounds and face a stiff jail sentence, or flee the country.

68 The Border War was not unpopular amongst the majority of the white populace or conscripts while it was being waged. The moral ambiguity conferred on the war has happened retrospectively with these groups. Even those who once supported the war do not now think it was worth fighting.

69 J. Breytenbach has published *They Live by the Sword*, Alberton: Lemur, 1990; *Eden's Exiles: One Soldier's Fight for Paradise*, Cape Town: Queillerie, 1997; and *The Buffalo Soldiers: The Story of South Africa's 32 Battalion, 1975–1993*, Alberton: Lemur, 2002. As a conservationist, he is at least critical of the senior politicians and SADF officers who benefited from the pillaging of animal resources in Angola. See also P. Nortjé, *32 Battalion*, Cape Town: Zebra Press, 2004.

70 J. Geldenhuys, *A General's Story: From an Era of War and Peace* (Johannesburg: Jonathan Ball, 1995). Originally published in Afrikaans as *Dié Wat Wen: 'n Generaal se Storie uit 'n Era van Oorlog en Vrede*, 1993.

71 Malan, *My Lewe saam met die SA Weermag*.

72 F. van Zyl Slabbert, *The Other Side of History* (Cape Town: Jonathan Ball, 2006), 17–19.

73 Gear, *Wishing Us Away*, 123–5

74 T. Bopela and D. Luthuli, *Umkhonto we Sizwe: Fighting for a Divided People* (Alberton: Galago, 2005).

75 Gear, *Wishing Us Away*.

76 Many ex-combatants have left the armed forces and have found employment in the burgeoning privatized security industry; others have resorted to providing such services as far afield as Iraq or have been engaged

as mercenaries. See Gear *Wishing Us Away*.

77   *TRC Report*, v. 2, 62.

78   D. LeBeau, *An Investigation Into Namibian Ex-soldiers Fifteen Years After Independence*. (Windhoek: Peace Centre, 2005). See http://www.peace.org.na/PEACE_Full%20Research%20Report.

79   R. Kössler, 'Public Memory, Reconciliation and the Aftermath of War', in *Re-examining Liberation in Namibia*, ed. H. Melber (Uppsala: Nordiska Afrikainstitutet, 2003), 107.

80   There have been a few exceptions. These include some stories in C. Leys and S. Brown, eds., *Histories of Namibia: Living Through the Liberation Struggle – Life Histories Told to Colin Leys and Susan Brown* (London: The Merlin Press, 2005).

81   P. Stiff, *Nine Days of War: South Africa's Final Days in Namibia* (Alberton: Lemur Books, 1991).

82   L. Metsola and H. Melber, 'Namibia's Pariah Heroes: SWAPO Ex-Combatants Between Liberation Gospel and Security Interests', in *The Security-Development Nexus: Expressions of Sovereignty and Securitization in southern Africa*, ed. L. Buur et al. (Uppsala: Nordiska Afrikainstitutet, 2006 and Cape Town: HSRC Press, 2007), 85–105.

83   Now in its sixth reprint in almost as many months.

Chapter 2

The Cold War and South Africa: Repetitions and Revisions on a Prolegomenon[1]

Peter Vale

South Africa is unequivocally the symbol of anti-Communism in Africa. Although often abused, we are also still a bastion in Africa for Christianity and the Western world
– Hendrik Verwoerd

South Africa was a cause célèbre in the life and times of the Cold War. A single example helps to explain why this was so. A divided country ruled by a minority where near feudal politics were cast by a racial fault line which almost perfectly paralleled the Cold War divide; a rich white minority seemed to enjoy the support of the West while an impoverished black majority looked to the Soviet Union and its allies as a source of support – intellectual, financial and military.

Although South Africa's racial divide has ended, certainly formally and constitutionally, the Cold War lingers in the country's politics and its daily life. South Africa's ruling party, the African National Congress (ANC), remains in an alliance with a Communist Party; aspects of security legislation still bear the stamp of apartheid's strain of anti-Communism; and school textbooks, especially in history, often bear the scars of the once-powerful Cold War register. Then, the trope, 'Cold War' resurfaces again and again – for instance, some Right-wingers used the theme 'Cold War against Afrikaners' on their website. Less immediate Cold War ideas and images often reappear: the notion of a 'Marshall Plan' for southern Africa is a recurring theme in public discourse over both the country's economy, and the revival of Africa.[2]

In some instances, the cloud of Cold War thinking still confuses crucial understandings of the past. For example, did the Central Intelligence Agency (CIA) turn in Nelson Mandela in August

1962?[3] Was the pay-off really an obscure tit-bit of apartheid's grand scheme? And does the Cold War explain why the central motif in the trial that followed, and which lead to Mandela's conviction and 27-year imprisonment, was the threat that communism and revolution posed to 'Western values' in South Africa? Other troubling issues have been resolved, however. The minority did have nuclear weapons; they manufactured seven fission gun-type devices. Fortunately, these were never used, and South Africa signed the Nuclear Non-Proliferation Treaty on 10 July 1991.

Borrowing loosely from Michel Foucault's notion of the 'capillary functioning power', this chapter explores some themes of a story that has been surprisingly slow to emerge. It begins with the local, or Foucault's 'smallest details of everyday life' [4] – the idea that modern power is most effective as 'micropower'.[5]

The local

In July 1986 four white women activists were arrested under the second of two States of Emergency. While they were not formally charged under any law, their incarceration did come to enjoy the attention of the courts even though the arrests took place during a bleak moment of apartheid repression. How? Why? Under administrative law procedures, it was possible to bring an appeal for the release of 'emergency detainees' if bad faith or personal animus could be shown on behalf of the state. On some such occasions, high court judges could order their release. From the judge's point of view, the most taxing part of the case at hand was the claim that the man from the 'Branch' (as the security police were colloquially called) had been spurned in a love affair by one of the claimants; collectively, the claimants wished to show that this arrest, like the others, was an act of vindictiveness. My immediate interest does not lie in the outcome of the case, but rather in the documents served before the court on this occasion which offer an interesting insight into the mind of apartheid at a crucial moment in South Africa's history. For the purpose of this chapter, I want to analyse one of these documents to illustrate some points about the Cold War in the mind of the apartheid state, because it offers an interesting insight into the worldview of those charged with maintaining apartheid.

In their statement to the court, the police revealed a world structured around binaries. Pure, clean, and decisive, the South African government represented a force for progress and order on a chaotic continent. Its opponents were confused rabble, conspiratorial in their social goals and intent on perpetuating regimes of violence.[6] This was the most familiar of all Cold War rhetorical devices with the accompanying assumptions of the superiority of one world over the other. The polarity providing, as Raymond Williams once suggested, coherence in the face of threatened social disorganisation.[7] In apartheid's case, however, there was not one, but two, divides – the first racial, black/white, and the second, the more familiar Cold War, east/west – were superimposed one upon the other. And at times, especially in the 1980s, it was difficult to isolate which of these was dominant.

Was the intention of the police in detaining these women to sustain the policy of racial domination? Or was their objective to save South Africa from the 'scourge of communism'? The answer is not all together clear.

For the police, the detainees were dupes of 'the world outside', who had misled a black community that could itself exercise no political or social agency: in a technique all too familiar in South African history, they set out to suggest that black people had no politics. This confirms a familiar theme in politics: in oppressive regimes, state functionaries, like the power they serve, often believe that victims have no interest in politics. Instead, politics is 'imported' or manipulated by outsiders with nefarious intent.

The security police went on to suggest that 'the . . . detentions and arrests were absolutely necessary in order to maintain public order and safety and for the termination of the state of emergency'. But closer inspection reveals that this conclusion was rooted in stylised interpretations – both of the behaviour of the detainees and the institutions that carried their professional lives. So, an adult educator had a strategy for 'socialising the youth and adults for the structuring of a so-called alternative society . . . [her] . . . teaching was aimed at the dismantling and rejection of the then system of education by revolutionary means and revolutionary educational teaching'. The police statement continued, 'alternative education, also known as "People's education" . . . is the left wing answer to the Government Education System'. This tactic of building conspiracy upon fragmentary evidence and the reaching of conclusions continued throughout the statement. As another example of this tactic, a copy of a pamphlet that was 'distributed' at a meeting in Johannesburg was attached to 'show how the so-called Democrats intend . . . to recruit the masses and organise the take-over of power'.

As they addressed the work of another organisation, one aimed at ending the conscription of young white men into the military, the police invoked the Cold War. The 'prime objective of this organisation is to break down the military system in the country . . . [this] . . . will make it easier for the ANC to take over, especially in regard to the townships'. They continued, the End Conscription Campaign 'is viewed by politicians as potentially the most dangerous political movement to emerge in the current crisis . . . It is heavily foreign-financed and has in recent months established overt personal links with the Helsinki-based War Resisters International, an identified adjunct to the vast Soviet "Active Measures" apparatus [sic]'. Having drawn upon one of the Superpowers, the document turned to the other making the appeal through the power of the personal: '[S]ources in America inform . . . [us] . . . that one of the applicants had sent anti-South

African propaganda to the United States of America, New Zealand and the United Kingdom. She also sent information on the state of emergency in South Africa to these countries.'[8]

As in many political conspiracies, the role played by individuals is important to its unfolding. Nelson Mandela – who by then had been in prison for 24 years – appears in this version of South Africa in the mid-1980s, but he is more foil than direct participant. The embodiment of evil is reserved for Joe Slovo, General Secretary of the South African Communist Party and leading member of Umkhonto we Sizwe (MK), the ANC's military wing, who was then in exile in Zambia. In this (and other state constructions of the 1980s), Slovo is a Svengali-type figure intent on manipulating the foolish 'masses' for reprehensible ends.

Absurd, conspiratorial and plainly stupefying though these views may appear to be, they offer an insight into the mind of the apartheid state. They are no different from the thinking – again, absurd, conspiratorial and plainly stupefying – that emerged from the country's white leaders. South Africa's then president, for instance, constantly argued that the country faced a 'Total Onslaught' from the Soviet Union and its allies, and that the Kremlin/Soviet Union/The Russians (the terms were often simply substituted one for the other) was intent on overthrowing white, Christian rule. In response, his 'good government' was compelled to embark on a 'total national strategy' which would prevent 'chaos and a government controlled by the communist-dominated ANC'.[9]

How was this kind of thinking possible in a distant corner of Africa? For this, I return to Foucault, and his idea of Panopticism.

Security states

A series of disciplinary routines helped to embellish Security Studies as a fixed point of knowledge in international relations, and the Cold War played an important role in this consolidation. Work presented by others in Critical Security Studies locate the origins of the idea of 'National Security' in the United States (US) National Security Act of 1947 – legislation which aimed to provide integrated policies and procedures for departments, agencies and functions of the US Government relating to the issue of national security. This interpretation is confirmed by a collection edited by Norman Graebner which broadcast the proceedings of a conference organised at West Point in April 1982. The conference focused on the 'efforts of the Truman and Eisenhower administrations to come to terms with the consequences of the Allied defeat of the Axis powers and the ensuing failure of the victors to disentangle their interests in a militarily and politically divided world'.[10]

Fixed by the practice of knowledge and the managerial and policy processes that they sanction, state security takes on a life of its own; a life which is largely unencumbered by the contestations of public politics. In apartheid South Africa of course all discussions on state security, critical or other, were silenced by legislation and the threat of incarceration.

But what role did the Cold War come to play in bringing this about? This question must be set within wider theoretical questions. Is it inevitable that metropoles frame and authorise development and behaviour on the periphery? Why is it that states on the global periphery always act in terms of the power of the centre? Can states on the periphery, like South Africa, ever define themselves outside of a frame authorised by a metropolitan centre?

For two centuries South Africa's centre of political universe was Britain – through the successive administrative codes of Colony, Empire and Dominion. After World War II, this cosmos was replaced by the US with the Cold War providing the organisational frame. The crude genealogy that now follows is intended to help the reader think systematically about theoretical issues, and simultaneously set a frame for a deeper argument.

Notwithstanding obvious parallels between the early frontier and other experiences of white settlement in the US and South Africa, until the mid-twentieth century, there were few direct links between the two countries. As a British Colony (and later a Dominion), South Africa was linked to the wider world through London; the US saw southern Africa as a British sphere of influence,[11] and 'in that capacity it had limited *political* importance for the Americans'.[12]

This changed after 1948, though, the year the National Party came to power and the point from which legalised apartheid commenced. South African pilots participated in the Berlin air-bridge of 1948–49, and a squadron (made up of F-51D Mustangs and later F-86F Sabre jets) flew ground attack and interdiction missions as part of the USAF's 18th Fighter Bomber Wing in the Korean War. This was the closest the US and South Africa came to having a formal combat co-operation during the Cold War. The example is instructive because South African forces could have exercised an option to serve under Commonwealth command. As these actions showed a commitment to accept Western interests as their own, South African defence and security thinkers turned their attention towards reinforcing their strategic importance to the global metropole although it is not surprising that 'the US also exerted pressure for a direct military contribution'.[13]

The British remained of prime importance, however. When the Royal Navy withdrew east of the Suez Canal in 1967, for instance, an emotionally charged debate arose in defence circles in Britain and South Africa over the strategic significance of the naval facilities at the Simonstown base, near Cape Town.[14] The sea route around the Cape (of Good Hope) had been valued by the Royal Navy since 1806, but in the late-1960s Britain's Labour government was under increased public pressure to abrogate these responsibilities because they sustained a link to apartheid South Africa. In response, the South Africans were determined to show that they were capable of 'filling the void' (to use the language of the debate); to do so, however, they needed to purchase ships and aircraft. This ignited a discussion about the issue of arms sales to the apartheid state ending in a United Nations Security Council (UNSC) Resolution which was vetoed by Britain and France. Britain wavered; it sold some weapons, but not others. In the event, apartheid South Africa did acquire submarines and other defence equipment from the French.

What finally ended any maritime role for South Africa in the Cold War was a visit by the USS Franklin Delano Roosevelt to Cape Town in February 1967; its multiracial crew were not allowed ashore because the ship's command refused to comply with South Africa's policy of racial segregation. The price to be paid for continued access to apartheid's strategic facilities was simply too high, whatever possible Cold War security argument could be made. This was a clear case when opposition to racial ideology trumped Cold War strategic calculations.

The Cape Sea Route issue was invariably tied to a discussion around access to South Africa's strategic minerals – primarily vanadium, platinum, chromium, manganese – where the Soviet Bloc was the only alternative source of supply. Here the argument, like many of the time, was a simple either/or trade-off: either the West secured these from South Africa, or the Soviet Union would deny access and so bring its economy and, more importantly perhaps, defence preparedness to its knees.

Infinitely more important than this residue of Britain's maritime glory (or strategic minerals, for that matter), was the idea that white minorities represented a bulwark against the advance of communism on the African continent – while the idea had some following in the US, it was more attractive in anti-decolonisation circles in Britain, France and Belgium. In response to these, South Africa's first Nationalist Prime Minister, Dr D. F. Malan, had proposed a form of co-operation between the colonial powers and South Africa; he called this the 'African Charter'.[15] While the immediate resonance with the Atlantic Charter is obvious, Malan's purpose was in the opposite political direction. The African Charter had 'five main aims for Africa – to protect it from Asian domination; to preserve it for Africans; to ensure that its development was on Western Christian lines; to keep out communism; and to make it "non-militarised"'.[16] Pursuant to these goals, South Africa's military participated in several conferences that brought together the colonial powers to discuss the issue of 'African Defence'. So, at a conference held in Dakar, Senegal, in 1954, South Africa's Minister of Defence indicated that the country's participation in any defence of Africa would be 'with only limited manpower. Her chief contribution would consist of war material and general supplies'.[17] But because the African Charter was opposed to the tide of African independence, it is difficult not to see the coincidence between racial prejudice and a strain of anti-Communism – both strong themes, incidentally, in the unfolding of race relations in every corner of the world. But in South Africa, where race was everything, this perspective had an obvious appeal. It also made apartheid South Africa a ready target for every conservative crackpot, conspiracy theorist and con-artist in the world. And this brought the ideas of 'Counter-enlightenment' thinkers into both the Cold War and South Africa's place in it.

Counter–enlightenment

In 1965, the South African government-supporting publishing house, Nasionale Boekhandel, published a book by the American writer, Anthony Harrigan, who was then Director of the Foreign Policy Research Institute in South Carolina. Ordinarily this book, like many on the country's security and politics which were published at that time, should have stayed in well-deserved obscurity. However, in excavating it, I want to show how its message to South Africans, especially the country's ruling Afrikaner community, was a peculiar and attractive interpretation of thinking around the idea of national security as this was positioned within Cold War thinking.[18]

There are four further reasons for reappraising the book nearly four decades later. First, it was issued in the year that the then Rhodesia's white minority made a Unilateral Declaration of Independence (UDI): a moment of some anxiety for the white community throughout southern Africa. Second, it was issued in English by a publisher whose list, at that time, was mainly aimed at promoting South Africa's then other official language, Afrikaans – this suggests that its message was intended for wider international dissemination which, undoubtedly, would have included free distribution abroad to make a propaganda case for minority rule in South Africa, a common practice during the Cold War.[19] Third, the book suggested how deeply the Cold War and its cultural representations spread from the US and how effectively these had been taken up in other parts of the world, especially in minority-ruled South Africa[20] and in other residues of colonialism in Africa. Finally, the book's title *Defence against Total Attack* captured an idea which, with the passing of the years – but especially in the late-1970s and 1980s – strongly resonated both within South Africa's security circles and in the everyday life of the country. This especially followed the proclamation of the Total Strategy – the political doctrine, which as already seen, guided official South African security thinking during the leadership of P. W. Botha (Prime Minister 1978–1983; President 1983–1989) and which shaped South Africa's policy of destabilisation of its southern Africa neighbours.

The spirit of Harrigan's book, and the messianic response of South Africa's growing security establishment to its message (and others of the same ilk), is caught in a single sentence which reads: 'There is a world-wide significance to the struggle of the South African people to escape engulfment by barbarism, which has been the fate of most Europeans who have made their home in Africa.'[21] To arrive at this conclusion the author begins with the immediacy of the

1961 Congo Crisis and, thereafter, rehearses a set of routine and well-worn impressions on the nature of man, contemporary society and plain pessimism. These are drawn closer to the holding idea of security in a line that reads: 'A nation's security . . . is never permanently won because the world is permanently in convulsion.'[22] The narrative pays passing deference to the work of the existential philosopher Karl Jaspers, but the political and propaganda point is carried forward by some familiar intellectual devices used in Realist International Relations theory – the timelessness represented by the Melian dialogue from Thucydides, for instance, and credential support – mainly in the form of disjoined quotations – from International Relations scholars such as James D. Dougherty and the Harvard economist, Thomas C. Schelling.

These genuflections to academe aside, the text is redolent with crude racism and vulgar anti-Communism which, at that particular time, characterised contributions to a variety of establishment defence journals[23] in which, as Harrigan notes, earlier versions of chapters from the book had appeared. These include *NATO's Fifteen Nations*, *The Australian Army Journal*, *Proceedings of the U.S. Naval Institute*, *Quarterly Review* (London), *Europa-Archiv* and *The Royal United Service Institution Journal*. Reading the Cold War (especially its military culture) through these quite respected publications provides insights into the ideas that carried the Cold War and their understandings of the importance of South Africa. Not the everyday, to be sure, but certainly the everyday world of military – and other security – professionals.

Looking back across the four decades which separate that writing from this, it is still quite easy to judge Harrigan's work: although drawing upon the academe, it is patently not an academic text; its pseudo-scientific setting has offered the patina of intellectual respectability to an immediate political text, and a wider project which aimed to shore up the case for minority rule in South Africa by employing the legitimacy offered by the engineered body of knowledge which (all too-recently) was called Strategic Studies and which, in time, would shade into Security Studies. In South Africa, certainly, the role played by this body of knowledge in fostering the ideological purpose of the national security state and the support it enjoyed from the Cold War's bifurcated explanation of the global predicament, cannot be under-estimated.

The licence afforded by the emergence of the latter and its role as a means to the politics of state security for the white minority in South Africa becomes plain in Harrigan's final chapter which draws together the issue areas represented by eugenics, the idea of state and the narrative of Cold War struggle in advancing the cause of modernity. Particular significance is registered in the country's 'skyscrapers and modern highways'[24] and these are drawn backwards towards the foundational myths of Afrikaner ideology and identity – in particular the '[Great] Trek that was a march toward the fulfilment of South Africa's destiny for greatness'.[25] In his effort to provide political opportunities for Afrikaner ideology at an increasingly embattled time, Harrigan contrasts the momentum offered by South Africa's quest for modernity against the 'lesser breeds'[26] represented in Africa and in southern Africa. Harrigan's work, like most of the writing on security at the time, establishes three things: a bridge to history, a sense of place and the permanence of threat.

It may seem unfair to single out this work by an American publicist, instead of focusing on the work of South African writers who may, at the same time, have produced interpretations that were, perhaps, less ideologically-directed.[27] Nevertheless, Harrigan's book is emblematic of the knowledge represented both by embryonic Security Studies and, indeed, International Relations within apartheid South Africa. It is not surprising, then, the book was glowingly received in the country. The daily propaganda broadcast, *Current Affairs*, described the book as a 'timely reminder that we live in a world of hard realities'.[28] In order to overcome a difficulty in classifying this genre of anti-Communism, I will refer to my own earlier judgment of the type of work which Harrigan inspired in South Africa which I have described as ' "boldly sectarian and crudely simplistic" where the cumulative impression is one of "archaic reasoning, unsubstantiated impressions and arcane deductions"; where scholarship was characterised by its "vulgar anti-Communist message" which demonstrates the missionary nature of [much mainstream] scholarship in South Africa" '.[29]

Harrigan's book and others in its genre were crucial in transporting the post-World War II discovery and production of security knowledge and the Cold War ideology to South Africa where it was used to assuage the fears of the country's ruling white minority. Its impact on regional politics in southern Africa was devastating – for South Africa's minority, the idea of security came to be the one – perhaps, the only – acceptable form of social organisation. By locating the Cold War at the centre of political discourse, all alternative efforts to explain and expand understandings of international relations, especially in security, were silenced by the authority of Cold War interpretations. Within the sanction that this offered, the country's policy agenda was set; and within the same coda, 'research and knowledge falling outside . . . [this] . . . agenda was dismissed as "unscientific" and not really as security knowing'.[30]

This may be so. Security had entered the domain of policy in a form that was inarticulate but, paradoxically, highly persuasive to President Botha and imbibed by security apparatchiks. Listen to its form as it emerged in a government appointed commission into the Press under apartheid.

The Soviet Union has launched a fierce multidimensional and rapidly intensifying onslaught on the Republic of South Africa . . . it operates preferably by the process of proxy forces, such as the South African Communist Party, the ANC and the PAC, to conduct the revolutionary war in order to neutralise Western Europe by denying it access to strategic minerals and oil before finally tackling the USA.[31]

Epistemic communities

The construction of a 'Total Onslaught' against the Republic of South Africa as a security discourse and its role in setting the agendas for both racial inclusion and exclusion, were both politically satisfying and rich with the possibilities offered by positivist social science. Thus, for many in South Africa[32] (and in the metropoles of academic legitimacy) it was politically satisfying, intellectually engaging and career-advancing to pronounce upon these matters. The latter observation owes its place in this essay to the power exerted on the construction of security – Cold War and other – by the power of credentialed expertise and the influence of epistemic communities.

In South Africa, both during apartheid and in the post-apartheid period, the holding power of credential authority has played an astonishingly influential role in efforts to explain and manage social relations. In this process, the place occupied by expertise that was located at the metropoles of learning – Britain initially, but from the late-1960s onwards, the US – was central. Giving ease of access and government and private sector funding to a ready audience, often quite bizarre interpretations of the world, wrapped in Cold War thinking, came to enjoy wide acceptance in white South Africa circles. This process of conformity was speeded by the unquestioning role often played by the country's universities and the further complicity of academic disciplines, such as International Relations.[33] These built on the accepted bipolar script, tip-toeing round the issue of race in South Africa, bringing little more to the local than the same old message dressed in the security and strategic-speak of their favourite Cold War policy journal.

Local determination to advance this narrow, but apparently academically respectable, position that linked apartheid, through security, to the Cold War was furthered by the creation of the Institute for Strategic Studies at the University of Pretoria in 1977. In a search for an 'operational universe', a symposium launching the institute suggested that the 'central concept in the modern study of interstate relations is national security, an inclusive concept which, apart from traditional "defense [sic] policy", also includes the non-military actions of a state to ensure its total capacity to survive as a political entity in order to exert influence and to carry out its internal and international objectives'.[34]

Two conceptual points are important: first, rather than follow the American route and naming the epistemological project National Security; South Africa drew from the British roots of its educational system and called it Strategic Studies. Second, the chief security referent was with states and so it fostered and secured the country's needs. However, the gathering in Pretoria was not an endpoint in the making of security knowledge in South Africa; it marked, rather, a moment in the development of scholarly institutions that stabilised the master concepts of the Cold War and integrated these into the politics of race and minority power. The book of the conference proceedings, *National Security: a modern approach*, was well received in South Africa: Fredrick Clifford-Vaughan of the then University of Natal – a retired British officer – called it 'a necessary and interesting book' and described the formation of a think-tank on 'National Security' to be a 'worthwhile project'.[35] The establishment of centres of expert knowledge which took the Cold War as their organisational frame continued unabated in South Africa throughout the 1970s and 1980s: the Institute for the Study of Marxism at the University of Stellenbosch and, at the then Rand Afrikaans University, both the Centre for the Investigation into Revolutionary Activities and the Institute on the Total Onslaught.

But the power of knowledge generated in the metropoles, had a paradoxical affect on local endeavours to construct their universe within Cold War logic. It weakened the possibility that South Africans, especially the minority, could develop an independent capacity to interpret international politics, or even to make an independent 'threat analysis' of it. Let this second anecdotal story carry this point. At a conference – cut off from the prying eyes and ears of the press, and organised under the so-called Chatham House rules – held in a magnificent Tudor-style hotel above Pietermaritzburg in the early 1980s, I asked the then senior bureaucrat in the South African government's Ministry of Foreign Affairs, how many people in his department read or spoke Russian. 'Not one', was his unabashed answer!

From the Nixon to the Reagan doctrine

This makes it easy to explain why it was that American and South African interests so readily coincided over the war that both preceded and followed the independence of Angola. It also explains the absolute conviction in South African military circles that Washington had abandoned them in Angola; that it had left them to face *their common* enemy alone. Here is the view of a former SADF General, Chris Thirion:

> I was told by two gentlemen from the CIA, and they were working alongside
> National Intelligence. They came to me one day and they said, 'We want you to
> know that we know that the military are involved in certain activities inside this country
> (Angola), which – if it had to come out in the open – would be very detrimental to the
> (US) government as a whole.[36]

This also explains why the same military insisted that the politicians and their own bureaucratic rivals in the intelligence community, certainly at the time of the Angolan affair, were the stooges of the CIA.

This is an interesting, although not entirely new idea. Its recognition, however, does suggest how the Cold War optic helped to reinterpret the international relations of apartheid South

Africa. To see these it is necessary to look beyond the accepted narrative that endlessly juxtaposes apartheid's unacceptable racial policy against a world increasingly intent on supporting, certainly rhetorically, non-racialism. This move may also build towards revisionist understandings of US approaches to Third World issues in general. So, the Nixon Doctrine, which effectively replaced Containment as a Cold War strategy, meant that the US would no longer serve as the world's policeman. Instead, its allies and other regional powers would be encouraged to take responsibility for their own security.[37] In a compelling essay, Mahmood Mamdani uses the Southern African case to illustrate how it was that the US 'harness[ed] . . . even . . . cultivate[d], terrorism – [South African and other] – in the struggle against regimes it considered pro-Soviet'.[38]

This is not the only interpretation: for the immediate purpose, the following complementary spin on the same moment could be considered. In the interests of American power, the Nixon Doctrine once again chained the periphery to the political goals of the centre, especially in security studies, where geopolitics counts for everything and local centres of power determine the course of immediate inter-state politics.

This revived an understanding that South African military should help to anchor Western interests in a distant corner of the world. South Africa had long experienced this so-called political sub-contracting and would do so again. As a Dominion (to use the formal name), South Africa had helped to secure the British Empire, and (at the end of the Cold War and apartheid) it would be named as a possible 'pivotal state', and would help to secure George H. W. Bush's 'New World Order'. Although separated by nearly 60 years, these proposed roles relied on the ready compliance of ideologically-sympathetic states in distant places to protect the interests of the powerful and, simultaneously, to project their power into far corners.

For Henry Kissinger, the notion of South Africa as a 'dominion' or a 'pivot' was a key to the world he hoped to restore. In his National Security Memorandum (NSM) 39 document, correctly dubbed 'Tar Baby' by his opponents, he looked towards the maintenance of white power in southern Africa. '[T]he whites are here to stay and the only way that constructive change can come about is through them,' was the core conclusion. This view sanctioned significant forms of clandestine co-operation – military, intelligence, economic and even the exchange of spies. All of these gave apartheid South Africa the status of a reliable (even if sometimes embarrassing) Cold War ally.[39]

The cinematic vistas that Cold War intellectuals like Kissinger brought to surrogate states were seamlessly transmitted deeper into the periphery. If Rhodesia (now Zimbabwe) was one, the other was South West Africa (now Namibia) – a territory that had been mandated to South Africa at the end of World War I. A war of national liberation, itself cast in a Cold War binary, had commenced in that country in 1962 and would continue for 30 years. Still another war of liberation was fought in neighbouring Mozambique on the east: here the language of freedom was forcefully cast in the language of decolonisation (this time from Portugal) with strong overtones of European Marxism. But it was the torrent of war on the other side of the sub-continent, in Angola, which was to absorb increasing resources from South Africa and which was, on the arrival of the Cubans in 1974, to assure them, albeit momentarily, that they were a lynchpin (a word much loved by local security buffs) in global anti-Communism.

Ironically, it had taken a major political event in the metropole, the April 1974 coup in Lisbon, to shift the political and ideological map in the periphery. This was a moment of great import to Kissinger, even though initially he failed to grasp its significance for the world beyond the global core. But why was Kissinger was far more concerned about Portugal than South or southern Africa? Portuguese re-fuelling facilities on the Azores archipelago had proved crucial to US efforts to reequip Israel during the Six Day War of 1967. But as Piero Gleijeses' book shows, even the latter-day disciples of Metternich and Castlereagh eventually had to turn their attention to the sovereign states that had been constructed in the south.[40] As Kissinger wrote to US President Gerald R. Ford on Angola: 'I favor action. If the U.S. does nothing when the Soviet supported group gains dominance, I think all the movements will draw the conclusion that they must accommodate to the Soviet Union and China. I think reluctantly we must do something.'[41] A day later, Ford told Kissinger: 'I have decided on Angola. I think we should go . . . if we do nothing, we will lose southern Africa.'[42] This recognition amplified the importance that the apartheid government felt within the organising frame offered by the Cold War and, not surprisingly, its domestic conversation became littered with Cold War rhetorical forms.

Kissinger would visit South Africa twice. In an effort to settle the colonial (and essentially constitutional) problem in the neighbouring country of Rhodesia, he arrived in 1976 with an entourage which would have made the Rolling Stones Global Tour retinue seem modest. The tilt towards the white South was no longer possible; a victim of the events in Angola. At a meeting held in Pretoria in late September, Kissinger, John Vorster, South Africa's Prime Minister, and Ian Smith, Rhodesia's leader, hammered out a breakthrough to end UDI. This agreement acknowledged the principle of majority rule for the country.[43] However, after the British fumbled a follow up conference, Smith drew back, and UDI limped on for another four years essentially under two banners – anti-Communism and the white man's burden. Kissinger was to return to South Africa when he was out of office in 1981: this time he did not bring an entourage, but his wife, Nancy, and billeted with Harry Oppenheimer, the country's richest man. At a paper delivered to the establishment at the South African Institute of International Affairs, he almost raised questions about the durability of race-based politics in South Africa, but mainly beat the familiar Cold War drum.

After the Nixon Doctrine had run its course, the right of surrogates to roll back communism was reinforced by the Reagan Doctrine. More than any other Cold War development, this doctrine helped to filter South Africa's deepening domestic insecurity into the region and legitimised apartheid's two-decade long silent war on South Africa's neighbours: a strategic doctrine that unabashedly mimicked US policy in Central America.[44] By this time, however, South Africa's people had taken to the streets and the popular struggles were redolent with revolutionary and Marxist rhetoric; as were the many symbols of popular insurrection – tee-shirts, posters, graffiti. Not one, however, was as visually powerful as the photograph that appeared on the front-page of the mass circulation, *Sunday Times*, in July 1985. This showed the Soviet flag being carried high at the funeral of four slain anti-apartheid activists in the small Eastern Cape town of Cradock.[45] Events like these suggested how the Cold War had entered the everyday lives of South Africans, on both sides of its insidious divide.

Cultural forms

In compulsive, even obsessive, ways the Cold War and race were written and re-written on the psyche of white people. Take the so-called 'Veld Schools': these school outings were a rite of passage for white youths who were taken to nature camps at which the importance of environmentalism, and a romantic love of nature were drawn towards the security threat that the Russians/the Communists/Black people/African states were said to present to the white state. This was a kind of Rousseau meets the Russians; it would appear elsewhere, too. In the literature of the Afrikaans language, a number of books – *bildungsromans*, really – drew on themes of which Harrigan would have approved by presenting black South Africans as puppets in the hands of a master plan orchestrated by the Kremlin. Invariably, the plot was carried by Christian heroes and Communist villains, but the stakes of the contest were desperately high – the very 'survival of western civilization' in an alien and hostile continent.[46]

If this was one mode of social compulsion, another was the universal conscription of young white South African males – the only form of discrimination they faced! As the 1980s lengthened, conscripts faced stints of combat on the 'border' (read: in Angola). As the vocabulary of combat grew, South Africa was known as 'The States' and Namibia, which was used as the staging post for the occupation of southern Angola, was known as 'Nam'. The appropriation of these powerful, even evocative, terms from another anti-Communist war, in a distant corner of Africa, seems more symbolic than anything that has been encountered this far. But this projection of Cold War as culture (or is it the other way around?) had commenced far, far earlier. In early 1966, for instance, the song 'Ballad of the Green Berets',[47] with its vivid opening lines '[f]ighting soldiers from the sky, fearless men who jump and die', topped the South African music charts for weeks.

While the distance between this remnant of Cold War culture and the events on the ground may seem, especially to structuralists, vague and entirely inconsequential, it is worth pointing out that the training of South African Staff Officers at American facilities continued until the late-1960s. Magnus Malan, destined to become successively Head of the South African Army, the South African Defence Force and Minister of Defence when the Total Onslaught paranoia was at its height, attended the United States Command and General Staff College at Fort Leavenworth, Kansas; during this time he visited the White House and was the introduced to President John F. Kennedy with whom he later corresponded.[48]

The acceptance of the Cold War as the framework of international relations was reinforced by the power of television, which was introduced into the country on 5 January 1976. Months later, the country's only channel broadcast the BBC's epic 26-part series called *The World at War*. Its popularity often occasioned complaints from the restaurant industry that an absence of customers meant they had to close on the nights that it was screened. The credited cast of this series included World War II luminaries drawn from the West: 'interviews were from all sides, except the Russian'.[49]

The development of the film industry also helped. A number of state-subsidised films, such as *Kaptein Caprivi* (1972) dealt with South Africa's anti-Communist war.[50] As is known, counter-culture is the inevitable bed-fellow of all state propaganda even in the most reactionary places and at the bleakest moments. So, the idea of a heroic border war was to return to haunt the protagonists of the Total Onslaught in the mid- and late-1980s. The rise and flourishing of an anti-war campaign, drew literature[51] and music together in the very language, Afrikaans, which had been used to enunciate its importance. The literature was known by the term *grensliteratuur* (border literature). One short-story title, *My Kubaan* (*A Cuban of My Very Own*), perhaps more than any other, caught the ambiguity of the country's relationship with the threat on the border. This move entirely revitalised this language and helped to secure, in my view, its lasting future for an apartheid-free South Africa.

Conclusion

Certainly, these thoughts have rambled far and wide, and they are too busy, perhaps, to be of any possible didactic use. The aim has been to show that the Cold War provides an absorbing 'take' on the construction of contemporary South Africa because it offers a compelling account of the robust contest for a state on the global periphery. Sadly, the tussle reinforced the idea that South Africa as state, as place, even as nation, can only define itself through a metropolitan centre. It offers, therefore, an account of the way in which the binary of race and the Cold War both inter-twined and conflicted on the global periphery.

So what was it that allowed apartheid to survive for so long? Reason? Race? Reaction? The Russians? In apartheid South Africa, security knowledge as racial knowing and the Cold War – irrespective of whether its target was local, regional and/or international – was created and invariably reinforced by the psychology of maintenance. The kind of quotient routine that makes for the very stuff of politics and, in Hannah Arendt's terms, banality; where the daily grind determines life and death; where security police make decisions not on knowing, but on conspiracy. This move turns away from the grim details of state of emergency politics and the meta-narratives of Cold War towards the everyday.

This was the . . . habit that made prejudice a standard mode of perception . . . It . . . flourished in its crude aspects among members of the white, mainly Afrikaner, working class, for whom jobs were reserved in the police force, the army railways and harbours, the civil service, and small-scale farming. Ruling elites, in both the political and industrial sectors, satisfied that they had bought the compliance of the white electorate, gave a blank cheque to the military and law-enforcement establishments.[52]

One core question remains: why did apartheid end? Many writers have fingered the impact of the ending of the Cold War on change in South Africa. Indeed, one of the core explanations for the ending of apartheid – indeed, it is almost an article of faith – turns on the idea that the ending of the Cold War compelled South Africa's embattled minority government to recognise that the great game was up. Here is the argument:

> While the white minority's sovereignty had prevailed, its long-term prospects for survival, notwithstanding the powerful anti-Communist rhetoric, were poor. In crucial areas, changing technology had left South Africa's military further and further behind; as a result, the capacity to sustain a war, even (or especially) an African one, was faltering as the Battle of Cuito Cuanavale in Angola showed, and influential circles raised serious questions about the wisdom of continuing a war on the country's borders. So, the newspaper of the Dutch Reformed Church (Nederduitse Gereformeerde Kerk (NGK)), *Die Kerkbode*, published an editorial on 8 July 1988 that raised questions, for the first time, about the present and future role of South African troops in neighbouring Angola.[53] More seriously, almost, the struggle for South Africa had come home – delivering an outcome that the Cold War strategists most feared. Increasingly the battle for the country's future was fought on the streets of the dusty townships, rather than through the gun-turrets of those weapons that the minority, despite an arms embargo, was able to export. This was one side of the dumb-bell – to use a code word from Cold War strategic studies – however; the other side of the great South African divide faced a mirrored set of imponderables. There was no hope that the majority could prevail by force of arms. New forms of surveillance and global relations had overtaken the idea of wars of

national liberation, with their roots in the romance of the Cuban experience. Then, old allies – the Russians more importantly than anyone else – faced changing priorities. If there had been doubts about the direction of *Perestroika*, it was *Glasnost* with its near water-tight agreement over the division of the world into spheres of interest – especially after the 1986 Reykjavik Summit – which confirmed that things could never be quite the same again.[54] As the Cold War world ended, therefore, it was inevitable that peripheral conflicts, like the one over apartheid, would also draw to a close.

This foreclosing explanation offers a range of conceptual and political worries, as can readily be appreciated. And it almost entirely misses how deeply the Cold War was engrained – and certainly, why it still lurks – in the routine life South Africans have created for themselves, both in their new state and in the world. The opening of archives, in South Africa but elsewhere too, will enable some of this past to be exposed, and this will ease the task of research. But my worry is that a hurriedly written diplomatic history will hide the wrong of using people on the periphery as a pummel-horse for the great and the good in the metropoles of learning and political power.

This briefly brings me back to Foucault's capillaries. The new South Africa, the 'New World Order' and the new 'realities' of market economics, like the Cold War, are rhetorical devices used by the powerful to discipline and punish social deviance. The ready acceptance of these three 'news' into the discourse of politics transmits and produces routines of power from the global to the local. In this process South Africa, as it was in the Cold War, is a compliant state in a world whose course, once again, is set by metropolitan power and influence.

Notes to Chapter Two

1   A version of this chapter was delivered at a Seminar at the International Centre for Advanced Studies, New York University on 8 November 2002, and can be found at http://www.nyu.edu/gsas/dept/icas/Vale.pdf.

2   See, for example, R. Mkhondo, 'Nkuhlu unpacks Nepad', *Leadership* (December, 2003–January, 2004), 17.

3   See 'The Mandela File' at http://www.africa2000.com/BNDX/BAO110.htm.

4   M. Foucault, *Discipline and Punish: The Birth of the Prison* (Harmondsworth: Penguin, 1979), 198.

5   Ibid. 222.

6   This is a technique in much political rhetoric and has been used to embellish the narrative of white power. The images on the friezes of the Afrikaner shrine, the Voortrekker Monument, reflect the same images. The 'Voortrekkers . . . [are presented] . . . as pioneers of civilization; the Christian nation; imaging community; the unified nation; and the authentic nation. In contrast, the natives [sic] are consistently presented as a warring barbarous rabble. While Voortrekker soldiers stand in straight and ordered lines, natives [sic] are chaotic, undisciplined and unordered . . .', A. Crampton, 'The Voortrekker Monument, the Birth of Apartheid, and Beyond', *Political Geography*, 20 (2001), 228–9.

7   R. Williams, *The Long Revolution* (London: Chatto & Windus, 1961).

8   All these quotations are taken from '"Louise Vale and others" versus The Honourable The Minister of Law and Order and the Commissioner of Police etc.' Case heard in the Supreme Court of South Africa (Eastern Cape Division), September, 1986.

9   On this issue see K. W. Grundy, *The Militarization of South African Politics* (Oxford: Oxford University Press, 1988).

10   N. Graebner, ed., *The National Security: Its Theory and Practice, 1945–1960* (Oxford: Oxford University Press, 1986), v.

11   There is a brief account of this by T. Sisk in *The Encyclopedia of U.S. Foreign Relations* (New York: Oxford University Press, 1997), 96–101.

12   J. Brits, 'Despatching Apartheid: American Diplomats in South Africa', *South African Historical Journal*, 46 (2002), 177.

13   F. J. Nöthling, 'The Search for Defence Co-operation', in *History of the South African Department of Foreign Affairs 1927–1993*, ed. T. Wheeler (Johannesburg: South African Institute of International Affairs, 2005), 373.

14   For an orthodox account of this see T. Potgieter, *The Geopolitical Role of the South African Navy in the South African Sphere of Influence after the Second World War* (Pretoria: Institute for Strategic Studies, University of Pretoria, 2002). Recently these notions have been subjected to some revisionist thinking. See A. Thomson, 'Balancing Interests Beyond the Water's Edge: Identifying the Key Interests that Determined US Foreign Policy Towards Apartheid South Africa', *Politikon*, 32, 1 (2005), 123–37.

15   On this see G. R. Berridge, *South Africa, the Colonial Powers and "African Defence": The Rise and Fall of the White Entente, 1948–60* (London: Macmillan, 1992).

16   J. Barber and J. Barratt, *South Africa's Foreign Policy: The Search for Status and Security 1945–1988* (Johannesburg: Southern Books, 1990), 36.

17   Cited in R.F. Pfister, *Apartheid South Africa and African States: From Pariah to Middle Power, 1961–1994* (London: Tauris Academic Studies, 2005), 33.

18   This section is drawn from P. Vale, *Security and Politics in South Africa: The Regional Dimension* (Boulder, Co.: Lynne Rienner Publishers, 2003).

19   Professor Marius J. Swart, a leading Afrikaner public intellectual, recommended this to the publishers in a review of the book. See letter from Marcus de Jong to Mr Herman Steytler of Nasionale Boekhandel dated 11 January 1966.

20   On this see J. Bacon, *Flannery O'Connor and Cold War Culture* (Cambridge: Cambridge University Press, 1993).

21   A. Harrigan, *Defence Against Total Attack* (Cape Town: Nasionale Boekhandel, 1965), 89.

22   Ibid. 29.

23   It seems clear that these journals offer a compelling insight both into the ways of the Cold War but also into the ways of today's strategic culture. South Africa equivalent magazines, called *Paratus* and *Militaria*, remain to be tapped.

24   Harrigan, *Defence Against Total Attack,* 92.

25   Ibid.

26   Ibid. 95.

27   There are various South African examples at hand. See L. D. Barnard, 'Die Magsfaktor in Internasionale Verhoudinge' (The Power Factor in International Relations), 2 Vols. Unpublished PhD thesis, University of the Orange Free State. Also see C. Vale and I. van den Ende, eds., *The Loss of Innocence: International Relations Essays in Honour of Dirk Kunert* (Pretoria: HSRC Publishers, 1994). For a policy-oriented sample of this kind of thinking see C. J. Maritz, 'Pretoria's Reaction to the Role of Moscow and Peking in

southern Africa', *Journal of Modern African Studies*, 25, 2 (1987), 321–44.

28   Book Discussion: 'Defence against Total Attack' by Anthony Harrigan, *SABC Survey, Current Affairs*, 28 January 1966, 7.15 pm English Service.

29   P. Vale, '"Whose World Is it Anyway?" International Relations in South Africa', in *The Study of International Relations: The State of the Art*, ed. H. C. Dyer and L. Mangasarian (London: Macmillan, 1989), 208.

30   J. N. Rosenau et al., *Global Voices: Dialogues in International Relations* (Boulder, Co.: Westview Press, 1993), 13.

31   Cited in T. Lodge, 'Soviet and Surrogates: Black Nationalism and the Steyn Commission', *Critical Arts*, 2, 3 (1982), 23. The roots of these interpretations of South Africa are to be found in the work of a number of other 'counter enlightenment' writers. See, for instance, D. H. McClure, *The Soviet Threat to Europe and South Africa* (Cape Town: Jeremy Spence, 1979).

32   There are many examples of this, but let this single one stand for others, F. Clifford-Vaughan, *Force and Peace: Four Introductory Lectures on Strategic Studies* (Durban: University of Natal, Department of Political Science, Occasional Papers Series, 1979).

33   See Vale, 'Whose World Is it Anyway?'

34   M. H. H. Louw, ed., *National Security: A Modern Approach* (Pretoria: University of Pretoria, 1978).

35   Book Reviews, *International Affairs Bulletin*, 2, 1, (1978), 49.

36   http://www.mnet.co.za/CarteBlanche/Display/Display.asp?Id=1768

37   This is culled from G. Cleva, 'Kissinger, Henry' in *The Oxford Companion to Politics of the World*, ed. J. Kriger et al. (New York: Oxford University Press, 1993), 469.

38   M. Mamdani, 'Good Muslim, Bad Muslim: A Political Perspective on Culture and Terrorism', in *Critical Views of September 11: Analyses From Around the World*, ed. E. Hershberg and K. W. Moore (New York: The New Press, 2002), 49. See also M. Mamdani, *Good Muslim, Bad Muslim: America, the Cold War and the Roots of Terror* (Johannesburg: Jacana Media, 2004).

39   Adapted from *South Africa* 2, 22 (January 1997), http://www.foreignpolicy-infocus.org/briefs/vol2/v2n22saf_body.html.

40   P. Gleijeses, *Conflicting Missions: Havana, Washington and Africa, 1959–1976* (Chapel Hill: The University of North Carolina Press, 2002).

41   H. Kissinger, *The Years of Renewal* (New York: Simon and Schuster, 1999), 808. [While updating this piece on 31 December 2005, I happened upon notes – which included this, and the next reference – made by Dr John Seiler. A day later my friend, John Seiler, died of complications arising from Parkinson 's disease. On this occasion, I want to remember him with much gratitude and fondness.]

42   Kissinger, *The Years of Renewal*, 809.

43   On this see J. R. T. Wood, *So Far and No Further. Rhodesia's Bid for Independence During the Retreat from Empire* (Johannesburg: South Publishers, 2005).

44   On this see W. Minter, *Apartheid's Contras: An Inquiry Into the Roots of War in Angola and Mozambique* (Johannesburg: Witwatersrand University Press, 1994).

45   J. Seekings, *A History of the United Democratic Front in South Africa 1983–1991* (Cape Town: David Philip, 2000), 148.

46   On this issue see M. Crewe, '"Sunny Skies and Total Onslaught" – Youth Preparedness and Veld schools on the Highveld', in *The Proceedings of the Kenton Conference 1985*, ed. W. Morrow (Bellville: Faculty of Education, University of the Western Cape, 1996), 129–46.

47   I remembered this when paging through M. B. Young, J. J. Fitzgerald and A. T. Grunfeld, eds., *The Vietnam War. A History in Documents* (New York: Oxford University Press, 2002).

48   M. Malan, *My Lewe saam met die SA Weermag* (Pretoria: Protea Boekehuis, 2006), 42–6.

49   From *The World at War* (1974) (mini) http://www.imb.com/title/tt0071075/ (accessed 5 January 2006).

50 There is a neat history of the South Africa film industry by Keyan Tomaselli at <u>www://und.ac.za/ccms/</u> <u>publications/articles/cinemasa.htm</u>. Also see K. Tomaselli, *The Cinema of Apartheid: Race and Class in South African Film* (London: Routledge, 1989) and D. Craig, 'The Viewer as Conscript: Dynamic Struggles for Ideological Supremacy in the South African Border War Film', MA thesis, University of Cape Town, 2003.

51 A. Coetsee, *Letterkunde en die Krisis* (Johannesburg: Tauris, 1990).

52 N. Ndebele, 'Memory, Metaphor and the Triumph of Narrative', in *Negotiating the Past: The Making of Memory in South Africa*, ed. S. Nuttall and C. Coetzee (Oxford: Oxford University Press, 1998), 23.

53 'Troepe in Angola', *Die Kerkbode*, Cape Town, 8 July 1988.

54 For a dissident view from South Africa at this time see 'A View from the Summit. "The Centre of the Universe"', by P. Vale, *Sunday Tribune,* (Durban), 12 June 1998.

Chapter 3

Mirrorings: Communists, Capitalists and Voortrekkers of the Cold War

Monica Popescu

'Communism [is] the highest form of capitalism' – the head of the South African Security Branch, Major-General Hendrik van den Bergh declared in 1966, in a nonchalant statement that short-circuited the staple binaries of Cold War discourse.[1] The officer's political illiteracy aside, his oxymoronic formulation may actually unwittingly reveal points of convergence in the discursive strategies created by supporters of communism and capitalism alike. Singular as it might seem, this curious little sentence speaks of a larger conundrum that placed South Africa in an uneasy ideological spot between the Scylla and Charybdis of the Cold War. With its uncomfortable position in relation to Western capitalism and Soviet communism, South Africa becomes a privileged site for exploring Cold War contradictions. These contradictions become most explicit in the simplified ideological positions distilled for young Afrikaners, who were trained into proper citizens of the nation during the apartheid years. Surprisingly, there are not many literary texts written after the fall of the Iron Curtain that engage with the impact of the Cold War in South Africa. During the early 1990s, with the effects of *Perestroika* and *Pretoriastroika* in full swing, the binaries that had haunted political thinking across the globe for more than four decades were dismissed as self-evident positions or silenced as uncomfortable memories of a too recent past.[2]

In search for answers to this prolonged silence, in this chapter I discuss Mark Behr's *The Smell of Apples* and its engagement with educational models intended to respond to the Cold War context. Its protagonist, Marnus Erasmus, is enrolled in the Voortrekker Youth Organisation (Voortrekkers), a movement intended to create proper white citizens. First fleshing out the history of this group, I then consider the political training Marnus receives at home, at school, and with the Voortrekkers. In enacting strictures of Afrikaner culture, the novel's youthful protagonist unwittingly reveals contradictions that his culture and his government faced in their battle with enemies both imagined and real. Marnus' trajectory, from Voortrekker camps and seemingly innocent childhood games, to service in the army and death in combat during the Angolan War, is supported by Cold War slogans. Far from clarifying and demystifying the identity and values of the opposing camps, these slogans complicate these positions to such a degree that they become iconic of larger ambivalences. Where a plain dichotomy (capitalists against communists, Americans against Russians) is supposed to be at play, an uneasy triangulation emerges in its stead, and the rival camps mirror each other's discourses in uncanny ways.

White children in apartheid-era South Africa were usually assumed to have lived innocent, peaceful, and largely de-politicised lives; however, children's literature, the Boy Scouts, the Voortrekkers, and adult role models aimed to transform them into obedient citizens of the apartheid state. An anecdotal episode from J. M. Coetzee's memoir *Boyhood: Scenes from Provincial Life* testifies to the strength and coerciveness of dichotomies imposed equally by the apartheid culture and the global Cold War structures. Playing with lead soldiers and 'spring loaded cannons that fired matchsticks', the young Coetzee discovered with stupefaction that certain choices were heavily codified and polarised:

When the Russians and the Americans were first set before him as antagonists between whom he had to choose ('Who do you like, Smuts or Malan? Who do you like, Superman or Captain Marvel? Who do you like, the Russians or the Americans?'), he chose the Russians as he chose the Romans: because he likes the letter r, particularly the capital R, the strongest of all letters . . . Then came the realization, from the disapproval of his parents, from the puzzlement of his friends, from what they reported when they told their own parents about him: liking the Russians was not part of the game, it was not allowed.[3]

If as a child, Coetzee stubbornly insisted on having his own private rules of the game, which were not restricted by the politicised dichotomies of historical contingency (he secretly preserved his collection of snapshots representing Soviet soldiers), this was not the case with most white children. Those co-opted by youth organisations such as the Voortrekkers were indoctrinated in the spirit of nationalism, and, according to the movement's statute, were educated to 'accept authority' and 'the virtues of a Biblical Christian life'.[4] Releasing children from school for Friday afternoon training and summer camps, the Voortrekkers seemed to break patterns of authority, give full reign to the children's spirit of adventure, fair-play, and comradeship. However, the quasi-military structures of the organisation and its involvement in public celebrations and historical commemorations with an explicit nation-building character, make obvious its ideological patterns. Milestones of Afrikaner history were lavishly commemorated with pageants, festivals, and parades. These elaborately staged historical re-enactments that I shall discuss later in this chapter, have predictably resulted in the creation, modification, and re-enforcement of national mythologies: they articulated a central role for Afrikaner settlers in South Africa's history. Yet from the 1970s onward, they also took on a more improvised character, as they enacted the country's position within larger global structures. In other words, the diachronic national vector of cultural memory at work in such public ceremonies intersected with a synchronic, trans-national counterpart that addressed South Africa's position within the dichotomies created by the Cold War. It is this latter shaping force that reveals a triangulation of positions instead of the expected binaries of political thinking on either side of the Iron Curtain. The role models handed down to Afrikaner youth both by such extraordinary ceremonies and by quotidian cultural narratives were overlaid with anti-communist features sometimes at odds with the national epic they originally set out to mould.[5]

Cold War silences

Historians and political scientists alike rightly complain of insufficient attention being paid by their disciplines to Cold War relations in southern Africa. In literary criticism and cultural studies the picture is even more desolate: there is an outright lack of interest in the tensions and biases generated by the descent of the Iron Curtain.[6] A search in academic databases for the relevance of the Cold War in studies addressing contemporary South African literature leads to virtually no results. The Cold War does not figure as the structuring thread or overarching explanatory principle for recent articles written on apartheid-era literature. After decades of internal colonialism – as the apartheid regime has rightly been termed – a great deal of energy needed to be invested in dismantling knowledge structures that reinforced white supremacy, in recuperating alternative histories, and in giving a voice to the silenced. Yet this post-1990 omission resonates with the apartheid regime's own uneasy position within the binaries created by the Cold War.

The dilemma posed by communism and capitalism to the old Pretoria government arose from the National Party's economic and cultural values. On the one hand, South Africa had the highest percentage of state-owned economy outside the socialist bloc, making the country dangerously akin to communist polities.[7] On the other hand, the Afrikaner abhorrence of leftist atheism and their embrace of the cultural values of the West (the government saw itself as a last bastion defending Occidental values in Africa) made it reject the Soviet Union and its allies as the ultimate enemies. The Marxist bent of many freedom fighters provided sufficient ground for labelling the African National Congress (ANC) and the South African Communist Party (SACP) as puppet extensions of the Kremlin authorities. The conundrum was not solved, but merely deferred, by the options opened up in the 1990s. White people's initial fears of a socialist revolution were allayed by the ANC's decision to integrate the country in the global market economy. As the so-called Second World bid farewell to communist utopias with previously unsuspected alacrity, there was no credible socialist model left standing after 1989 for the leftist members of the post-1994 government. Under pressure to make the South African economy viable and to garner Western support, the ANC changed its leftist discourse to open up to the requirements of a global economy.[8] As the ANC deftly bypassed some of its former political goals, South African society as a whole deferred the debate on the impact of the Cold War. Concerned with the more pressing goal of decolonising knowledge systems previously controlled by the apartheid regime, cultural and literary criticism left Cold War tensions and incongruences brewing below the surface.

The silence surrounding Cold War discourse could find an easy explanation in the apparent explicitness of its dichotomies. After the Iron Curtain descended and divided not only Europe, but political allegiances throughout the world, the two camps were taken for granted if not as the absolute representatives of good and bad political and moral choices, at least as necessary positions that even sophisticated writers were forced to take. Under the added pressure of a polarised Cold War situation, in South Africa any opinion not associated with the leftist forces was automatically relegated to the opposite camp. At the beginning of the 1980s, Nadine Gordimer decried this Manichean dynamic which forced intellectuals to make unsubtle choices. In her essay 'Living in the Interregnum', Gordimer points to an impasse of categories, an impasse generated equally by apartheid dichotomies and by even larger Cold War binaries. In a political world where to win is to drive a simple and simplified message home, there is sadly little room for nuances, concessions about inadvertencies, and elaborations on exceptions. Admitting to nuances of grey in a black and white world can unwittingly betray the cause one supports. 'Manichean poisons' (a term Gordimer borrows from Czeslaw Milosz) had to be absorbed in order to ensure a safe and direct sailing into the home provided by the future.[9] Yet, it was these 'Manichean poisons' that gave Gordimer much trouble and forced her to explain her position. Why would a well-read, intellectually keen, politically savvy writer lean towards 'an alternative communism' as the political solution in South Africa? Was Gordimer not aware of the troubles African adaptations of socialism had encountered? Was she not in the know about atrocities committed in the name of communism in the Soviet Union, China, and the eastern European states? On the contrary, Gordimer was a passionate reader of Czeslaw Milosz, Milan Kundera, and other dissident writers from Eastern Europe, and was fully aware of the mechanisms of censorship set in place throughout the Soviet Union and its eastern European satellites. Yet on a globe polarised by Cold War binaries, criticism directed at communist regimes was interpreted as collusion with capitalist exploitation:

> It is difficult to point out to black South Africans that the forms of Western capitalism are changing towards a broad social justice in the example of countries like Sweden, Denmark, Holland, and Austria, with their mixed welfare economies, when all black South Africans know of Western capitalism is political and economic terror. And this terror is not some relic of the colonial past; it is being financed now by Western democracies – concurrently with Western capitalist democracy's own evolution towards social justice.[10]

Gordimer thus recognises the intellectual's conscription into either of the battling camps, and acknowledges the ambiguities ready to explode out of this forced dichotomisation. She also defends her choice to dream of an ideal form of communism that South Africans black and white alike would be able to call home, in the temporal dimension beyond apartheid. Yet she pushes her exploration of Cold War tensions no further.

After the 1989–1990 moment, writers and critics' energy alike went into debunking apartheid ideology, and almost nothing was done towards analysing the discourse patterns produced by the Cold War. The anti-colonial rhetoric of the liberation struggle turned into the post-colonial discourse analysis deployed essentially to identify the mechanisms of oppression under the apartheid regime. There was a strong need to recover the voice of the silenced, to disclose the epistemological structures which favoured the white people, to identify the many ways in which the black and coloured population had been marginalised, discounted, and disempowered. Thus during the 1990s, the past decades still seemed too close for scholarship to reveal not only the apartheid government's involvement with Cold War rhetoric, but also the freedom fighters' indebtedness to the same discursive patterns.

Behr's *The Smell of Apples* is among the few texts that directly engage the Cold War discourse.[11] A *bildungsroman*, Behr's work has been celebrated for revealing the structures of indoctrination that transformed South African white children into subjects that acquiesced to state ideology.[12] The quasi-military rhetoric of the endangered nation is reflected by the family and social structures within which Marnus, the narratable voice in the novel, is enmeshed: he has to display soldier-like patience and endurance while fishing with his father, he is enrolled in the Voortrekkers, he receives military epaulettes for his birthday, and, of course, when he grows up, he participates as a lieutenant in the Angolan war. The rites of masculinity into which both the state and the father attempt to initiate Marnus are revealed as physically and psychologically violent processes aimed at creating obedient citizens.

Voortrekkers of yore and of today

Established in 1931, the Voortrekker Youth Organisation was named after the nineteenth century Boer pioneers and therefore was meant to re-enact their trail-blazing role and speculate (on) their core values, in the double sense of mirroring and deriving ideological profit from these values. It was intended as an Afrikaner counterpart to the Boy Scouts organisation. In the 1930s, the latter had attempted without success to bring the young descendants of Dutch settlers into their organisation; yet the required allegiance pledged to the King of England was a deterrent for the Afrikaner nationalist spirit on the rise, as was the suspicion that the Scouts and Guides movements would grant full membership to the coloured and black Wayfarers and

Pathfinders groups.[13] During the latter half of the twentieth century, the Voortrekkers focused on preparing proper citizens of the apartheid state: biblical values and patriotism were inculcated in the same breath during camp training, with uniformed parades, flag raising, *skriflesing en gebed* (scripture and prayers) every morning and evening.[14]

There is a striking scarcity of documentation on the Voortrekkers, despite the organisation's continued existence beyond the end of apartheid. Their acknowledged goal of inculcating, developing, and spreading Afrikaner cultural values explains the slim number of publications in English, but does not account for the equal shortage of resources in Afrikaans. The Voortrekkers are tangentially mentioned in studies on white youth culture and education that critically engage the formation and perpetuation of apartheid mentality. These mostly post-1994 studies are matched in the previous decades by the odd enthusiastic essay that actually praises the ideological apparatus underlying the organisation. For instance, in an educational treatise on the role of the Voortrekkers as a therapeutic measure for the improvement of the mental health of youth, J. P. C. Meyer praises the organisation as a palliative to 'behaviour deviations' in teenagers and demonstrates that, once enrolled in the movement, the school children improved their 'discipline and sense of duty' and 'developed a healthier attitude towards the church, fellow beings and parents'.[15]

If the core of the Voortrekkers' activities consisted in learning nature skills twinned with leadership abilities and patriotic feeling, these young pioneers also participated in events carrying an overt ideological component. Accompanying ox wagons loaded with settler nostalgics, these young pioneers marched into Pretoria during the 1938 centenary celebrations of the Great Trek, where the foundations of the Voortrekker monument were laid. The grandiose festivities for the inauguration of this edifice in December 1949 gave the young Voortrekkers the opportunity to hoist and strike flags, carry the torch, while the adults enacted historical tableaux and gave ardent thanks to God. More flag-carrying and torch-bearing opportunities were generated in 1988, with the one hundred and fiftieth anniversary of the Great Trek. However, these occasions did not lend themselves only to round figure anniversaries: more mundane activities, such as waving little orange, white, and blue flags on Parliament's opening day through the 1980s kept the Voortrekkers initiated into the continually adjusted narratives of nationhood shaped in South Africa.[16]

Several excellent studies, most notably *Apartheid's Festival: Contesting South Africa's National Pasts* by Leslie Witz,[17] as well as articles by Peter Merrington and Loren Kruger have shaped the field of research on historical re-enactment in South Africa.[18] Yet instead of focusing on the Voortrekkers' participation in parades and ceremonies, I would like to take a more textual approach and point out the wide variety of cultural texts (literature, children's books, educational tomes, and visual texts) that directly or implicitly prescribed the normative behaviour of Afrikaner youths. If Voortrekkers' commandos participated directly in historical re-enactments of crucial moments of Afrikaner history, the majority of the white youth were also involved in daily enactment and re-enactment of the roles prescribed for them by the apartheid state. These roles did not only solidify the concept of Afrikaner nationhood based on a reinterpretation of past events, but also shaped and modified it in accordance with the larger global political context of the latter half of the twentieth century. With the advent of the Cold War, a new feature was thus added to the already palimpsestic Afrikaner sense of nationhood: this was its anti-communist identity, with South Africa projected as an anti-Soviet bastion and embracer of Western values. In this way the Voortrekkers, with their seemingly innocent emphasis on nature-skills, provided excellent training grounds for later participation in the compulsory military service and preparedness for the anti-red war as national service conscripts deployed to Angola attested:

My best preparation for the army was the *Voortrekkers* . . . During school holidays in the autumn and spring they offered camps, mostly teaching fieldcraft and campcraft. This was a[n] introduction to living in tents, queuing for food, and sharing bathrooms. I was never taught to pitch a tent in the army, but it wasn't needed, for I already knew. (The easiest way to pitch a tent is the way I was taught in the *Voortrekkers* . . . *Voortrekker* leaders had often been to the army and applied what they had learned at these camps. The Defence Force knew that, and readily supplied tents and water carts for these camps. It was part of the total defence against the total onslaught.[19]

The connection between Voortrekker training and anti-communist preparedness was emphasised in another account:

I was a member of the Voortrekkers. It was [a] very nice paramilitary organisation, supposed to be the Afrikaans version of the Boy Scouts, with very much the same uniform, but by the time I was there the uniform was brown shoes, knee lenght [sic] socks, brown shorts, a dressy sort of shirt with all your badges you could earn sown to your sleeve, a brown tie and a beret. At all the camps there was flag raising parades with '*skriflesing en gebed*' (scripture and prayers) every morning and evening. Sometimes when they were feeling generous the parade was in normal clothing, but mostly it was in uniform. We had lectures in fieldcraft and survival, slept in army tents (on the ground of course), and had inspection every morning. I didn't think those camps would have been possible without the logistical support of the army because all the catering equipment, the tents, generators and lights were supplied by the army. In 1983 my father was called up for the Buttermilk camps, when all the older men who weren't drafted or did military service were militarised. A two week camp with some drill training and lectures and they were all given R1's to take home and a set of browns, ready for the '*rooi gevaar*'.[20]

Feeling increasingly trapped among countries with Marxist sympathies, by 1975 South Africa secretly sent troops to Angola.[21] This anti-communist emphasis in foreign policy resulted in an adjustment of the good citizen model that the youth were supposed to internalise and emulate. Thus, the biblical Christian lifestyle that Voortrekkers, like the nineteenth century Boer pioneers, pledged to enact in their daily life was expanded to include anti-communist values. But this moral and physical preparedness for the so-called 'total onslaught' unleashed by the Russians did not come without its inherent self-contradictions.

Uneasy binaries

Behr's *The Smell of Apples* is one of the very few texts that explicitly foreground the impact of Cold War rhetoric on children's imagination. Marnus Erasmus, its central character, takes the already mentioned route from Voortrekker camps to service in the army, from internalising the values of Afrikanerdom to acting them out in the war against the Popular Movement for the Liberation of Angola (MPLA) and Cuban forces in Angola. The narrative strides two timeframes: while most of the events take place in December 1973, as 11-year-old Marnus prepares for the end of the school year and the Christmas vacation ahead of him, this storyline is interspersed with 1988 episodes from the main character's service in the army during South Africa's secret war in Angola. Much of the novel's narrative energy is directed at unmasking the nationalist and masculinist culture in which Afrikaner children were raised. As Rita Barnard has argued, both the Erasmus family microcosm and the Afrikaner macrocosm rely on a code of secrecy that binds characters together.[22] The novel's climax is reached when Marnus peeps through the chinks in his floor and witnesses his father sexually assaulting Frikkie, the boy's trusted friend and play mate. Far from bringing the expected rebellion, this shocking revelation leads to collusion between the father's values and the son's goals for the future.

The child of the youngest general in the SADF and of a beautiful opera singer turned dedicated housewife, Marnus trusts the political knowledge he imbibes from his parents and never fails to reproduce it for the benefit of the readers: 'Dad says things are looking bad up north. They've even started planting bombs in South West Africa. Things are worse than when dad was in Rhodesia. The Communists muddle up people's brains so that in the end you can't trust anyone. The Communists indoctrinate everyone.'[23] Indoctrinated himself with the values of Afrikanerdom, Marnus is less a self-determined agent than a performer of the role of obedient, respectful, and hard working child assigned to him by his parents. 'Quietpoliteandinthebackground,' Marnus repeats over and over again and internalises the conduct rules set out by his mother, which are echoed by school instructions and Voortrekkers strictures.

The process of ideological cooptation has given rise to numerous theoretical interpretations, from Althusser's interpellation and his ideological state apparatuses to Homi Bhabha's triad of church, classroom, and barracks as the locus of nationalist indoctrination.[24] Given the theatrical nature of the Voortrekkers' participation in public celebrations, I emphasise the usefulness of re-enactment theory to understand the *frisson* that public recreations of historical moments offer to their participants. The thrill of making history anew, of traversing time to re-live and re-conceptualise a symbolically-charged moment might not be immediately transparent to participants in all its political ramifications, but it offers theoretical food for thought regarding the efficiency of ideological cooptation by means of elaborate public celebrations. The Voortrekkers, with their uniforms, berets, oaths, and command hierarchies gave Marnus the elaborate ceremonies a child raised in a general's household came to adore. Yet Marnus is equally attentive to information delivered by school teachers, newspapers, the church, and later, when he grows up, the army.

The Erasmus family are selective in their reading tastes: 'Dad only reads *Die Burger* . . . We don't read the *Cape Times* or *The Argus*,' Marnus explains, because the latter are written by English 'foreigners' who are unconcerned with the fate of South Africa.[25] If the English-speaking South African journalists are thought to deliver only 'propaganda' and are therefore to be avoided by any self-respecting Afrikaner, the information delivered by the nationalist daily *Die Burger* is absorbed with much interest, especially when it confirms Afrikaner opinions about other South Africans. Its journalists are quick to label the political awareness campaigns and the rise of the Black Consciousness movement at the University of Western Cape as 'savage goings-on' that lower the standard of coloured education.[26] Presiding over the white-washed version of the past that children are being offered is the figure of the schoolteacher. If Frikkie Delport has heard about the genocidal campaigns white settlers and hunters carried out against the San population, the teacher authoritatively dismisses this information: '[I]t wasn't the Boers that killed off all the Bushmen, it was the Xhosas.'[27] Furthermore, Leonore Erasmus sings in the church choir and Marnus has been taught all that a good Christian needs to know: taking the name of the Lord in vain will propel one's family into the everlasting fire of hell, while scorching the back of a coloured boy and mutilating him for life will barely provoke any commotion in the white family the child's mother serves. If Behr's novel touches on all the institutions of ideological cooptation that shape the life of Marnus, in this chapter I focus mainly on the Voortrekkers and the discursive dilemmas they faced during the Cold War.

In proposing national narratives and devising role models for the youngsters to enact, state ideology reveals its inner contradictions. To oppose communism during the Cold War meant to embrace Western capitalist culture. Yet the conservative Christian nationalist outlook of the Erasmus family rejects the West as debauched and immoral. American politics are regarded as muddled backwaters, with leaders lacking the vision they preach to their allies:

> Dad says Nixon will be out of the White House before Christmas and it looks like the
> Americans are going to lose the war against the communists in Vietnam. Dad says it's

typical of the Americans to try and prescribe to the Republic how we should run our country while their own president is such a rubbish. Dad says you don't tell someone else how to make his bed when your own house looks like a pigsty.[28]

Apart from the repeated assertion of paternal authority, as Marnus argues by means of quotation, what transpires from this fragment is South Africa's imperfect alignment with the American camp within the binaries established by the Cold War. General Erasmus treats 'communist terrorists' like hunting trophies (he tortures, murders, and displays them for photo shoots) without any signs of uneasiness, while his Christian morality shivers at the thought of entering a jazz bar, considered to be a site of American depravity. Furthermore, the most powerful textual subversion comes from the identification of signifiers supposed to belong uniquely to the Afrikaner culture in the discourse of the opposing camp. Afrikaner culture shared strategies and discursive patterns with the very ideologies it combated most fiercely. Thus, many of its authoritative patterns are characteristic not only of patriarchal, militarist systems, but of the communist dictatorships they despised and feared so much.

Similar uprooted forms of language have circulated both under apartheid and communist dictatorships. The inflexible *langue de bois* of totalitarian national ideologies thrives at the expense of children, who are both optimal surfaces, ready to be inscribed, as well as enactors and disseminators of a rhetoric they cannot fully comprehend. For little Afrikaner boys such as Marnus and his friend Frikkie, to be a Voortrekker was cool, while the English-speaking Boy Scouts was deemed unpalatable:

On Friday afternoons we have *Voortrekkers*. I'm the team leader and Frikkie is my deputy. Our team is the Lions and our motto is: *Voorwaarts*. The Spiro twins are Boy Scouts and we always fight about which is better: Voortrekkers or Boy Scouts. We always say the Boy Scouts is naff. Ilse used to be a Voortrekker until last year. But when she came back from Holland, she said she was lagging behind in her school-work because of her activities. When she stopped Voortrekkers, Dad was very disappointed, because Ilse would definitely have become a *Presidentsverkenner*; only the top Voortrekkers become *Presidentsverkenners*. [29]

The moral and intellectual distance between reader and narrator upon which the effectiveness of this episode is based, displays a gradation of levels of ideological awareness: from the fully naïve Marnus, who takes the organisation's award structures as tokens of success, to the awakened yet dissimulating older sister, who does not want to worry her parents with her newly gained political insight, to the reader, who is supposed to decode the ideological charge of the seemingly inconspicuous movement. As part of his Voortrekker training, history is passed down to Marnus in the abstracted form of military uniforms displayed in museums which masquerade the violence of the wars against the British and Zulu as tales of Afrikaner valiance. Voortrekkers dressed up national ideology as attractive tales of valiance and resourcefulness, and infused the youth organisation with quasi-military structures. Even from the cultivated and more aware, these structures elicited an ambiguous response: Behr himself confessed to have 'both loathed and adored' these masculinist codes.[30]

The conflation of contradictory ideologies under one heading is a characteristic strategy of monoglossic discourses, which reduce everything to a set of binaries. For Mrs Erasmus, liberals and communists are the same anti-Christian anarchists ready to destabilise her family and nation. For General Erasmus, jazz and hippie clothing, such as bellbottoms and platform shoes, are communist instruments that attract and corrupt the serious Afrikaner youth. According to General Erasmus, Tannie Karla, Marnus' nonconformist aunt, got mixed up with the liberals while attending university. 'When she started wearing platform shoes and jeans', the Erasmus family suspected her to have been influenced by a 'Moscow on the Hill' fashion, a fad arising from the rebellious University of Cape Town.[31] What (American) jazz, jeans, and platform shoes had to do with the eponymous Soviet style – which, quite contrarily, was fond of drab asexual clothing – would be difficult to fathom beyond the pseudo-logic of these conflations.

In search of ironic moments when the well-entrenched binaries of Cold War discourse are dismantled as lacking a real referent, I find the final touch in the interchangeable and free-floating signifiers between the opposing camps. A simple process of substituting 'communism' for 'capitalism' would show that the following slogans in *The Smell of Apples* could easily change camps: 'Communism is raising its ugly head everywhere'[32] contemplates General Erasmus with the determination to help get 'rid of this cancer';[33] for the Eastern bloc the same 'ugly head' belonged to capitalism. Terrorists have 'Moscow training', while at the same time 'the destabilizing elements' held responsible by the Eastern Bloc for infiltrating and subverting the socialist economies were raised and trained by American imperialists. All the dangers seem to be lurking from the opposing camp and the first targets are the ready-to-be-lured youth. Marnus is repeatedly told that 'pop music can cause you to become a drug addict. Before Lucifer was thrown out of heaven, he was the angel of music, and so it's only logical that the Communists will use pop music to take over the Republic'.[34] The same laments were simultaneously heard from the communist camp, where party propagandists pontificated about the dangers of pop music, associated with drugs, hippies, and the corrupt American lifestyle.

Although Behr is a controversial figure in South Africa (he confessed that he was co-opted as an informer by the security police), his novel has nonetheless been celebrated for unmasking the ideological structures which transformed young children into docile subjects of the apartheid state.[35] However, the novel is equally important in conveying the interrelations between apartheid and Cold War structures. It reveals the similarity of discursive strategies between the capitalist and communist camps during the Cold War, while displacing South Africa from the well- entrenched dichotomies established by the descent of the Iron Curtain. With their equal fear of red atheism and capitalist debauchery, Afrikaner culture as presented in the novel short circuits the gap between East and West. It conveys the inherent contradictions of the good citizen model that Afrikaner youths were supposed to enact on a daily basis. The triangulation that shows South Africa as falling between the discursively neat yet practically inaccurate dichotomous positions occupied by the American and Soviet camps could also provide the explanation behind the many silences that mark this field of study. The absence of the Cold War as a topic of interest in recent scholarship and literary texts on South Africa reveals less its self-evident character than its many tensions and ambiguities that still need to be comprehensively engaged.

Notes to Chapter Three

1   Delivered at an international congress on the dangers of communism, this statement issued by the head of the Security Branch was intended as an explanation for the high number of Jewish people attracted by the South African Communist Party. What it demonstrated, in fact, is the kinship between German Nazi ideology and apartheid politics. See B. Bunting, *The Rise of South African Reich* (London: International Defence and Aid Fund for southern Africa, 1986), especially chapter 4.

2   *Pretoriastroika* is a term that Rob Nixon unearthed from journalistic lingo describing the new orientation brought about by Frederik de Klerk's administration in South Africa, a current that eventually led to the first democratic elections in 1994.

3   J. M. Coetzee, *Boyhood: Scenes from Provincial Life* (London: Vintage, 1998), 27–8.

4   These values are still reflected by the Constitution (*Grondwet*) of the Voortrekker Youth Organisation, which can be found on the movement's website: http://www.voortrekkers.org.za/. For instance, one of the many repetitive promises (*beloftes*) that members have to pledge is phrased as follows: 'Ek sal oral en altyd probeer om 'n Voortrekker te wees, om gehoorsaam te wees, om my volk, my land en my medemens te dien en bo alles die Here lief te hê.' *An English translation would read: 'I will always and everywhere try to be a Voortrekker, to be obedient, to serve my nation, my country and my people, and above all, to love God.' I am indebted for this translation to Henk Rossouw.*

5   Certain terms mentioned above need to be contextualised. I obliquely invoke a terminology introduced by recent scholarship on historical re-enactment, which highlights the problems arising from the reduplication of events long past. The ideological benefits of making history come alive are obvious: such commemorations establish historical landmarks and settle ways of interpreting them while at the same time they persuade the public that something useful and authentic can be learnt from history. See A. Cook, 'The Use and Abuse of Historical Reenactment: Thoughts on Recent Trends in Public History', *Criticism*, 46, 3 (2004), 487–96; V. Agnew, 'Introduction: What Is Reenactment?' *Criticism*, 46, 3 (2004), 327–39; I. McCalman, 'The Little Ship of Horrors: Reenacting Extreme History', *Criticism*, 46, 3 (2004), 477–86. In this chapter I give a wider interpretation of historical enactments to include the emulation of tacit or explicit role models in the day-to-day life of Afrikaner youth. With respect to *The Smell of Apples*, this model allows, first and foremost, for an understanding of the political orthodoxies absorbed by children, while avoiding the already explored field of established theories of ideology (see R. Barnard's important article on Althusserian models of ideology

in Behr's novel '*The Smell of Apples*, *Moby Dick* and Apartheid Ideology', *Modern Fiction Studies*, 46, 1 (Spring 2000): 207–26). Second, these slogans reveal the ambiguities contained by these narratives handed down to children to be internalised and replicated.

6   The most notable exception is constituted by the work of R. Nixon, whose *Homelands, Harlem and Hollywood: South African Culture and the World Beyond* (New York: Routledge, 1994) displays a strong interest in the impact of the collapse of the communist regimes on the dismantling of apartheid. See also M. Popescu 'Translations: Lenin's Statues, Post-communism and Post-apartheid', *Yale Journal of Criticism*, 16, 2 (Fall 2003), 406–23.

7   A. Sparks, *Beyond the Miracle: Inside the New South Africa* (Johannesburg: Jonathan Ball, 2003), 170.

8   Internal criticism from its political allies has not been much delayed, as frictions between the leading party and the SACP and COSATU became more and more visible under Thabo Mbeki's second mandate.

9   N. Gordimer. 'The Essential Gesture', in *The Essential Gesture: Writings, Politics, and Places* ed. S. Clingman (London: Penguin, 1989), 270.

10   Ibid. 82.

11   For a comprehensive discussion of texts that deal with the war in Angola see G. Baines, 'South Africa's Vietnam? Literary History and Cultural Memory of the Border War' *Safundi: The Journal of South African and American Studies* 15 (July 2004), 1–21.

12   Several articles that discuss this novel stand out for their innovative approach. Barnard's essay, '*The Smell of Apples*, *Moby Dick*, and Apartheid Ideology', provides a compelling analysis of the process through which Marnus Erasmus and other characters in the novel are shaped by the state into obedient citizens. In 'The Whole Country's Truth: Confession and Narrative in Recent White South African Writing', *Ariel*, 27 (January 1996), Michiel Heyns engages the theme of confession and absolution within the national frame set up by the Truth and Reconciliation Commission, while in 'Fathers and Sons: Structures of Erotic Patriarchy in Afrikaans Writing of the Emergency', *Modern Fiction Studies*, 46, 1 (Spring 2000) he revises the Oedipal triangle as one involving the father, the son, and the fatherland, in a homoerotic relationship based on an 'erotic short circuit that fuses rivalry and love'.

13   T. Proctor, 'A Separate Path: Scouting and Guiding in Interwar South Africa', *Comparative Studies in Society and History* 42, 3 (July 2000), 618.

14   J. Malan, SADF National Service (1989–90) See http://uk.geocities.com/sadf_history2/jm10a61m.html as well as note 16 below.

15   J. P. C. Meyer, *Die Voortrekkerorganisasie Gesien as Terapeutiese Middel ter Bevordering van die Geestesgesondheid van die Jeug, met Spesiale Verwysing na 'n Empiriese Ondersoek.* [The Voortrekker Youth Organisation viewed as therapeutic measure for the improvement of the mental health of youth, with special reference to an empirical investigation.] (Pretoria: University of Pretoria, 1960), 103.

16   Several sources attest to the Voortrekkers' participation during commemorations and parades. In *The Official Programme for the Inauguration of the Voortrekker Monument: December 13 to 16, 1949*, the Voortrekkers are listed in the programme with flag carrying and flag striking tasks. Movietone's Online Newsreel Archive (<www.movietone.com>) contains two brief films covering the preparations for the 1938 centenary of the Great Trek (Stories 35024 and 35190). Finally, a South African photo database contains snapshots of members of the movement taking part in public commemorations. See, for instance, www. iafrikaphotos.co.za/site/AddToLightBox.asp?pic=25505&Dealer=5606& showcat=959.

17   L. Witz. *Apartheid's Festival: Contesting South Africa's National Pasts* (Bloomington: Indiana University Press, 2003).

18   P. Merrington, '*Masques, Monuments and Masons: The 1910 Pageant of the Union of South Africa'*, *Theatre Journal*, 49, 1 (March 1997), 1–14; L. Kruger, 'Acting Africa', *Theatre Research International*, 21, 2 (1996), 132–40.

19 'Total defence' and 'total onslaught' were governmental terminology to justify the militarisation of the country in order to withstand an allegedly imminent Communist invasion. This account of a former soldier on national service during the late 1980s is signed with the family name Daniel and posted on a website of South African conscripts titled *Sentinel Projects Presents 'Bad Guys'*, ed. Barry Fowler, 1997, http://www.geocities.com/sadfbook/bgtoc.htm. The cited paragraph can be found at http://www.geocities.com/sadfbook/6sai.htm (accessed 3 December 2005).

20 See http://uk.geocities.com/sadf_history2/jm10a61m.html.

21 Although South Africa sent troops to Angola in 1975, they were not maintained there until the 1980s.

22 Barnard, *The Smell of Apples*, 207–26.

23 M. Behr, *The Smell of Apples* (New York: Picador, 1995), 81.

24 See L. Althusser, *Lenin and Philosophy and Other Essays*, trans. B. Brewster (New York: Monthly Review, 1971) and H. Bhabha, 'The Other Question: Stereotype, Discrimination and the Discourse of Colonialism', in *The Location of Culture* (London: Routledge, 1994), 83.

25 Behr, *The Smell of Apples*, 85.

26 Ibid. 32.

27 Ibid. 8.

28 Ibid. 12–13.

29 Ibid. 46.

30 M. Behr, 'South Africa: Living in the Fault Lines', *Common Sense*, 60 (October 1996), 339. http://www.nd.edu/com_sens/october/behr.html (accessed 18 November 2005).

31 Behr, *Smell of Apples*, 105. The University of Cape Town was nicknamed 'Moscow on the Hill' due to its rejection of apartheid orthodoxies.

32 Ibid. 172.

33 Ibid. 116.

34 Ibid. 67.

35 At a conference held in Cape Town in 1996, Mark Behr confessed that as a student at the University of Stellenbosch he was co-opted as an informer by a high-ranking officer in the South African Police Force. 'From the end of 1986 to 1990 I received money for reposting mostly on the activities of the student organisation, NUSAS, at the University of Stellenbosch. In 1990 I brought this to the attention of the ANC in Lusaka and from then, until the end of 1991 I gave the ANC whatever information I gained access to.' (See 'South Africa: Living in the Fault Lines'.) His disclosure raised new questions about the confessional structures of *The Smell of Apples* and their persuasiveness.

Chapter 4

'Total Justification': Ideological Manipulation and South Africa's Border War

Dylan Craig

In this chapter, I am concerned with understanding *how* the apartheid state manufactured and buttressed its legitimacy, and attempted to justify the Border War. I propose to show how the collapse of the apartheid state was accompanied by shifts in the nature of the security threat to South Africa, and that the National Party (NP) government became increasingly desperate to answer charges that it was embroiled in an unjust war both at home and against the Frontline States. This placed ideological manipulation high on the government's agenda.

Conceptions of the state that posit the notion of a social contract or institutionalised relationships between rulers and ruled, take for granted the idea that the former are permitted to extract whatever resources are required for them to operate, in exchange for their provision of sufficient collective goods to the latter.[1] In this social contract collective goods are generally taken to be concrete and quantifiable (i.e., 'real'). However, it is well recognised that this relationship can be modified or manipulated to suit the peculiarities of a specific ideological environment. In the case of apartheid South Africa, cost-benefit analyses by supporters of the NP government were sometimes undertaken in abstract terms (such as a belief in racial segregation for its own sake rather than its utilitarian value), or by allowing such abstractions to modify decisions relating to real phenomena (such as the role of civic duty in convincing the electorate to maintain the apartheid state despite a shrinking relative share of the communal goods it provided).[2]

The mantle of legitimacy which the apartheid state needed to remain in power could thus be attained in two ways: either *directly*, through positive gains in various real indices such as personal wealth, international prestige, collective security, and regional stability; or *indirectly*, through the modification of domestic perceptions of the South African context, the dangers associated with mass rule, and so on, as well as a growing reliance on entirely abstract collective goods. It is argued here that *apartheid* survived only as long as it could convince its various foreign and domestic support bases (economic, ideological, political, and military)[3] that they were better off with than without the system. The foreign dimension of South African diplomatic strategy in this regard is dealt with elsewhere.[4] This chapter, instead, deals directly with (1) the growing need to sell apartheid to its support bases; (2) the mechanisms created to facilitate this, and the symbolic forms deployed by the mass media in service of this goal; (3) the degree to which this deployment enabled, sustained, and can be argued to have valorised[5] white South Africans' support for counter-revolutionary strategy, and (4) the link between the government's mounting failure to justify the Border War and the widespread withdrawal of support for the war in the late 1980s.

Selling apartheid to its support bases

The advent of NP dominance in South Africa in 1948 took place within a context of pre-existing white minority rule. What the NP added to this racial division of power was an ethno-cultural bias; in other words, a mandate relating to the revival of (white) *Afrikaner* primacy justified as an act of God.[6] This was to be achieved through an extension of the existing distribution of racial power beyond politics into the economic, ideological, and military spheres, both domestically and regionally.[7] Before 1948, black South Africans had been oppressed and politically disenfranchised; but under apartheid they were relentlessly stripped of economic agency and the capacity for self-improvement, and subjected to a fracturing socio-economic regime aimed at subverting any nascent sense of unity, transforming them from the anonymous inhabitants of Native Reserves into an amorphous labour pool for the mining industry and other sectors of the economy.

Meanwhile, for white South Africans, a series of benefits were being derived from the same system: individual and collective prosperity, personal and national security, and a growing coherence (in cultural and lifestyle terms) of an identity predicated on '*braaivleis*, rugby, sunny skies and Chevrolet'. Each of these gains was dependent (in different ways) on apartheid's subjugation of the black labour force, and as an examination of electoral records through the first 25 years of NP rule shows, this consolidated support for the ruling party.[8] Indeed, the trade-off must initially have seemed highly profitable for the white electorate. Until the mid-1970s, almost none of the direct costs of maintaining minority rule south of the Zambezi were being borne by the white South African taxpayer. This was due to the effective suppression of internal dissent by the South African Police (SAP) and intelligence services, as well as the co-operation of Rhodesian and Portuguese forces in neighbouring states in patrolling the borders and intercepting provisions destined for South African revolutionaries.[9] In addition, the country was enjoying a moderate rate of industrial growth, high (albeit fixed) prices for its gold exports, and the relative absence of cohesive international attention to its domestic affairs.[10]

Nonetheless, for the first time since the *Gesuiwerde Nasionale Party* ('Purified' NP), had broken from the Smuts–Hertzog alliance in 1936, the NP began to experience internal cleavages. A split occurred between the NP's centre-right (*verligte*, or 'enlightened') and far-right (*verkrampte*, or 'conservative') factions.[11] Taken together with the splintering-off of Andries Treurnicht's *Herstigte Nasionale Party* ('Reconstituted' NP) in 1969, by the mid-1970s the NP was being torn in two directions: one representing secular pressures for a firmer response to domestic and international insecurity, and the other demanding a return to the exclusivist and culturally-bounded NP of the Malan era. These tendencies were nothing if not contradictory; indeed, one of the greatest ironies of apartheid was the degree to which it required the (albeit firmly supervised) co-option of black people into the system.[12] At the same time, the NP's reliance on the *Nederduitse Gereformeerde Kerk* (NGK) [13] for a moral sanction of apartheid was being challenged. Following the resolutions of the World Council of Churches (WCC) Conference at Cottesloe in December 1960, the NGK had elected to withdraw from the WCC rather than address criticisms of apartheid. But this did not mean that the NGK and other Afrikaner churches continued to give unqualified support to apartheid. Dissenters such as Beyers Naudé, a former NGK pastor and *Broederbond* member, swelled the ranks of the anti-apartheid movement.[14] At a time when a survey of Afrikaners showed the desire to 'lead an upright and moral life' to be the most important of nine possible options pertaining to their lifestyles and dreams for the future,[15] the loss of its religious mandate posed a grave challenge to the NP's legitimacy. So, too, did the first indications of a slowdown in economic growth caused both by a combination of endogenous (largely, the market effects associated with the bloated Afrikaner-empowerment public enterprises) and exogenous (such as the oil crisis of 1973) shocks.[16]

The NP government's response to these challenges occurred at many levels, and on multiple fronts. It developed a 'total strategy' with which to face the 'total onslaught' directed at South Africa by its enemies. P. W. Botha encapsulated this view in a 1971 White Paper when, as Minister for Defence, he stated:

> Defence strategy embraces much more than military strategy. It involves economy, ideology, technology and even social matters, and can therefore only be meaningful and valid if proper account is taken of these other spheres . . . [this,] in fact, is the meaning of 'Total Strategy'.[17]

The apartheid state's reliance on dynamic and closely synchronised combinations of covert, semi-covert (or quasi-official), and overt action in the political, military, and economic spheres amounted to an extensive undertaking that cannot be fully treated here. It will suffice to note that the military played an increasingly intrusive role in governance and civil society in South Africa during the 1980s. With the installation of a State Security Council that could overrule cabinet, the securocrats effectively assumed charge of national policy and strategy under Botha. Thus, it is possible to speak of militarised apartheid or a 'garrison society' which has been defined as follows:

> A garrison society is one in which it makes no sense to ask whether or not civilians control the military. It is a society in which the institutions and the men who hold military, economic and political power have become so dependant on one another; in which their goals and interests are so complementary; and in which the traditional boundaries between military and civilian spheres have broken down to such an extent, that the very conception of civilian versus military control has no meaning.[18]

Apartheid South Africa followed the 'garrison state' model to the extent that civil and military power became indivisible. Well-known anti-apartheid figure and former *Daily Dispatch* editor, Donald Woods' appraisal of the hold of white minority rule and of the militarisation of the apartheid state in the mid-1980s led him to conclude that: '[W]hite control of South Africa is complete and comprehensive; . . . Pretoria's military might guarantees the status quo permanently, and . . . black opposition is neither significant nor strong enough to challenge it effectively.'[19]

Against this background, ideologues of the apartheid state invoked 'just war' theory to justify waging the Border War. In outlining the traditional definition of a just war, Robert Phillips distinguishes between the just *initiation* of war ('*jus ad bellum*') and the just *conduct* of war ('*jus in bello*'). Briefly, the requirements for the former are that it is: (1) a last resort after all other reasonable avenues have been exhausted; (2) declared by legitimate, representative, and accountable authority, and (3) morally justifiable in terms of self-defence, support of legitimate foreign authority, or intention to further justice and bring about peace. The requirements for the just conduct of war are: (1) proportionality, by which force must be responded to with proportionate counter-force, and (2) discrimination, by which non-combatants must not be deliberately targeted, and any action which runs the risk of collateral damage to non-combatants must be able to justify this risk in terms of the greater good.[20] These conditions, in effect, directed the ways in which the apartheid state had to be legitimated and the Border War justified. Selling apartheid to its support bases, however, carried the seeds of its own destruction.

Propaganda and media manipulation

Clearly, any authoritarian state is able to clamp down on its domestic media and suppress alternative voices in favour of its own version of 'the truth'. One of the many writers who has paid particular attention to the apartheid government's attempts at ideological manipulation, is the abovementioned Donald Woods. His examination of externally (i.e., internationally) presented government-backed views of South Africa in the print media elicited the opinion that: 'Pretoria works partly through indirect or subliminal methods, but most visibly and challengeably through media statements, both editorial and advertising.'[21] The government's propaganda efforts with respect to the popular broadcast media are examined in the work of Keyan Tomaselli and Eric Louw. In their analysis, the central discursive features are given as follows: marginalisation of the extreme right; increased prominence of tactical/military terminology; depiction of the liberation movements as lacking popular support; avoidance of any depictions of overt racism, and strengthening the 'influence of military strategists' definition of reality' and the 'rhetoric of siege'.[22] The attainment of these objectives, they claim, was crucial in concealing the 'fractionalisation' (splitting into interest groups and power blocs) of the apartheid regime and getting the public to internalise the idea of total war, thereby legitimising the apartheid state's cross-border raids and the conscription system, as well as convincing the public of the need to invest in an expensive domestic arms industry in order to overcome sanctions.[23]

To this end, propaganda was manufactured for domestic consumption. In 1980, the South African Defence Force (SADF) revealed that it was then either involved in, or directly responsible for, the production of no fewer than 20 separate print publications at a total cost to the government of over R300 000.[24] These publications included a glossy magazine for each of the branches of the security forces, propaganda comics and brochures aimed at black and white South Africans alike, an orientation guide for conscripts featuring a cartoon character called *Roger Raakskiet* ('Roger Shoot-Straight'), and other pro-war items.[25] According to a 1989 assessment by the End Conscription Campaign (ECC):

> The white community is exposed to pro-conscription propaganda daily . . . [there] are countless television and radio news reports, documentaries and dramas that portray military service as a worthwhile personal experience and as essential for the defence of the country. SADF publications are sold through news agencies, glossy pamphlets are sent to conscripts with their call-up papers, and the Chief of the SADF writes open letters in the press to incoming National Servicemen . . .[26]

The government's attempts to win the hearts and minds of the white public included a strategy of gaining firm control over the mass media thereby framing their perceptions of the security situation in South Africa and on its borders. This agenda was realised in a variety of ways: from crude propaganda to the more subtle (indeed, subliminal) effects achieved by the consistent use of certain types of images in news reports dealing with internal violence, as detailed by Deborah Posel.[27]

Whereas Woods, Tomaselli and Louw, and Posel concur that control of the South African media was crucial in influencing public opinion (both in the foreign and domestic contexts) during this time, their analyses are narrowly focused on government and/or security force-produced propaganda. This perspective must be extended by showing how the private sector became complicit in the production of propaganda. It is not simply that the apartheid state disseminated propaganda which is of interest here, but rather the manner in which the government's ideologues not only ensured an overwhelming dominance of pro-government views in the mass media, but could rely on the reinforcement of such views by the private and semi-private sectors. This was achieved through various combinations of overt and covert controls, alternately coercive and compulsive in nature, which characterised the apartheid state's attempts to shore up its support. The NP government's manipulation of the media is neatly summed up by John Phelan's American analogy:

> Imagine, if you will, a United States Department of Public Media, which would operate all the radio and television stations in the country and make all the programming decisions . . . [further] imagine a Federal Media Appeal Board, which would review the censorship decisions of the government, now gently chiding the department as too narrow-minded, now castigating excessive leniency. Finally, picture these agencies of repression presiding over a plethora of varied media that in no way resemble the great gray yea-saying of totalitarian states, but rather remind one of our own vulgar and sassy, bright and brave, deep and honest confusion of voices . . .[28]

Disinformation and censorship

The apartheid state established a monopoly not simply over the expression of opinion, but also over the manufacture of opinion – in other words, over the generative components as well as the distributive apparatus of the norm-creation process. Prior to the declaration of the first State of Emergency in 1986, this was achieved in three main ways: disinformation, concealment from the public eye through censorship, and 'censorship by proxy', i.e. the ostensibly undirected alignment of private media with government agendas, and by way of control over subsidy payments and other incentives in the film industry. These processes by which troublesome media content was concealed from the public and replaced with information justifying the status quo will be examined in order to expose the lengths to which the apartheid government was willing to go to exercise ideological hegemony in South Africa.

Disinformation implies the creation of 'false news' in order to broadcast the government's views and advance its aims. The apartheid state's use of disinformation predated the Botha government. Indeed, the Information Scandal of 1978–79 which allowed it to seize power had been occasioned by the exposure of the Vorster government's involvement in shady deals in respect of public media companies which were intended to serve as fronts or mouthpieces for the NP. Disinformation was, however, used more cautiously by the Botha government than its predecessor – perhaps because the control of existing news sources was seen as more important than creating them from scratch. Nonetheless, the Botha government enthusiastically used disinformation to promote its relationship with its internal and external support bases. For instance, the Botha government provided extensive radio facilities and logistical support to Jonas Savimbi's Union for the Total Independence of Angola (UNITA). The movement's propaganda radio station 'The Voice of the Resistance of the Black Cockerel' (VORGAN) was supposedly located at Savimbi's base in Jamba, but actually broadcast from South African soil.[29] Brittain describes how the South African government ensured a steady supply of sympathetic international media attention for Savimbi:

> [The] centrepiece of the Jamba experience was Savimbi himself. He honed his public relations skills in press conferences and interviews, mainly with the lazy and compliant Johannesburg press corps or selected European and American journalists keen on the anti-communist cause of the time. His fluent duplicity was swallowed uncritically by many journalists who should have known better . . .[30]

Although disinformation was part and parcel of the white South African public's experience, it was more often aimed at overseas audiences less able to distinguish fact from fiction.

Censorship had two main forms. One was outright suppression of reports by both the domestic media and foreign news services that included material contrary to the provisions of the Defence Act.[31] The very fact that suppression was occurring was itself often concealed, usually through complicity between private-sector media producers and the government censors. An instance of this occurred during Operation Savannah in 1975 when an 'inner circle' of newspaper editors were gathered together and bound to secrecy regarding the (as yet undisclosed) South African involvement in Angola. In this case, the suppression was justified by the government's claim that divulging details of the operation while it was being carried out might 'cause panic or harm the country's international relations.'[32] The second form of censorship was suppression of certain forms of media, such as music, that were considered capable of contaminating South African society by publicising the international protest culture which had arisen in the 1960s. For this reason, many well-known anti-establishment anthems of the time – including 'We Shall Overcome', 'If I Had a Hammer', 'Blowin' in the Wind', and 'The Times they are a-Changing' – were branded as subversive by the South African Broadcasting Corporation (SABC) and consequently denied airplay.[33] A similar attitude was taken to locally produced protest music.[34] Given that the SABC had a virtual monopoly of the public broadcast of audio and visual media, such control of the dissemination of music constituted a potent form of suppression.

Censorship also screened South African audiences from media that was critical – even inadvertently so – of the government's ideology. For instance, the 1976 locally produced film *Terrorist* could only be released after several government-ordered cuts and additions had been effected to the original version. These cuts were not aimed at those elements of the movie that might shock or offend the viewer, such as graphic depictions of violence or sex, but rather at the movie's treatment of the three terrorists who attack a white farm. This treatment was considered too positive; the filmmakers were told to re-edit the movie so that '[the] emphasis is thus changed from a successful to an unsuccessful terrorist attack'.[35] Viewing even an incomplete version of *Terrorist*[36] suggests that the government intervention was successful, as the film manages to portray the terrorists as somehow both menacing and incompetent. Noteworthy is the movie's depiction of household servants as potential allies of the terrorist cause. Paulus and Selina undergo a change from caricatures of innocent and loyal workers busying themselves with their daily tasks, to inscrutable agents of the enemy, all within a few minutes of film running time. No other stimulus is needed for this transformation than the arrival of the trained terrorists at the farm – a clear reference both to the idea of the black population as fundamentally untrustworthy, and to the idea that terrorism posed an ever present danger. As such its eradication served the best interests of all South Africans regardless of race. Direct censorship of this kind existed side by side with a more subtle form involving the withholding of critical production assistance. One of the three most widely distributed Border War films of the 1970s, *Grensbasis 13* (1979), had to undergo five script re-writes before the security forces would approve the script and extend their considerable prop and location aid to the production of the film.

Disinformation and censorship were, however, only a prelude to the much harsher set of media regulations introduced with the State of Emergency, a nation-wide declaration of martial law enacted in July 1986.[37] Under these regulations, many types of information gathering previously vetted by editors or censors were outlawed altogether. This included reporting on the conduct of the security forces, promoting a 'subversive statement', or reporting from any black residential area without prior permission.[38] The application of these procedures benefited from a neat set of circular definitions, enshrined in law, which allowed the authorities to forbid any media activity in an 'operational area' under the Defence Act, and declare any area as an 'operational area' under the Police Act.[39] Therefore, to screen a certain area from media attention and render any media coverage thereof illegal, all that was needed was this two-step redefinition process.[40]

Subsidies and Border War films

While the State of Emergency enabled the government to conduct its disinformation campaigns and implement censorship, a variety of incentive schemes were put in place to buy the complicity of private media. The relationships between authoritarian governments and 'hostage' media producers has been well documented, both in a variety of case studies and as a matter of theory.[41] With particular reference to the Border War, though, the particular methods deployed by the government to assert remote control of the South African film industry provide a comprehensive example of the partially coercive, partially co-optive character of this relationship more generally. Such an explication informs a general understanding of the apartheid state's attempts to assert control of one particular medium but which has wider implications for understanding its (ab)use of power.

Initially implemented under the Vorster government, by the early 1970s, the film subsidy made available to domestic filmmakers was routinely being used to support those films perceived to be pro-government and pro-military. Conversely, it could withhold financial incentives from any filmmaker projecting critical messages.[42] The exponential growth in government support for the local film industry after Botha's succession as Prime Minister in 1978, along with the introduction of television, indicates the extent to which visual media were considered an important part of his total strategy. After allocating just R10 million between 1971 and 1977, the film subsidies board dispensed well over R100 million between 1979 and 1981 alone, with R50 million going to 'A-Scheme' films directed at white audiences and R34 million to 'B-scheme' films directed at black audiences.[43]

Critical to the subsidy's coercive function, however, was the fact that this money was not provided up front. To acquire an A-Scheme subsidy, which could cover up to 70% of costs, a film had to make at least R100 000 at the box-office within two years. The percentage covered dropped off as box office revenue increased, but overall the benefits remained high, with a minimum subsidy of 30% guaranteed even if the film earned over R500 000. To encourage Afrikaans-language filmmakers, the subsidy scale was more generous for their films than for their English counterparts. In addition, South African cinema theatres relied heavily on the two-movies-a-week ritual of the loyal Afrikaans-speaking families who accounted for 50 to 60% of their revenue.[44] These factors combined to make the viability of local films a delicate process based heavily on distribution deals and the projected popularity of the movie. Poor box-office revenues would leave the financiers unable to recoup most of their costs, and any failure to appeal to the movie-watching core of Afrikaner filmgoers was tantamount to financial suicide. The inevitable result, as M. Botha and M. van Aswegen put it, was that: 'During the 60s and 70s, the subsidy system undermined the production of socially critical movies more than anything else . . . self-censorship played a big role: few financiers were prepared to give money to a film which ran the risk of being banned or being a commercial failure.'[45]

Ostensibly put in place to encourage the growth of the local film industry, the subsidy system in fact punished dissent and rewarded affirmations of the status quo as comprehensively as the processes of disinformation and censorship examined above. Amongst other things, it ensured the release of numerous 'politically correct' (judged in the relevant, ideological terms of the day) locally made films on the circuit. The messages of such films, dependent as they were on government goodwill and security force support for any project involving the military, could then be more easily controlled. Moreover, films featuring Afrikaans dialogue and recognisable local scenes also provided a cost effective means of communicating with the heartland of the NP support base – the primarily Afrikaans-speaking rural areas. Movies were a highly popular media in these areas, with takings providing around 25% of the film industry's annual national revenue, and thus any message aimed at such an audience was almost certainly assured of a favourable reception by a well-disposed constituency.[46]

The pro-war message was achieved through a parallel demonisation of the liberation movements and lionisation of the security forces, combined with an explicit scorn for members of the liberal media, draft dodgers, and females active in the anti-conscription movement. The rank-and-file of the security forces depicted in these films are likeable, noble individuals who respond to terrorist atrocities (almost exclusively against innocent civilians) with measured, precise, overwhelming force. Furthermore, their immediate superiors (i.e., the generals and politicians) are shown to be not only reasonable, but also well informed enough so as to suggest semi-omniscience. Foreign governments, the films suggest, are either in league with the terrorists and naïvely incompetent, or both capable and secretly sympathetic to the South African cause. Moreover, the rationality (and, indeed, the moral imperative) of opposing the forces of terror is incontrovertible. If made-for-TV documentaries such as *The Battle for Bridge 14* and *The Infantryman* are included, no fewer than 18 pro-war films depicting military service as either heroic, an opportunity for personal growth, or at the very least a necessary sacrifice for the common good (and often a mix of all of these) were made between 1971 and 1987.[47]

Challenging apartheid's legitimacy and discrediting the Border War

The period of relative quiescence in South Africa's international relations did not endure beyond the 1970s. By 1980, both Rhodesia (now Zimbabwe) and the Portuguese colonial presence had vanished from the regional landscape, and South Africa was under fire both in the United Nations (UN) for its illegal occupation of Namibia and its creation of the 'Bantustan' system,[48] and more generally for its heavy-handed suppression of opposition following the 1976 Soweto uprising. Equally resounding were local and international condemnations of the series of South African Defence Force (SADF) incursions into Angola in late 1975, which culminated in an ill-fated drive towards Luanda – Operation Savannah – in August of that year.[49] In the international arena, Savannah was denounced as barefaced adventurism but, more importantly, the operation also came under fire domestically from hardline factions of the NP who accused State President Vorster of not going far enough. General Magnus Malan, future head of the SADF and Minister of Defence, said of the period that '[we] were let down by our politicians'.[50]

In the increasingly unstable (and hence costly, in a variety of ways) local and international contexts of the 1970s, the apartheid state faced a growing challenge to its legitimacy in the eyes of its supporters. Yet, paradoxically, this climate also provided South Africa with an opportunity. Garrison states' tendency to respond well to visible adversity, reinforces and in many ways make possible a discourse of defiant resistance, which provides exactly the kind of ideological justification needed to defend its actions. In addition, the state was being forced to take an increasingly active role in asserting its own legitimacy, in order to replace the validation once provided by non-governmental institutions such as the NGK and the support provided by the regional white minority governments of Rhodesia, Angola, and Mozambique.

South Africa's fortunes declined from a peak in the early 1970s to an absolute low in the mid-1980s. To arrest this decline, the apartheid state would have required: handing the war in Angola over to a stable surrogate; extracting a profit from the overly-bureaucratic parastatals founded to sustain the emergent Afrikaner middle class, and parlaying its ostensible commitment to 'constructive engagement' with the West into something other than a delaying game. But its failure to do so meant that the gulf between perception and reality could only widen, and this forced the state to resort to ever more elaborate propaganda ploys. This ideological manipulation eclipsed any attempt to advance, in the face of almost universal condemnation, the wealth- and status-creation goals which had constituted the initial apartheid mandate. It may have made good, if somewhat melodramatic, copy for Botha to declare in 1986 that South Africa's choices had now come down to 'war and a dishonourable, fearful peace'.[51] Yet even the mainstream *Financial Mail* had difficulty in making sense of the State President's ill-defined threats: 'The world is also frightened of the Nationalists' *götterdämmerung* stance: "Don't push us too far . . ." Or what? Or we'll impose martial law, wreck the economies of our neighbouring states, nuke Lusaka? What did the man mean?'[52]

By the mid-1980s, the government's rhetoric thus was not only out of touch with contextual realities, but almost nonsensical in terms of the strategies the apartheid state was advocating in order to defeat its enemies.

Given the seemingly impenetrable set of justifications for the Border War, it is indeed remarkable that they became discredited as quickly as they did. However, the behaviour of national servicemen throughout the 1980s indicates that these justifications were increasingly being rejected as lacking validity (due, in no small part, to the conscientisation efforts of organisations such as the ECC).[53] A character in one of only two anti-war films made during this period, namely Darryl Roodt's 1987 film, *The Stick*, expresses disdain for the government's threats that Cubans would 'rape our sisters', mirroring the widespread failure of government scare mongering among conscripts. Increasing numbers of white South African youths left the country rather than fulfil their national service obligations, and of those that did not flee, between 30 and 40% were found – in an SADF study conducted in 1985 – to routinely use drugs ranging from *dagga* (marijuana) to ethyl nitrate, sodium seconal, synthetic adrenaline, and anything else that could be stolen from base medical stores. Apart from substance abuse, many conscripts resorted to suicide to avoid national service. Indeed, three times as many soldiers attempted suicide in 1986 as were killed in combat, with the preferred method being drug overdose.[54] To some extent, pro-war films attempted to face up to these difficulties, discarding the (at that point well-developed) 'noble sacrifice' theme in favour of films which depicted military service as an opportunity to engage in boyish high-jinks and coming-of-age rites of passage.[55] But even these well-funded responses could not undo the SADF's – and the NP government's – loss of legitimacy in the eyes of conscripts and their families. In an examination of conscription in Rhodesia during the *Second Chimurenga*, Louise White shows how quickly a loss of vertical legitimacy within a state (to adopt Kalevi Hosti's concept)[56] can spread laterally into the nexus of relationships – familial, patriarchal and otherwise – that render young men willing to risk death in war.[57] Almost overnight, in such cases, support for resource intensive regimes that rely on such networks can be withdrawn; and this is precisely what white South Africans began to do.

The loss of support and failure to justify the Border War

Three reasons for the failure of the efficacy of NP government propaganda to justify the Border War emerge from this analysis.

First, government propaganda about 'total onslaught' notwithstanding, the Border War was clearly not a last resort for the South Africans. The government's apparent unwillingness to parley with 'terrorists', set the scene for a confrontation that could have been avoided. And as the casualties mounted and the inability of the SADF to achieve decisive victories at battles such as Cuito Cuanavale (1988) became clear, the view that – inverting Winston Churchill's famous statement – 'war-war' made for a better strategy than 'jaw-jaw', proved harder and harder to sustain. This was further exacerbated through the prominence of high-profile rapprochements between the African National Congress (ANC) and the Afrikaner elites such as those at Dakar in 1987.[58] Instead of attempting to find an equitable settlement in SWA/Namibia and South Africa, and against the recommendations (later, the resolutions) of international bodies such as the UN, the South African government took the lead in initiating military action against the ANC, the South West Africa People's Organization (SWAPO), and regional governments that supported the liberation movements. This course of action specifically served to expose the illegitimacy of the apartheid state to the deleterious effects of operating as a Cold War pariah state and to international condemnation.

Second, convincing the public that the war on the border had been declared by a representative, accountable, and legitimate authority proved to be an increasingly difficult task for the SADF and the NP government alike. We have seen that the NP's domestic legitimacy had been crumbling since the mid-1970s in the eyes of right-wing splinter groups such as the HNP and (after 1982) the Conservative Party, and had long been the case amongst the Marxist and/ or liberal left. The prominence of ex-soldiers in the ranks of the ECC voicing dissent, and of growing unease amongst the general public, can also not be discounted. Internationally, the war had proved even less defensible despite the South African government's various attempts to position the Border War as a critical conflict theatre of the Cold War. It had, after all, been invoked in clear defiance of international law, and it was the precisely the legal indefensibility of the occupation of Namibia and the apartheid system that undermined the international support South Africa would have needed to achieve its objectives in the region. But while apartheid's very illegitimacy provided SWAPO and the MPLA with access to a level of foreign support (political, military and humanitarian) without which they would not have been able to survive the South African onslaught, attempting to conceal SADF activities from international scrutiny meant concealing information from or lying to the white electorate. As early as 1976, the government's propensity for concealing the truth from its citizens was being questioned by elements of the media, to the consternation of the censors.[59] How could the war be justifiable if the government would not even admit to fighting it?

Third, the Border War was not justifiable in moral terms. The essential right of the state to act in self-defence may have justified 'hot pursuit' operations into Angola, but this clearly did not extend to supporting UNITA, attempting to seize Luanda in 1975, or destabilising the frontline states. At a time when South African and international news sources alike publicly mused about Military Intelligence's role in the death of Mozambican president Samora Machel, few in South Africa could have considered destabilisation to be a morally acceptable defence against a total onslaught, whatever its source of origin.[60]

All this goes to show possible grounds for the tension between politico-military and ideological agendas examined in this chapter. Not only did the unjustness of the war require the NP government to conduct ongoing and extensive campaigns of propaganda and disinformation to convince its own electorate and the world at large that the war was worth fighting, it also rendered the question of 'what must the security forces do in order to win?' unanswerable. They could try to cultivate regional allies' military support and/or coercion (e.g., Smith, Kaunda – and Machel after the Nkomati accords), but none of these détente measures proved of any lasting value, because those willing to cooperate thus lacked political status. They could incite or sponsor civil wars to keep their enemies weak, as occurred in Angola and Mozambique, but (once again) that only served to intensify condemnation of South Africa. They could turn the border zone into a no-man's-land and hunt down People's Liberation Army of Namibia

(PLAN) infiltration squads, but that did not stop the SWAPO diplomats on the international cocktail circuit from reinforcing their legitimacy in the eyes of the world. Whichever way the security forces turned, the alternatives became less attractive.

In addition, the harder the regime in Pretoria pushed, the harder its enemies – and, specifically, its enemies' patrons – pushed back. Not only could the Soviet Union and Cuba share the cost of the war between them, they could also extract dollar payments and oil concessions from the Angolan government to defray their costs. Locating advanced air-defence systems in southern Angola enabled the Soviet Union to cheaply and effectively prevent the South African Air Force (SAAF) from exploiting its air superiority over the Popular Armed forces for the Liberation of Angola (FAPLA). Deploying its surplus military manpower to aid the Angolan government enabled Castro's Cuba to establish itself as a global anti-imperialist force. The only participants in the Border War playing on borrowed time and diminishing resources were the South Africans. As early as 1980–82, during the intensified fighting initiated by the Botha administration, defence spending already stood at 20% of the overall budget,[61] and one in every two white male South Africans was either in the army or eligible for reserve call-up.[62]

The predictable result of this increasingly desperate situation, given the difficulty associated with matching the war's ostensible and actual aims, was vacillation and equivocation. Short-term strategies would be mooted then cancelled; security force objectives would be re-formulated in mid-operation to accommodate some change in the larger military or political environment.[63] And all through this the patience of the domestic support bases and the economic reserves of the pre-1973 boom shrunk steadily until, in 1988, the Border War can be considered to have become too costly in terms of the financial burden and the loss of young white conscripts. Thereafter, the apartheid system imploded due to internal inconsistencies, political and social schisms, and a growing inability to deliver on its minority-advancement mandate, as much as it collapsed in response to both internal and external opposition.[64]

The apartheid state was therefore increasingly unable to motivate prospective soldiers and their families to support the war effort. Unpopular regimes can almost always be tried in the court of international opinion, but unpopularity *per se* is rarely enough to convince states to abandon courses of action in which they are deeply invested.[65] Moreover, the decision to seek resolution to an ongoing conflict invariably hinges on domestic considerations and depends on the embattled regime's assessment of its own chances of survival (or even triumph) in the face of its enemies. It is only when this assessment returns a zero (or at the very least, fast-diminishing) probability of success in a cost-benefit analysis of available options – including unilateral action – that the willingness to consider change will follow.[66] Such an assessment is rooted in the regime's ability to maintain the loyalty of those it derives support and draws resources from. Thus, it is clear that the end of the Border War, and fast on its heels the collapse of the apartheid state, represented the unravelling of a garrison state in which ideological consensus had become too fractured to maintain a semblance of legitimacy and power.

Conclusion

It has been pointed out that the entry of the increasingly militarised NP government into the field of media manipulation in the late 1970s coincided with a widely perceived slump in both the real-world fortunes and the ideological underpinnings of the apartheid state. Furthermore, it has been shown that this move involved both the coercion and voluntary compliance of private media, through the processes of disinformation, censorship and incentives such as film subsidies. As a corollary, it was argued that having opted to underpin, primarily by means of ideological and normative structures, (1) its extensive requirements for military manpower, and (2) its subordination of civilian needs to military ones, the apartheid state essentially gambled everything it had, and lost. In less dramatic terms, when the state's ideological scaffolding was undermined in the late 1980s, the NP government's civil-military support bases collapsed soon thereafter.

Notes to Chapter Four

1   C. Tilly's *Coercion, Capital and European States AD 990–1992*, (Oxford: Blackwell, 1992) and M. Olson's *Rise and Decline of Great Powers* (New Haven: Yale University Press, 1982) provide one theoretical foundation for this position, although the nexus of relationships that constitute the state have become increasingly debated in the last fifteen years.

2   P. Regan, *Organising Societies for War: The Process and Consequences of Societal Militarization* (Westport: Praeger, 1994), 111–12 and 144.

3   My appropriation of Mann's four sources of social power is intended, and his terminology will be used throughout the analysis which follows. For an exploration of the logic behind these divisions, see M. Mann, *The Sources of Social Power* (Cambridge: Cambridge University Press, 1986).

4   See Peter Vale's chapter in this volume, as well as his 'Pivot, Puppet or Periphery: The Cold War and South Africa', Paper delivered at the International Studies Association Convention, Portland, Oregon, Feb–March, 2003.

5   This term, developed by J. B. Thompson in his *Ideology and Modern Culture* (Stanford University Press, 1990), refers to the ascription of value (i.e. normative weight) to certain symbolic forms in a dynamic social context.

6   This refers to D. F. Malan's characterisation of the coalescing of Afrikaner nationalist sentiment, which facilitated the Nationalist Party's 1948 victory, as 'an act of God'. See W. Saayman, 'Rebels and Prophets: Afrikaners Against the System', in *Resistance and Hope: South African Essays in Honour of Beyers Naudé*, ed. C. Villa-Vicencio and J. W. de Gruchy (Cape Town: David Philip, 1985), 52.

7   Apartheid's self-depicted status as a civilising mission, backed by divine right and the Covenant of Blood River, obscured (and continues to obscure) this instrumentality. Nonetheless, the ongoing struggles

within the NP to define the system's most desired output (segregation versus profit, simply put) are clear testimony to the existence of a strong *secular* rapaciousness alongside apartheid's more *abstract* [religious?] narratives of *volk* and destiny.

8   Specifically, the collapse of one after the other English-supported political parties, from the United Party until its dissolution in 1977 to the Progressive (later, Progressive Reform and finally Progressive Federal) Party between 1959 and 1989, indicate the degree to which English-speaking South Africans were gradually brought into alignment with the NP's aims. See M. Álvarez-Rivera, 'Election Resources on the Internet: The Republic of South Africa Electoral System', http://electionresources.org/za/system/ (accessed 19 April 2004) for a more detailed breakdown of voting percentages.

9   Salient details of the South African contribution to these efforts can be found in W. van der Waal, *Portugal's War in Angola* (Rivonia: Ashanti Publishing, 1993), and P. Stiff, *The Silent War: South African Recce Operations 1969–1994* (Alberton: Galago, 1999).

10   For an exploration of economic data for this period and an analysis of why South African growth peaked and then (after 1970) began an inexorable slide, see G. Maasdorp, 'Economic Survey, 1970–2000', in *The Decline of the South African Economy*, ed. S. Jones (Cheltenham: Edward Elgar Publishing, 2002).

11   The history of the NP's difficulty in resolving tensions between, these factions is well detailed in H. Giliomee, *The Afrikaners: Biography of a People* (Cape Town: Tafelberg, 2003), 557–87. Other perspectives appear in R. I. Rotberg, *Towards a Certain Future: The Politics and Economics of southern Africa* (Cape Town: David Philip, 1981), 48–60 and T. Bell and D. Ntsebenza, *Unfinished Business: South Africa, Apartheid and Truth* (Cape Town: RedWorks, 2001), 60–7.

12   Giliomee, *The Afrikaners*, 587 points out that by the early 1980s only one third of public sector employees in the apartheid state were white. C. Cooper examines a particular dimension of this collaborationism in 'The militarisation of the Bantustans: control and contradictions', in *War and Society: The Militarisation of South Africa*, ed. J. Cock and L. Nathan (Cape Town: David Philip, 1989).

13   'Dutch Reformed Church'.

14   The Broederbond is examined in minute detail in Giliomee's *The Afrikaners* and elsewhere. Details on the life of Beyers Naudé were sourced from C. Villa-Vicencio, 'A Life of Resistance and Hope', in *Resistance and Hope*, ed. Villa-Vicencio and De Gruchy, although a large volume of tributary material was generated by his death in 2004.

15   Giliomee, *The Afrikaners*, 617.

16   Maasdorp, 'Economic Survey', 10–14.

17   Cited in G. Cawthra, *Brutal Force: The Apartheid War Machine* (London: International Defence and Aid Fund, 1986), 27.

18   Definition by Vernon Dibble cited in Regan, *Organising Societies for War*, 5–6.

19   D. Woods, *Apartheid – The Propaganda and the Reality* (London: Commonwealth Secretariat International Affairs Division, 1985), 3.

20   For a fuller treatment, see R. L. Phillips, *War and Justice* (Norman: University of Oklahoma Press, 1984), 12–70, and R Holmes, 'Can War Be Morally Justified? The Just War Theory', in *Just War Theory*, ed., J. Elshtain (Oxford: Basil Blackwell, 1992), 197–233, and R. Skidelsky, 'The Just War tradition', *Prospect*, 105 (December 2004).

21   Woods, *Apartheid – the Propaganda and the Reality*, 3.

22   K. Tomaselli and E. Louw, 'Militarization, Hegemony and the South African Media, 1976–1986', Paper presented at the 19th Annual ASSA conference, University of Durban Westville, July 1988.

23   Ibid. 39–42.

24   Cawthra, *Brutal Force*, 44.

25 For an examination of depictions of the war in SADF periodicals of the time, see C. Erichsen, 'Shoot to kill: Photographic Images in the Namibian Liberation/Bush War', *Kronos*, 27, (November 2001), 158–82.

26 CIIR, *Out of Step: War Resistance in South Africa* (London: Catholic Institute for International Relations (CIIR), 1989), 54. The End Conscription Campaign (ECC), a human-rights oriented anti-draft organisation, was eventually banned under the State of Emergency – according to Minister of Law and Order Adriaan Vlok, because of the '. . . dangers posed by the ECC to the safety of the public, the maintenance of the public order, and the termination of the State of Emergency' (*Cape Times*, 23 August 1988).

27 D. Posel, '"A Battlefield of Perceptions": State Discourses on Political Violence, 1985–1988', in *War and Society*, ed. Cock and Nathan.

28 J. Phelan, *Apartheid Media: Disinformation and Dissent in South Africa* (Westport, Conn.: Lawrence Hill & Company, 1987), 9.

29 E. Windrich, 'The Laboratory of Hate: The Role of Clandestine Radio in the Angolan War', *International Journal of Cultural Studies* (August 2000) 3, 2, 208–11. VORGAN was eventually classified as hostile propaganda during the UN-mediated ceasefire 1998–99, and was briefly shut down. However, with the resumption of the civil war, VORGAN was soon back on the air.

30 V. Brittain, *Death of Dignity: Angola's Civil War* (London: Pluto Press, 1998), 11–12.

31 R. Harvey, 'SABC TV', in *The Great White Hoax: South Africa's International Propaganda Machine*, J. Burgess et al. (London: Africa Bureau, 1977), 19.

32 H. Hamann, *Days of the Generals* (Cape Town: Zebra Press, 2001), 34.

33 Phelan, *Apartheid Media*, 118.

34 M. Drewett, 'It's my Duty, Not My Choice', in *Telling Wounds: Narrative, Trauma and Memory*, ed. C. van der Merwe and R. Wolfswinkel (Stellenbosch: Van Schaik/Content Solutions, 2002), 127.

35 K. Tomaselli, *The Cinema of Apartheid: Race and Class in South African film*. (London: Routledge, 1989), 20–1.

36 This was the only copy that could be located for viewing at the National Film Video and Sound Archives (NFVSA), Pretoria which is a repository of South African made film materials.

37 A partial State of Emergency had been declared the year before. However, the 1986 declaration was the first time that such a proclamation had been extended to cover all of South Africa.

38 G. Slovo, *Subverting Apartheid: Education Information and Culture under Emergency Rule* (London: International Defence and Aid Fund, 1990), 12.

39 Cawthra, *Brutal Force*, 49.

40 The government did not always succeed in silencing independent media groups such as the publishers of the *Vrye Weekblad*. In addition, far beyond the censors' reach, the ANC merely switched to less formal media such as taping broadcasts from their own clandestine radio station, Radio Freedom, and smuggling them into the country for later distribution. For more information on this topic, refer to Unknown, *Addendum to ANC Submission to TRC on The Role of Media Under Apartheid* (ANC Dept of Information, Johannesburg, South Africa).

41 Regan, *Organizing Societies for War*, 101. See also Y. Peri, 'The Media and the Military', in *Democratic Societies and Their Armed Forces*, ed. S. A. Cohen (London: Frank Cass, 2000) and (for a wider examination of the co-opted South African media system) K. Tomaselli, '"Adapt or Die": Militarization and the South African Media 1976–1982', *Reality*, 16, 1, (January 1984).

42 K. Tomaselli, *The South African Film Industry* (Johannesburg: University of the Witwatersrand Press, 1980), 19.

43 J. Blignaut and M. Botha, eds., *Movies – Moguls – Mavericks: South African Cinema 1979–1991* (Cape Town: Showdata, 1992), 80.

44   M. Botha and M. van Aswegen, *Beelde van Suid-Afrika: 'n Alternatiewe Rolprentoplewing* (Pretoria: Human Sciences Research Council, 1992), 16–17.

45   Ibid. Author's translation.

46   Tomaselli, *The South African Film Industry*, 95.

47   I have analysed these films on an individual basis, and shown how their evolution matched political and military developments in South Africa and on its borders, elsewhere. These films tend to endorse the Border War and shows that the NP government spent a great deal of time and resources asserting its own legitimacy through mass media such as film, and that it paid particularly close attention to the public's assessment of the costs of the Botha administration's 'total strategy.' See Dylan Craig, 'Screening the Border War, 1971–88', *Kleio: A Journal of Historical Studies in Africa*, 36, (2004), 28–46 and 'The Viewer as Conscript: Dynamic Struggles for Ideological Control in the South African Border War film, 1971–88', MA thesis, University of Cape Town, 2003.

48   For information on the SWA/Namibia conflict resolution process, I. W. Zartman's *Ripe for Resolution: Conflict and Intervention in Africa* (New York: Oxford University Press, 1989) provides an excellent summary. My analysis of the Bantustan system draws from Maasdorp, 'Economic Survey', and Bell and Ntsebeza, *Unfinished Business*, 107–17.

49   H-R. Heitman, *War in Angola: The Final South African Phase* (Gibraltar: Ashanti Publishing, 1990), 10. Savannah was the second large-scale South African entry into post-independence Angola, although small bands of special forces troops had been operating across the border for several years. In August, three companies of South African mechanised infantry had occupied the Calueque pumping stations in southern Angola, ostensibly to protect South Africa's R261 million investment in the Ruacana hydro-electric scheme (Stiff, *The Silent War*, 107–08).

50   Hamann, *Days of the Generals*, 44.

51   *Cape Times*, 13 July 1986.

52   *Financial Mail*, 6 September 1985, quoted in P. Moorcraft, *African Nemesis: War and Revolution in southern Africa 1945–2010* (London: Brassey's, 1994), 368.

53   For an in-depth treatment of the ECC's role, see L. Nathan, 'Marching to a Different Beat: The History of the End Conscription Campaign', in *War and Society*, ed. Cock and Nathan, 308–23.

54   G. Cawthra, G. Kraak and G. O'Sullivan, eds., *War and Resistance: Southern African Reports* (London: Macmillan Press, 1994), 177–80.

55   Of particular notoriety in this regard were Regardt van den Bergh's *Boetie Gaan Border Toe* ('Little Brother Goes to the Border', 1984) and *Boetie op Manoeuvres* ('Little Brother on Manoeuvres', 1985).

56   K. Holsti, *The State, War, and the State of War* (Cambridge: Cambridge University Press, 2001), 98–119.

57   L. White, 'Civic Virtue, Young Men, and the Family: Conscription in Rhodesia', *The International Journal of African Historical Studies* 37, 2004, 103–21.

58   Bell and Ntsebeza, *Unfinished Business*, 229–36.

59   Harvey, 'SABC TV'.

60   From the signing of the Nkomati Accords, the South African government had been unable to use the excuse that Machel was harbouring terrorists to sustain its secret war against FRELIMO. Ironically, the SADF's Mozambican proxy, Alfonse Dhlakama, went on to end his struggle against the Mozambican government and convert RENAMO into a political party after being abandoned by the South Africans. The least 'legitimate' of South Africa's proxy forces was thus also the first one to surrender its arms and demobilise.

61   P. Frankel, *Pretoria's Praetorians: Civil-military Relations in South Africa* (Cambridge: Cambridge University Press, 1984), 72.

62   *IDAF Fact Paper on southern Africa No. 8: The Apartheid War Machine* (London: International Defence and Aid Fund, 1980), 112–13.

63 The clearest examples being Operation Savannah, in which troop transport flights were literally redirected in mid-air, and Operation Moduler, which was extended three times in response to fluctuations in the climate of the ongoing peace talks.

64 The enormous sacrifices made in bringing down apartheid are often allowed to obscure the question of whether South Africa could have lasted significantly longer than it did, had it been able to address problems such as those mentioned here. The question of whether (and if so, under what circumstances) autocratic regimes can be induced to abandon power and accept a negotiated settlement has been widely debated. Contributors to the debate include C. Crocker, F. O. Hampson, and P. Aall, eds., *Grasping the Nettle: Analyzing Cases of Intractable Conflict* (Washington: United States Institute of Peace, 2005).

65 Admittedly, policymakers in third party states may seek political gains by aligning themselves with such protests, thus 'articulating' the energies of public opinion through concrete actions taken by their government (such as participation international sanctions and boycotts); this articulation, in turn, places very real pressure on even the most authoritarian and repressive regime. For a detailed investigation of the role of globalised protest in prompting local change, see M. Keck and K. Sikkink, *Activists Beyond Borders: Advocacy Networks in International Politics* (Ithaca: Cornell University Press, 1998).

66 Zartman's *Ripe for Resolution* refers to this moment, which draws on several other stages in the broader field of actor perceptions, as the moment of 'ripeness'. His analysis of South Africa's actions during the peace talks that ended the Border War provides a good summary of the brinkmanship exhibited by the South African negotiators right up to their agreement to withdraw from Angola.

Chapter 5

'Somewhere on the Border – of Credibility': The Cultural Construction and Contestation of 'the Border' in White South African Society

Daniel Conway

South Africa's Border War had profound implications for the social and political organisation of white society. Indeed, maintaining the credibility of South Africa's presence in Namibia and the prosecution of the Border War was an important political project for the National Party (NP) government. The discourse of 'the border' became a powerful cultural sign in white society and underpinned a mythology[2] that sustained and intensified South Africa's militarisation. As a cultural mythology, 'the border' was not a complete fabrication of reality (there was indeed a war conducted on and close to the Namibian border), but white society attached political and social meanings to 'the border' that appeared to be 'common sense' and self-evident and yet were partial and contingent on the existence of a number of socially constructed discourses. It seemed, however, self-evident to the majority of white people that the border between Namibia and Angola had to be militarily defended if the Republic and all that was familiar were to survive. It is, therefore, unsurprising that dissent or criticism of the Border War emanating from within the community was met with rhetorical vitriol from NP and military leaders and punitive legal sanctions.[3] This chapter will focus on the cultural construction of 'the border' and its contestation by a small group of white men who refused to serve as conscripts and their supporters in the End Conscription Campaign (ECC). The analysis reveals that gender norms were central to the operation of 'the border' as a cultural sign in white society and the most effective means for critiquing 'the border' were also gendered. Changing political and military circumstances, the realities of the effects (both psychological and physical) on white men returning from 'the border' and the discursive spaces opened by anti-conscription activists in South Africa, all challenged the credibility of the Border War and helped to hasten the end of the conflict in 1988.

The South African state defined the Border War in terms that made its prosecution seem natural and essential. As such, the discourse of 'the border' underpinned the militarisation of white society. White people's perceptions of the security situation, particularly on 'the border', could be manipulated by the state. Seventy per cent of white South Africans relied on electronic media for news. The state-controlled South African Broadcasting Corporation (SABC) therefore had a monopoly on the majority of white South Africans' access to news and information.[4] Philip Frankel wrote in 1984:

> Most whites hold the Defence Force in high esteem for its role in upholding the state in the face of internal revolution, in protecting the national frontiers against the apparent southwards march of international communism. Most, to use the metaphor employed by white parliamentarians, see it as a necessary 'shield' for the Republic behind which order is upheld and possible constitutional reform can take place. The majority of whites, if not the majority of South Africa's population, also wax enthusiastic about Defence Force actions conducted over national borders.[5]

The metaphor of the SADF as 'a shield' at 'the border', protecting the Republic against communist incursion, was frequently invoked and this aided the perception of maintaining the integrity of and defending 'the border' as essential to the continuation of the South African state. Existing opinion poll evidence suggests that the majority of the white population accepted the basic tenets of the government's security paradigm.[6] Indeed, one white opinion survey, conducted in 1982, found overwhelming support for the Border War: 72.3% of the white population believed South Africa could defeat the South West Africa People's Organization (SWAPO) in the long term and 60% opposed any attempt to negotiate over Namibian independence; 79.9% felt the threat of communism was not over-exaggerated by the government, and 81.1% endorsed the SADF's policy of attacking 'terrorist' bases in neighbouring states.[7] Such was the hard-line attitude of the white public that the author of the report believed the South African government's political manoeuvrability regarding 'the border' conflict was severely restrained: any attempt to negotiate or compromise with SWAPO could provoke a severe backlash from the white electorate.[8] As the following discussion will elucidate, white opinion shifted with the changing circumstances of the apartheid state and the bullish attitude towards defending 'the border' waned as the 1980s progressed.

The geographical distance of 'the border' from white South African society helped create a romanticised ideal of military service on 'the border'. The state relied on maintaining a considerable degree of secrecy and subterfuge regarding SADF activities on 'the border' (particularly when they were taking place in Angola) and South African popular culture aided the perception of 'the border' as a distant yet heroic place. Patricia Kerr, host of the popular SABC radio programme *Forces Favourites*, regularly dedicated messages from white families to their conscript relatives 'somewhere on the Border', emphasising 'the border' as a self-evident yet mysterious entity.[9] 'Military operations' at 'the border' also helped to rally the white nation and were a symbol of South Africa's prowess and defiance of United Nations sanctions. Successful military operations on 'the border' (and, of course, in Angola) were celebrated in the white social realm. The symbolism of the SADF's 'victories' in the Border War was regularly invoked by the SABC. For example, in 1981, the SABC commented:

> As over the weekend, South Africans rejoiced at the splendid victory of the Springboks in New Zealand, other of the country's representatives were returning from the battlefield in Angola. Their mission, too, was splendidly accomplished . . . There is good cause for pride in the performance of our men in New Zealand and Angola.[10]

The Border War was geographically distant from urban white South Africa, yet psychologically much closer. It was an arena in which national identity could be affirmed and celebrated in much the same way as competitive sport. Furthermore, defending 'the border' symbolised the maintenance of the white status quo and the continued existence of capitalism, Christianity and 'civilisation'.

'The border' and white men

An essential factor in South Africa's waging of the Border War was the institution of compulsory conscription for all white men. By the 1980s, white men were obliged to serve an initial period of two years continuous service in the SADF (at least six months of which would be in, or near, the 'Operational Zone' on 'the border'). This would be followed by 15 years of periodic 'camp duty' (which frequently involved active service on 'the border'). The existence of such onerous responsibilities required the militarisation of white society and in particular, the militarisation of white gender identities. Cynthia Enloe notes that '[g]endering and militarisation are inseparable':[11] governments waging military conflicts must ensure that men consider military service as an essential duty as *men* and women must believe that it is their duty to support men as soldiers. Cultural discourses of white masculinity and femininity were therefore militarised in an effort to make conscription appear a natural and essential facet of every white man's life-course. Conscription was constructed as a performance that was a 'rite of passage' that positively changed the attitude, capabilities and prospects of the man who undertook it. Essentially, military service was a rite of passage that turned boys into men. Linda Price, commented that serving as a conscript in the SADF was, symbolic of the transition from youth to adulthood. Within the context of a social world, which reinforces the importance of the army both as protector and as a vehicle for the attainment of manhood, it is possible that the individual would perceive it as a pivotal point in his life. In addition, young men preparing themselves for armed combat and the defence of their country reinforce the status quo.[12]

The state designed the white education system to prepare boys for their impending 'duty' as conscripts and a considerable proportion of white civil society, the media and the business community aided the legitimisation of military service.[13] The legitimacy of conscription was heavily vested in the credibility of the Border War. However, the militarisation of gender identities made this interlinked social and political project appear both inevitable and sensible, yet vulnerable to individual dissent.

For white men, serving as troops on 'the border', constituted the ultimate marker of hegemonic masculinity[14] in white South Africa. Indeed, the image of the *grensvegter* (border fighter) became common currency in social discourse. The iconic image of the South African soldier resonated throughout South African culture and encouraged many men and their families to relish the prospect of sharing in an esteemed masculine endeavour where they would be transformed from boys into men. Conscripts were popularly acclaimed as 'troopies', 'Our Boys': the collective sons of South Africa. It was possible to purchase troopie cuddly toys (labelled with the epithet – 'I'm a winner'). The 'Ride Safe' campaign for national servicemen wishing to travel across the country was publicised on radio with the following song which reinforced the troopie construct:

> He is just a troopie, standing near the road.
> He's got a weekend pass and he wants to go home.
> Pick him up, take him with.
> He's still got a long way to go,
> That troopie who stands by the 'Ride Safe' sign,
> His hair is short, his shoulders broad and strong,
> And his arms are tanned brown,
> With pride he does his national service,
> Respected wherever he goes, he's more than just a number,
> He's a man's man . . .[15]

The troopie was admirable and masculine, a 'man's man'. It was active service on 'the border' that provided the ultimate symbol of militarised masculinity in white culture, however. It was the *grensvegter* who, in the words of *Paratus*, the SADF's official magazine, was '[s]hrouded in myth and legend, a Rambo-type figure. Essentially one who has been in the Operational Area'.[16] The *grensvegter* had supposedly been at the heart of the action, had participated in dangerous guerrilla warfare and proved his mettle. The symbolism of 'combat' as the ultimate performance of military hegemonic masculinity infused the *grensvegter* myth. *Grensvegter* was a popular picture book hero in Afrikaans culture.[17] A number of South African films were made focusing on *grensvegters* on 'the border', the most popular of which were the *Boetie Gaan Border Toe* (Little Brother goes to the Border) series of films.[18] The *grensvegter* image also drew from contemporary global discourses of militarised masculinity, namely Rambo, the famed anti-communist military hero in a series of Hollywood movies. White anti-apartheid activists noted the sexualised and hyper-masculinist basis of the *grensvegter* identity: 'The *Boetie gaan border toe* mentality is aimed at male sexuality and encourages a feeling of inadequacy amongst national servicemen who do not serve on the Border'.[19] The *grensvegter* imagery served to create and police a hierarchy of masculinities within the SADF and even when troops were stationed on 'the border', an internal politics of masculinity developed: troops kept at the SADF bases on 'the border' were derided as 'base *moffies* (gays/effeminate men)' by troops deployed in active combat on the frontline.[20] The images of serving soldiers created cultural icons by which white men were judged by others in society. Troopies were the affectionately regarded sons and protectors of white South Africa and *grensvegters* were the revered warriors defending the Republic's borders against Communist takeover. The latter image also helped create an internal sexualised hierarchy within the SADF pressuring men to be seen to be involved in combat at 'the border'.

'The border' and white women

White women also played an active role in constructing and sustaining 'the border' myth. A 1978 NP pamphlet declared that white women 'are indispensable "soldiers" within our country's borders and their spiritual power is South Africa's secret weapon'.[21] SABC actress, Monica Breed encapsulated the state's attitude towards white women and militarisation when she said:

> You can't separate the man from the woman as far as safety is concerned. The one cannot be safe without the other . . . She mustn't think she's in 'paradise' just because her husband or her relatives are fighting in the Operational Area, keeping her safe.[22]

Essentially, white women in society were addressed as 'mothers, sweethearts, wives and friends' of conscripts and were encouraged to actively identify and support 'their men' as *grensvegters*.[23] Enloe recognises that militarisation relies on 'surrogate militarized motherhood': women, who are far removed from the theatre of conflict, but contribute to morale and gain prestige by their support and encouragement of soldiers from the confines of femininity.[24] The South African example of 'surrogate militarised motherhood' was undoubtedly the Southern Cross Fund (SCF). The SCF was a women's group that boasted over 15 000 members and had over 250 branches. Above all else, the women of the SCF focussed on the importance of supporting the troops on 'the border'. The SCF gave a gift pack to all servicemen (which was inscribed with 'The Southern Cross Fund Thanks Our Men at the Border') and raised funds for recreational equipment for SADF troops stationed in Namibia. The Fund's motto was 'They Are Our Security', and the women's 'Dial and Ride' scheme, which gave soldiers free car rides, used the slogan, 'They keep us safe in our homes. Let's give them a safe ride to theirs'. The slogans underlined the women's clear identification with their position as the 'protected' and the necessity of a large-scale military protector.[25] Founder and President of the SCF, Elizabeth Albrecht, described the Fund as 'the channel between the people and the forces, who receive in this way not only recreational equipment, but also the assurance of the gratitude and moral support of the people at home . . . As a nation we must all stand together in this conflict'.[26] An SCF tee-shirt, depicting a map of Namibia and an arrow pointing to its border with Angola, was regularly given to all financial donors to the Fund. The slogan 'He is There', beneath the arrow on the tee-shirt, underlined the SCF's role in defining 'the border' as a self-evident, common sense line of defence for South Africa and military service as a vital and admirable duty for all white South African men. Popular culture also helped to emphasise the importance of white women supporting men on 'the border'. Popular Afrikaans songs such as '*Daar's 'n Man op die Grens*' (There's a Man on the Border) and the aforementioned radio programme *Forces Favourites* (and also the Afrikaans medium SABC programme *Springbok Rendezvous*) helped to further celebrate the role of sons and husbands in the army and encouraged women to support and admire them.[27] 'The border' myth helped to create and sustain militarised gender identities by white society.

Conscription and white society

The performance of conscription in any society is a disciplinary mechanism that aims to engender conformity and obedience. It is unsurprising that in such a highly militarised environment as white South Africa, the majority of white men 'complied' with military service.[28] However, despite the considerable energy spent on militarising white identities, compliance with national service should not be misinterpreted as widespread enthusiasm for duty. Indeed, even the then Prime Minister, P. W. Botha, estimated that only 20 to 30% of conscripts were positively enthusiastic soldiers and disciplinary problems amongst troops rose considerably during the 1980s.[29] Challenging militarisation in apartheid South Africa was possible. As Enloe notes, 'militarisation is a potent set of processes. But it is not the well-oiled, unstoppable development that it is frequently portrayed as being'.[30] Conscription may have served to engender discipline and widespread compliance to militarisation in white society, but it also exposed the South African regime and made Nationalist rule vulnerable to political and social shifts in white society. The South African government's political manoeuvrability was limited by white social reaction to the state's changing military fortunes, as was demonstrated by the rapid end of the Namibian conflict after an increase in conscript casualties in 1987–1988. ECC activists Sue Britton and Paul Graham wrote in 1989:

> Conscription appears to have had the following effects – entirely unintended and subversive of the rationale of those who govern. It confronts all white South Africans with a moral dilemma and a choice, ensuring that there can be no apathetic acceptance of reality; it provides white South Africans with an opportunity to demonstrate their

commitment to the oppressed majority without paternalism – conscription is the "cross" they alone bear; it forces the government to be sensitive to the public.[31]

The existence of conscription confronted white South Africans with the realities of apartheid as in no other context. While conscription represented the pinnacle of South Africa's militarisation, it could also be seen as introducing a fundamental weakness in apartheid governance. Merran Phillips concludes:

> Racially based conscription was . . . ultimately a self-limiting strategy, creating continuous manpower problems as well as fracturing white political consensus by the extent and nature of SADF deployment . . . as the burden of conscription grew it was increasingly difficult for the National Party to demonstrate sufficient benefits to offset the costs of its conscription demands on whites.[32]

The deepening political and security crisis of the apartheid state and the concomitant changing use of conscripts exacerbated these inherent tensions and also destabilised the acceptance of waging the Border War in white society.

Although the majority of white men were conscripted, a minority chose to 'challenge' and conscientiously object.[33] A combination of factors: the advent of P. W. Botha as Prime Minister, South Africa's deteriorating regional security situation and the advancement of militarisation, made the issue of conscription politically prescient after 1978. A small number of politically motivated political conscientious objectors (COs) began to be tried from the late 1970s onwards. These public and highly politicised stances reflected a burgeoning trend of conscripts failing to report for duty. Estimates suggested that between 1975 and 1978 an average of 10% of the call-up failed to report; this rose to 50% by 1985 (over 7 000 people).[34] This in itself was symptomatic of a rapidly increasing number of men who avoided conscription by emigration, deferment or by simply not providing the SADF with their current address.[35] Even white political support for the extension of conscription to white immigrants, political calls for conscription to be widened to the Coloured and Indian population groups and evidence that there was public support for white women to be conscripted, suggested the white population felt conscription was a burden that should be shared by others and not by white men alone.[36] Conscription was an accepted part of white South African life, but was not necessarily enthusiastically embraced. Eventually resentment grew.

In 1983, the conference of the Black Sash (a white women's anti-apartheid organisation that had been in existence since the 1950s), passed a motion that stated:

> South Africa is illegally occupying Namibia and this is cause for many in conscience to refuse military service. When South Africa withdraws from Namibia there would be

no need for a massive military establishment unless there has been a political failure to respond to the desires of the citizens, and that army will be engaged in civil war, which is a good cause for many to refuse military service. In such a civil war, if the state has to rely on conscription to man its army, the war is already lost . . . We maintain there is no total onslaught against the people of South Africa and that the total strategy demanded of us is not the military defence of a minority government but the total all out effort of all South Africa's people to bring about democratic government.[37]

White liberal groups in civil society began to debate how to respond to the call. The decision was taken to form the ECC, an umbrella organisation that incorporated a number of smaller white anti-apartheid and church organisations. The ECC was particularly active on white English-speaking university campuses. Although the ECC never became a mass-political movement, it did succeed in creating considerable press interest and in generating a cultural movement focused on the opposition to conscription and apartheid. Individual COs were also a mobilising catalyst for ECC activists, a good vehicle for creating press interest and allowed the ECC to develop themes of its campaign. Contesting the Border War was a central theme of ECC campaigning. Demanding an end to the Border War was one of the first ECC national campaigns, yet it had little impact beyond English-speaking university campuses precisely because of the power of 'the border' imagery. The ECC's later campaigns, focusing on the effects of militarisation on white masculinity, had greater impact (particularly in the English-speaking press) and reflected the wider social destabilisation of militarised gender norms.

The changing nature of South Africa's militarisation gave the ECC and the CO movement its impetus and also signified profound changes in white society. The ECC had an increasingly broad set of issues which it could use to highlight its case, issues which struck at the heart of white society and were of concern to white people who had never had reason to question apartheid before. Senior ECC activist, Janet Cherry, recognised the opportunity apartheid's crisis offered the ECC:

> There is an incredible difference between South Africa and Rhodesia before independence. There you had an almost homogenous white population, with very few voices of dissent. The whites were prepared to just fight unquestioningly until the end, not actually knowing at any stage what was really happening and what the black community thought. Here it is different because we have got that room to move and to change white people's attitudes.[38]

As Phillips notes, 'the oppositional force of the ECC did not lie in its ability to mobilise large sections of the white community to oppose conscription, but in its publicising the essential divisive issue of conscription': conscription was an issue for white people whether they were aware or supportive of the ECC or not and the ECC was able to use white self-interest as an oppositional tool.[39] CO trials in the late 1980s served as forums to highlight these issues: the imprisonment of professionals such as Dr Ivan Toms, Saul Batzofin and David Bruce appeared reckless and inexplicable in the face of emigration and an escalating war. However, the depth and efficacy of militarisation also served to isolate and stigmatise COs and the ECC, restricting their manoeuvrability and strength.

Contesting 'the border'

There were a number of social factors that destabilised white social consent for the Border War and enabled the ECC to contest service on 'the border' as an essential rite of passage for white men. The actual experience of men serving on 'the border' introduced dissonance for many white men and wider white society and the ECC was quick to highlight this. 'Most people with call-ups aren't into going,' claimed the ECC, 'two years, in some camp up north, getting bored out our skulls, is not our idea of fun.'[40] Whilst the claim that 'most' white South Africans were not 'into going' to 'the border' was difficult to assess the claim that service on 'the border' was 'boring' was an insightful strategy for the ECC, because it reflected emerging anecdotal evidence of conscripts finding border duty boring and not the *grensvegter* arena of macho excitement the SADF claimed it would be.[41] Annette Seegers cites compulsory conscription as the 'worst thing' a pro-militarist could institute, because it 'ruins the entire scheme' of militarisation by exposing young men to the reality of war and the military, a reality that would not correspond with the positive cultural myths in society.[42] Whilst this is a contestable claim, it is certainly true that a number of COs in South Africa became politically conscientised and radicalised because they had served as conscripts on 'the border'. For example, Batzofin, who was imprisoned for refusing to serve 'camp duty' in 1989, explained that whilst stationed in Namibia:

> Going on the patrols you realised that you drive into a village and every person hated you and everyone feared you and the soldiers, the trained infantry that were with us, they would go into these villages and just kick everyone on the pretext of 'Where's SWAPO?' and you realised that whatever we were being told back at the camp, we weren't there for these people, we were there for some reason, I didn't know what, but it certainly wasn't to protect these people, they were dead scared of us.[43]

CO Toms was also struck by the hostility and fear his presence evoked from the Namibian population (even though he was an unarmed SADF medic).[44] Experiencing the Border War at first hand exposed conscripts to the reality of apartheid's war and for some, this turned them into political radicals who were willing to oppose South Africa's militarisation. Furthermore, COs and the ECC consistently ensured that the trials of men refusing the call-up were used to describe atrocities committed by the SADF in the Namibian/Angolan conflict (either through the direct testimony of objectors who had served on 'the border' or other former conscripts who had returned).

The heroic *grensvegter* image of the SADF soldier at 'the border' also began to be questioned by mainstream white society and the ECC capitalised on this. The main impetus for this questioning was the experiences of individual white men and the discernable effects military service was having on them. A number of disturbing trends began to emerge as 'veterans' of 'the border' conflict returned home. By the mid- to late-1980s there was increasing comment in the press and academia on the rise of white male suicide rates, instances of interpersonal violence and the phenomenon of 'family murder' whereby white men would inexplicably murder their families and then commit suicide (Pretoria, in fact, had the highest number of 'family murders' anywhere in the world).[45] In 1987, General Malan told parliament (in response to a parliamentary question) that 326 national servicemen had attempted suicide during the previous year and that 18 killed themselves, as opposed to 116 who died in operations over the same period.[46] The reality of these developments began to influence white popular culture. The slang word *bosbefok* (bush fucked/bush mad) entered common currency as a term of abuse, yet actually its origins were influenced by the symptoms of post-traumatic stress disorder (PTSD) exhibited by troops who had served on 'the border'.[47] The metaphor of 'bush fucked' itself contested the army as a masculinising experience and 'the border' as an exciting and heroic landscape: men were 'fucked' by the experience, demeaned and driven 'mad' as a result. The realities of the negative effects of conscription (particularly when serving on 'the border') became increasingly difficult for the government to hide and the ECC exploited this. ECC leader Laurie Nathan explained to the Truth and Reconciliation Commission (TRC) that he believed conscripts were 'both victims and perpetrators' and this influenced much of ECC campaigns.[48] CO Charles Bester told a student audience at the University of Cape Town:

> I believe that, in as much as discrimination and injustice harm the oppressed, so, in the same measure, is the oppressor spiritually and mentally damaged. There is abundant proof of this in the astonishing escalation of murder, family killings, child abuse, alcoholism, drug addiction and unwarranted aggression amongst White South Africans in recent years – all manifestations of a society in stress. In addition, the danger to young white conscripts lies not only in physical maiming or death during National Service, but in spiritual scarring due to their experiences.[49]

The ECC was highly creative and artistic in many of its campaigns and posters were a common means for disseminating its message on university campuses and student areas. ECC imagery frequently represented white masculinity as restrained and restricted by the SADF – with white conscripts being depicted as tied up, gagged or slumped and dejected. The discourse that men were not only restrained by conscription but warped and perverted by it was incorporated into the ECC's visual images. One ECC cartoon depicted a white man being warped into a brutal sadistic killer by the SADF. The poster showed a naked white man in darkness and then being thrust into an SADF uniform. The conscript stood on a South African flag holding the legs of a dead baby and the caption read, 'Please I am terrified of what I will be forced to become for our country'. Animalistic images were also frequently used by the ECC in newsletters and pamphlets and emphasised the damaging effects military service on 'the border' was having on white men: one such image that was used numerous times contained a series of pictures of conscripts slowly metamorphosing into pigs. Men were turned into animals by the SADF: their rationality, free will and agency was replaced by base instincts of survival, brutality and effectively, of inhumanity. The *grensvegter* image of white men as troops on 'the border' began to disentangle as the evidence of the real physical and psychological effects of military service on white men became apparent.

The ECC not only contested conscription as a beneficial rite of passage, using visual images and cartoons. It also did so with written discourse in mainstream public forums such as newspaper letters pages. The letters sent by ECC activists were an effective means of contesting directly the claims made by those supportive of military national service on 'the border'. The following example comes from letters to the *Natal Witness* that centre on the claims of one correspondent that juvenile delinquents would benefit from military conscription. ECC activists and those sympathetic to objectors were quick to respond. Fidelia Fouché wrote:

> Is it not fairly well known that persons returning from their spell of compulsory military service tend to be psychologically disturbed, violent, anti-social, that many are depressed and that there is a high rate of alcoholism among them? . . . Military camps are sterile and unutterably boring places (everyone complains of the boredom); they are also places of fear in which bullies are peculiarly at home. Conscripts yearn for release from the army and no doubt idealise the real world . . . Are unemployed ex-army misfits not more likely to be delinquents than are young persons who have been establishing themselves in careers and forming normal relationships?[50]

Contained in this extract are multiple criticisms of the military as a rite of passage. Indeed, Fouché defines conscription as a transformative process that is entirely negative for the men who perform it. Men are warped and 'disturbed' by military service, a process which is 'boring' and unpleasant. Finally, conscripts graduate as 'misfits' who are 'unemployed' and at a disadvantage to those who were pursuing careers instead of serving in the military. Fouché also attacked the concept of army discipline, which she branded, pseudo-discipline . . . obey senseless rules senselessly . . . Army "discipline" relies on fear and not on rational choice, is not only worthless but harmful . . . should we really deplore the fact that protest comes mostly from young people – at our universities and in our townships? Is it bad that people should protest and indeed rebel against what they perceive as unjust?[51]

ECC activist S. Spanier-Marsden wrote on the same page that, 'conscription evokes emotions such as fear, irrational patriotism and resigned acceptance. These emotions are hardly noble . . . to defend conscription in this country is to defend mindless social convention at the expense of human dignity and wasted life'.[52] In letters such as these, ECC activists contested some of the tenets of militarised masculinity and citizenship: portraying the performance of conscription as the antithesis of a beneficial rite of passage.

The worsening circumstances of the apartheid state required the more extensive use of conscripts across the Republic and an increased level of conflict on 'the border' area (and in Angola). The use of SADF troops to control unrest in the townships, particularly during and after the State of Emergency in 1985, undermined the image of the SADF acting as a shield against outside aggressors posted at a distant perimeter and introduced doubt about the legitimacy of SADF activities in the minds of some conscripts and their families. Furthermore, the heroism of the *grensvegter* was simply not transferable to township duty. In a widely quoted statement in the press, given during the trial of CO Philip Wilkinson, one former conscript described the rationale behind the random acts of violence committed by his former colleagues in the townships as the antithesis of heroism: 'There is a tremendous sense of power in beating someone up: even if you are the most put upon, dumb son of a bitch, you are still better than a *kaffir* (offensive term for black person) and can beat him up to prove it.'[53] The deployment of the SADF in townships allowed the ECC to appeal to conscripts directly. ECC activist Cherry explained, 'We [the ECC] do not condemn the individual soldier who is forced into a situation in which he has no choice. But in this situation, all conscriptees should consider the moral implications of their actions' by serving in the townships.[54] Nathan claimed that support for the ECC by conscripts had dramatically increased during the State of Emergency and that some of supporters did not necessarily come from an 'anti-apartheid position'. Nathan believed that:

> The thought of going into a township and taking up guns against the people has been terrible for many people . . . conscription is one aspect that is an imposition on all white South Africans. They realise there is a difference between enjoying privileges and propping up the system with a gun. People are asking whether it is worth it and many are concluding it is not.[55]

The ECC recognised that the use of conscripts in the townships destabilised one of the fundamental premises of the cultural portrayal of the justifications for South African conscription; that of the SADF defending society from an outside aggressor on the Namibian border. National ECC leader Alistair Teeling-Smith said:

Potential conscripts never had much problem with the idea of going to the border to fight the unknown enemy. But now they are fighting in townships where their maids and gardeners live, and for many it has become a personal and emotional issue . . . for a young white South African the choices are stark; serve, go to prison, go underground or flee overseas.[56]

The use of troops in the townships allowed the ECC to interrogate the use of 'the border' as an unquestioned discursive sign in white society. The distant, tightly controlled environment of 'the border', classed into 'Operational Zones' controlled by military discipline and power, evaporated in the noisy, chaotic and unruly townships. *Waar is die grens nou?* (Where is the Border now?) asked an ECC leaflet distributed in Stellenbosh. The ECC subverted the *Boetie Gaan Border Toe* cultural symbol by producing posters, stickers and tee-shirts emblazoned with *Boetie gaan Athlone Toe* (Little brother goes to Athlone). As an ECC sponsored collection of short stories noted, 'Now the border goes all over the place. Sometimes straight through the middle of families which is, I suppose, what civil war is all about.'[57] A musical genre that appealed to white student and youth anti-conscription music started to flourish in the bars of Johannesburg, Durban and Cape Town. This music also focussed on many of the gendered themes of ECC campaigning.[58] The State of Emergency and conscripts deployed in the townships gave the ECC a relevance and power that they would not have otherwise had and destabilised the myth of 'the border' in white society.

The ECC also addressed militarised constructs of white femininity and women's role in supporting conscripts on 'the border'. Appealing to white women as mothers who were harmed by apartheid rule was a theme present in progressive women's activism stretching back to the 1950s. Indeed, the Black Sash had been established by a group of white mothers who sought to portray themselves as the true mothers and guardians of the South African nation.[59] In 1987, the exiled ANC National Executive Council stated, 'these black and white mothers must reach across the divide created by the common enemy of our people and form a human chain to stop, now and forever, the murderous rampage of the apartheid system'.[60] The ECC sought to embody this appeal. The ECC organised a conference on 'mothers' perspectives' of SADF conscripts deployed in the townships. White mothers of conscripts gathered with black mothers from townships. At the conference, 'one [black] woman said she had to live with the fear that she might not find her two sons alive when she returned home from work each evening' and a white mother said, 'I know it may sound cowardly, but we just don't want our son to go into these areas'.[61] The ECC cleverly played on white families' fears of the township conflicts in particular (as opposed to 'the border' campaign that was much more readily accepted by the white community) and also tried to link it to wider themes of the damage apartheid was doing to families and the common fears mothers had about their sons, regardless of race.

The ECC also addressed the issue of how the manifestation of PTSD symptoms in conscripts returning from 'the border' might impact on friends and family. An ECC leaflet entitled 'Women and Conscription' sought to destabilise the image of the hegemonic male soldier and present the process of conscription as a direct threat to women as wives and mothers of conscripts. The leaflet explained that the army's culture of 'making a man' out of conscripts was premised on a type of masculinity that was 'authoritarian, violent and brutal. It is no accident that there are reports of increased crimes of rape and wife-beating from men who return from their military service'.[62] The leaflet also explained women's complicity with conscription, a complicity that made the militarisation of South Africa possible: white women were expected to keep the 'homefires burning' and groups such as the SCF existed to aid women's complicity in militarisation. Former CO and ECC activist Dr Ivan Toms recalls that in the ECC:

> There would be an active way in which people would be talking about girlfriends, mothers, sisters, so they would be quite actively talked about as a political reason. Helen Zillé [a senior ECC activist] had got involved in ECC because she had a little son, four years old, and she didn't want him to go to the army and she often spoke on platforms about that, very effectively. It was quite obvious. She saw what was going on – she saw what [the] ECC was and she thought, 'I'm going to join this organisation that's going to protect my son from going to fight in this army that's defending apartheid'.[63]

The ECC produced literature aimed at white families and mothers, in particular, in the weeks leading up to bi-annual call-ups. The ECC addressed women as mothers and wives and particularly stressed the importance of family bonds and what conscription could do to damage this. The ECC focused on white mothers' fears of how military service could harm their sons, physically and psychologically and stressed white people's self-interest in not performing conscription.

Unravelling 'the border' myth

The critical moment in 'the border's' cultural destabilisation was the Cuito Cuanavale offensive of 1987–1988. The loss of SADF air superiority and the concomitant rise in conscript deaths provoked a sharp backlash from white society and played a significant factor in the South African government's decision to call a ceasefire and negotiate. The revelation of the SADF's activities in Angola, as opposed to their presence in the 'Operational Area' in Namibia, was a particular source of opposition. The unravelling of 'the border' myth is remarkable, considering the widespread support for the military conflict in the early 1980s, yet it reflects the multiple stresses white society had become subject to. Michael Mann notes that although militarisation may appear all encompassing and unassailable; 'If the nation is called to real sacrifice, we see that its militarism is not rooted deep', if living standards in a militarised society begin to fall, or should 'our boys' be perceived to be 'pointlessly sacrificed', militarism is profoundly threatened.[64] Influential groups in white society began to openly discuss whether conscript deaths in Angola were 'pointless' and this critically undermined the ability of the state to continue 'the border' conflict. Even the hitherto loyal Dutch Reformed Church questioned the presence of South African troops in a neighbouring country.[65] What was most significant in the backlash against 'the border' conflict following the increase in casualty rates was its gendered nature: women, as mothers of conscripts, were especially vocal in their hostility to the Border War. The white social response to the rising casualty rates from the Cuito Cuanavale operation removed the ability of the apartheid state to define 'the border' as a *carte blanche* for offensive military operations and critically threatened white support for conscription.

The concept of the patriotic, dutiful, militarised white mother began to be questioned in mainstream white popular culture. Women's magazines began to publish articles that were hostile to the SADF's activities in Angola. The mass-market women's magazine, *Fair Lady* published one such article in 1988. One mother, whose 19-year-old son had been killed in Angola, wrote:

> Isn't it terrible that it should be my son? . . . Personally I feel that our children should not be fighting in that war. It is our duty to give our sons to the army – nobody really wants them to go, but it is our duty to send them. But . . . we are not told that our children are being sent into Angola. We think they are in South West Africa.[66]

What made this commentary so powerful was not the woman's rejection of South Africa's militarisation (indeed she endorses her 'duty' as a mother to 'give' her son to the army), but rather her opposition to 'the border' conflict in particular, prosecuted as it was on Angolan territory. General Malan reacted furiously to women's magazines criticisms of the SADF and pledged to ban any such publications in future. *Cosmopolitan* consequently dropped the testimony of a mother whose conscripted son had been killed in an accident shortly before the end of his tour of duty in Namibia. The article was, however, published by the magazine of the Black Sash. Although being published in this niche medium meant that its impact was much reduced, the article vividly demonstrated the process of how 'the border' myth had come to be questioned and eventually rejected by a previously compliant white woman. Margaret Biet's son had been conscripted shortly after the deaths of her husband, mother and brother. Biet's pleas to have her son posted in his home area of Cape Town were ignored by the SADF. After being posted to 'the border', Biet's son (Sean) returned for a weekend visit deeply traumatised by his experiences and talked of absconding from duty. However, he returned and was killed some weeks later. The SADF were uncooperative with Biet's requests to see the body of her son and were hostile to her questions as to why the military had no record of her numerous applications to have him transferred. Even the State President's wife, Elize Botha, became involved in the case. The article ended with Biet's words:

I accepted the death of my husband, my brother and my mother. I cannot accept his death. Elize Botha sent a printed card, 'Presented to the guardians of our borders'. She had added the words 'and one who gave his life. Sean Biet'. He didn't give his life. It was taken.[67]

The recognition that lives lost in the Border War were 'taken' and not heroically sacrificed was a radically destabilising one for the state and Biet's testimony represents an individual rejection of 'the border' myth. This rejection was a critical one, for the apartheid state was as dependent on white mothers embracing their militarised gender identities as much as it was reliant on men doing the same

Conclusion

The SADF announced the halving of the period of duty required of conscripts in 1990 with the proclamation that 'We Won!'. In reality, however, SADF commanders had pressed NP leaders for a swift end to the Border War as the credibility of perpetuating the conflict began to be questioned. There had been widening concern about the levels of conscript causalities, the potential for further white social dissent and the prospect of SADF losses at the hands of superior Soviet weaponry. 'The border' had become a commonly accepted social myth in white South African society by the early 1980s. Yet changing political and social circumstances created political fractures in the white community and enabled individuals and groups to critique South Africa's militarisation and the blind acceptance of the legitimacy of the Border War. The ECC may not have become a mass political force in white society, nor did it successfully 'end conscription' before 1994, but it did manage to highlight and exacerbate growing white unease about the impact and rational of conscription and the Border War. Without the willingness of white men to serve as conscripts and the complicity and support of white women in this process, the state would become dangerously vulnerable in both ideological and military terms. The ECC's effectiveness in highlighting conscription and the Border War as contentious political issues exposed this vulnerability. The state's ability to wage the Border War indefinitely and in relative secrecy was thus undermined by the ECC's activism and particularly the press interest that was generated thereby. Popular culture had effectively created and sustained the myth of 'the border' and was creatively garnered by the ECC to contest and destabilise it. Furthermore, the ECC accurately discerned the gendered nature of South Africa's militarisation and subverted hegemonic tropes of militarised gender identity in some of its most successful campaigns. The phrase 'somewhere on "the border"' that encapsulated a powerful social discourse of militarisation, and the acceptance of the ideological imperatives that lay behind it were an essential facet of apartheid rule, was challenged.

Notes to Chapter Five

1   *JODAC News: Official Bulletin of the Johannesburg Democratic Action Committee*, no. 1, (1988). The phrase refers to Anthony Akerman's 1983 play of the same name.

2   R. Barthes (trans. A. Lavers) *Mythologies* (New York: Hill and Wang, 1972).

3   For an analysis of the apartheid state's response to political objectors to military service and the End Conscription Campaign see D. Conway, 'The Masculine State in Crisis: State Response to War Resistance in Apartheid South Africa', *Men and Masculinities*, 9, 2 (2006).

4   D. Posel, 'A "Battlefield of Perceptions": State Discourses on Political Violence 1985– 1989', in *War and Society: The Militarisation of South Africa*, ed. J. Cock and L. Nathan (Cape Town: David Philip, 1989).

5   P. Frankel, *Pretoria's Praetorians: Civil-Military Relations in South Africa* (Cambridge: Cambridge University Press, 1984), 132.

6   G. Cawthra, *Brutal Force: The Apartheid War Machine* (London: International Defence and Aid Fund, 1986), 42; J. Gagiano cited in *Truth and Reconciliation Commission of South Africa (TRC) Report*, Vol. 4 (Cape Town: Juta & Co, 1998), 222–3; D. Geldenhuys, 'What Do We Think? A Survey of White Opinion on Foreign Policy Issues', (Johannesburg: The South African Institute of International Affairs, 1982).

7   Geldenhuys, 'What Do We Think?'.

8   Ibid.

9   Cited in J. Frederickse, *South Africa: A Different Kind of War* (Boston: Beacon Press, 1986), 61.

10 Ibid. 137.

11 C. Enloe, 'Beyond Steve Canyon and Rambo: Feminist Histories of Militarized Masculinity', in *The Militarization of the Western World* (New Brunswick: Rutgers University Press, 1989), 119.

12 L. Price, 'A Documentation of the Experiences of Military Conscripts in the South African Defence Force', Unpublished MA thesis, University of Natal, Durban, 1989, 136.

13 G. Evans, 'Classrooms of War: The Militarisation of White South African Schooling', in *War and Society*, ed. Cock and Nathan; J. Cock, *Women and War in South Africa* (Cleveland: Pilgrim Press, 1993).

14 R. Connell, *Masculinities* (Cambridge: Polity Press, 1995), 77.

15 Frederickse, *South Africa,* 67.

16 P. Delmar, 'Learning the Language', *Paratus*, (February 1986), 23.

17 Cawthra, *Brutal Force*, 51.

18 D. Craig, 'Screening the Border War, 1971–88', *Kleio*, 36 (2004): 28–46.

19 K. Tomaselli, 'The Border War: Cinematic Reflections', *South African Outlook* (April 1985), 16–17.

20 Price, 'A Documentation of the Experiences'.

21 D. Gaitskell and E. Unterhalter, 'Mothers of the Nation: A Comparative Analysis of Nation, Race and Motherhood in Afrikaner Nationalism and the ANC', in *Woman-Nation-State* (London: Macmillan, 1989), 60.

22 'Conscription: SABC Personalities Speak out on why Every South African Should Serve his Country', *Paratus*, (September 1980), 47.

23 Advertisement for *The Citizen*, in *To The Point*, (28/7/1978).

24 Enloe, 'Beyond Steve Canyon'.

25 Cock, *Women and War*, 3.

26 A. Nelson, 'In Conversation with Elizabeth Albrecht', *SA Digest* (March 1979), 6.

27 M. Drewett, 'Battling Over Borders: Narratives of Resistance to the South African Border War Voiced Through Popular Music', *Social Dynamics*, 29, 1 (2003): 78–98; M. Drewett 'Satirical Opposition in Popular Music within Apartheid and Post-apartheid South Africa', *Society in Transition,* 33 no. 1 (2002): 80–95.

28   J. Cock, 'Conscription in South Africa: A Study in the Politics of Coercion', *South African Sociological Review*, 2, 1 (1989): 1–22.

29   Cawthra, *Brutal War*, 45.

30   C. Enloe, *Does Khaki Become You?: The Militarization of Women's Lives* (London: Pandorra, 1988), 215.

31   S. Brittion and P. Graham, 'The Conflict of Conscription', in *Conscientious Objection: Occasional Paper No. 8*, (Cape Town: The Centre of Intergroup Studies, 1989), 78–9.

32   M. Phillips, 'The End Conscription Campaign 1983–1988: A Study of White Extra-Parliamentary Opposition to Apartheid', Unpublished MA thesis, University of South Africa, 2002, 22.

33   Cock, 'Conscription in South Africa', 9.

34   Catholic Institute for International Relations, *Out of Step: War Resistance in South Africa* (London: CIIR, 1989), 61.

35   Cock, 'Conscription in South Africa', 9.

36   Geldenhuys, 'What Do We Think?'; Gagiano, *TRC Report*, Vol. 4, 222–3.

37   K. Spink, *Black Sash: The Beginning of a Bridge in South Africa* (London: Methuen, 1991), 219.

38   J. Frederickse, *The Unbreakable Thread: Non-racialism in South Africa* (Bloomington: Indiana University Press, 1990), 214.

39   Phillips, 'The EEC', 224.

40   Undated ECC Leaflet, ECC Collection, William Cullen Library, University of the Witwatersrand (File B1.4.526).

41   Price, 'A Documentation of the Experiences'.

42   Truth and Reconciliation Commission (TRC), *Special Submission on Conscription: 23 July 1997*, http://www.org.za/special/conscrip/conscr01.htm (7/17/01).

43   S. Batzofin, Interview with the author (5/12/2002).

44   I. Toms, Interview with the author (27/1/2003)

45   S. Marks and N. Andersson 'The Epidemiology and Culture of Violence', in *Political Violence and the Struggle in South Africa* (London: Macmillan, 1990), 61.

46   P. MacLennan, *Saturday Star*, (22/2/1987).

47   J. Branford, ed. *Dictionary of South African English* (Cape Town: Oxford University Press, 1994), 100.

48   TRC, *Special Submission*.

49   University of Cape Town, *Orientation Times*, February 1988.

50   F. Fouché, 'Army and Delinquency' letter to *Natal Witness* (26/11/1985).

51   Ibid.

52   S. Spanier-Marsden, 'ECC', letter to the *Natal Witness* (26/11/1985).

53   L. Nathan, 'The Troops in the Townships' in *War and Society*, 75.

54   J. Cherry, cited in *City Press* (29/9/1985).

55   B. Streek, *Cape Times* (7/6/1985).

56   S. Perkins and L. Brooks, *Sunday Times* (7/8/1988).

57   J. Whyle 'Sappeur Fijn and the Cow', in *Forces Favourites* (Emmarentia: Taurus, 1989), 70–1.

58   Drewett, 'Battling over Borders'; 'Satirical Opposition'.

59   Spink, *Black Sash*.

60   Cock, *Women and War*, 50.

61   C. Capel, *Sunday Tribune* (29/5/1985).

62   Undated ECC Leaflet, 'Women and Conscription', ECC Collection (File B1.7.13).

63   I. Toms, Interview with the author (27/1/2003).

64   M. Mann, 'The Roots and Contradictions of Modern Militarism', *New Left Review,* 162 (1987), 49.

65   B. Wood, 'Preventing the Vacuum: Determinants of the Namibian Settlement', *Journal of Southern African Studies*, 17, (1991), 751.

66   Nathan, 'Marching to a Different Beat', 319.

67   M. Biet, *Sash*, (September 1988).

Chapter 6

The Construction and Subversion of Gender Stereotypes in Popular Cultural Representations of the Border War

Michael Drewett

The South African Border War of the 1970s and 1980s was justified in Cold War terms, as a fight against the 'red danger', but it was essentially a war in defence of the apartheid system. In need of soldiers to fight in the South African Defence Force (SADF), the government instituted conscription for all white males. By the 1980s the period of conscription was two years. Through a programme of propaganda, the government attempted to convince South Africans to support the war and compulsory military service. As has been the case with war the world over, the South African government and defence force regularly framed the war and support for it within gender terms. Conscripts were told that it was their duty to serve in the military to protect their families, particularly their mothers, wives or girlfriends and sisters. National service was seen as a rite of passage into manhood, turning immature boys into reliable fighters who could be trusted to defend their country and their families against external danger. The government's propaganda about gender roles and the military were quickly taken up by the popular culture industry, so that militarised masculinity was popularised through the mainstream media in South Africa.

This chapter considers the gendered forms of popular culture representations in support of and in resistance to the war. For the government, the articulation of gender binaries was a critical foundation upon which to build support for the war. In response, resisters tackled not only the injustices of the war in general, but they undermined the gender binary logic of supporters of the war. This not only made support for the war questionable, but also made resistance more acceptable and courageous. It also posited alternative forms of desirable masculinity, as opposed to the militarised masculinity advocated by the state.

Gender binaries in defence of militarisation

In apartheid South Africa white boys were socialised into a militarised form of masculinity, and taught that it was their duty to become soldiers in order to protect white women and children from the threat of a black and communist take over. Schools particularly encouraged a conformist acceptance of prescribed gender roles, 'masculine, aggressive defender roles'[1] for boys and more supportive and admiring roles for girls, proud of their 'boys on the border'. These expected roles were not only propagated at school level but at institutional level throughout society. It thus became apparent that the processes of gendering and militarisation were inseparable[2] so that meanings about gender and sex differentiation were 'produced, reproduced and circulated back into society'.[3] Jackie Cock discusses how soldiers need to learn to dehumanise the enemy and turn them into targets.[4] Their survival as soldiers is dependent on this process. Ultimately, military training is an extreme form of masculine socialisation. Carol Cohn argues that this leads to the dismissal of all things marked as feminine in the binary dichotomies of gender discourse.[5] The discourse is based on the very stereotypes set up to justify militarisation to begin with, sustaining a cycle of self-perpetuating gender binaries.[6]

The essence of the militarised gender dichotomy lay in the separation between the frontline and the home front, a separation which correlates with the division of home and workplace whereby men have traditionally been regarded as the protectors and providers (breadwinners) while the place of women has traditionally been viewed as based in the home, bearing and rearing children and performing the caregiver role for bread-winning males. These stereotypical roles have strongly influenced gender roles in militarised societies, especially in times of war. This leads Lynda Boose to conclude that the separation of frontline and home front 'has not only been a consequence of war but has also been used as its justification'.[7] Certainly, the concept of the military man was central to the South African government's male-only conscription propaganda and became an integral component of the ideal masculine male within South African society more generally. Gender binaries were encouraged in order to map out a clear gender division, separating masculine from feminine in relation to the idea of the 'war effort'. There was no mistaking the state's ideology that men were the protectors and women and children the protected.

In terms of this division, only men were conscripted into the SADF as protectors. However, the new recruits had to be trained to become dependable soldiers. During basic training the bodies and minds of conscripts were worked on in order to construct a militarised masculinity so ingrained that being a soldier was 'not an occupation but a male identity'.[8] Michel Foucault's discussion of docile bodies, in particular the disciplined military body, reveals that through a process of productive power, conscripts (in general) were persuaded to willingly submit to military disciplinary practice, believing that it was in their interests for the military to transform their bodies and minds.[9] Indeed, the possibility of being turned into a real man – a fighting machine – became widely regarded as a service offered to white South African men by the SADF. In addition, not only did many conscripts accept the ideal of militarised masculinity, but made a fetish of it, in the process reproducing it on a general level so that it became an intrinsic component of a hegemonic white South African male identity. Thus parents would proudly send their sons to the army to turn them into real men, and it became the mother's duty to support her son. Her patriotic duty was to supply sons for the country's defence. Furthermore, younger white South African women were encouraged to admire the strength, bravery, patriotism and discipline of white soldiers serving in the SADF. This admiration was to be demonstrated though support in various ways, as discussed below.

Women set up numerous support organisations and initiatives for men serving in the military. The most important of these was the Southern Cross Fund (SCF) which built morale for men in the military primarily through providing material and emotional support. The idea was that those protected at home needed to stand behind their men in uniform.[10] Another significant support organisation was the Defence Force Ladies Association to which all wives of military men automatically belonged. The purpose of the Association was to promote 'sympathetic understanding and active support for the husband's duty as defender of the Republic'.[11] Women, in these supportive roles, actively promoted the 'war effort' and supported their military men. It is within this context that female musicians on the home front recorded numerous songs dedicated to their men, especially, but not exclusively, to those fighting on the border.

A 7-inch single released by the SCF in the 1970s was an Afrikaans song called 'Soldate–Seun' ('Soldier, Son') sung by Esmé Solms.[12] As was often the case with SCF projects, the song both promoted the idea of support for the men on the border and raised funds for the SADF Fund. The sleeve notes made the claim that:

> In many homes this Christmas there will be an empty place at the family table – a place vacated by one of our menfolk who has gone far afield to patrol our borders and defend our freedom. It is to ensure that these loved ones can share in the joys of Christmas that we women – safe at home – are donating all proceeds of this record to the SADF Fund. Women from all walks of life, drawn from many sections of our society, have willingly come forward to help distribute the record.

The cover of the 7-inch single depicts a soldier, sitting against a tree with his rifle resting on his shoulder. He is reading a letter (presumably from home). In the background there is a large image of the South African flag. The image clearly depicts militarised masculinity as a patriotic act and perpetuates the division between home and frontline (see Fig. 1).

Figure 1: Cover of Esmé Solms' 'Soldier, Son'; 7-inch single record

The words of the song further stereotypical ideas about gender binaries with regard to the war:

At night as the stars shine so bright

Then longing and danger is my sky above

I miss you my son on the border

As your wish is for me to fall asleep tonight

But your protector looks after you through the night

To protect you against the forces of evil

And maybe this will be heart-warming

Enabling you to fight undaunted and fearlessly for your country

Know that your mother is by your side day and night[13]

The message that women should write letters to their absent loved ones serving in the military was a common theme in pro-military songs. John Edmond in 'Forgotten Soldier'[14] reminds the listener that all that prevents soldiers from feeling forgotten are the letters they receive from their loved ones at home. The soldier in the song tells his girlfriend or wife:

So when I feel like a forgotten soldier

And when the night is extra long

That crumpled letter is my inspiration

The words they just push me on

Marie Van Zyl, a singer and South African Broadcasting Corporation (SABC) radio presenter (including the presenter of a request programme for men serving in the military) explored a similar theme in 'Daar's 'n Man op die Grens'[15] (There's a Man on the Border). The lyrics depict the role of the woman at home, faithfully waiting with a deep longing and admiration:

> The waiting for that letter with that special handwriting
> Every minute I wonder where he is and what he's doing –
> My thoughts are always with him . . .
>
> I will wait for him
> Night and day for him
> My prayers will keep him safe
> And I'll wait until he's back by my side
> Oh my darling come back quickly[16]

Many songs like this were regularly requested and played on various request programmes for men serving in the military on the state-owned and controlled SABC. The programmes were given names like *Forces Favourites*, and *Fun with the Forces* and fulfilled an important propaganda role by providing emotional support for those involved in the Border War. Requests stressed the man as protector of supportive women and children back at home. This is clearly evident in a series of examples taken from a *Forces Favourites* programme (broadcast on the SABC's English Service in August 1981), in which the home/front gender dichotomy is clearly demonstrated:

> 'Remember I love you stacks and always will. Waiting for you faithfully. Not long anymore . . . from Connie';
>
> 'Love you honey. Miss you stacks. And it's min dae (few days), look after yourself and God bless. From your loving wife Bridget and baby son, Patrick';
>
> 'No words can describe how much I miss you, Robert, and I love you; and counting every minute to your first pass. Take good care of yourself, very proud of you and can't wait to see you in uniform. Lots of love from Elsa.'

All three examples remind the soldier of the protected back at home, described in sentimental and loving terms, assuring him of their faithfulness and support. The third message specifically emphasises the importance of the military man, looking forward to seeing the soldier wearing his uniform, the badge of his attained militarised masculinity.

Compilation albums commemorating the military request programmes were released, comprising cover versions of some of the most popular songs requested. One of these was 'Soldier Boy and other Forces Favourites'[17] which included a sleeve note message from the presenter of the programme, Pat Kerr. The SADF so appreciated Pat Kerr's contribution through the *Forces Favourites* programme that in 1982 the State President awarded her the Order of the Star of South Africa for exceptional service of military importance.[18] Another compilation was called 'Forces Favourites'[19] and included a skimpily dressed blonde woman wearing a military helmet, holding a rifle and smiling at the camera (see Fig. 2a). The suggested symbolism is that sexy women back at home supported the war effort and were attracted to military men. In the photograph the woman cradles a rifle in the absence of her loved one. Sexual connotations linked to the rifle are probably also implied. Indicative of the widespread nature of militarisation within South African society is that even albums having nothing in particular to do with the military songs sometimes showed models appearing in military gear suggesting support for the war and soldiers. An example of this is the *Music for Pleasure* (mfp) session compilation album 'Hit Power 1',[20] which shows a white woman on her knees, clad in a camouflage shirt with rolled-up sleeves. She is resting on a rifle for support and looks at the camera, smiles at the viewer (see Fig. 2b). The image is clear: the uniform and the rifle are sexy, as are the men who usually possess them. By association she is supportive of the 'war effort' and is attracted to military men. In the absence of men who are presumably away on the border, she waits faithfully, perhaps invitingly, in the meantime making do with a symbol of their profession. Importantly the women in these images are single, emphasising (or at the very least suggesting) their availability to military men on their return from duty.

Figure 2a and b: Pro-military compilation album covers

Following the same pattern as the radio request programmes, some newspapers printed request columns. For example, every Tuesday *The Citizen* (a government-funded daily) printed a weekly supplement called *Forces News*. An advert for the supplement called on 'Mothers, sweethearts, wives and friends (to) keep in touch through Forces News'[21] (see Fig. 3). The SADF magazine *Paratus* also encouraged correspondence between the home front and SADF recruits through its regular pen friend page.

Figure 3: Forces News advertisement

A similar initiative, backed strongly by the SADF was the 'Ride Safe' campaign, launched to make the public feel that they were contributing to the 'war effort' by giving lifts to members of the military as they made their way to or from home while on pass. Advertisements appealed to drivers to 'Help Johnny come marching home' and to 'Give our country a lift'. Numerous Ride Safe pick-up areas were demarcated on roadsides all over the country. Soldiers could wait at these signs for a lift. Matt Hurter recorded 'Ride Safe',[22] a country music-styled song framed in gender terms and sung with a deep voice seemingly projecting masculinity:

> He's just a boy in uniform trying to get home
> With a heavy kitbag and
> Not much hair to comb . . .
> If you pick him up and talk to him
> You'll find he's quite a man
> And he can tell you army stories like only a soldier can . . .

The song clearly depicts the soldier as a real man, with short hair, strength (to cart around a heavy kitbag)[23] and the tough army stories which set him apart from civilians. Although the song was aimed at patriotic men and women, urging them to give soldiers lifts to their destinations, it also urged listeners to send messages on the radio and to send 'that perfumed letter in the post'. Women were obviously targeted by the songwriter, who reminded them that it was their patriotic duty to support men in uniform in whatever way they could.

While women were clearly expected to play a supportive role for their men by waiting faithfully for their return, single women (as suggested by images on the record covers discussed above) were encouraged to support military men by offering their good looks and charm to the men protecting them on the border. A radio programme presented by Gail Adams featured a 'radio centrefold' involving a chat-up with a reigning beauty queen.[24] All over the country newspapers and other publications published pin-ups of women supporting 'the boys on the border'. For example, an issue of *The Daily News* featured 'the girl of the month' wearing a 'For the boys on the border' sash.[25] Winners of the Miss South Africa beauty pageant regularly toured the operational area on the Namibian/Angolan border[26] and many female singers (including Irish singer Geraldine)[27] gave concerts for the troops on the border.

In the mid-1970s the government introduced a programme of youth preparedness and the school cadet system whereby South African boys were prepared for service in the military (in those instances where teachers took these functions seriously). Apart from indoctrinating school children with anti-communism and apartheid ideology, notions of militarisation as a core part of masculinity were strongly stressed. It became commonly accepted that a boy could only really become a man if he underwent military training. This is borne out in the song 'Troop Train' by Buddy Vaughn[28] where the sergeant tells the new recruits' girlfriends: 'Don't worry about your boyfriend cause we'll bring him back brand new'. The new man would be, according to a Bles Bridges song ('Tawwe Tienies')[29], a 'tough guy':

> Do you see each man, standing there
> Brave heroes each and every man
> There's a task to complete
> And with pleasure, it's our duty
>
> Because we're tough guys, the tough guys
> We do battle on the frontlines
> The tough guys, the tough guys
> It's not hard to see[30]

The truly masculine man was one who was brave, courageous and prepared to fight on the border, as depicted on the front of a South African Border Patrol tee-shirt which proclaimed 'Be a man among men'.[31] The army was clearly constructed as a profoundly gendered space occupied by men performing masculine acts. The SADF thus engaged itself in a process of 'dispelling gender ambiguities and maintaining clear distinctions between masculinity and femininity'.[32] Within this unambiguously masculine space the SADF undertook to make men of new recruits.

The journey into militarised manhood commenced with basic training. This began with a condemnation of anything which did not conform to the hegemonic white masculine ideal. On arrival in the SADF any sign that someone was not a model soldier was met by a retort about his failure to be masculine. This usually took the form of name-calling. Patrick Hopkins has noted that within strong masculine cultures, any failure to conform to stereotypical masculine categories is regarded as a form of gender treachery, a threat to masculine identity, and is met with derision.[33] Name-calling as a form of labelling takes place, signifying 'failure of masculinity, a failure of living up to a gendered standard of behaviour, and a gendered standard of identity'. Hopkins specifically focuses on the term 'girl'. Apart from the obvious sexism of using the term 'girl' as an insult, Hopkins is aware that the term robs the young male of his identity, given that the term means 'not-male', 'not me'. This form of behaviour was commonly practised in the SADF. For instance, a former conscript in the SADF who was assigned to administrative duty for medical reasons, was called 'moffie' (a derogatory term for a homosexual) and 'girl', while another noted that his instructor often reacted to a his section's failure to complete a task by saying: 'You are just like a bunch of women with wet pants.'[34] Cartoons drawn in support of the army often made similar references. In one 'Vasbyt' cartoon an overweight male tells off a younger 'alternative' male (presumably his son) who is wearing ear rings and bangles: 'Look what you look like! I can't wait till the army makes a man out of you!' (see Fig. 4a). In a comic series for new recruits issued by the SADF, Corporal Shootstraight complains to new recruits: 'Silly civvies! You look like a bunch of meisies (girls)! I'll make you into real manne (men)' (see Fig. 4b).

'Look what you look like!" I can't wait till the Army makes a man out of you!"

Figure 4a and b: Pro-SADF cartoons

Similarly, anyone who refused to serve in the SADF was systematically denounced and ridiculed by the state as feminine and cowardly. For example, in a series of anti-End Conscription Campaign (ECC) posters, resisters were repeatedly portrayed as weaklings afraid to join the army. One poster (see Fig. 5a) shows a puny looking ECC member dwarfed by a strong rugged-looking soldier. The ECC member uses language traditionally associated with 'sissies'. In another poster (see Fig. 5b) a weakling ECC member is depicted as a puppet controlled by the KGB. On this poster 'ECC' is said to stand for 'Every Coward's Choice'. Similarly, a 'smear' poster was created out of an ECC poster publicising conscientious objector (CO) Philip Wilkinson's stand against conscription (see Fig. 6). The subversive version of the poster has the words 'or coward?' typed across Wilkinson's photo so that the poster reads 'Conscientious objector or coward?' The object of these posters was to associate membership of the ECC with cowardice and failure to achieve masculinity. This was certainly the message the SADF wanted to convey to the South African public. For example, an SADF military chaplain attributed conscientious objection to mothers who unfortunately 'would rather see their sons' fingers on the piano than offer a year in preparing to serve their country'.[35] The then Minister of Defence, Magnus Malan, called the men in ECC 'mommy's little boys'.[36]

Figure 5a and b: Anti-ECC posters

Figure 6: Anti-ECC 'smear' poster

These examples emphasise not only that a hegemonic understanding of masculinity was a fundamental requirement for new recruits, but that femininity and femaleness were scorned and rejected. In a juxtaposition of the frontline and the home front, women and the feminine were to be admired, but only in a sexual sense, as the 'opposite sex', helpless and defenceless people to be protected by real men, fighting on their behalf. Certainly, the image of the masculine soldier as protector was regularly part of the message put forward in various pro-military media. A monthly photo-comic celebrated the exploits of the lead character *Grensvegter* (border fighter) a stereotypical Rambo-type muscular brave soldier who regularly single-handedly fought and defeated the enemy, in the process rescuing a white female who then invariably accompanied him on a romantic liaison to the coast (see Fig. 7).

Figure 7: Cover of Grensvegter magazine

The man as protector of helpless women on the home front was also the subject of pro-military songs. In 'Jungle Green',[37] John Edmond sang of a soldier who had seen a beautiful woman while he was on pass. The next day the soldier is sent to the border where he goes into battle and where there is:

> No one to tell her that he fought and fell there
> Thinking of the blue eyes he was really fighting for

Clearly, the pressure was to be a strong, disciplined soldier, whose heterosexuality and masculinity were not in question. Even corporate advertisements for products and services appealed to gender binaries in the military. An advertisement for First National Bank advised: 'How to get it together for your first pass' with a picture of a happy heterosexual couple below. The double meaning is clear. The Allied Building Society also made use of a similar play on words when offering a free Allied Armed Forces Combo kit wallet to all SADF customers. The advert exclaims 'Hey guys? Get it together with the Allied'. One slot in the wallet is available for a photograph and in it a photo of a woman is shown with an arrow indicating 'What you think about all day' (see Fig. 8a). The Perm Building Society aimed an advertisement at women with the caption: 'The reason I save is in uniform and puts kisses at the bottom of his letters'. There is a photograph of a smiling woman who is then quoted as saying: 'When he pops the question, I know I'll say yes. That's why I'm bringing a little Permanence into my life with a savings account at The Perm'. Caress Jewellers offered a 15% discount to members of the SADF. A young returning solider is pictured embracing and kissing a blonde woman. The heading says: 'He saved his Caress just for you'. Below the advertisement continues: 'Homecoming: A kiss, a soft touch, three whispered words. And a beautiful Caress. A diamond ring as flawless as your wedding day. Caress makes it easy for young lovers' (see Fig. 8b). The MILBO housing association advertised houses for members of the SADF. The advertisement claimed that: 'MILBO helps you own our dreamhouse'. Pictured below is a sketch of a soldier and his wife imagining a cosy newly-built home (see Fig. 8c).

Figure 8a, b and c: Corporate advertisements promoting militarised heterosexuality

In all these examples the frontline and the home are once again depicted in gender binary terms. The same theme is portrayed in the picture cover to Dennis East's 'Love Manoeuvres',[38] a comic song from the soundtrack to the film *Boetie op Manoeuvres*. It portrays a white gun-wielding military male being pursued by a white female. The two straddle an army tank, with a fair degree of sexual innuendo suggested in the pose (see Fig. 9). In an earlier film, *Six Soldiers*, a left wing female student confronted an SADF soldier in uniform at a party. Initially she mocked him, asking him if he enjoyed 'playing army'. He responded very frankly, putting her down, saying that he was looking forward to the border where there would be beer and, importantly, no women. She was suddenly impressed with the soldier, and turned down an offer to dance with her lefty boyfriend, choosing rather to ask the soldier to dance with her. Quite clearly the message was that intellectual non-conformist men are not as attractive, even to intellectual women, as brave straight-talking military men are.

Figure 9: Cover of Dennis East's 'Love Manoeuvres'; 7-inch single record

Fracturing gender binaries: resisting military stereotypes

In response to the very persuasive propaganda in favour of conscription and the SADF, COs opposed service in the SADF. Many would-be conscripts went into exile, some avoided the system for as long as possible, while a very select few went to jail rather than leave the country or serve in the SADF. In the 1980s the central organisation in resistance to conscription was the ECC. Some of the examples of resistance considered here were ECC projects, but many – especially music recordings – were more individualised. Just as gender binaries regularly formed part of pro-SADF ideology concerning the war effort so, too, did many anti-SADF campaigns and popular cultural examples oppose gender binaries including militarised masculinities as an ideal type to be pursued by white South African men. Thus many resisters became engaged in a struggle to reconstruct gender and war as fluid categories, thereby fracturing rigid binaries. Given the anti-conscription position which resisters adopted, the sex/gender position ascribed by gender activists opposed to the war and conscription was not in favour of women's conscription, but rather against the idea that men needed to join the army in order to be truly masculine, or that women should support such notions. The underlying rationale of resistance to gender/war binaries was to present the war and conscription as negotiable, countering hegemonic ideas about what roles men and women were to play in the conflict.

In their opposition to conscription and the SADF, many conscientious objectors (COs) focused on this silencing of conscripts' important emotions and characteristics. Robert Morrell argues that 'masculinities are constantly being protected and defended, are constantly breaking down and being recreated.[39] For gender activists this conceptualisation provides space for optimism because it acknowledges the possibility of intervening in the politics of masculinity to promote masculinities that are more peaceful and harmonious'. While many resisters were not necessarily gender activists per se, resistance to conscription and the SADF was often gendered. The form of gender politics was a response to the extreme version of masculinity (militarised masculinity) which the SADF and its supporters promoted as the ideal form of white South African masculinity.

The ECC in particular targeted the SADF's ideal type of masculinity, criticising and challenging it as part of its campaign against the SADF. The ECC brought out a series of posters and cartoons in the mid-to-late 1980s which stressed the non-thinking, conformist nature of the military. In a sense their argument was that real men are creative and thinking, not prisoners of a non-questioning system. Often stereotypically strong and disciplined male soldiers would be shown to be incomplete, dehumanised or disturbed because of militarisation. A cartoon picture designed by the ECC shows a young boy dressed in an adult's military uniform with a rifle that is bigger than him (see Fig. 10a). The picture is disturbing because of the innocence of childhood being so overly and uncomfortably cloaked in the garb of militarised masculinity. Furthermore, the young boy is so obviously not ready for the horrors for which he is in the process of being socialised, especially the military preparedness of the school cadet system. In a poster with the heading 'Stop the call up', a manly soldier in uniform and holding a rifle is masked (gagged) by the South African flag (see Fig. 10b). The strength of the soldier is undermined by the lack of choice, the control exerted over him. The unjust context of the war is revealed through a series of snapshots which reflect various atrocities committed by the SADF. Similarly, an ECC poster with the caption 'Free us from the call up' shows a soldier on his haunches, bound up and with his head down, defeated (see Fig. 10c).

Figure 10a, b and c: ECC anti-conscription posters and images

Another ECC poster shows two contrasting images, one emerging from the other (see Fig. 11a). The first is of a cadet subversively saluting with his left hand and the second is of a deranged looking soldier also in uniform whose head is actually a hand grenade. The saluting hand is replaced with one about to pull the pin of the grenade. The caption says 'Man, didn't they tell you, cadets make you mad' ('Mannetjie, didn't they tell you, cadets maak malletjies'). This is in contrast to the government idea that cadets makes a man of you. A similar idea is put across in a poster showing a man in a state of frightening metamorphosis with a gun in a holster at his hip. The caption says 'Please – I am terrified of what I will be forced to become for our country' (see Fig. 11b). Once again the lack of freedom is stressed, but simultaneously questioning the make-up of the solider, whether he really is a real man if he is turned into a thoughtless, demented fighter?

Figure 11a and b: ECC anti-conscription posters

The contrast between mindlessly obeying military orders and creative freedom of expression is also depicted on the cover of the ECC and Shifty Records' anti-military compilation long playing record ironically entitled 'Forces Favourites'[40] (see Fig. 12). In the picture, a tape recorder-radio playing the ECC compilation separates an image of conformist masculinised military from an image of a colourful and diverse group of men and women dancing. Amongst the men are two barefoot dancers wearing their SADF uniforms, suggesting that they have left the former context for the latter.

Figure 12: Cover of Shifty Records' 'Forces Favourites' album

Amongst progressive musicians there was strong resistance to the dehumanising, conformist machine of the SADF. This is clearly expressed in the Cherry Faced Lurchers' 'Warsong'[41] which is very similar in sentiment to the posters discussed earlier:

> The old men in the top storeys
> Organise another war
> All this blood and guts and glory
> Is this what life is for?
>
> How can they make me feel like somebody else when I'm already myself?
> How can they make me act like somebody else when I can act for myself?

The Kalahari Surfers (in 'Don't Dance')[42] parodied the conformist person the soldier was expected to be when in the army. White men were supposed to unquestioningly adopt a military identity, obey military commands and march in defence of apartheid. In opposition to this narrow form of masculinity, the Surfers called on South Africans not to dance to the SADF's tune. A military beat emphasised the theme of conformity dealt with in the lyrics:

> Hey white boy get your feet off the floor
> The Lord gave you legs to march to war

Your leaders want you in a sporting affair
So put on your boots and cut your hair
Don't talk back or stop to think
Don't dance

The Aeroplanes also used a marching beat to ridicule the conformity of the militarised 'South African Male'[43] in a song which casts doubt on the hero image of the soldier as propagated by the South African government. The lyrics that appear in parenthesis are spoken by the male protagonist, spoken in an unintelligent white South African accent, except for the last line which is shouted out by an army officer.

South African male, you're a South African male
You've got a uniform
South African male (I've got a new car)
You're a South African male (And a big tape deck)
South African male (Go out on Friday night)
You're a South African male (Get pissed)
South African male (Pick up some chicks)
South African male (Wait for your next order)

As I have suggested elsewhere,[44] the song mocks the image of the stereotypical South African male who unthinkingly appropriates the dominant white South African masculine characteristics and waits for his next order. Given the equivocation of the lyrics it is not clear whether the South African male is wearing the army uniform, or has donned the dominant form of masculinity. The prevailing image portrayed in the song is of a conformist masculinity of which the singer is critical.

These images and songs confirm David Morgan's argument that the masculine body is in part constructed to become a dominating and disciplined body.[45] It is controlled through training and marching and regimented through the use of a uniform. The uniform and marching divert attention away from the particularities of individual bodies and persons and focuses instead on the general public conformist role of the soldier. Being disciplined means becoming someone else, being transformed from an individual into a part of the non-thinking brutal military machine. The songs referred to here cleverly parody the gender binaries which for years had been used to encourage support for the aparthied government's military endeavours.

On the matter of body politics, Morgan also notes that not only are bodily differences major sexual signifiers of difference between men and women, but they become the reference points for differences between masculinity and femininity.[46] The penis is linked to strength, hardness, action and potency and to 'have balls' is to be courageous, a man of strength and action. Thus only the truly masculine man has earned the right to possess particular body parts. This was clearly demonstrated by the symbolism of the moustache in the army. New recruits were not allowed to grow moustaches. As with stripes, the right to grow a moustache had to be earned, so that the moustache became associated with notions of the masculinised and the militarised body. As a matter of routine, many national servicemen grew a moustache as soon as they had earned the right to do so. In response to the mentality that led to this mass grooming of moustaches, Bernoldus Niemand (aka James Phillips) wrote the song 'Snor City'[47] ('Moustache City') which was about Pretoria, a city teeming with moustachioed men. The song parodies the disco fusion style as a means of satirising the military macho stereotype which the moustache represents.[48] For Phillips, moustaches represented conformist army mentality. He commented: '[T]hey all go to the army and the only hair you can grow in the army is a moustache. So of course everybody grows a moustache because that means that now they're better than all the other new *ous* (blokes) and then they just never shave it off. And it's just there forever. They don't even know that it's there.'[49] Phillips' ridicule of the moustache went even further on an insert to the album *Wie is Bernoldus Niemand?*[50] (Who is Bernoldus Niemand?) on which the song appeared. The album insert includes a drawing of a face being attacked by a moustache which has grown out of control (see Fig. 13). Rather than being attacked by the enemy in a 'total onslaught', the person is attacked by a 'total onsnort' (pun on *snor* – moustache). The image suggests that the military mentality (unthinking conformity) is more dangerous to the soldier than is the mythical total (black and communist) onslaught. Similarly, the Kalahari Surfers debunked the image of the *grensvegter*,[51] a South African Rambo (as discussed above) describing him in anti-hero terms as someone spat out amongst the weeds by 'some reluctant womb' who grows up to fill hungry mouths with bullets.

Figure 13: Bernoldus Niemand's 'Total Onsnort' image

In contrast to the state's view of COs as cowards, the ECC put forward a view of them as intelligent and brave people. An example of this was an ECC cartoon which shows a military commander giving a lecture. He points at the brain of a CO drawn on a board. He says: 'And HERE is where they hide their weapons' (see Fig. 14).

Figure 14: ECC cartoon emphasising the intelligence of COs

A similar idea was pursued by the group Bright Blue who wrote a song called 'The Rising Tide'[52] about the brave decision made by David Bruce, who was sentenced to six years in prison for refusing to serve in the SADF. The song held Bruce up as a hero, someone to be admired, a role model. The song's lyrics flew in the face of government propaganda about masculinity and bravery:

David, now that your eyes don't shine anymore
People will know
And always, always remember that you were the one
Telling it so

. . . You know where you stand, you have raised your hand
You're the first, you're the first of a new generation...
And always, always remember your words have been heard,
We're on your side . . .
Walking side by side
We're the rising tide

Through these various efforts, a strong case was made for alternative forms of (respectable and admirable) masculinity, based on different understandings of what it meant to be brave, and which proffered intellect and creativity as key components of alternative masculinities, rather than simple brute strength and non-questioning conformity. However, despite espousing alternative masculinities, the underlying tenet of the ECC's conceptualisation of masculinity still rested on strength and courage. Indicative of the pervasiveness of the hegemonic position on masculinity, the ECC and its sympathisers did not promote weaker forms of masculinity which excluded the necessity for bravery and courage. Nevertheless, given that the ECC's campaigns were waged within a context where militarised masculinity was widely accepted by white South Africa, its message not only boosted the morale of resisters, but also questioned the status quo, paving the way for alternative masculinities to be considered within South Africa's political and cultural landscape.

Not only were hegemonic forms of masculinity criticised, but some resisters also advocated a different model of ideal feminine behaviour within the context of the Border War. As has been discussed, white South African women were supposed to play a supportive role for their men in the military. They were meant to wait patiently and faithfully at home, reminding their men of their presence by sending them parcels and letters through the post and requests via the airwaves. Jennifer Ferguson provided the strongest critique of this role in her satirical song 'Letters to Dickie'.[53]

> Dickie baby
> This one's for you
> Wherever you may be
> Tonight sleeping cold
> Fighting for your country and for me
>
> Dickie Baby
> Your mother and me
> We been talking 'bout a white dress
> For our wedding
> And I'm saving for a colour tv
> A lot of men are phoning me
> Asking me to parties
> But I only smile and say no
> Cos I'm waiting for you Dickie
> I'll always be faithful
> And true to only you . . .

In the end, the woman singing the song tires of waiting for Dickie, goes out with another man and falls pregnant. On hearing the news, Dickie shoots himself. In a moment of critical poignancy, the singer notes that the bullet he used was really meant for her. The song both mocks the ridiculous expectations placed on women (and their men) during the Border War, yet also points to the problematic nature of the war and the sex-specific sacrifices that it entailed.

Other musicians also made fun of the stereotypical position that women were expected to adopt with regard to their relationships to men in the army (and which many women did indeed adopt). As noted earlier in this chapter, female singers who supported the war sang about the honour and the glory of their men fighting to protect them. The women in Marie Van Zyl's 'Daar's 'n Man op die Grens'[54] ('There's a Man on the Border') and Esmé Solms' 'Soldier, Son'[55] imagined the border as a place of danger and bravery and they prayed for their loved ones to be protected from the enemy. However, Illegal Gathering parodied these sentiments in 'Willie Smit',[56] sardonically suggesting that far from involving themselves in heroic battles, all military men did in the army was develop a smoker's cough and 'balles bak' (sit around sun tanning their balls, something only men could do). Similarly, Bernoldus Niemand (in 'Hou My Vas Korporaal'[57] – 'Hold Me Tight Corporal') did not turn to prayer but ironically asked the corporal to hold him tight, to help him through his army experience while sitting around, playing war games during what ought to have been the best time of his life. Importantly, he noted that he was there out of duty and not by choice.

While many pro-military songs (including some of those discussed earlier in this chapter) focused on the importance of the male as protector, Roger Lucey voiced the scepticism of those who questioned this role. In 'The Boys are in Town',[58] he sang of a soldier who doubted the government's insistence that it was his duty to protect women back at home:

> They say 'think of your family
> Think of your friends'
> But he knows that sentiment won't make it end

Songs with this sort of message assisted in the task of breaking down the myth of military service as a brave undertaking by males engaged in defending their country. On the contrary, such songs demystified the military, in a sense opening the way for a counter discourse in which meanings attached to sex and gender roles and military activities were open to wider interpretation.

This was also borne out in an ECC support book for conscripts serving in the SADF. It was called *Know Your Rights in the SADF*. The cover depicted a blonde woman giving a copy to her boyfriend about to leave for military service (see Fig. 15). At first appearance the cover picture plays right into the hands of those who uphold the stereotype, thus giving the book greater acceptance. But it had more subversive intentions. The woman supports her boyfriend by handing him a book produced by the ECC which itself undermines the SADF's authority and control over new recruits. The critical message of the book and its subversive cover once again questioned gender roles in relation to the SADF. The support which women were expected to provide to conscripted men was undermined, as was the ideal type of masculinity – towards one in which men were educated, aware and thought for themselves, rather than simply acting out a non-thinking conformist role as expected by the SADF and Nationalist government.

'Know Your Rights' . . . ECC booklet for soldiers.

Figure 15: Cover of the ECC Know Your Rights booklet

Conclusion

The aim of this chapter was to illustrate that resistance to the SADF and conscription in South Africa often took the form of questioning traditional gender dichotomies. The SADF and its supporters established a self-perpetuating gender binary discourse according to which gender stereotypes were constructed and reified. The discourse justified the SADF's approach to legitimating war while itself being partly dependent on the SADF's propaganda for its continued existence.

The position of many resisters was that the binary dichotomies of gender discourse set up by the SADF and South African government were problematic. The SADF's fixed notion of a male/masculine and female/feminine dualism entwined with corresponding notions of heterosexuality was too restrictive, as was its entire approach to society. Resistance discussed in this chapter disrupted the rigid gender oppositions cherished by the SADF and its supporters. They suggested a more complex understanding of gender. This position asserts, following Judith Butler, that militarised masculinity is part of 'an ongoing discursive practice currently structured around the concept of heterosexuality as the norm'.[59]

Ultimately militarised masculinity and corresponding ideas about femininity consist simply of 'the stylised repetition of particular bodily acts, gestures and movements',[60] including mental processes. Hence both body and mind can be inscribed with cultural messages. This chapter has shown that by undermining and questioning components of that masculinity and femininity, resisters were able to fracture representations of militarised masculinity and expected feminine roles, opening alternative gender spaces for South Africans to occupy without having to feel that they were either unpatriotic and/or gender traitors. Resisters importantly stressed that it was only the powerful position of the SADF and its ability to conscript young men that made militarised masculinity seem to be the only socially acceptable option available to men. Resistance involved a process of transgression. The more the gender boundaries were contested, the more acceptable the alternatives became, and in the process the more resisters became empowered.

Acknowledgments

The Rhodes University Joint Research Committee is thanked for providing funding enabled the research for this chapter. The late Pat Kerr supplied some very interesting archival material and Julie Frederikse helped in tracking down some of the archival evidence used. The Cory Library at Rhodes University, Mayibuye Centre at the University of the Western Cape and Cullen Library at the University of Witwatersrand were extremely helpful in locating archival evidence. Shifty Records and Third Ear Music provided some of the music referred to in the chapter. Thanks, too, to David Bruce who inspired many white South African men who harboured their own objections to conscription.

Notes to Chapter Six

1   D. Conway, ' "In the Name of Humanity, Can You as a Woman, as a Mother Tolerate This?" Gender and Militarisation of South Africa', Unpublished MA thesis, University of Bristol, 2000, 26.

2   C. Enloe, 'Beyond Steve Canyon and Rambo: Feminist Histories of Militarized Masculinity', in *The*

Militarization of the Western World, ed. J. Gills (New Brunswick: Rutgers University Press, 1989), 119.

3   L. Boose cited in *Gendering War Talk*, ed. M. Cooke and A. Wollacott (Princeton: Princeton University Press), ix.

4   Cited in J. Cock, *Colonels and Cadres: War and Gender in South Africa* (Cape Town: Oxford University Press, 1991), 58.

5   C. Cohn, 'Wars, Wimps and Women: Talking Gender and Thinking War', in *Gendering War Talk*, ed. Cooke and Wollacott.

6   Boose cited in ibid. ix.

7   Ibid.

8   J. Gibson, 'American Paramilitary Culture and the Reconstitution of the Vietnam war', in *Making War Making Peace: The Social Foundations of Violent Conflict*, ed. F. Cancian and J. Gibson (Belmont, CA: Wadsworth. 1990), 96.

9   M. Foucault, *Discipline and Punish* (Harmondsworth: Penguin, 1977).

10   Cock, *Colonels and Cadres,* 106.

11   White paper on defence cited in Cock, *Colonels and Cadres*, 120.

12   Esmé Solms, 'Soldate–seun' (Brigadiers, c. 1970 (exact year unknown)).

13   Author's translation.

14   John Edmond, 'Forgotten Soldier' off *Troopiesongs R..S.A.* (Jo'burg Records 1977). Quote used by permission ROAN ANTELOPE MUSIC. www.johnedmond.co.za.

15   Marie van Zyl, 'Daar's 'n Man op die Grens' off *Potpourri van Afrikaanse Treffers* (EMI 1984). Used by permission Gallo Music Publishers.

16   Author's translation.

17   Various Artists, *Soldier Boy and Other Forces Favourites* (Brigadiers, 1971).

18   Personal correspondence from the SADF to Pat Kerr, 22 January 1982.

19   Various Artists, *Forces Favourites* (Dynamite Records, 1979).

20   Various Artists, *Hit Power 1* (Music for Pleasure, 1973). Used by permission Gallo Music Publishers.

21   *To the Point* (1978), 46.

22   Matt Hurter, 'Ride Safe' (Gallo 1980). Used by permission Gallo Music Publishers.

23   The Afrikaans army slang for a kitbag is *balsak* or 'ball bag'. Thus one who has the strength to carry around a *balsak* in a sense has earned the right to be regarded as 'male'.

24   *Paratus*, cited in Cock, *Colonels and Cadres*, 127.

25   In J. Frederikse, *South Africa: A Different Kind of War* (Johannesburg: Ravan Press, 1986), 168.

26   Cock, *Colonels and Cadres*, 126.

27   *Anti-Apartheid News* (1982), 10.

28   Buddy Vaughn, 'Troop Train' off *Troepie Tunes* (Music For Pleasure, 1985).

29   Bles Bridges, 'Tawwe Tienies' off *Potpouri van Afrikaanse Treffers* (EMI 1984).

30   Author's translation.

31   Frederikse, *South Africa: A Different Kind of War*, 69.

32   M. Cooke, 'Wo-man, Retelling the War Myth', in *Gendering War Talk*, ed. Cooke and Wollacott, 178.

33   P. Hopkins, 'Gender Treachery: Homophobia, Masculinity and Threatened Identities', in *Rethinking Masculinity*, ed. L. May and R. Strikwerda (Maryland: Littlefield Adams, 1992), 111.

34   Cock, *Colonels and Cadres*, 59–60.

35   *South African Outlook* (1978), 143.

36   Cock, *Colonels and Cadres*, 73.

37   John Edmond, 'Jungle Green' off *Troopiesongs R..S.A.* (Jo'burg Records, 1977). Used by permission ROAN ANTELOPE MUSIC. www.johnedmond.co.za.

38   Denis East, 'Love Manoeuvres' (Gresham Records, 1985). Used by permission David Gresham Music
      Publishing.

39   R. Morrell, 'The Times of Change: Men and Masculinity in South Africa', in *Changing Men in South
      Africa*, ed. R. Morrell (New York: Zed Books, 2001), 7.

40   Various Artists, *Forces Favourites* (Shifty Records, 1985). Used by permission Shifty Records.

41   Cherry Faced Lurchers, 'Warsong' off *The Otherwhite Album* (Shifty Records, recorded in 1986, released
      in 1992). Used by permission Shifty Records.

42   Kalahari Surfers, 'Don't Dance' off *Forces Favourites* (Shifty Records, 1985). Used by permission Shifty
      Records.

43   The Aeroplanes, 'South African Male' off *Greatest Hits* (Shifty Records, recorded in 1986, released in
      1997). Used by permission Shifty Records.

44   M. Drewett, 'Battling Over Borders: Narratives of Resistance to the South African Border War Voiced
      Through Popular Music', *Social Dynamics*, 29, 1 (2003):92.

45   D. Morgan, 'You too Can Have a Body Like Mine: Reflections on the Male Body and Masculinities', in
      Body Matters: Essays on the Sociology of the Body, ed. S. Scott and D. Morgan (London: Falmer Press,
      1993), 72, 80–1.

46   Ibid. 70–1.

47   Bernoldus Niemand, 'Snor City' off *Wie is Bernoldus Niemand?* (Shifty Records, 1984). Used by
      permission Shifty Records.

48   B. Smit, 'Afrikaans Alternative Popular Music 1986–1990: An Analysis of the Music of Bernoldus
      Niemand and Johannes Kerkorrel', Unpublished B.Mus. thesis, Durban, University of Natal, 1992, 38.

49   Doxa Productions, *South African Music: Unreleased Interviews and Concert Coverage* (video) (Cape
      Town: Doxa, 1989).

50   Bernoldus Niemand, *Wie is Bernoldus Niemand?* (Shifty Records, 1984). Used by permission Shifty
      Records.

51   Kalahari Surfers, 'Grensvegter' off *Living in the Heart of the Beast* (Recommended Records, 1985). Used
      by permission Shifty Records.

52   Bright Blue, 'The Rising Tide' off *The Rising Tide* (Gallo, 1988). Used by permission Gallo Music
      Publishers.

53   Jennifer Ferguson, 'Letters to Dickie' off *Hand Around the Heart* (Shifty Records, 1986). Used by
      permission Shifty Records.

54   Marie van Zyl, 'Daar's 'n Man op die Grens' off *Potpourri van Afrikaanse Treffers* (EMI, 1984).

55   Solms, 'Soldate–seun'.

56   Illegal Gathering, 'Willie Smit' off *Voice of Nooit* (Shifty Records, 1986). Used by permission Shifty
      Records.

57   Bernoldus Niemand, 'Hou my Vas Korporaal' off *Wie is Bernoldus Niemand?*. Used by permission Shifty
      Records.

58   Roger Lucey, 'The Boys Are in Town' off *Half Alive* (Third Ear Music, 1980). Used by permission Roger
      Lucey/Third Ear Music.

59   See T. Spargo, *Foucault and Queer Theory* (Cambridge: Icon Books, 1999), 54.

60   Ibid. 56.

Chapter 7

Borderline Cases: Madness and Silence in the Representation of the Border War in the Works of Select South African Novelists

Mathilde Rogez

Across generations as well as across time, the war in Namibia has left a deep impact on many South African novelists, an impact which is mostly to be read in what is absent from the page. Whether the result of post-traumatic stress disorder (PTSD) or of wilful amnesia, what prevails in these accounts of the Border War are understatements, a failure to reach a real dialogue with the Other or even to express fully the writer's consciousness. Silence and a form of madness gnaw at the heart of all the works under study, be they published as a warning, before the start of the hostilities, or years after the end of the conflict and even after the demise of apartheid. This chapter examines the nature of the silences at work in various novels and short stories: J. M. Coetzee's *Dusklands*,[1] Etienne van Heerden's 'My Kubaan', 'My Afrikaner' and 'Slap Grensdrade';[2] Damon Galgut's 'The Clay Ox', *The Beautiful Screaming of Pigs* and *The Good Doctor*,[3] and Mark Behr's *The Smell of Apples*.[4]

Not all the works in this selection strictly fit into the category which has come to be known as *grensliteratuur* ('border literature'): Coetzee's *Dusklands* was published in 1974, at the time of the fall of the Portuguese government, and although skirmishes had already occurred on the Namibian border, the brewing conflict had not yet been dubbed the Border War.[5] On the other hand, Galgut's *The Beautiful Screaming of Pigs* and the Afrikaans version of Behr's *The Smell of Apples* (*Die Reuk van Appels*) were published only a couple of years before the end of apartheid (1994), after the independence of Namibia (1989). Galgut's *The Good Doctor*, published in 2003, also deals with reminiscences of the war. It is telling in itself that novels and short stories spanning almost 30 years should all obsessively go back to the events in Angola and Namibia, revealing in this manner the deep impact the war left on South African minds. The changes thus brought with time obviously affect the perspectives adopted by the writers, who resort to different modes of writing, and of course, because of their origins, to different languages. Yet beyond these superficial divergences, it will be interesting to see how language itself suffers from the same long-lasting disabilities, and how these disabilities stem from the self's own incapacity to grapple with its own identity in the midst of a frontier landscape. The imaginary partitions that years of foul rhetoric and perverted discourses have carefully erected on South African soil and mind criss-cross this part of the territory, as well as the characters' selves. Not only are peoples and nations pulled apart: this chasm seems to be reflected in the characters' split identities in the works studied, therefore precluding any possibility of bridging the gap between self and the Other.

Borderline cases: Madness and hysteria on the frontline

Most writers are first and foremost concerned with the psychological traumas caused by the war. *The Beautiful Screaming of Pigs* is perhaps the most explicit on the topic of PTSD: the central part of the book is devoted to the mental breakdown of the main character, Patrick Winter, who does his service on the 'Border' towards the end of the conflict, in 1988. The process of 'cracking up', of 'go[ing] *bossies*', is described in great detail in the first-person narrative, in all its violence.[6] While experiencing a kind of elation, of foolhardiness when on patrol, the character gradually feels estranged from the world and aggrieved by it, to the point of contemplating suicide.[7] He attempts to describe his fits several times, as in the following passage:

> A desolation had entered me, scraping my bones of their flesh . . . It was a universe and world to which I did not belong: its scents and sounds appalled me. I desired to flee, bawling, into the bush. More often than not I remained, the palms of my hands jammed into my eyes . . . Once, in line for dinner, my metal tray caught the light. Splintered, refracted, this glint of light burst into my head.[8]

The violence of the sensations expressed by the verbs ('scraping', 'appalled', 'jammed') is compounded by that of the prepositions, suggesting a violation of the integrity of the self: the splinters of light parallel the feeling of 'intense dislocation'[9] and fragmentation[10] the character experiences, which are reflected in turn in the fragmented nature of the narrative, which alternates family scenes and truncated reminiscences of the war.

Yet the other works tend to convince the reader that madness is not so much an exceptional consequence of the war, as its intrinsic characteristic. It is of course the fate which awaits prisoners of war, submitted to torture, as is developed, among other things, in Van Heerden's short story 'My Afrikaner', but it also and more generally befalls most soldiers because of the very nature of this war, secret and sporadic as it is. Both Van Heerden and Behr lay the stress on the way the particular conditions of the conflict lead to a growing feeling of unease among the troops. At the beginning of *The Smell of Apples*, the 'aimless waiting' and the orders 'riddled with contradictions' are testing the nerves of the soldiers,[11] and find an echo in the very disconnectedness of the various vignettes interspersed at random intervals in the main narrative.[12] When something does happen in 'My Kubaan', the troops react with 'simultaneous thrill and fear', as Van Heerden elaborates:

> *Wat doen 'n soldaat wat hom voorberei? Hy groet eintlik wat nie te groete is nie. Hy's nie soos ['n] ou in Death Row nie. Hy weet nie. Wat jy eintlik groet, is die sekerte. Jy groet die sekerte en dít vat lank. Dit vat baie nagte. Dit vat baie dink, of baie wégdink. Sommige ouens dink dit weg. Hulle raak wild, die kamp raak wild voor 'n operasie. Hulle drink en baklei soos tiere. Hulle vloek en bemors die latrines. Hulle steel die Bedfords en jaag deur die vlugtelingkampong. Hulle maak die moffies kaalgat vas op jeeps se neuse en ry dorp toe met hulle. Hulle drink, drink, drink.*[13]

The rhythm of the sentences and once again their disconnectedness, partly due to the narrator's irony, and to his willingness to boast in front of his captive interlocutor, do nothing to hide the cruelty of some of the soldiers' acts, nor their growing sense of insecurity and uncertainty. Death is mentioned somewhat offhandedly, but the understatement is counterbalanced by the accumulation of negatives, the mounting sense of deprivation, and the strong contrast between reason and madness. '[T]he border between the two' is 'as incidental and fine as' a mere suffix, just as that between death and life was as fine as a mere typographical sign, a mere slash a few pages earlier in the short story.[14]

The episodes described do not add any sense of specificity to the war: the conflict remains an abstraction when considered at a general level, as the use of indefinite plurals and juxtaposed short sentences in another excerpt from *The Beautiful Screaming of Pigs* intimate:

> Stories were spread about fights in the dark; about bullets and battles and guns . . .
> Planes were sent out. Mortars were fired. Bodies were rushed in by chopper and rushed out again in black bags. With diligence and haste, we fought our strange war.[15]

When the character is personally and directly involved, however, 'the firing, the cursing, the terror' seem just as aimless.[16] It is no wonder that most of the texts should focus on defeats, or at least on events which did not turn into feats of glory the South African regime could boast about: Patrick arrives on the 'Border' in 1988, 'when it was no longer glorious to be there' – and his contact with the enemy occurs, it should be noted, in November of the same year, some months after the ceasefire had been officially proclaimed.[17] Similarly, the soldiers in *The Smell of Apples*, traumatised by the battle of Cuito Cuanavale,[18] are depicted as running *away* from the enemy, only to reach the Cunene River at Calueque and be trapped there under the enemy's fire which destroyed the dam on 26 June 1988, killing at least 12 soldiers. It is perhaps to compensate for these disillusions that the narrator in 'My Kubaan' tries to delude himself and his reader, and invents the existence of a captive Cuban brought back to camp after a South African victory – or, at least, invents the conversation he has with him. The short sentences and self-assured tone at the beginning of the novel are intended to make the reader and the narrator himself, certainly, believe that the South African side came out of 'Operasie Koedoe' victorious. Yet the end of the narrative gradually escapes the narrator's control: the stream of consciousness technique, the rush of words and the gradual disruption of the syntax signal the collapse of this imaginary order. The sentence seems almost open-ended, leaving the reader in doubt as to the fate of the narrator, and underlining again the difficulty in granting credence to any report of the war.

Language defeated: Understatements and silences

What these passages therefore put into relief is how untrustworthy most accounts of the war are. Not only is this mistrust present as an element of the narrative, as in *The Smell of Apples* for instance, the false declarations of Marnus Erasmus' father claiming on the radio that 'there wasn't a single South African soldier inside Angola';[19] they contaminate the narratives themselves and the very act of story telling. It is language itself and the possibility of expressing oneself, and one's own identity and consciousness, which are simultaneously threatened, as in Van Heerden's aforementioned short story. Language is falling apart because of the war, and this again is another sign of madness and hysteria. This pathological sign is in part acknowledged, when it is as obvious as in Patrick's fits. 'My illness grew stronger,' he explains, adding: 'When I spoke, my language defeated me: I forgot common words, couldn't finish sentences.'[20] Yet this is more than just a symptom, since he cannot even speak of his malady. Oftentimes, when he or some of the other characters attempt to refer to it, they stop abruptly in the middle of their sentence. This happens at the beginning of the novel, when Patrick's illness has not yet been fully explained to the reader, and could be justified to maintain a sense of suspense. Yet this strategy is somehow redoubled when he cannot even explicitly name the source of his ill-being when asked by his Commandant to explain himself. The reasons he gives remain vague; he refers elusively to '. . . all this'.[21] The three dots and the generic pronoun do not point to anything clearly identifiable, and they even become a manner of speech over the course of the narrative. Thus, his disorder is never directly named, even after it has been duly identified, as if mentioning it were taboo.[22] The dialogue he has with Godfrey much later is a case in point:

> 'I'm just trying to . . . recover.'
> 'From your . . .'
> 'Yes,' I said. 'Yes.'[23]

The pervasive use of understatements, the silences boring holes in the texture of the narrative, imply that the symptom has become a cause of madness. The characters lose their grips on reality because they are not allowed, not able, to name this reality. Their maladies are a result of PTSD or of voluntary amnesia, as in the case of Frank Eloff in *The Good Doctor*, who for some reason, after being unable to face Commandant Moller with the truth, is later unable to tell what truly happened in this cell on the 'Border'. This was partly the case, too, of Guy in Galgut's earlier short story: a character who, willingly or not, seems unable to give any details of his life on the 'Border' and of his escape from it. The dialogue between the deserter and the young woman who gives him a lift is almost pathologically 'weird', full of non-sequiturs and heavy with things left unsaid.[24]

Notwithstanding the fact that Frank and Guy's situations cannot be equated, nor that Frank's guilt and silent collaboration with the regime by refusing to stand up to Commandant Moller can be ignored, it must be acknowledged that on the whole the possibility for real dialogue is flawed from the start. All the works studied suggest the impossibility of reaching the Other through words, partly because the Other remains absent from the page, leaving the characters to their solipsism. With the use of first-person narratives, the authors restrict the characters' grip on reality to their own limited point of view. This partly explains the silence weighing on Eugene Dawn in *Dusklands*: the reader is never party to anybody else's thoughts but his, and no other voice but that of his inner mind can be heard. Similarly, the dialogue between the South African soldier and his Cuban captive in Van Heerden's short story can be considered as the figment of the former's imagination. It may be that the Cuban keeps quiet voluntarily, or that the soldier cannot understand him because of his gross ignorance of his culture (such as not knowing which language is spoken in Cuba), but it is more likely that he never actually intended to speak to the Cuban (if there were a Cuban, that is), but only wanted to stage a little scene for his own benefit. This is of course a way of negating the Other's existence, of relegating him to the margins; and it should be added that such scorn for 'unknown things' and 'Other Ideas'[25] is not the prerogative of one side in the political struggle: the black soldier in 'My Afrikaner' mirrors his military counterpart in many ways. The authors themselves seem contaminated: remarkably little is said of the feelings of the people on the other side of the border, as if even after the end of the war, language and literature still remained maimed. Patrick does not understand much of his former South West Africa People's Organization (SWAPO) enemies, nor does he really try to get more information when he meets them during the elections, and Galgut's attempt to show the other side of the story after the end of the conflict remains partly unsatisfactory.

The roots of this evil, however, seem to lie in the very structure of the militarised society which gave birth to the conflict, as Behr's *The Smell of Apples* testifies. Marnus, the young narrator, constantly and almost unconsciously allows many of his parents' opinions to inform his own thinking and discourse: each paragraph is thus introduced by 'Dad says' or any similar structure, and often ends with the same kind of expression, such as 'says Dad' or 'says he'. The frame consequently created by this almost chiastic structure emphasises the tightness of the ideological hold on Marnus' mind. The young boy internalises these thoughts so much that he ultimately becomes a mere ventriloquist for a number of clichés and racist proverbs, which are in themselves, linguistically, a form of violence.[26] Not only is this detrimental to the boy during his youth; its damaging effects persist through adulthood, and it is in part because of this kind of education that Frank Eloff in Galgut's *The Good Doctor* cannot answer back, and because of these prejudices and ready-made theories that communication fails even between allies, as the grown-up Marnus is repeatedly unable to trust and talk to his Xhosa section leader. He ends up fleeing from his own men, and is forced to acknowledge that '[t]hose' like himself 'that arrive alone look the worst'. They were '[t]he ones who ran alone, hearing the enemy in the bush all around them. And the few who discovered the enemy tangled in their own entrails and heads'.[27]

An education built on distrust and fear of the Other, and therefore on veneration of strength, embodied in the military force, is shown to have contributed to a gap between the self and other people. This ultimately results in a split identity; and this gap, widened by the war, cannot be filled by common language. Patrick acknowledges the inability of language to express some of the horrors witnessed on the 'Border', a language which 'falls short of describing those minutes' – a statement significantly in the present tense as if to discard words more completely.[28] Notwithstanding its explicitness, Galgut's *The Good Doctor* is not the most severe indictment of such traumatic effects of the Border War. In this respect, Behr's *The Smell of Apples* and Van Heerden's 'Slap Grensdrade' are undoubtedly the most trenchant in their criticism, the impact of the war being all the stronger for the number of blanks left on the page and the omissions in the narratives. Behr rejects both the paranoid climax of the war and the ideology on the home front from which it stems in the same breath, while Van Heerden is intent on showing how devastating the conflict has become on the frontline as well as at home. 'Boet . . . is Grens toe,' Oom Isaac manages to answer after some time to his inquiring nephew.[29] But that is all he will say for much of the short story: he evades further explanations as best as he can, but this short confession, in its curtness, speaks volumes. A single sentence, a single word, magnified by the use of the capital letter, are enough both to convey the full tension of the situation, while again reducing the speakers to powerlessness symbolised by the three dots and the ensuing silence. Later, when he eventually confesses the full story, it is '*met sy stem hees en sy oë op die grond*' (with a gruff voice and eyes on the ground),[30] in a voice which is not even strong enough to reach the level of the narrative. A blank paragraph follows his revelation, which will never be disclosed openly, but only indirectly hinted at by the means of the narrator's nightmare and the last sentence of the short story, so strong is the taboo both of going to the 'Border' and of crossing racial barriers. It even becomes forbidden to utter Boet's name; the very existence of the self (and perhaps, of life and natural human feelings as the word 'Boet' also means 'brother') is imperilled.

That a person's life should be endangered by the war is a truism. Rather, what is striking here is that it is language itself which becomes threatening and that the perils on the front are further expressed through an extremely violent imagery, which transforms the 'total onslaught' into human slaughter. The symbol of the slaughtered animal recurs almost obsessively: it is by exerting their power over animals that the soldiers want to prove their control of the battlefields. Both are linked in the young Marnus' mind, whose favourite pastimes are participating in the activities of the Voortrekkers, watching American 'Westerns', and listening to the serial 'Die Wildtemmer' on Springbok Radio.[31] These types of leisure form part of his education just as the verbal indoctrination at the hands of his parents, and no doubt equally contribute, albeit unconsciously, to his decision to join the Defence Force and fight on the border – even if the landscape there proves less tameable than that of radio serials. Patrick does not ponder therefore the sight of the 'corpse of an elephant', 'murder[ed]' 'by soldiers for cruelty or fun'.[32] These men merely repeat the gesture of the first explorers, and in *Dusklands* of Jacobus Coetzee among them, who in his raving confessions to Klawer, equates the control exerted by the eye/I (the organ as well as the subject) over the landscape with that of the gun over wildlife and other peoples: 'I am a hunter, a domesticator of the wilderness.'[33] His actions are not dissimilar from those of Eugene Dawn who, two centuries later, will have no qualms in advocating napalm bombings to tame the luxuriant forests of Vietnam and the insurgents it hides. Patrick himself is aware that in killing a man on patrol, he is repeating the moves of those 'men' who, like his father, 'hunted animals with guns' in the bush.[34] What is more surprising is the vocabulary resorted to: the animals' deaths are in fact as shocking as the unnecessarily high toll of the Border War, and they do not so much embody the power of the soldiers as their fragility, pointing to the human slaughter being performed daily on the 'Border'. The quivering iron pig-sticker planted on Jonas' grave casts an ominous shadow on Patrick and the reader's minds,[35] as dark as the one left by the carcass of the ewe hanging in the slaughter shed in 'Slap Grensdrade' when Jac realises that his cousin has been sent to the 'Border' like a lamb to the slaughter – a lamb not so pure, though, as he is shown to have first sacrificed the maid on the altar of his lust. In this distortion of the ritual of common sacrifices for reconciliatory feasts, in which the oxen are not roasted on fire pits for *braaivleis* or bodies laid in the family graveyards to rest, but 'left to rot' in the bush, there is no redemption for which to hope.[36]

From borders to frontiers: An enduring chasm

That the narrators should resort to so violent an imagery, which forces them to fall silent afterwards, bears witness to the deep traumas left by the war, which contaminate language itself. Just as this imagery itself is reminiscent of earlier episodes in the history of South Africa, the source of this failure of language lies deep in the ideology on which the apartheid regime was built at an earlier stage, and from which the Border War later sprung. Indeed, the texts being studied reveal that the obsession with the border itself harks back to the very foundations of South African society and identity: the twin concepts of border and frontier, evoked in the same breath by Patrick when he goes back to Namibia.[37] This is already hinted at in the later works which have been the main focus of attention so far, particularly, as has been shown, in the structure of Behr's novel. However, for a better and fuller understanding of how the debunking of this ideology works, and how this identity is questioned, it is necessary here to return to Coetzee's *Dusklands* dealing with Namibia, and to analyse how he lays bare the roots of South Africa's troubles.

The parallel drawn in *Dusklands* between the Vietnam War and the exploration and colonisation of Namibia in the late eighteenth century is blatant enough. What is less obvious is the way in which Coetzee weaves a web of correspondences between the two events, and what these equivalences aim to show.[38] Coetzee indeed proceeds by allusions and confusions in order to conflate different historical periods and their respective political contexts and, via a series of tropes and displacements, to destabilise all the more deeply an ideology built on fixity and well-drawn boundaries. So the first part of the story deals with contemporary but geographically remote events, while the second part deals with historically remote events that occur on African soil. It appears, therefore, that Coetzee does address local concerns, but somewhat indirectly, a tactic which finds echoes in other parts of the text, on a smaller scale. Whereas both Eugene Dawn and Jacobus Coetzee revere the gun, 'the only copula we knew of between ourselves and our objects',[39] 'the hope that there exists that which is other than oneself',[40] it is worth noting here how the play on tenses creates further confusion, making what is remote close in time, and relegating to the past what is contemporary. The novel is structured in such a way that from a logical and chronological point of view, the situation in Vietnam, or the Border War, is seen to stem from 'frontierism',[41] and centuries of colonial expansion and exploitation, as if in answer to Eugene Dawn's last expressed hope 'of finding whose fault [he is]'.[42] Yet from a narrative point of view, it is as if the second part were an actualisation of the first. The deaths envisaged on a conceptual, abstract level in the first part, find a real, concrete manifestation in the second, the structure of which further confuses logic and chronology and mingles genres and targets without blunting the criticisms of the ideology they represent.

As a matter of fact, it is no wonder that Coetzee should favour stylistic tropes and displacements in a country so obsessed with fixity, with 'erect[ing]' boundaries and fences, with the Siamese concepts of frontier and border.[43] Both served as national myths in the South Africa of the apartheid regime and more generally of the colonial era: the main myth was that of the frontiersmen embodied in those trekkers who (in the words of Dr S. J. Coetzee author of the 'Afterword') 'scattered the seeds of civilisation' and simultaneously 'extend[ed]' the white

'Empire'[44] into 'the naked plains of the interior'.[45] This justification was used to legitimise the occupation of the land: 'the boundaries of the settlement' in the Cape Colony at first, thereafter the buffer zone in the 'Frontier Country' of the Eastern Cape,[46] and years later the border of the South African state in Namibia, itself 'a mythical site'.[47] Indeed, the phrase 'Border War', as well as the name South West Africa (or Namibia as it was renamed by the United Nations (UN) in 1968) were used by those who approved Pretoria's control over the territory, because of the connotations attached to the word 'border'. The dialogue between Patrick, Ellen and Ouma de Bruin in the opening chapter of *The Beautiful Screaming of Pigs*, as well as Patrick's squeamishness every time the word 'border' is used (in italics on page 66 for instance) are quite telling in this respect. Indeed, although 'border' and 'frontier' are often used interchangeably, they actually do not have the same connotation. Broadly speaking, 'border', as Dorian Haarhoff and others have pointed out, has a geographical import and conveys the idea of a limit agreed upon, of mutually recognised fixed and legitimate boundaries, whereas 'frontier' rather suggests the idea of interaction, more often than not of con*front*ation and instability, and it is therefore generally envisaged as the first step before borders are drawn and accepted.[48]

Of course, the same myth holds true for America, and the text makes it clear through the juxtaposition of the two stories and histories. This kind of juxtaposition is also present, although more subdued, in *The Smell of Apples*, where the reader is invited to make a connection between Marnus' favourite radio serial 'Die Wildtemmer', the Voortrekkers, and the western *Trinity*.[49] To the American thrust westwards, would therefore correspond a South African movement northwards, something which had been proposed after the 1948 elections and was still on the agenda when Coetzee wrote *Dusklands*. This is illustrated in the text by numerous references to the ideas of exploration and penetration, as well as an abundance of the prepositions 'into' and 'out'. But thanks to the contrived web of correspondences and reversals, the myth is not so much endorsed as debunked from within: what the myth tries to prove is in what way the frontier was a first step to legitimise the border that replaced it. What the text does, by conflating both concepts, by resorting to tropes and displacements of various kinds, and by reversing and confusing the chronology, is to deflate the notion of stability implied in the idea of a border, and that of progress which lay at the core of 'frontierism'. The latter is here equated with mere colonisation, as when Eugene Dawn laments that he should have been born 'two hundred years ago' and that, '[he] would have had a continent to explore, to map, to open to colonization'.[50] The comma explicitly likens exploration to colonisation. The conflation of times and places also makes the trek not so much an instrument to 'scatter the seeds of civilisation', but always a tool to exert violence, as is suggested by the replacement of the word 'travel' (borrowed from William Burchell's writings which form the basis of 'The Narrative'), with that of 'journey', laden with military connotations.[51] Similarly, it transforms the so-called Border War into a mere sequel to the imperialist urge, to this search for ever new frontiers: the implication is that, far from being a legitimate war to protect the Republic of South Africa's integrity, as the word 'border' insinuates, the conflict in Namibia is but another form of expansionism, of a confrontation which originates in the inability to assert oneself in any other way than by destroying the Other.[52] The frontier spirit did not lead to the legitimacy of the border but to the paranoia of a *laager* community.

Discourses of division: Obsession and hysteria

The pervading ideology of white supremacy thus finds its way into all the texts discussed in this chapter. But this ideology is adapted and transformed in various ways, although it may not always be only or simply to fit the aims set by the authors, be they English or Afrikaans. It seems that no language escapes the taint of guilt, the influence of these discourses of division, which threaten to become a ranting obsession.

The mythic trekkers are thus conjured up rather irreverently by both Patrick in *The Beautiful Screaming of Pigs*,[53] and by Guy who in 'The Clay Ox' makes the journey back to the Drakensberg.[54] But it is in Van Heerden's more restrained short story 'Slap Grensdrade' that the *laager* mentality is more scathingly attacked, in a manner reminiscent of Coetzee: the fences of the title first appear in the narrative in the full form of *grensdrade*;[55] but once Boet's fate has been revealed and the awesome *Grens* to the north evoked, it is the word *drade* alone which appears a few lines further on.[56] The quick juxtaposition of the different stakes simultaneously involved makes the link between the Boer mentality, with its insistence on taming the land, and on upholding the colour bar, and its disruptive effects at the time of the Border War, on the frontline as well as on the home front, obvious enough. It is because of this obsession with well-drawn boundaries that the fences of the farm ultimately go slack, and that the narrator, who is subject to nightmares, collapses as if on the other side of reason. There is but one (metaphorical) step between Jamesy, who actually dies of 'cowhide shrinkage' on the 'Border',[57] and Guy, who on the home front where people blow themselves up in front of public buildings, 'see[s] the perimeters of [his] existence shrinking at incredible speed'.[58]

Yet what is more striking is the speed of the juxtapositions of those feelings: some characters become mad because of the dominant ideology, and this madness finds its expression in a disrupted language. However, language itself becomes mad as if contaminated by the perverted logic of this ideology. Some critics attribute the convoluted narrative in *Dusklands* to postmodernism, but a closer look at some passages prompts the reader to arrive at other conclusions. '[T]he forking paths of the endless inner adventure' envisaged by Jacobus Coetzee when he meets the delegation of the Great Namaquas all lead to confrontation.[59] There is no way out of this maze which is always pushing towards both literary and literal dead ends. The syntax is insane, but so is the discourse it encapsulates. The distortions perpetrated by Coetzee the writer on the original texts at his disposal, especially the pseudo-rational essay of Dr S. J. Coetzee, exemplify the madness of apartheid's rhetorical apparatus.[60]

Madness is no longer a mere symptom caused by the stress of the war; its shrillness creeps into the narrator's voice and insinuates itself into the writings themselves. This is mostly true of Van Heerden's short stories, in particular 'My Kubaan' and 'My Afrikaner', both built on the ramblings of a single character, with the addition of several digressions in the former. The English translation attenuates in part the writer's original intentions, at least in the version edited by André Brink and J. M. Coetzee who invert the order of the two paragraphs about Jamesy and make them sound more logical. The alternative sequence of paragraphs in the Afrikaans original could have been prompted by the horror of the events recounted.[61] Similarly, the minor changes Behr introduces in the translation of his own work into English smooth out some of its original abruptness: sentences are added to several of the vignettes which are to a certain extent less incisive as they become less concise. This is particularly true of the first vignette. The first chapter in the Afrikaans version ended on a note of total hopelessness, heightened by a blank before the chapter which follows it: '*Niemand weet meer wat om te glo nie*' ('No one knows what to believe any longer'). The English version does not sound so desperate, since the vignette which is not separated from what follows, ends not with this but another paragraph, which was originally part of the second episode about Angola.[62] Yet some English texts on the war are no less unsettling: the traumas run so deep that someone like Galgut, who did not even experience the conflict in Namibia at first hand, returns to it almost obsessively in writings that span more than a decade and were all written after the end of the hostilities. It seems that despite the time that has elapsed since the end of the conflict, writings about the Border War are still hovering over the porous frontier between obsession and hysteria.

Conclusion

Neglected at the time and still a relatively taboo subject today, the Border War cannot be said to have been completely forgotten. The literature it gave birth to during the years of the conflict has branched out into other types of writings which, long after the independence of Namibia, continue to map the deep imprint left by those events on South African culture and society. The trauma experienced by the troops on the frontline, and by some of the characters on the page, reducing them to madness and speechlessness, was so overpowering that it seems to have affected the writers themselves and their very means of expression, whether they are of Afrikaans or English extraction. It presents a challenge to language itself, assailed by a long history of discourses which tried to justify successive frontier wars and barriers. As Haanchen E. Koornhoff pointed out as early as 1989, 'border literature' was concerned with more than just borders but with everything that was at stake in the conflict itself.[63] The writers rose to the challenge by taking advantage of all the nuances implicit in the very word *grens*: whereas the English equivalent makes the distinction between the two notions of border and frontier, the Afrikaans word subsumes the two under a single term. Following Coetzee, these writers attempted to transform *grensliteratuur* into more than a mere record of past events: making good use of the ambivalence of the word, they juxtaposed frontier/border, home front/frontline in order to question the rhetoric of confrontation lying at the core of the regime's legitimisation of its war.

In the final analysis, it is identity that is being questioned: Afrikaner identity of course, but also, at a more general level, South African national identity, as well as the personal identity of the authors and the characters who appear in their writings. The 'Border' is not just a line on a map, the 'border troubles' not just events of 'no significance', mere ripples in 'the history of the back of beyond', to quote another passage from *Waiting for the Barbarians*.[64] On the contrary, the authors are keen to stress the link between the frontline and the home front, to show that the ideology of separation and division impinges on every aspect of the characters' lives. The scar left by the war runs deep across the Chilean General's back in Behr's *The Smell of Apples*; the crack in the mirror which reflects this scar's presence, or absence, makes a deep impression on Marnus' split mind and a disturbing blank in the texture of the narrative. It is echoed almost ten years later in Galgut's *The Good Doctor*, when Frank Eloff, discovers through another crack in the darker mirror of a lake next to another former border, that of the previous Bantustans, that he cannot shrug off the burden of history.[65] He realises that the wilderness, a dual term that simultaneously refers to a dangerous desert and a refuge away from the world,[66] runs deep within himself. It is not something that he could wish to tame, to fence off in a web of 'grids', but forms part of his own self. The conclusion he comes to is that to ignore this darker side of his own personality, this disposition for madness, would be to repeat again the scene on another border, in a dark cell in Angola, and to condemn himself to silence and to a more dangerous form of madness. This may be the motive driving Galgut to write again and again about the Border War, however distant he might have felt from the conflict, a sign that obsession with the Border War is not the prerogative of war veterans only, because it in fact threatens all South African citizens if it is not properly addressed.

The centrality of language to the processes of rehabilitation and reintegration is a concern shared by all the writers studied.[67] In the course of this study the Afrikaans visions of things have sometimes been shown to be starker than, if not their English counterparts, then at least their English translations. Yet it is one of those translations that suggests the clearest sign of convergence of the aims of these writers. In a separate paragraph at the end of a vignette at the core of *The Smell of Apples*, Behr writes: 'But the one whose life ended yesterday, his parents will have to wait. And they won't ever know what happened to him'.[68] By adding this sentence to the English translation of his narrative, he suggests that there is little likelihood of closure for those involved in the Border War – not only the ex-soldiers but those who lost loved ones. Writers do not necessarily lay the memory of the conflict to rest or facilitate any form of healing by breaking the silence, or by describing the horrors of the war. Rather, they prevent further amnesia by contradicting the discourses which led to the paranoia and madness of the Border War.

Notes to Chapter Seven

1   J. M. Coetzee, *Dusklands* (London: Vintage, 1998).

2   E. van Heerden, *My Kubaan* (Cape Town: Tafelberg, 1983), for the references to the text in Afrikaans, except for the short-story 'My Afrikaner', for which there is apparently no Afrikaans edition available in France; *Mad Dog and Other Stories* (Cape Town: Africa South Writing, David Philip, 1992, translation by C. Knox), for the English version. Sometimes references will be made to the version of 'My Cuban' published in *A Land Apart, A Contemporary South African Reader*, ed. A. Brink and J. M. Coetzee (New York: Penguin, 1987), 240–8: although both versions are the work of the same translator, Catherine Knox, they vary significantly in some places.

3   D. Galgut, 'The Clay Ox', in *Small Circle of Beings* (London: Abacus, 1990); *The Beautiful Screaming of Pigs* (London: Abacus, 1992); *The Good Doctor* (London: Atlantic Books, 2003).

4   M. Behr, *Die Reuk van Appels* (Cape Town: Queillerie, 2002), for the Afrikaans version; *The Smell of Apples* (London: Abacus, 1998), for references to the English text.

5   The armed insurrection and its repression by 'Operation Blue Wildebeest' actually started in 1966. During the 1970s, tension mounted between the apartheid regime and the local population as well between the South African government and the UN. The first recorded incident of the decade occurred in May 1971 when two white South African policemen died after detonating a land-mine, allegedly laid by members of SWAPO. There was further violence in January 1972, during the miners' strike in Owamboland. Simultaneously, the opposition to South Africa's control of Namibia was gathering momentum at the UN: in June 1971 the International Court of Justice declared the South African presence in Namibia to be illegal. Cf. for example E. Riley, *Major Political Events in South Africa, 1948–1990* (Oxford and New York: Facts On File, 1991), 121–4. The text by the imaginary scholar S. J. Coetzee included as an afterword to 'The Narrative of Jacobus Cotzee' bears the date '1951': two years before, in the year 1949 following the victory of the National Party, the South West African members of Parliament took their seats in the South African Parliament.

6   Galgut, *The Beautiful Screaming of Pigs*, 121. For more details on PTSD, see for instance D. Sandler, 'The Psychological Experiences of White Conscripts in the Black Townships', in *War and Society: The Militarisation of South Africa*, ed. J. Cock and L. Nathan (Cape Town and Johannesburg: David Philip, 1989), 79–89, and G. Baines, 'South Africa's Vietnam? Literary History and Cultural Memory of the Border War', *Safundi, The Journal of South African and American Comparative Studies* 15 (July 2004) (an earlier version of this article was published in *Telling Wounds: Narrative, Trauma and Memory, Working Through the South African Armed Conflicts of the Twentieth Century*, ed. C. van der Merwe and R. Wolfswinkel (Proceedings of the conference held at the University of Cape Town, 3–5 July 2002, 159–70).

7   Galgut, *The Beautiful Screaming of Pigs*, 113–14, 117.

8   Ibid. 112–14.

9   Ibid. 116, 122.

10   Ibid. 28.

11   Behr, *The Smell of Apples*, 12.

12   Or so it seems; but to analyse the links between the main narrative and all the different vignettes and Behr's strategy in the intertwining of the two layers of events would require much more space than this chapter allows.

13   Van Heerden, 'My Kubaan', 96 for the Afrikaans version. The English reads: 'How does a soldier prepare himself? He takes leave of things which cannot be left. He isn't like a man on Death Row because he

doesn't know for sure. He says goodbye to certainty. Saying goodbye to certainty takes a long time. It takes many nights. It takes a lot of thinking or a lot of blotting out. Some guys blot it out. ['a lot of thinking away. Some guys think it away', in the David Philip edition.] They go crazy, the camp goes crazy before an operation. The men drink and fight like tigers. They swear and vandalise the latrines. They steal Bedfords and dice through the refugee compound. They strip the queers naked and tie them on the bonnets of jeeps and race off to town with them. They drink, drink, drink' (in Brink and Coetzee, *A Land Apart*, 79–80).

14 '*Dood/lewe. Net só, met die grens tussen die twee so toevallig soos die graadverskil in 'n geweerloop se mik.*'(Van Heerden, 'My Kubaan', 94); 'as fine as the degree of the variant in the aim of a gun barrel', in the English version (Van Heerden, *Mad Dog*, 77). The translation published in Brink and Coetzee, *A Land Apart*, 242 reads slightly differently: 'the *borderline* between the two as fine as the siting on a gun'. In this latter version, the emphasis seems to fall even more on this deep-rooted link between the Border War and madness, on borderline cases in both senses of the term.

15 Galgut, *The Beautiful Screaming of Pigs*, 73.

16 Ibid. 75.

17 Ibid. 66.

18 Behr, *Die Reuk van Appels*, 35, for the Afrikaans version; *The Smell of Apples*, 28 for the English version.

19 Behr, *The Smell of Apples*, 83.

20 Galgut, *The Beautiful Screaming of Pigs*, 116–17.

21 Ibid. 116. The pause and the three dots are in the original text.

22 Ibid. 116.

23 Ibid. 132.

24 Galgut, 'The Clay Ox', 166.

25 To use Patrick's phrases to describe the regime's fear of anything different and deviant (Galgut, *The Beautiful Screaming of Pigs*, 66). Note again the derogatory tone behind the use of the indefinite plurals, and the significant use of capital letters.

26 See J-J. Lecercle, *The Violence of Language* (London: Routledge, 1990), as well as his article on clichés, 'Du cliché comme réplique', in *Le cliché*, ed. G. Mathis (Toulouse: Presses Universitaires du Mirail, 1998).

27 Behr, *The Smell of Apples*, 178.

28 Galgut, *The Beautiful Screaming of Pigs*, 74.

29 Van Heerden, 'Slap Grensdrade', 7 for the Afrikaans version. The English version tones the narrative down to a certain extent, by dropping the capital letter: 'Boet . . . has gone to the border' (Van Heerden, *Mad Dog*, 107).

30 Van Heerden, 'Slap Grensdrade', 9 for the Afrikaans version; *Mad Dog*, 109 for the English version.

31 Behr, *Die Reuk van Appels*, 48, 53, 54; *The Smell of Apples*, 41, 46–7.

32 Galgut, *The Beautiful Screaming of Pigs*, 117.

33 Coetzee, *Dusklands*, 79–80.

34 Galgut, *The Beautiful Screaming of Pigs*, 74–6, 14–15. See as well how the narrator moves from 'the onslaught of pain' to a description of a hunting scene in 'My Afrikaner', in the space of a few lines (Van Heerden, 'My Afrikaner', 85–6).

35 Galgut, *The Beautiful Screaming of Pigs*, 31.

36 Ibid. 110.

37 Ibid. 39.

38 It would be interesting to draw a parallel between the texts studied and the literature of previous wars, particularly the fiction written about the Vietnam War, as it is known. For instance, Coetzee resided in the

US and started to write his first novel towards the end of the conflict, and he sometimes took part in the protests against the war. I could not, however, find any evidence that the writers mentioned here had read, or had consciously borrowed from, such texts as Michael Herr's *Dispatches*.

39 Coetzee, *Dusklands*, 17.

40 Ibid. 79.

41 The term is borrowed from D. Haaroff, as developed in his book, *The Wild South-West: Frontier Myths and Metaphors in Literature Set in Namibia, 1760–1988* (Johannesburg: Witwatersrand University Press, 1991).

42 Coetzee, *Dusklands*, 49.

43 Ibid. 27.

44 Ibid. 111.

45 Ibid. 109.

46 See for instance the mention of the missionary John Philip (Coetzee, *Dusklands*, 111). Dr S. J. Coetzee would have us take Philip as a fervent supporter of the colonial expansion, whereas he was one of the main religious authorities to protest against the extension of the white people's influence and the increased risks of conflict with the native populations. For more information on the role played by Philip in South Africa and in Britain, with respect to the Frontier Wars, see for instance, A. Lester, 'Constructing Colonial Discourse: Britain, South Africa and the Empire in the Nineteenth Century', in *Postcolonial Geographies*, ed. A. Blunt and C. McEwan (New York and London: Continuum, 2002), 29–45, and C. Strobel, '"The History of the Cape is Already Written in that of America": The Colonisation of America in South Africa's Discourse of Empire, 1820s–1850s', *Safundi, the Journal of South African and American Comparative Studies* 20 (October 2005):1–15. William Burchell of course also travelled through the Eastern Cape, at about the time of the beginning of the Great Trek which Dr S. J. Coetzee is keen to see as the foundation of the South African society. For a more thorough analysis of the role of the Eastern Cape frontier in *Dusklands*, see M. Rogez, 'Variations on a Frontier: J. M. Coetzee's Novel *Dusklands* in Context', *Commonwealth, Essays and Studies*, 28, 1 (Autumn 2005):40–52.

47 Galgut, *The Beautiful Screaming of Pigs*, 66.

48 Cf. Haarhoff, *The Wild South West*, 7, as well as the work of geographers and historians such as L. Febvre, 'Limites et frontières', *Annales ESC (Economies, Sociétés, Civilisations)*, 2 (April–June 1947) (Paris, Millwood, New York: Krauss reprint, 1977): 201–07; J. T. Juricek, 'American Usage of the Word "Frontier", From Colonial Times to Frederick Jackson Turner', *Proceedings of the American Philosophical Society* 10 no. 1 (February 1966):10–34; and D. Nordman, 'Des limites de l'Etat aux frontières nationales', in *Les Lieux de mémoire*, tome II, *La Nation*, vol. 2, ed. P. Nora (Paris: Gallimard, 1986), 35–61. The latter writes, for instance, that 'The word *frontier* refers to a zone which can shrink, expand, or move according to territorial changes . . . If *frontier* belongs to a vocabulary of aggression, *limits*, on the other hand, belongs to that of peace' ('La *frontière* désigne une zone qui peut se rétracter, s'élargir ou se déplacer au gré des modifications territoriales . . . Si la *frontière* appartient au registre de l'agression, la *limite* appartient à celui de la paix'; Nordman, 'Des limites de l'Etat aux frontières nationales', 50, my translation). An illustration of this shift from 'frontier' to 'border' can be found in Coetzee's *Waiting for the Barbarians* which can also be read as an analysis of these two notions and of the Border War. The growth of the settlement bears similarities with the history of American frontier settlements analysed by Juricek, as when the Magistrate observes that 'what was once an outpost and then a *fort* on the *frontier* has grown into an agricultural settlement', later to notice that those settlements are now the scene of 'clashes with *border* patrols' (J. M. Coetzee, *Waiting for the Barbarians* (New York: Penguin, 1982), 5 and 8, my emphasis).

49 The reader should not forget that this same frontier background is to be found as well in *Moby Dick*, the novel Ilse is reading at the time of the General's visit. R. Barnard has commented on the presence of that

novel in her article '*The Smell of Apples*, *Moby Dick*, and Apartheid Ideology', *Modern Fiction Studies*, 46, 1 (Spring 2000):207–26. For an analysis of the use of Frontier ideology in *Moby Dick*, see R. Slotkin, *Regeneration Through Violence: The Mythology of the American Frontier, 1600–1860* (Middleton, Connecticut: Wesleyan University Press, 1973), chapters 1, 9 and 14 in particular. He also devotes several chapters to the study of Western movies (though not to *Trinity*) in the third tome of his trilogy, *Gunfighter Nation, The Myth of the Frontier in Twentieth Century America* (New York: Atheneum, 1992).

50   Coetzee, *Dusklands*, 31–2. I have here kept the original American spelling, since the American narrator positions himself as, precisely, an American.

51   Coetzee thus parodies the genre of travel writing at the very beginning of the 'Narrative' for instance, and, in the same vein, he subtly re-arranges the allegedly true version of Jacobus Coetzee's deposition given as an appendix to the story: the final part is a fairly accurate translation of the original document, except that J. M. Coetzee replaces 'astonishment' with 'suspicion', and omits two other expressions: 'friendly disposition' and 'Great Amacquas who desired to travel hither with him'. 'The effect of these alterations and omissions is another form of historical distortion as the co-operation of earlier frontier contact is played down and the potential enmity heightened. The J. M. Coetzee encounter becomes one of the forking paths, a conflict prototype operative in a frontier model.' (Haarhoff, *The Wild South West*, 222–3).

52   He did not have to look far and wide for a validation of such a thesis. See Haarhoff's analysis of Eschel Rhoodie, the author of *South West: The Last Frontier in Africa* (Johannesburg: Voortrekkerpers, 1967) and (later) Secretary of the Department of Information during the Information Scandal.

53   Galgut, *The Beautiful Screaming of Pigs*, 40.

54   Galgut, 'The Clay Ox', 169, 181.

55   Van Heerden, 'Slap Grensdrade', 6.

56   Ibid. 7.

57   Van Heerden, *Mad Dog*, 78 for the English version; translation of *beesvelinkrimping* (Van Heerden, 'My Kubaan', 95).

58   Galgut, 'The Clay Ox', 179.

59   Coetzee, *Dusklands*, 65–6.

60   For an analysis of J. M. Coetzee's sources, see D. Attwell, '"The labyrinth of my history": J. M. Coetzee's *Dusklands*', *Novel, A Forum on Fiction*, 25, 1 (Fall 1991):7–32. The reader should, however, be wary of inferring from this overwhelming sense of madness that the decision to go to war was, in itself, irrational, although it may seem so to the characters directly involved in the novels studied: the war may have been ill-prepared, tactical errors may have been made, but the decision itself was rational and calculated, as is revealed in the main narrative of *The Smell of Apples*. To use Jim Neilson's comments on the literature written about the Vietnam War, such a transposition runs the risk of "mak[ing the war] seem an aberration rather than an extension of cold war militarism, irrationality rather than a coldly calculated policy of aggression". See J. Neilson, *Warring Fictions, American Literary Culture and the Vietnam War Narrative* (Jackson: University Press of Mississippi, 1998), 137–45.

61   Van Heerden, in Brink and Coetzee, *A Land Apart*, 243. The David Philip edition keeps the original order (Van Heerden, *Mad Dog*, 78).

62   Behr, *Die Reuk van Appels*, 19 for the Afrikaans version; *The Smell of Apples*, 12 for the English version.

63   H. E. Koornhoff, 'Works of Friction: Current South African War Literature', in *Society at War*, ed. J. Cock and L. Nathan (New York: St Martin's Press, 1989), 275–82

64   Coetzee, *Waiting for the Barbarians*, 114.

65   Galgut, *The Good Doctor*, 73–5.

66   'Wilderness' indeed suggests both the untameable, savage, open space, and the desert as a refuge from the world and a place of revelation. The revelation is first and foremost personal, as the writer puts the true

meaning of the frontier into use, making the con*frontation* work both ways: Frank is challenged by the duality of his inner self, imagining as he does that he has some kind of double, that he is faced, there and afterwards, by a 'dark' reflection, a kind of 'ghost', the embodiment of the complexity of one's character which can never be fully one-dimensional only (Galgut, *The Good Doctor*, 73, 75). Notice that the soldiers significantly go 'wild' before an operation in 'My Kubaan' (Van Heerden, 96). Both English translations miss this underlying meaning – and the repetition – by simply translating 'wild' by 'mad' or 'crazy' (Van Heerden, *Mad Dog*, 80 for the David Philip edition; Brink and Coetzee, *A Land Apart*, 245 for the Penguin edition).

67   Although perhaps not so by their readers. Surprisingly enough, it is not the representation of the Border War which seems to have drawn the interest of most readers and critics of a novel like *The Smell of Apples*. A vast majority of the articles on Behr's novel kept at the National English Literary Museum in Grahamstown, for instance, focus on the indictment of the system generally speaking and the everyday aspects of apartheid, and not on its military consequences as depicted in the vignettes, which are somehow seen as an accessory to the main narrative.

68   Behr, *The Smell of Apples*, 101.

Chapter 8

Writing from Within: Representations of the Border War in South African Literature

Henriette Roos

In several of the interviews granted by Deon Opperman during April 2006, the playwright – who had just been named the winner of the prestigious Hertzog Prize[1] for Afrikaans Drama – referred directly to his participation in the Border War and the influence of that experience on his personal life and his writing. Opperman told a reporter from the daily newspaper *Beeld* that 'I will rather leave South Africa than ever be conscripted again, but I also will never want to be rid of that experience' (author's translation).[2] At about the same time a review appeared of the memoir of two now quite prominent officials of the South African Government and the South African National Defence Force (SANDF), Thula Bopela and Daluxolo Luthuli. The book *Umkhonto we Sizwe: Fighting for a Divided People* is a tale of being trained in Tanzania and the then Soviet Union, fighting with Umkhonto we Sizwe (MK) in the former Rhodesia, being imprisoned on Robben Island and afterwards moving in very different directions. One soldier became an esteemed and academically trained businessman; the other joined the Inkatha Freedom Party in a treacherous partnership with the South African Defence Force (SADF).[3] And then in June 2006, the publication of *An Unpopular War* was announced. This collection of personal stories by ex-servicemen thrown together from all walks of life and (white) cultural groups in the SADF, including accounts of life-changing experiences,[4] became a top-selling non-fiction title.

All three events occurred during the final phase of my writing this chapter, and it strikes me as remarkable that the recollections and aftermath of the Border War are, about two decades after that conflict had reached its climax, still part of (a literary portrayal of) our ordinary lives, and that there have been so many indications of a resurgence of interest in a conflict that has long since passed. The latest publications also demonstrate an awareness of how porous the categories of 'us' and 'them', 'right' and 'wrong', and 'true' and 'false' become once they are depicted in retrospective writing. Coupled to this perception is the question of why this is happening, and then of what has, and has not, been written about this war.

These observations touch upon the key concerns of this chapter. I wish to look at the articulation of the historical, ideological and emotional significance of the fiction and drama of specifically Afrikaans authors of that time who have produced a substantial output of texts focusing on the representation of the Border War. But I will also discuss the (small) body of 'border' texts produced by other South African authors. Most of the work has been written by people who were personally involved, often using a young soldier as narrator or central intelligence. Generally they presented their work in a realistic, almost documentary style, and revealed a subversive point of view. The political and cultural impact of this group on the reading public of that time, their place in literary history, and the return to that era in recent South African literature, are also discussed.

The face of Border Literature

The South African government became involved in armed conflict with several neighbouring countries from the end of the 1960s (in the erstwhile Rhodesia) up to April 1989 (after which South West Africa would gain independence as Namibia). This Border War included incursions into Botswana, Lesotho and Mozambique, and reached its greatest intensity in ongoing battles fought in Angola during the 1980s. Representations of the Border War have featured prominently in a large number of South African literary texts. The system of compulsory military service which underpinned the war effort, forced all white males to spend two years as fighting soldiers, and shaped the context in which this Border Literature was written.

In his essay linking the personal accounts of South African soldier-authors with the American literary and cultural memory of the Vietnam War, Gary Baines identifies four categories of literature about the Border War.[5] He first mentions the descriptive writing, presented as military history but often politically biased and in most instances sanctioned by the SADF. In the second place there is 'a body of left leaning academic writing . . . critical of the apartheid regime',[6] and then there are the literary works. Baines describes one of these latter categories as texts 'representative of the experiences of White, English-speaking national servicemen', in many cases strongly confessional and filled with nostalgia for military life.[7] About this category, as well as the recurring themes that are noted as characteristic of both South African, American and international war literature, more later.

It is a fourth category, one which Baines describes as written 'almost exclusively by young white male Afrikaner intellectuals . . . seldom written by those with first-hand experience of the war',[8] which constitutes the main corpus of what is known in Afrikaans as *grensliteratuur* (border literature). These specific, well-profiled books – the short stories and novels by a small group of authors – created a distinctive trend in Afrikaans literary history. It was indeed produced mainly by male authors, though female authors did write some seminal texts. But contrary to Baines' assertion, the best known and most prolific of these authors were soldiers themselves. Their personal experiences as, for instance, voluntary *recces* (the feared, because they were regarded as merciless, Special Reconnaissance Battalion), or conscripted foot soldiers, or dedicated members of the End Conscription Campaign (ECC), lurching between going *awol* or going mad, lie at the base of the traumatic events they narrate. Although some stage plays about the war were also written, published and performed, these narrative works, published at the height of the Border War, captured the essence of the moral and ideological chaos of the time.[9]

What was not published, despite the conscription of nearly all white males in some or other form (apart from the army, also as national servicemen in the police, navy or air force), with very few exceptions, was a distinctive body of English language texts. While he foregrounds the writings of these 'reluctant soldiers' in a separate category, Baines' description mentions only four texts and all were published in the late 1990s or even afterwards. To place this hiatus into context, the research done by Karen Batley could perhaps be investigated. She collected the unpublished writings of young (mainly English-speaking) soldiers: poems, diary inscriptions, notes and short narratives. The texts arrived in bushels full in response to Batley's radio appeal and a letter she wrote to several popular magazines inviting young soldiers to contact her. That the urge to articulate their experiences was there was very evident. Batley realised that these teenagers, spending their most formative years in foreign, war torn regions, were 'striving for the appropriate means of expression to escape this alien landscape and its personal significance to them'.[10] It is interesting to note that – decades later – the 'Legacy project' (the efforts to preserve war letters dating back to the American Civil War) gained momentum and eventually reached international status after a similar popular appeal was launched in 'Dear Abby' columns during 1998. Internet postings since the start of the war in Iraq gave added impetus to the project. The project leader's evaluation could just as well be applied to Batley's harvest:

> Letters like these represent the first, irreplaceable drafts of history – immediate, raw, unfiltered. [But] erase the names, dates and geographical references in these letters, and it would be difficult, if not impossible, to determine the nationalities of the writers. Their words transcend boundaries, offering insights that are timeless and universal . . . the letters remind us of our capacity for violence – and our potential compassion.[11]

That the young South Africans writing in English were rarely approached or published by the mainstream press, in contrast to what had happened in the case of Afrikaans writings, could not have been because they lacked talent. A plausible explanation is that publishing these war stories at a time when a strong anti-war and anti-apartheid culture existed among English-speaking intellectuals was not only regarded as politically incorrect,[12] but probably also as economically unviable.

However, in the midst of the war era some notable texts did appear. From Peter Wilhelm's pen came three works which focused on different stages of the armed conflict: *LM and Other Stories* (1975), *At the End of a War* (1981) and *Some Place in Africa* (1987). In the story 'Veterans' from *Some Place in Africa,* the main character is a soldier wounded in a landmine explosion, experiencing great difficulty in handling civilian life, and finding it impossible to speak about his experiences on the border. This recurring motif is also encountered in many other 'border' narratives, for instance in Peter Rule's 'A Return', but also in the majority of the Afrikaans texts. In 1991 Damon Galgut's *The Beautiful Screaming of Pigs* was published; a narrative in which, from the context of the Namibian election of 1989, the first person narrator looks back at his involvement in the war and its devastating impact on his personal life. A few short stories, many of which had first appeared in magazines, such as *Contrast, The Bloody Horse, Staffrider* and *Stet* were published in collections and anthologies. The part these 'little magazines' played in giving the young writers publishing space, especially in the case of the Afrikaans magazine *Stet*, must not be underestimated. *Armed Vision* (1987), compiled by Martin Trump, consisted of translations of Afrikaans stories, and in the same year *Forces Favourites* presented ten stories by English-speaking authors and eight translations of Afrikaans writings. But this latter collection – its title ironically referring to the then hugely popular radio 'request' programme for the 'troops' – was published by the (alternative) Afrikaans publishers Taurus, and in association with the ECC.

With these stories the focus was already turning inwards; the terror that reigned in the townships and which increased after the State of Emergency was declared in 1985, came under the spotlight. The war stories appearing in *The Vita Anthology of New South African Fiction* (1989) reflected this spatial shift, as was also evident in the novels of the young Megan du Plessis: *A State of Fear* (1983) and *Longlive!* (1989). Susan Kriel mentions that in these published texts, in contrast to the majority of Afrikaans stories, the narrators often convey a clear political message.[13] In Andrew Donaldson's 'On the Sidelines' (published in *Forces' Favourites)*, the soldier who gave a short talk on the African National Congress (ANC) is treated as a security risk by his superiors. When Anthony Akerman wrote his play *Somewhere on the Border* in 1982 while he was an expatriate in Holland, years had elapsed after his own military service. But the play was a huge hit at the Grahamstown Festival of 1986, after it had been 'banned' from being published, but not from being performed. The reason given for the 'banning', that is that the 'the play was prejudicial to the safety of the state',[14] was probably also a motivation for refusing the author a visa to attend subsequent performances.

English texts by underground or insurgent black soldiers were completely absent during the war period. A novel like *A Rainbow on the Paper Sky* (1989) by Mandla Langa could be mentioned, but this was published in London, and not written by an active soldier. Mbulelo Mzamane wrote *The Children of Soweto* in 1982, and Miriam Tlali *Amandla* (first published in 1980, but 'banned' until 1985). Both texts gave the view from the 'inner frontier . . . where the actions of "terrorist" and "security forces" are seen from the other side, from a black perspective'.[15] The obvious explanation for this silence is that there was neither time nor opportunity for writing (as is indicated by the publication only many years later of *Umkhonto we Sizwe* by Bopela and Daluxolo); yet it is also true that large numbers of the guerrillas were not part of a literary culture. In addition, combat strategies would have placed a prohibition on the combatants publishing their war experiences during the conflict. Texts such as Ronnie Kasrils' *'Armed and Dangerous': My Underground Struggle Against the Apartheid State* (1993), and Mongane Wally Serote's *Scatter the Ashes and Go* (2002) only appeared after the installation of the new government and when fighting had completely ceased.

The nature of grensliteratuur

Recently, whilst going through some forgotten boxes filled with yellowed paper, I came across a thin booklet, the 'Annual Magazine' of 'Sector 70', a region in the Eastern Caprivi so designated by the then SADF. The text reveals a treasure chest of stereotypes. With no title, author/editor or publisher indicated, the mysterious origin of *Sector 70 Annual* stands in telling contrast to its carefree contents. The lavish colour photographs of nature and wild life are interspersed with upbeat messages by generals; the glowing reports on schools, hospitals and entertainment opportunities provided by the SADF for the 'indigenous population' are illustrated by pictures of happy looking black children. On the front cover there is an artful photograph of a trumpeting elephant against a dramatic sunset. On the back cover, an image appears of a young military chaplain reading the Bible to four attractive, attentive soldiers of his own age. Some implied dating puts the year of publication as sometime during 1983; the portrayal of the war zone as calm and peaceful ('Die atmosfeer is een van rustigheid en vrede') is at complete odds with what is now known about the actual military situation.[16]

This picture of a 'peace force' ('Ons soldate is nie net in staat om vrede af te dwing nie, maar ook om vrede te bewaar')[17] operating in harmony with man and nature, manned by handsome, morally upright and socially conscientious soldiers, was a construct that not only existed in military publications, but was also disseminated in popular fiction.

Although generally not accepted as 'high-brow' literature, there were quite a few Afrikaans narratives that reflected and strengthened the then dominant social discourse – specifically amongst Afrikaans-speaking white people, but not exclusively so – of a general acceptance of official policy and its related military propaganda. In her Master's dissertation, Kriel discusses the phenomenon in broad terms.[18] She mentions one such narrative from the early years, the 1978 text by Johan Coetzee, *Verby die Wit Brug, Kortverhale oor die Grens*, which can be said to have set the scene for fostering the romantic image of a just and necessary war. Other novels of a similar ilk were *Kruisvuur* (1978) by Adriaan Snyman, Andrew McCallaghan's *Jampie*

Gaan Grens toe (1983), *Tweede Prys is 'n Houtjas* (1983) and *Half Boom, Half Mens* (1986) by Bertrand Retief, *Dag van die Reuse* (1985) by Pieter Pieterse, Maretha Maartens' *Verste Grens* (1986) and *Engele op Stelte* (1990) by Marietjie Kotze. In addition, there were the numerous short stories published in popular 'family' magazines and collections such as At van Wyk's *Honoris Crux: Ons Dapperes II* (1985) and Maretha Maartens' *Ses Wenverhale* (1988). H.P. van Coller lists 75 such popular stories, most of them appearing in *Die Huisgenoot* and the widely read *Radio en TV Dagboek*.[19] Besides the traditionally romanticised image of war as a site for heroics, male bonding and patriotism, these texts – in some cases directly linked to SADF initiatives[20] – served to keep up morale amongst the troops' next of kin[21] by painting a fictitious world held in place by male power, supportive women and the divine right to victory.[22] It is noteworthy that very few, if any, of the authors of these stories were active soldiers themselves.[23] Closely related to this phenomenon was the release of a number of Afrikaans films on the Border War. In Dylan Craig's informative dissertation he gives a detailed description of this visual propaganda. The blatant indoctrination present in these films made from 1971 onwards, was followed by the irreverent 'Boetie'-films of 1984–85 (*Boetie Gaan Border toe, Boetie op Manoeuvers*) which diverted attention from the dangers of war and propagated the message that 'fighting is fun'.[24]

The most distinctive characteristic by which intellectually accomplished *grensliteratuur* could be distinguished from these popular pieces, would be the way in which they contested (with very few exceptions) the dominant stereotypes. Koos Prinsloo was the Afrikaans author identified most closely with the subversive nature of Afrikaans border literature, and 'Fighting for Peace' is the title of one of his best known 'border' stories. It appeared in Prinsloo's first published collection of short stories, *Jonkmanskas* (1982), shortly after he had returned from a compulsory spell of 'border duty'. Prinsloo's writing introduced into the then contemporary Afrikaans literature a totally new tenor: contemptuous of the pretences of middle class society, subversive of the official communiqués, menacing in its personal despair.[25] The recurring figure in his border stories is the gay conscript who rejects authority in all its guises; who experiences life inside and outside the military as an outcast; who is completely alienated from those at home. When the young soldier is picked up along the beach and told by the cruising yuppie that "'fighting for peace is like fucking for virginity'" (29), he turns his assault rifle on the man with the same impersonal brutality he has been practising in the war zone. Prinsloo kept returning to the Border War in his subsequent publications, although in his later books the focus fell on the violence and marginalisation rife in everyday life, and of being gay in such a world.

It is striking that in the majority of the texts the word 'grens' appears in the title. The multivalence of the term *border/grens* which became evident in Prinsloo's writings, was also characteristic of the other literary texts in this genre.[26] The very existence of many of southern Africa's borders was part of a colonial heritage of delimitation as a sign of conquest and exclusion aimed at disempowering the Others; geopolitical issues were therefore self-evidently part of the bigger message of these texts. However, the concept was most distinctively augmented through being transposed from a historical space into the metaphysical realm. The theories of Karl Jaspers – himself so involved with questions of war, soldiers and guilt – on self-definition and boundary experiences seem to be very relevant in this case.[27] According to Jaspers, an individual only attains complete identity when opening up to border experiences: those involving conflict, struggle, guilt and death. In these situations the limits of existence are reached, and although a person can not see the other side, they become aware of what exists there.[28] In *grensliteratuur*, whilst the texts primarily announce, chronicle and interpret the pervasive war exploits of the time, there is a constant return to these 'boundary situations' of individuation.

A person could read two texts by decidedly non-combatant authors as being prescient of the forthcoming *grensliteratuur*. In 1963 Elsa Joubert, now the doyenne of Afrikaans literature, published *Ons Wag op die Kaptein*. This story of the horrifying culmination of racial strife in colonial Angola on one specific farmstead is a precursor to the historical events of two decades later. But in its articulation of how physical, emotional and ethnic boundaries were transgressed on that day of reckoning, her text also hints at the multifaceted meanings the 'border' concept would attain. In later works like *Melk* (1980) and *Die Laaste Sondag* (1983) Joubert portrayed reactions to the Border War of the time, and in the latter novel gave a chilling account of a small town *dominee* inciting the community to mass hysteria and vengeance after his own traumatic confrontation with a young soldier. It is interesting that it was Joubert who first gave prominence to the term *grensliteratuur* when she wrote a review of contemporary publications.[29]

The second text is *Op Pad na die Grens* (1976) by Jaap Steyn, a conservative intellectual still active in language politics today. This collection of short stories focused directly on the characteristic war environment that would prevail in South Africa from 1975 onwards. The recurring use of the word 'grens' throughout the collection is notable; the final story, 'Die dag toe ons agtergekom het dis oorlog', incorporates real newspaper reports announcing the 'first' (publicised) military incursion into Angola. Steyn links this event to the South African War of 1899, and his main character in the title story – a policeman departing for the border – visits the farm cemetery to take leave of those family members who had died in that earlier war. Critics have referred to the essayistic, stylised structure of the narratives, pointing out that the text can also be read as a debate about ideological questions concerning momentous future changes in Afrikanerdom and the validity/righteousness of the response to that changed future.[30] There were also some texts by Piet Haasbroek (the gruesome 'Anatomieles' and 'Aardrykskundeles' from his collection *Roofvis* in 1975, as well as 'Afskeid' from *Verby die Vlakte* of 1982), and others by Peet van der Merwe (some of the episodes in *Vir 'n Lewe*, 1974) that, despite the thematic links, appeared to be peripheral to the Border War. But most of these stories, including P. H. Roodt's war narratives in *Afrika is Blou Soos 'n Lemoen* (1990), were told by men who had been drafted for military service in the 1960s and were still very much part of the pervasive military culture.

In my view, what constitutes the core of *grensliteratuur* are those texts written over a period of less than a decade by a group of authors who themselves, in one way or another, were involved in the Border War. Amongst these Alexander Strachan's *'n Wêreld Sonder Grense* (1983) is exemplary. Although Strachan returned to the Border War in his subsequent *Die Jakkalsjagter* (1990) and *Die Werfbobbejaan* (1994), this first collection of stories became his signature. The collection displays a remarkable cohesion. The nine separate stories are linked by the cover illustration, the ambiguous title, the cold blooded soldier/narrator, the enumeration of brutalities as part of a developing plot, the military jargon and the explicit autobiographical grounding. In the last story there is a complete and sinister rejection of all conventional forms of authority and tradition as the narrator enters a new form of existence.[31] Strachan has sometimes acted as mouthpiece for his generation of writers; perhaps his most telling remark was that these authors did not write about the war situation, but from within it. Their primary aim was to *report* what was happening.[32] In his survey of films made about the Border War, Craig identifies the film based on this Strachan book as 'unique among Border War films . . . and [an examination of it is] highly rewarding in terms of its subversions of, rather than adherences to, the Border War filmic template'. His assessment corroborates my interpretation of the book.[33]

The debut of Gawie Kellerman in late 1988, *Wie de Hel het Jou Vertel*, just after completing his military service, is in many ways reminiscent of Strachan's work. Once again the stories are linked by the typographical layout, the insidious tenor and the recurring themes. The title suggests that something which should have been kept hidden is being revealed.[34] The Namibian environment – as was the case with two earlier narratives by George Weideman, 'Gelykenis' and 'Nagelaat' from his book *Tuin van Klip en Vuur* (1983) – is prominently featured.

Louis Krüger, a military chaplain and vocal opponent of government policies who left South Africa after his military service, published *'n Basis Oorkant die Grens* in 1984. This novel relates an episode in the warfare between, on the one hand infiltrating white Rhodesian and South African soldiers, and the Mozambican government forces, on the other. The narrator is one of the infiltrators, a dead soldier who, from beyond the border between life and death, tells of what has happened as he is being carried back over the geographical border by his retreating compatriots. Indications that the narrative is based on real events appear more than once.

Several other young authors published their first prose fiction during this decade, among them Harry Kalmer and Victor Munnik, both closely involved with the ECC. In Kalmer's *Die Waarheid en Ander Stories* from 1989 some of the narratives describe secret incursions into Mozambique and Lesotho. His 'Die nag steek op soos 'n seer tand; 'n grensverhaal in die jongste styl' offers an ironic look at the border genre as such. Kalmer's novel published in 1993, *X-Ray Visagie en die Vingers van God*, depicted the political violence and social disorder of 1982. From Victor Munnik came another collection of short stories, *Die Oog van die Nyl* (1983) in which one of the texts,

'Mej. Augustus' – also appearing in translation in *Forces' Favourites* – was based on the same story material as Prinsloo's 'Grensverhaal'. In Prinsloo's story the situation of a young soldier being informed that back home a loved friend had just died after a horse riding accident, interrogates the different meanings of 'limitation', 'border' and 'cry' with the use of the Afrikaans word 'grens'. André Letoit (this pseudonym changed in a later incarnation to Koos Kombuis) the iconoclastic singer and musician, wrote 'Grenssoldaat in die Suburbs', a story from his *My Nooi is 'n Tikmasjien* (1983). Like Eben Venter's 'Die Donner in Boetiefanie se Kop' (*Witblitz* 1985), it portrayed an outcast, freaked out soldier back at home. One of the most frightening depictions of soldiers 'gone mad', is perhaps the short novel *Beertjie en sy Boytjies* (1990) by R. R. Ryger (pseudonym of Michael Green). Hansie Pienaar wrote *Die Lewe Ondergronds* (1986), the story of a young man's 'growing up' on the border, and with Hein Willemse he published *Die Trojaanse Perd* (1985), which documented through interviews in both English and Afrikaans one of the horrifying episodes of betrayal on the Cape Flats. Revealing the cruel torture to which the 'enemy' was subjected – MK soldiers as well as civilian supporters – formed the contents of many of the war narratives. Not only Kellerman's stories but also some in André le Roux's *Sleep vir Jou 'n Stoel Nader* (1987) dwelt on these torture scenes which were very often of a sexual nature. The poet Henning Pieterse, another winner of the prestigious Hertzog Prize, published one book of short stories (*Omdat Ons Alles Is,* 1998) in which his experiences as a conscripted soldier are also recounted. 'Laaste Taptoe' especially, is a burlesque account of the seemingly innumerable burials the irreverent Army Band had to attend. These texts informed a society in denial about that which was censored by newspapers at the time, and thus contributed to capturing a history of the horrifying times.

Etienne van Heerden may be regarded as perhaps the most successful writer of this generation because of his prominent position in the Afrikaans literary canon. Although not an active soldier, as he spent his compulsory military service being trained as a dog handler at the military headquarters then named Voortrekkerhoogte, his writing is firmly rooted in documented historical situations and events. The collection *My Kubaan* (1983), and specifically the title story, captured the burden of guilt that the young soldiers had to carry. They might have been conditioned and trained to be merciless killers, but when confronted with the enemy as fellow human beings, the knowledge and memories of their own inhumanities followed them around – just as if the dead Cuban soldier had been tied to them for life. In Van Heerden's later works, *Om te Awol* (1984), *Liegfabriek* (1988), *Toorberg* (1986, translated into English as *Ancestral Voices)* and *Casspirs en Campari's* (1991), the war and its aftermath figured in different degrees. Discussing some of Van Heerden's works, Kriel concludes that his border narratives were more stylised, more consciously fictionalised texts than most of the work of other authors.[35] The focus was on the writer in his role as author, and not primarily on the experiences of the writer as a young soldier.

In identifying Joubert as one of the earliest literary voices heard in the border discourse, it is necessary also to be aware of other, just as important, female voices. In some instances they would articulate the concerns and doubts of the 'home front'. Lettie Viljoen with *Klaaglied vir Koos* (1984) told the highly unusual story of a woman whose husband had deserted the SADF to join the enemy, the South West Africa People's Organisation (SWAPO). In Petra Müller's short story 'Etmaal', a more conventional view is given of those who stayed at home. Welma Odendaal, on the other hand, adopted a male point of view and many of the stories in her *Keerkring* (1977) are acted out amidst the battle. This collection was deemed to be subversive and was one of the few Afrikaans texts to be declared 'undesirable' and 'banned' by the then Directorate of Publications.[36] Emma Huisman's *Berigte van Weerstand* (1990), Jeanne Goosen's *'n Kat in die Sak* (1988), and *Sitate om 'n Rewolusie* (1985) by Jeanette Ferreira all portrayed the Border War and its fall out. Almost every one of these authors was sensitive to feminist issues and this attitude also informed their literary texts. In her book *Colonels and Cadres: War and Gender in South Africa* (1991), Jacklyn Cock argued that an ambiguous feminist attitude existed towards war. On the one hand, females demanded to be treated on an equal footing and allowed to become combat soldiers; on the other, they considered women's nurturing nature as superior to any male, military role.[37] It is interesting that in the narratives mentioned above the female characters were never portrayed as soldiers, but they all subverted the SADF through their active or passive support of the resistance. The equation of the military with a vehicle for male power is clearly present in these texts.

In his class-based analysis of Afrikaans border literature, Robert Gordon states that 'in a milieu of silence, rumour and myth fostered by draconian press censorship, "border literature" as a bourgeois creation is used not so much to expose the technologies of control of indigenes, as to regulate the settlers'. He adds that 'this literature serves in the last analysis to fortify the state and the occupying power, for it is not concerned with the destruction of the indigenes, but of the Afrikaners or the Whites . . .' Gordon makes several valid and illuminating points, amongst others his indication of the apolitical stance, the literary tradition of the frontier/colonialist concept, the process of individuation and the sense of alienation from the self as recurring themes in *grensliteratuur*. The validity of his arguments notwithstanding, he underestimates and even fails to recognise the great impact of this literature on its Afrikaans readership. With the supercilious statement that 'what *Scope* and *Grenswagter* [sic; I presume this is a reference to the macho photo romance *Grensvegter*] do for the white working classes, *grensverhale* make acceptable for the middle and upper classes',[38] he misread the radical core of these texts and the subversive nature of their literary discourse.

At the time of their publication every one of these new Afrikaans texts was received with considered reviews; general discussions in magazines and essays in journals preceded several post-graduate studies and even large research projects.[39] But a wary literary establishment and a shocked and sceptical reading public remained uncertain about how to receive *grensliteratuur*. The conflicting reactions are indicated not only by actual 'banning' and rumours of pre-censorship at publishing houses, but also by the uproar surrounding some of the most prestigious literary prizes of the time. In 1988 the *Rapport* Prize, the biggest in monetary terms, was awarded to Koos Prinsloo's collection of short stories *Die Hemel Help Ons*, but the grand prize-giving ceremony was cancelled less than 36 hours beforehand. The reason was the furore caused by Prinsloo's description of a bored soldier calling the then State President P. W. Botha 'die meidenaaier'.[40] That the narrator of the title story also noted graffiti exclaiming 'Fuck Mandela, Free Tsafendas', was never mentioned in any of the newspaper reports. Etienne van Heerden, the more acceptable face of *grensliteratuur,* was awarded the Hertzog Prize in 1988. He did attend the prize-giving ceremony, but used his acceptance speech to deliver a scathing attack on the political and literary establishment.

I regard these texts as the harbingers of the postmodernist era in Afrikaans literature. Undermining of the *status quo*, rejecting authority, hierarchy and stereotypes, fragmenting the narrative structures, forsaking aesthetic norms, crossing textual boundaries: these are the essential characteristics of postmodernism in literature. In what is certainly the best known Afrikaans drama about the Border War, Deon Opperman's *Môre is 'n Lang Dag* (1986), the dialogue is in both English and Afrikaans, the young soldiers are their own worst enemies, and playing games – uncompleted games – becomes their main activity. In Dan Roodt's *Sonneskyn en Chevrolet* (1982), with its fragmented structure and cynical point of view, the postmodernist attitude is very evident. The testimonial of a drunken soldier is interspersed with (unacknowledged) reproductions of seventeenth century graphics depicting scenes of rape and torture. That Roodt was one of the very few who wrote about the atrocities of the Border War without ever being there (he fled military conscription for France where he studied Philosophy), and today is back in South Africa as one of the 'intellectual' king pins of the far right movements, is perhaps another postmodernist prank. But in contrast with the playful, and essentially superficial, if not nihilistic nature of Western postmodernism, in Afrikaans literature in general the subversive tenor and sense of disillusionment conveyed a serious message of political and ideological commitment and a prefiguration of momentous social change. The attention to factual information and documentary references in the texts challenged the validity of what was disseminated as 'true' by official sources, but also implied the authors' own desire for validation. At the very least, *grensliteratuur* indicated that fiction could become a source of information, and in many instances it may have contributed to a revisionist history of atrocious events.[41]

Certain readers may regard the trend/genre that has become known as *grensliteratuur* as limited in scope and appeal, even amongst Afrikaans-speaking white people. The journalist Stephanie Niewoudt quotes various literary critics giving different reasons for this muted response: the narratives were too 'literary' to have a wide appeal, the readers too involved with the reality of war, the authors so traumatised that they could only glibly portray the terrible events.[42] I disagree with this verdict, although the unconvincing efforts to present the 'other' side of the war effort are clearly limiting aspects in achieving greater relevance. Van Heerden's story 'My Afrikaner' (1988), supposed to be the opposite of and companion piece to 'My Kubaan' from five years earlier, was no literary success.[43] Although *In die Tyd van die Uil* (1989) by Henk Rall there were farmers, a doctor, a white soldier, a military chaplain and a group of black insurgents acting as narrators, their narrative lacked cohesion and conviction. But the Border War left nothing and nobody in South Africa, and very few outside its immediate borders, untouched.[44] *Grensliteratuur* chronicled the history of one (albeit small) group of the many affected, and brought home some of the realities of that war to many who might otherwise have remained unaware. Notwithstanding changing attitudes towards war and specifically the Border War, these texts pushed the first hand experiences of what was – and still is – hidden, to the fore.

What has happened to grensliteratuur?

Since the texts were published at a specific historical moment by authors who were directly involved in the war, *grensliteratuur* is often dismissed as a body of work which has lost its relevance to post-apartheid democratic South Africa. Even the narrative structure most commonly encountered in *grensliteratuur*, the short story, seemed to have been chosen for a very specific use. Kriel developed a detailed argument that the short story was the most suitable narrative form to convey the momentary experiences and abrupt emotions so typical of most of these texts. A genre that was seen to be 'innovative' and 'rebelling against stereotyped forms' was tailor made to communicate a single compelling image or statement.[45]

When reading *grensliteratuur* within the larger context of (Afrikaans) literary history, however, it becomes evident that this was no fleeting trend, but part of a tradition of dissent in Afrikaans literature. Since the early years of the twentieth century successive generations of some of the best known Afrikaans authors vehemently opposed the then current regime and its policies. I am referring not to their personal political convictions, but to the articulation of dissent in their literary work. Eugène Marais, Johannes van Melle, the poets Peter Blum and Uys Krige, the *Sestiger*-group and especially André P. Brink, Breyten Breytenbach, Adam Small and Jan Rabie, and later Karel Schoeman and John Miles were perhaps the best known. It is also relevant to note that a long-standing tradition in Afrikaans publishing to (sometimes) serve the interests of language and culture – meant that manuscripts were often published even if they were unlikely to be profitable or supportive of the political *status quo*.

According to Baines, the Border War narratives written in English have their literary precedents in the American texts of the Vietnam War and share certain tropes with that corpus of literature. Experiencing the environment as an adversary, the futile attempts to co-opt the civilian population, the mood of demoralisation and disillusionment, and not being welcomed back home, are some of the most marked similarities. He also states that *grensliteratuur* 'tends to draw its inspiration from the country's own frontier history'.[46] Although the connection with earlier wars and the consequences of a (Namibian) frontier past are undeniably present, especially in the case of the work of George Weideman, Dorian Haarhoff's assertion that these texts 'demythologised a conscript culture rather than perpetuated the trekker myths' is valid.[47] I believe that *grensliteratuur* remains interesting because, apart from its unique characteristics, there is also a meaningful connection to universal war themes. Both Kriel and Baines have discussed what they consider to be general characteristics of modern war fiction.[48] That *grensliteratuur* is an integral part of this broad structure is indicated by a brief overview of the most noticeable themes: the ambivalent attitude towards killing, the dehumanisation of the enemy juxtaposed with recognising the Self in that enemy, the fatalistic mood, the sense of futility and betrayal, experiencing war as a rite of passage, and the focus on individual involvement in the war rather than representing it as an epic whole.

But *grensliteratuur* was not only heir to existing literary traditions; it also developed in new directions. During the latter part of the Border War, the troops moved into the township spaces, an inevitable historical process that also led to a parallel literary development – the theme being the 'crisis of increasing confrontation shifting from the periphery to the centre'.[49] The credibility of these subsequent publications also grew from their chronological link to the border conflict. Many of the fictional characters were portrayed as former or re-deployed soldiers, the once far off border being drawn into the South African state. Although the difference was one of degree rather than the emergence of a completely new genre, the focus now fell on the metropolitan scene, and the enemy was a fellow countryman or countrywoman. In announcing the publication of *An Unpopular War,* the author stated that the arrival of 'township service' was the turning point for many of the young soldiers who now realised that fighting the 'Red Menace' did not correlate with terrorising grandmothers and children in the dusty township roads.[50] Aside from the abovementioned English texts which depicted the period after the declaration of the State of Emergency, some of the female Afrikaans authors named above also focused on this period. Etienne van Heerden's *Toorberg* (1986) and *Die Stoetmeester* (1993), *Blaaskans* (1983) by John Miles and the rare book by a coloured author in this genre, *Verdwaalde Land* by Abraham Phillips (1994), were some of the other prominent Afrikaans texts portraying this period.

Another interesting development is the publication from the late 1990s onwards of texts in which, almost two decades after the war had ended, the war years and the author's involvement are relived. Late in 2005 I came across a collection of short stories, *The Small Bees' Honey*, which was published in the United States in 1997 and written by an ex-*recce* George Clark. The remarkable stories about ex-soldiers (the narrators are Angolan, South African, Rhodesian, Cuban) reliving the Border War in the midst of a new life in the New World, speak of indelible memories and of an indeterminable nostalgia. A former soldier now settled in Australia, Clive Holt, published *At Thy Call We Did Not Falter* (2005) – the title of the book an ironic reference to the then National Anthem.[51] This is a collection of personal recollections and diary inscriptions, as well as stories told to the author by his erstwhile comrades. The book is dedicated to all the soldiers of the 61st Mechanised Infantry Battalion who died during battle; the overbearing impression is that of confusion and stress that have never been fully overcome. Also in 2005 a reprint of Rick Andrew's *Buried in the Sky* (first published in 2001) appeared. The reviewer states in his closing paragraph that 'this book . . . will appeal to a lot of people . . . who can say "I remember the dust and the heat, the good, the bad, the brotherhood and the madness"'.[52] Discussing the earlier edition, Baines points out that some of Andrew's satirical lyrics were appropriations of Vietnam songs, articulating the same anti-war sentiments. He very convincingly argues that these texts form part of a cathartic literature: the tone is confessional, honest, self-deprecating and above all, nostalgic.[53] The playwright Greig Coetzee used different words but reached the same conclusion in describing his play *White Men with Weapons* which was first performed in 1997. It is to be presumed that apart from the confessional and nostalgic mood, less restrictive publishing policies and a broader reading audience also played a part in this re-emergence of English Border War texts.[54]

A noteworthy example of the confused emotional environment in which these post-war texts were written, is Mark Behr's *Die Reuk van Appels* (1993), which had achieved almost blockbuster status by the time it was translated into English as *The Smell of Apples* in 1995. The theme of betrayal by a father of his son and by a country of its young men is developed through the recollections of a young soldier in his dying moments. The rumours about and then confession by Behr of his own secret life as an agent for the Security Force spying on anti-apartheid activists, bring to mind Heyns' comments on the 'ambivalence of confessional fiction [as it is] often accommodating, and not confronting the culpability' of the author.[55]

Ambivalence is also noticeably present in a number of the Afrikaans texts that appeared towards the end of the nineties. In a detailed survey of the Afrikaans fiction published during this period, Van Coller describes the emergence of a 'male discourse' within a new generation of border stories.[56] He distinguishes as one broad category those texts which reveal the lies and futility of war as characteristic of male values and therefore also attack war as a male power game. With some texts written by female authors, these narratives portray the brutalities, sexual excesses and destructive boredom in the SADF as being responsible for a traumatised life which has become stunted and defeatist. In two full-length novels, Marita van der Vyver's *Die Dinge van 'n Kind* (1994) and Riana Scheepers' *Die Heidendogters Jubel* (1995), the stereotypical role of women as loyal homemakers or sexual objects in support of the Border War is rejected as a male chauvinist conception. A number of newcomers published short story collections in which the futility of war, in the sense that nothing is achieved while only terrible scars remain, takes central place. From Charles Malan came *Pan se Pretboek* (1996), the gruesome stories suggesting that the hit squads terrorising the suburban population in the pre-election period around 1994 were made up of former soldiers. These accusations would emerge again a decade later, when newspaper reports about crime syndicates and hijackings pointed directly to the involvement of former members of the SADF, and especially the feared 32nd Battalion.[57] The popular detective novels by Deon Meyer, and specifically *Orion* (available in an English translation as *Dead at Daybreak,* 2001), also dwell on the link between the old soldiers and the new criminals. In 1997 Jaco Botha with *In Drie Riviere,* Jaco Fouché with *Paartie by Jake's* and Herman Wasserman with *Verdwaal* revealed similar deceits. In the same year S. P. Benjamin published *Die Reuk van Steenkool,* a unique work as it represents the 'coloured' view in its portrayal of a young boy and his unstable family life during this period. The boy's experience of township violence is very personal: he nags his mother for a 'Casspir' toy; clearly confusing this military symbol with his absent father, Kasper, and the need for paternal and socio-political stability. Jan Vermeulen in *Die Laaste Dans* (1998) concentrates on the desolation experienced by a group of Bushmen trackers completely abandoned by the government and also spurned by their clan, revealing a less publicised aspect of the tragic aftermaths of this particular war. In Izak de Vries' *Kom Slag 'n Bees* (1998), the former soldier participates in an African ritual of sacrifice and exorcises his guilt. The prize-winning novel by Dine van Zyl, *Slagoffers* (2001), is a strongly autobiographical narrative that relives the experiences of a war reporter in the Angola of Jonas Savimbi. The narrative is presented in the form of interviews with four women who had endured the most gruesome violence – the reporter would only years later recuperate from the trauma; her cameraman committed suicide. Van Coller regards the novels of Eben Venter, and especially *Ek Stamel Ek Sterwe* (1996), as articulating some of the most vehement onslaughts on the SADF and the impact of the Border War.[58] In the latter text, the main character, who is dying from AIDS, is profoundly burdened by the conflict with his father and with family tradition. He has rejected the equation of manliness with violence, especially as it is realised through war and hunting, but eventually dies with great courage thereby lending new meaning to the concept of heroism.

The link between war and hunting (or related pastimes) characterises the second group of new border narratives as identified by Van Coller.[59] Although not necessarily displaying a positive attitude toward the Border War, these texts are not anti-war; rather they subscribe to a strong heroic ethos and focus on traits such as bravery, comradeship, self sacrifice, endurance and loyalty. Christiaan Bakkes' story of the almost inhuman endurance of an ex-soldier – now game ranger – suggests that this bravery originated in the Border War (*Die Lang Pad van Stoffel Mathysen,* 1998). This book would later be followed by *Skuilplek* (2002) with its similar accent on a 'macho' world and by *Moer toe die Vreemde in* (2001) of which his brother C. Johan Bakkes was the author. One of the most remarkable texts representing this 'retro-border' trend, *Agter die Suikergordyn* (1997), was written by Alexander Strachan. The stereotypical male activities of war, hunting, drinking, sexual pursuit and sport have been tempered by an increasing commitment to game conservation and eco-hunting(!).[60] But the narratives also describe extreme cases of post-traumatic stress disorder (PTSD), a return to the war zone to confront the past, and comradeship as the enduring legacy of war. One of the stories, 'Caprivi', is an autobiographical account of a soldier/author returning after about two decades to his former haunts and the old battlefields (probably the only text of this nature in Border War literature); the futility of it all, but also the enduring relationships, are convincingly portrayed.

In the course of 2004 the first reports of South Africans dying in Iraq suggested that these mercenaries – as was the case with the group arrested during March 2004 in Zimbabwe, allegedly on their way to stage a coup in Equatorial Guinea – were in many cases veterans of the Border War. Perhaps this would be the last stage of the continuing hostilities in which that generation of soldiers was involved. *War Dog: Fighting Other Peoples' Wars* published in 2005 by the prolific war writer A. J. Venter, who started his career reporting on the first battles in the Border War, describes in graphic detail the diverse activities on their own continent as well as abroad of successive groups of black and white (South) African mercenaries. The book is also the story of men who have been marked by their training for and fighting in – and by the inglorious ending of – the Border War.[61] In a personal account of her involvement with soldiers from the Border War over a period of 20 years, a well-known criminal psychologist tells a harrowing tale of PTSD, the overwhelming feeling of abandonment and marginalisation, and the lack of emotional and social support in adapting to a new life. The inevitable conclusion is to sell to the highest bidders the skills they learnt 20 years earlier; once again fighting other people's wars.[62]

Conclusion

The emergence, development and legacy of *grensliteratuur* are undeniably linked to contemporaneous socio-political and cultural developments. The texts published in the 1980s were written and read within an authoritarian state functioning in pervasive secrecy and deceit. The impact and meaning of these narratives must be evaluated in the context of contesting, or even rejecting, this state of affairs. Towards the latter part of the nineties the founding and sittings of the Truth and Reconciliation Commission (TRC) increasingly influenced also the literary discourse. The concept of publicly recounting misdeeds and suffering, in order to free both perpetrators and victims from the disabling past, was a political vision that translated into complex literary texts. Njabulo Ndebele once remarked that 'in few countries in the contemporary world do we have a living example of people reinventing themselves through narrative'.[63] Issues around the questions of guilt, confession and redemption, but also doubts about the collective nature of these acts, were articulated in a narrative return to the Border War. Apart from the Afrikaans texts discussed above, I could mention the novels by Mike Nicol (*The Ibis Tapestry,* 1998) and Galgut (*The Good Doctor*, 2003) where, in both cases, the central plot develops around the fate of former Border War soldiers. In Nicol's book the four parts of the narrative are titled: 'Reconstruction', 'Development', 'Truth' and 'Reconciliation'.[64] Van Heerden recounts the remarkable incident of a commissioner of the TRC asking him for names of writers of *grensliteratuur,* so that these authors could be summoned to a confessional panel. Van Heerden motivates his refusal with the statement that these authors – all of them mentioned in the paragraphs above – are there for the reading; 'in an era of cultural shallowness, these texts bear documented witness to the suffering of a whole generation. No new confession will surpass the intensity and complexity of the literary work'.[65]

The new millennium started in Afrikaner circles with a vociferous controversy, the so-called 'Boetman'-debate (Boetman being a patronising form of addressing a young boy, but perhaps also conjuring up memories of the 'Boetie' movies of the early eighties). This mainly generational conflict tapped into the conviction of many ex-soldiers that they had been deceived, betrayed and eventually patronised by the 'old men' of the Apartheid era: first into unwittingly fighting their wars for them, then in being abandoned to a bleak future whilst the old men flourished in a new dispensation. The furore played out in the media, on stage and in private discussions, perhaps reflecting a broader post-colonial disillusion, but specifically articulating the perception that this generation of Afrikaner males had been sold out by their elders. Once again it was Van Heerden who expressed surprise at the numerous professions of 'not knowing'. Why, he asked, were so many people in 2000 reading the 'Boetman' missives as if they had revealed unknown secrets about the war; why had the same people not read (or believed) those accusations and doubts when they were voiced during the 1980s in a 'whole arsenal of Border stories'?[66] It is very interesting that the main characters in recent novels by some of the best Afrikaans novelists today are cynical survivors of the Border War. Etienne van Heerden's *In Stede van die Liefde* (2005), John Miles' *Die Buiteveld* (2003), as well as *Die Avonture van Pieter Francken* (Jaco Fouché, 2005) and Jaco Botha's *Miskruier* (2005), all include characters that experience confession and guilt. But, they also convey the message that the past is past; it is the present that demands all those skills necessary to survive.

Perhaps the first new literary trend in Afrikaans fiction which is as clearly profiled as *grensliteratuur*, is that made up of the revisionist writings appearing around the centenary of the South African/Anglo-Boer War of 1899–1902. This is a large body of works, encompassing popular fiction as well as complex, serious narratives, also published in a variety of literary forms, and part of a very wide ranging discourse that sprang up around the centenary celebrations (or the absence thereof!). The narratives are characterised by their undermining of accepted myths about heroism, courage, and the moral high ground occupied by the Boer soldiers.[67] An interesting intertextual relationship can be discerned here. In the 1980s, in several instances border literature drew on the thematic echoes of the Boer War (for instance some texts by J. C. Steyn, Kellerman and Prinsloo); at the end of the century, the literary reappraisal of the Boer War could draw upon the subversive tenor of *grensliteratuur*.

In August of 2005 a glowing review appeared of the well-known journalist Lin Sampson's book of short stories *Now You've Gone 'n Killed Me* described as 'a book about ordinary people, people like us'. The accompanying interview mentions that Sampson was pondering about why so little had been written about the Border War, and the reviewer reckoned Sampson's story 'A Time to Mourn: A Community Loses Eight Young Men on the Border' to be one of the most poignant he had ever read. It is evident that Sampson was wrong in assuming that 'little' had been written about the war. Moreover, the interest amongst 'ordinary' people in the war is very much alive.[68] Then in late November 2005 the Border War was once again resurrected on the political front. The discovery of mass war graves in Namibia, probably linked to the final battles occurring in April 1989, resulted in ironically apt newspaper headings: 'Geraamtes in die kas' and 'Namibia graves unearth old wounds'.[69] This only goes to show that in literature, history and life, closure is not easily attained.[70]

Notes to Chapter Eight

1   The most prestigious literary prize in Afrikaans, awarded annually in rotation to one of the three genres.

2   J-A. Floris, 'Volpunte vir sy hart. Sukses kom toe Opperman doen wat hý wil', *Beeld,* 8 April 2006, 13. ('Ek verlaat eerder die land as om weer diensplig te gaan doen . . . Maar ek sal nooit die ervaring in die *army* weggee nie.')

3   J-J. Joubert, 'Uit Umkhonto se binnekring', *Beeld,* 13 February 2006, 13.

4   E. van Wyk. 'Boetie se afgryse op die "border". Boek werp lig op diensplig-nagmerrie', *Rapport,* 26 February 2006, 20. The compiler of this publication is the freelance journalist Jacqui Thompson. In the *Rapport* of a week later (5 March 2006), two angry letters appeared which disputed Thompson's statement that the Border War emotionally destroyed the young soldiers. Both writers, apparently without irony, repeated the old adage that 'War turns boys into men'. From late April onwards many more letters appeared on LitNet, the online Afrikaans (originally strictly literary) magazine, passionately stating conflicting perspectives on the after effects of the Border War., The letters were followed by several autobiographical stories, and Thompson's book had become a best seller. See Paul Ash, 'Bloody Africa. Military memoirs are filling the shelves', *Sunday Times Lifestyle,* 29 October 2006, 18.

5   G. Baines, 'South Africa's Vietnam? Literary History and Cultural Memory of the Border War', *South African Historical Journal,* 49 (2003):172–92.

6   Ibid. 176.

7   Ibid. 178.

8   Ibid. 177.

9   See also the survey of Border Literature by H. E Koornhof, 'Works of Friction: Current South African War Literature', in *Society at War: The Militarisation of South Africa,* ed. J. Cock and L. Nathan (New York: St Martin's Press 1989).

10   K. Batley, 'The Language of Landscape: The Border Terrain in the Writing of South African Troops', *English Usage in southern Africa* 23 (1992):14–27.

11   A. Carroll, 'War letters. The Lives Behind the Lines', *National Geographic,* 208, 5 (2005):78–95.

12 Announcing the pending publication of *An Unpopular War*, the compiler is quoted as saying that the young soldiers felt themselves to be part of a detested group, much like the German soldiers after the Second World War. 'They believe they have no right to talk about it' (author's translation). See Van Wyk, 'Boetie se afgryse op die "border"'. On the other hand, it also appears that no books by deserters or conscientious objectors have been published. It is only very recently that one such book has been published, namely, C. Yates, *Prisoner of Conscience. One Man's Remarkable Journey From Repression to Freedom* (2005) which tells of his trial and imprisonment because of his refusal to serve in the SADF.

13 S. E. Kriel, 'Vertellersmanipulasie in die Afrikaanse Grensliteratuur', MA Dissertation, University of South Africa, 1989.

14 D. Salter, 'Exile, Return and the New South Africa – An Interview with Anthony Akerman', *South African Theatre Journal*, 18 (2004):257.

15 H. M. Viljoen, 'Borders and Their Transgression in Recent South African Fiction', in *Proceedings of the 12th Congress of the ICLA, Munich 22–29 August*, Vol. 2, ed. D. W. Fokkema and R. Bauer (Munich: Iodicium Verlag, 1988), 118.

16 The quote appears on p. 5. Perhaps the best known, though openly biased historical documentations of this period are the books by W. L. Steenkamp, *South Africa's Border War, 1966–1989* (Gibraltar: Ashanti, 1989) and P. Stiff, *The Covert War: Koevoet Operation Namibia, 1979–1989* (Alberton: Galago, 2004).

17 Lieutenant General J. J. Geldenhuys as quoted in *Sektor 70 Jaarblad/ Sector 70 Annual* (1983):3. 'Our soldiers are not only capable of enforcing peace, but also of keeping peace' (author's translation).

18 Kriel, 'Vertellersmanipulasie in die Afrikaanse Grensliteratuur'. See also the supporting statements by Mabel Rossouw in her conference paper "'n Vernuwende blik op die verlede: Afrikaanse oorlogsliteratuur as (alternatiewe) bron van geskiedskrywing oor die indiwidu', in *Vernuwing in die Afrikaanse letterkunde, referate gelewer tydens die sesde hoofkongres van die Afrikaanse Letterkunde-vereniging by die Universiteit van Port Elizabeth, 29 September–1 Oktober*, ed. M. Hattingh and H. Willemse (Belville: University of the Western Cape, 1994).

19 H. P. van Coller, 'Afrikaanse Literatuur oor die Gewapende Konflik in Suid-Afrika Sedert 1963: 'n Voorlopige Verslag', *Acta Academica*, 22, 4 (1990):74–91.

20 Kriel, 'Vertellersmanipulasie in die Afrikaanse Grensliteratuur', 10.

21 Between 1980 and 1988 four texts written by Jan van Pletzen but published by different publishers, gained wide popularity. The thematic link was the story told through the upbeat letters written by a young soldier, Kleinjan, to his mother back home.

22 In his MA Dissertation 'Populêre vs. Literêre Grensverhale: Twee Beelde van die Angolese oorlog (1966–1989)', Konstant van Huyssteen goes into great detail in analysing this contrast, and provides a useful description of the many 'popular' texts.

23 H. Roos, 'Perspektief op die Afrikaanse Prosa van die Twintigste Eeu', in *Perspektief en Profiel. 'n Afrikaanse Literatuurgeskiedenis Deel 1*, ed. H. P. van Coller (Pretoria: Van Schaik, 1998), 90.

24 D. Craig. 'The Viewer as Conscript: Dynamic Struggles for Ideological Supremacy in the South African Border War Film 1971–1988', MA Dissertation, University of Cape Town, 2003, 90.

25 H. Roos, 'Die grens is inderdaad bereik', *De Kat*, 1, 5 (1985):90–2.

26 J. C. Cronjé, 'Die Grens as Meerduidige Gegewe in die Kontemporêre Afrikaanse Prosa', PhD Thesis, University of Pretoria, 1989. See also Kriel, 1989 and Van Coller, 1990.

27 Kriel, 'Vertellersmanipulasie in die Afrikaanse grensliteratuur'.

28 Tameri, 'The Existential Primer. 'Karl Jaspers'. http://www.tameri.com/csw/exist/jaspers.shtm/ (Accessed 30 November 2005).

29 E. Joubert, 'Die Afrikaanse "Grensliteratuur". Die Nuwe Afrikaanse Oorlogsliteratuur', *Die Suid-Afrikaan*, (Autumn 1985). In this contribution Joubert repeats the sentiments she expressed in a paper read during 1984. She not only uses the term *grensliteratuur*, but also expresses regret that there was no similar exposé

of what was happening in the Border War from the side of the black insurgent soldiers.

30   Kriel, 'Vertellersmanipulasie in die Afrikaanse Grensliteratuur', 56.

31   H. Roos, 'Van twee debute uit twee wêrelde', Review of Strachan's book in *Standpunte*, 184 39, 4 (1989):45–59.

32   A. Strachan. 'Die Suid-Afrikaanse Prosa Vandag: Ingesteldheid in die Tagtigerjare', *Tydskrif vir Letterkunde*, 23, (1985):128–43.

33   Craig, 'The Viewer as Conscript', 86.

34   H. Roos, 'Gruwelike getuienis oor ons tyd', Review of Kellerman's book in *Rapport*, 26 February 1989.

35   Kriel, 'Vertellersmanipulasie in die Afrikaanse Grensliteratuur', 170.

36   Roos, 'Perspektief op die Afrikaanse Prosa van die Twintigste Eeu', 87.

37   J. Cock, *Colonels and Cadres: War and Gender in South Africa* (Cape Town: Oxford University Press, 1991).

38   R. J. Gordon, 'Marginalia on 'Grensliteratuur': Or How/Why is Terror Culturally Constructed in Northern Namibia? *Critical Arts: A Journal for Cultural Studies*, 5, 3 (1991):91.

39   Van Coller, 'Afrikaanse literatuur oor die gewapende konflik'.

40   Prinsloo, 'Grensverhaal', 38. 'One who screws black women' (author's translation).

41   Roos, 'Perspektief op die Afrikaanse Prosa van die Twintigste Eeu'.

42   S. Niewoudt, 'Kartetse oor die grensoorlog moet nog bars', *Beeld*, 13 June 2001, 11.

43   Another interesting text in this group is J. Diescho, *Troubled Waters* (Windhoek: Gamsberg Macmillan, 1993). The author, a black man, tells his story from the perspective of a white SADF soldier. The novel had a very small readership.

44   An informative view on this pervasive effect is presented by Cock and Nathan, eds., *Society at War*.

45   Kriel, 'Vertellersmanipulasie in die Afrikaanse Grensliteratuur', 45–9.

46   Baines, 'South Africa's Vietnam?', 192.

47   D. Haarhoff, *The Wild South-West: Frontier Myths and Metaphors in Literature set in Namibia, 1760–1988* (Johannesburg: Witwatersrand University Press, 1991), 21.

48   Kriel, 'Vertellersmanipulasie in die Afrikaanse grensliteratuur'; Baines, 'South Africa's Vietnam?'.

49   Haarhoff, *The Wild South-West*, 205.

50   J-J. Joubert, 'Uit Umkhonto se Binnekring', *Beeld,* 13 February 2006, 13.

51   M. Ley, 'Persoonlike Vertelling oor Angola-oorlog', Review in *Beeld*, 27 February 2006, 20.

52   A. Beet, 'Border memories relived', Review in the *Pretoria News*, 20 June 2005, 16.

53   Baines, 'South Africa's Vietnam?', 174–8.

54   At a panel discussion on 'Writing and Publishing in South Africa' during the Spring Language Festival at Unisa from 28 September – 1 October 2005, the author Finuala Dowling stated that not only were publishing houses actively seeking out new authors, but in her experience a larger readership for English South African narratives has come into existence.

55   See Heyns as quoted in H. Roos, 'Die Afrikaanse Prosa 1997–2002', in *Perspektief en Profiel. 'n Afrikaanse Literatuurgeskiedenis*, Deel 3, ed. H. P. van Coller (Pretoria: Van Schaik, 2006), 98.

56   H. P. van Coller, ''n Eietydse Afrikaanse Prosaterugblik op die Grensoorlog, Deel 1', *Tydskrif vir Letterkunde* 37, 2 (1999), 31–9 and H. P. van Coller, ''n Eietydse Afrikaanse Prosaterugblik op die Grensoorlog, Deel 2', *Tydskrif vir Letterkunde* 37, 3/4 (1999), 22–30.

57   B. Viljoen, 'Gewese lede van SAW glo in roofsindikate: opgelei, aggressief en werkloos', *Beeld*, 26 January 2006, 12.

58   Van Coller, ''n Eietydse Afrikaanse Prosaterugblik op die Grensoorlog, Deel 2'.

59   Ibid.

60   In at least two recent issues (October 2005, January/February 2006) of the Afrikaans 'outdoors' magazine *Weg*, narrative texts on recollections of the Border War have appeared. While the general tone is one

of 'this experience lies at the bottom of our love for the great outdoors', the sense of ambiguity is very evident.

61   See the review of Venter's book by J. Cilliers, 'Boeiende boek oor hursoldate', *Beeld*, 27 June, 15.

62   The article recounts her personal acquaintance with these traumatised ex-soldiers, and is written by the well-known criminal profiler, Dr Micki Pistorius. 'As die Draak sy Kop Uitsteek', *De Kat* 19, 4 (2004):82–5.

63   See Roos, 'Die Afrikaanse Prosa 1997–2002', ed. H. P. van Coller (Pretoria: Van Schaik, 2006), 59–97.

64   Some accounts of the border experience also found their way into forms of autobiographical writing linked to the activities of the Truth and Reconciliation Commission, as for instance, T. Eprile, *The Persistence of Memory* (Cape Town: Double Storey, 2004).

65   E. van Heerden, 'Van Liegfabriek na Biegfabriek', *Die Burger*, 24 April 1997, 4 (author's translation).

66   E. van Heerden, 'Grensverhale moes Lankal Getref het', *Die Burger*, 25 May 2000, 4.

67   Roos, 'Die Afrikaanse Prosa 1997–2002', 75–78.

68   G. van der Westhuizen, 'Lin Sampson en die Gewone Mense', *Beeld PLUS*, 20 August 2005, 4.

69   L. Engelbrecht, 'Namibia Graves Unearth old Wounds', *Pretoria News*, 22 November 2005, 11; E. Gibson, 'Geraamtes in die Kas' ('Skeletons in the Cupboard' – author's translation), *Beeld*, 25 November 2005, 23.

70   When *Die Buffel Struikel* (*The Buffalo Stumbles*) was published early in 2007, it received a great deal of media attention. The author, Louis Bothma, had been one of the feared soldiers of 32nd Battalion, and he described his self-published book as 'a monument to the fallen comrades'. This claim was a direct reference to the debate on the refusal of the trustees of Freedom Park to acknowledge the fallen SADF soldiers on the wall of remembrance. See Pieter du Toit '32 Bataljon. Die dade van destyds – en die herdefinisie van 'helde' daarna' (The deeds of long ago – and the redefinition of heroes afterwards – author's translation), *Beeld (By)*, 10 March 2007, 10.

Chapter 9

Art and Aftermath in Memórias Íntimas Marcas: Constructing Memory, Admitting Responsibility

Wendy Morris

Growing up in Johannesburg in the 1970s my awareness of a place called 'the Border' came, to a degree, through the Saturday afternoon Springbok Radio request programme *Forces Favourites*. Dedicated to the 'boys on the border', the programme conveyed messages between parents, wives and girlfriends at 'home' and their sons, spouses or boyfriends in the army. My interest in the *Memórias Íntimas Marcas* (Memory Intimacy Traces), project, however, is unrelated to any nostalgia for dull Saturday afternoons in white suburbia, but relates to research that I am undertaking as part of a practice-based doctorate. This research is concerned with modes of engagement of artists with *event/s at the limits*. *Event/s at the limits* is a term used in the discourse in respect of the *adequate* representation of the Jewish Holocaust,[1] but one that I would argue usefully describes the dilemmas of representation of all war and its aftermath, of all atrocity, and of all state-legislated violence. An *event at the limits* is a practice of such magnitude and profound violence, involving such a degree of loss, that it tests conceptual and representational categories. This chapter considers the Angolan–South African war as an *event at the limits*, and examines, through the project *Memórias Íntimas Marcas* the ways in which artists have sought to think through its social and personal repercussions.

Following the attempted extermination of the Jews of Europe during World War II, debates around issues of representation of this Holocaust brought the notion of ethics in art into sharp focus. The record of this atrocity was not to be distorted or banalised by supposedly inadequate representations that could potentially redeem events by providing any kind of aesthetic beauty or mimetic pleasure. It was questioned whether even the very act of history writing (whether textual or visual) would not potentially redeem the genocide with the kinds of meaning or explanation that are reflexively generated in all narrative.[2] While artists or writers engaging with other *events at the limits* have not been subjected to the same prescriptive demands, the dilemmas raised for them by the intellectual obligation to remember such atrocities, combined with the ethical hazards of doing so, have been no less acute in the years since.

Artists' engagement with the Angolan–South African war first came to the attention of the art public at the Johannesburg Biennial of 1995 when a sculpture of a prosthetic leg, replete with human femur and burnt stumps of flesh and toes, was positioned outside the United States of America (US) exhibition space in MuseumAfrica. Labelled *Leg from Angola* and accompanied by the question, 'Can anyone find my body?', the work was a reminder of the high number of limbs that the 'civil' war in Angola was costing its citizens. Positioned as it was, it was also an allusion to US collusion in the Angolan 'civil war'. *Leg from Angola* was the work of Angolan artist, Fernando Alvim, and was the first in a series of *interventions* through which he sought to lift the veil of silence shrouding the Angolan–South African war. *Memórias Íntimas Marcas* became the project framework for these interventions.[3]

In 1997 Alvim invited Cuban artist Carlos Garaicoa and South African artist Gavin Younge to join him for 12 days in Cuito Cuanavale, Angola. The work that the three artists produced during this visit, and as a result of their stay, was shown in Luanda and at the Castle of Good Hope in Cape Town later that year. Other artists were then invited to participate. By the next showings in Johannesburg and Pretoria, 14 artists were exhibiting and there was a shift away from the earlier concerns with national guilt, construction of memory and post-traumatic stress that characterised the work of Younge, Garaicoa and Alvim, towards an exploration of notions of personal implication and lived experience in the South African Defence Force (SADF) and 'on the border'. Included in these exhibitions were Colin Richards, who had done 'border duty' in Angola; Jan van der Merwe, a soldier in the Permanent Force who had spent five years working as an artist in the propaganda department of the SADF; and Willem Boshoff. Boshoff eventually refused to carry arms or even follow orders during his repeated periods of call-up and managed instead to write what later became *Bangboek*, as a secret act of defiance on an army typewriter and official paper. The project underwent a further shift when it opened in Lisbon and then Antwerp with the inclusion of artists from further north. Congolese artist Toma Luntumbue's concern was with *human earthquakes,* the transnational repercussions of conflicts such as the Angolan–South African war. Bili Bidjocka of Cameroon explored the defence of the 'Border' as a defence of privilege, and Burundian Aimé Ntakiyica drew attention to the rationality behind the genocide in Rwanda. The tight focus on the Angolan war that had characterised the Southern African shows had given way to broader continental concerns.

This chapter examines the first two stages of the project: first, Alvim, Garaicoa and Younge's attempt to constitute memory through a physical engagement with the specific and historically charged site of Cuito Cuanavale and, second, the inclusion of the work of artists who had been conscripted into the SADF as well as those who had seen 'active service' in Angola. The third stage – the shift to Europe and the participation of artists from elsewhere on the African continent with their perspectives on other, though not unrelated, conflicts – is beyond the specific scope of this volume.

Memórias Íntimas Marcas is a constantly reconstituted work that is difficult to grasp as an entity. At every stage its meanings are elusive. Key issues of healing, exorcism and amnesia recur throughout, but their meanings are never fixed and as the event moves on their meanings become ever more opaque. More tangible, perhaps, is the extent to which a project that started out as an attempt to represent the unspeakable eventually brought that unspeakable into the range of the speakable. Alvim's working method of setting up a framework for the project involved not only the participation of artists, but also the endorsement of the project by government officials from the three countries involved, as well as officials from the United Nations (UN) and European Union (EU).[4] Politicians and army officials who had been involved in the war opened the exhibitions and talked of their experiences and of the amnesia surrounding the war.[5] For many speakers, soldiers, and artists who had been soldiers, it was the first time that a public space was created in which the war could be discussed. Even then it was difficult for veterans to talk about their experiences, as Richards noted when he recalled being at an opening of one of the exhibitions and watching a projection of SADF footage in Angola. He told of the deep, inarticulate feelings and sense of isolation brought on by the projection that prevented him from being able to talk to anyone present about his experiences. Nevertheless, he argued that *Memórias Íntimas Marcas* still 'made it possible for us to face these images in a way we can touch. And hold [them], at least for a while. In an uncomfortable, oblique and eccentric way, this exhibition offers its own articulation of living together on the mutilated ground of our shared histories'.[6]

Artists who engage with the memory of atrocity or the unspeakable have not always been caught up in the violence directly. The American artist Art Spiegelman, who drew *Maus: A Survivor's Tale* (1972–1985), is relating events told to him by his father, a Holocaust survivor. The work is not about the Jewish Holocaust itself, but about a survivor's tale and the artist–son's recovery of it. It is about what the son understands of his father's story. Marianne Hirsch terms it 'an aesthetics of post-memory', a narrative hybrid that interweaves events and the way that they are passed on to us.[7] Postmemory is a particular sort of memory whose connection to its object or source is mediated not through recollection, but through imaginative investment and creation. It investigates the artist's distance from the events as well as his or her relation to the fall-out of that event.

With a few exceptions, the artists who exhibited for the *Memórias Íntimas Marcas* project did not do 'active service' in Angola. Their connection to that conflict is at a remove, vicarious. It is mediated partly through the press – strictly controlled in both Cuba and South Africa at the time – and partly through stories, or hearsay of stories, of soldiers who were there.

Act I: Amnesia

In 2001 Alvim brought together material from the various interventions of *Memórias Íntimas Marcas* into two films, *Zinganheca Kutzinga: Blending Emotions* and *Gele Uanga: War and Art of Elsewhere*.[8] These combine interviews with artists, army officials and government representatives from all sides, poetic texts assimilated from various writings in and on the project, archive footage of SADF troops, and video filmed by the artists in Angola. Alvim describes the films as integral to the project.[9]

Gele Uanga opens with a list of all that *Memórias Íntimas Marcas* is against:

> Against the lapses of memory,
> . . . the omissions, the oversights,
> . . . the facile 'don't remembers',
> . . .the images erased or blurred
> . . . the lives anaesthetized,
> . . . the words ensnared,
> the lips sealed, the tongues tied . . .

Amnesia, or those 'lapses of memory' of the opening litany, is an issue central to Alvim's project. It refers not to the amnesia of those wounded psychologically or physically in the war – for who would deny victims the relief of no memory – but rather to a wilful amnesia of those who have colluded, directly or indirectly, knowingly or unknowingly, willingly or unwillingly, in the dismemberment and wounding of Angola.

South Africans have had to deal with a blanket of silence over the facts of the SADF ever having been in Angola. Conscripts who were sent there were intentionally kept disoriented or uninformed about their precise whereabouts. That they had travelled and fought deep inside Angola was never admitted. Richards describes how, on his platoon's retreat from Angola, they had to travel 'miles and miles southward' to reach the bridge at Ruacana, which was the border between South West Africa (now Namibia) and Angola. Once there they heard the then Minister of Defence, P. W. Botha, announce that South Africa was withdrawing from the border area. Botha assured those assembled (national and international press as well as the troops who had just left Angola) that the large number of military crossing over the bridge from Angola had been deployed within a defensive combat zone which 'hugged' the border. Richards notes that Botha 'said this straight-faced, with us all in earshot. Us, who had travelled so far'.[10]

Before returning to South Africa they were searched by the military police and any evidence of their having been in Angola was confiscated. They were forbidden from speaking about their experiences on their return home.[11] 'Later we all received "Pro-Patria" medals for what never really happened.'[12]

Little of what the SADF was up to in Angola filtered through to the majority of South Africans. The body count of those who died in combat in Angola was paced so as to reduce alarm, and news of death on the 'Border' dribbled home in 'palatable quotas'.[13] In 1975, in response to a question from the Opposition in Parliament, the National Party denied that there were South African troops in Angola. Even after 1994 no one from the old guard was prepared to lift the blanket of silence around the role of the SADF in that war. Desmond Tutu regretted, in the disclosures to the Truth and Reconciliation Commission (TRC), that so little was forthcoming from the SADF. 'Sadly,' he wrote, 'the military, represented in the old South African Defence Force, hardly cooperated with the Commission at all. This left a considerable gap in our truth-gathering process . . . There is much truth that the nation still needs to know if our healing and reconciliation are to be lasting and effective.'[14]

At the opening of the Johannesburg exhibition of *Memórias Íntimas Marcas* in April 1998, Brigitte Mabandla – then deputy minister of arts, culture, science and technology – noted that the project came at a critical time in which the country was confronted with a form of collective intellectual amnesia: 'As South Africans we are continuously confronted by a situation where nobody wants to take responsibility for the atrocities and aggression which took place under apartheid. [D]estabilization . . . and the wars waged against neighbouring states, as exemplified by the battle of Cuito Cuanavale, did not happen in some sort of political or historical cyber-space.'[15]

Despite the SADF and government's considerable effort invested in camouflaging the precise nature of their presence and deeds in Angola, the fact that South Africa was involved in the conflict was known to a great many South Africans and could be deduced by reading between the lines in the press. This knowledge could be said to function, in Michael Taussig's terms, as a 'public secret' – 'that which is generally known but cannot be articulated because of its inherent danger to the legitimacy of the State or to personal ideas of wholeness integral to conceptions of the self'.[16]

In Cuba, too, there was a silence. In his essay *Pincers to Remove Shrapnel,* Cuban art critic Orlando Hernández wrote:

> [B]efore us many also kept quiet, or had spoken by halves, hiding information, details. The 'vanquished' had been struck dumb by pain, or they did not speak out of anger,

out of shame. The 'victors' probably because they thought it unnecessary or because of unconfessed feelings of guilt. Cowards, traitors, the negligent, because they had no right to do so. And we know why the dead did not speak.[17]

On the wall of the Portuguese Cultural Centre in Luanda, where the first exhibition of *Memórias Íntimas Marcas* was held after the more private performances in Cuito, Garaicoa drew, in black paint, the image of a fist holding a whip. The tip of the whip touched the top of a head from which the skin had been flayed. The title of the image was *Instrument to dissolve memory*.[18]

Scene 1: Locating the wound

Prior to going to Cuito, Alvim spent a year setting up a framework for the project in which he raised finance from Angolan companies, institutions and the government, as well as from the EU. With that support in place, he invited Garaicoa and Younge to travel with him to Cuito Cuanavale. The artists had little idea of what they would do once there. Alvim says, 'We simply went there and found ourselves facing a reality, facing this space, which provided the impetus for everyone to start developing his own work.'[19] The site, the physical place of Cuito, became the thread that linked all their work. The third artist, Garaicoa, dug obsessively into the earth, making new scars in a landscape already scarred by the war. Alvim directed a small radio-controlled car with camera attached along roads and pathways, through long grass and in ravines, filming as it roamed. He buried a camera in a bottle and filmed the 'birth' of a two-headed baby doll. Younge positioned a camera on the back of a post-office bicycle and cycled through Cuito and the minefields of the surrounding countryside.

Garaicoa had been conscripted into his country's army. Given a choice of volunteering for 'service' in Angola, he had refused. His concern in Cuito, according to Alvim, was to attempt to understand why the large number of Cuban soldiers who had been killed in the area – some of whom had been school friends – had agreed to go there in the first place.[20] Using four portraits of friends who participated in the war as a point of departure, he set himself seven days of digging. 'To dig up answers. To dig up an answer. To dig in search of convincing reason.'[21] He dug from sunrise to sunset for seven days. Mounds of sand rose next to each of the holes that he dug out with a pick-axe. Hernández writes of this interrogative performance that Garaicoa did not expect to find anything, at least 'nothing physical, nothing visible . . . He knows very well that he will find nothing here that will allow him to shed more light on the history of this war. There are no pieces to complete this puzzle from the past'.[22]

Younge, too, had been conscripted for military 'service' but managed, by frequently changing addresses, to evade his call-up. He never attended any camps, never reported for 'duty', never underwent any training, nor wore a uniform of any kind[23]. Nevertheless he admits to a sense that he was in enemy territory when he arrived at Cuito. Introduced as *el sul africano*, he felt nervous and vulnerable, unsure as to how he would be regarded.[24]

The Border had become – to a white minority who seemed to prefer to remain ignorant – the *civilised* boundary of the southern-most tip of Africa, beyond which lay the dark and irrational continent. It was a line of division, the final line of resistance between a mythical 'us' and an equally mythical 'them'. With the change of guard in South Africa in 1994, the Border opened up and became again a crossing point rather than one of containment. Yet, in the 1990s, voluntarily crossing the border between South Africa and the rest of the continent was, for people from both sides, a novel and unsettling experience. In his essay, *Omelette with Rum*, Manuel Dionisio writes of the confusion that arises when people you have been taught to hate are no longer to be hated:

> There was a time when planes flew daily from Luanda to Havana, and vice versa, and we weren't even allowed to speak about South Africa, unless we spoke through bared teeth, vowing hate and death to the South Africans . . . And the Cubans, our buddies, flew in from Havana to help us aim the Soviet anti-aircraft batteries at Mirages and Buccaneers . . . Nowadays everything has changed. Almost the opposite picture, there are no more daily flights to Havana, but to Johannesburg . . . We have found out that, after all, there are some South African artists and that the Cubans are stubborn . . . We go on living – a bit confused – somewhere in between.[25]

In Cuito, Younge set a camera on the carrier of his bicycle and filmed the receding landscape and townscape of Cuito Cuanavale. Later, at the Castle of Good Hope in Cape Town, he formed a ring of post office bicycles into the form of a *laager*,[26] and projected the footage of Cuito on to monitors placed on the metal baskets on these bicycles (see Fig. 16). The soundtrack included the signature tune and archival recordings of the radio request programme, *Forces Favourites*.

Figure 16: Gavin Younge, Forces Favourites (1997). With permission of Lanoire Galerie.

Younge's images of war-torn Cuito stand in stark juxtaposition to the sentimental messages broadcast on *Forces Favourites*. This contrast of cruel realities and sentimental contact with home is one that Richards remembers of his experience in Angola. In the film *Gela Uanga* he talks about a hierarchy in the army – one that existed outside of rank – of masculine strength or power. Within this hierarchy certain soldiers who were thought to fall short of 'masculine' qualities, were 'feminized' and treated 'in a sense like women' – which meant badly, Richards adds. Amongst the same company of men, there was a sentimental other side that involved writing emotional letters home to mothers and girlfriends. Richards found the combination of sentimentality towards those at home with the extraordinarily cruel treatment of soldiers towards each other, 'really hard to take'.[27]

Scene 2: Unlived situations

If Garaicoa, Younge and Alvim had never been sent to fight in Cuito or elsewhere in Angola, why then should they feel an obligation to remember the Angolan war? In his reflective essay on his reaction to the Luandan exhibition of *Memórias Íntimas Marcas*, Hernández asks of himself: 'Why suffer retrospectively for something that I didn't suffer then? Why suffer as a duty, as an intellectual obligation?'[28]

Cuito Cuanavale was the site of a decisive battle that had ended in defeat and retreat for the South African forces. In the consciousness of many South Africans and Cubans, it took on a mythical status. To Brigitte Mabandla, Cuito 'will forever symbolize the sacrifice of the Cuban and Angolan people in the defeat of a brutal crime against humanity'.[29] To Garaicoa it is mythical in a more ambiguous way. He first heard of it when he was seven when an acquaintance who had lived nearby was killed there. He describes it as an imagined place: 'like a magic space where we would find truth'.[30] The idea that the truth, or truths, about the war were to be found in places such as Cuito, emerges too in the writings of Hernández. He notes that Cubans were prevented from knowing the truth – or large parts of it – about the war in Angola by the national press media and by the comments of some ex-combatants that he describes as 'falsified by fear'. He muses that had he not refused the call-up, had he become a soldier and volunteered for Angola, he might have come to learn the truth in Cuito.[31]

Both Hernández and Garaicoa's memory of Cuito and the Angolan war is vicarious. Garaicoa's obsessive digging and Hernández' self-searching essay are attempts at constructing memory of situations that they never experienced. But why remember a war in which you took no part? Hernandez writes: 'One war amongst all wars cannot matter to me at all. A distant, ancient war that is over. A war that doesn't appear in the papers or the newsreel any more. Why understand what I never understood before?'[32]

Hernández responds to his own question with the suggestion that 'to awake the memory of any attack is to dig up all battlefields with a pick, to exhume all the dead, to bring to light all the bones, to hear again the horrible music of all weapons. To remember everything'.[33] Garaicoa and Hernández reveal a concern with the necessity of *memory-work* – an ethical or intellectual obligation to attempt to know or imagine vicariously, and to make meaning out of experiences that they never knew directly. This bears out visual theorist Irit Rogoff's argument that politically informed intellectual work is founded on certain disenchantments and frustrations with existing ways of knowing and that it is the mobilisation of this discontent that is the driving force behind the need to arrive at new articulations.[34]

Act II: Exorcism

Artists who did have experience of the war, or at least of SADF military training, produced work that spoke of the difficulties of giving form to what Richards terms 'the paralysing intranslatability' of that experience.[35] These works admit to a lack of personal agency, to the frustrations of being caught in an iniquitous political system, and to the artist's unavoidable complicity with the crimes committed within that system.

Quite different in register is Alvim's work. In the opening sequences of *Blending Emotions* he issues the warning that the film 'contains images that could change the weight of human conscience'. His fetish-like objects suggest a belief in the ability of art to mediate in rituals of catharsis and the exhibition of trauma and tension.

Scene 1: Confession and complicity

Angola 1976, a work by Richards, was included in the *Memórias Íntimas Marcas* exhibitions from the Johannesburg intervention onwards. It shows three objects against a transparent field – a brace of cartridges that Richards removed from the clothes of a dead 'enemy soldier'; a metal flame from a Catholic relic found in a cemetery in Venice; and the 'Pro Patria' medal awarded to Richards for 'active service' in Angola (see Fig. 17). The artist describes *Angola 1976* 'as a fragment of past experience which will forever remain a source of distress for me'.[36]

Figure 17: Colin Richards, Angola 1976 detail. With permission of the artist.

In comments on his involvement in the conflict, Richards broaches the subject of an inevitable complicity in the atrocities of war. Complicity was a problem not exclusively for supporters of the apartheid regime and its policies, but also for its opponents. In the film *Gele Uanga* Richards says:

> There are moral decisions all the time about what you will and won't do, and they all go to shit anyway . . . because actually you've got no choice. Your choice, I realised when I started evading the call-up, was really not to be called up. It was ridiculous to sit in Angola, which we did do, and try and discuss what we would and wouldn't do, what we were capable of and what we would not condone. Because we weren't in that position. If we saw an atrocity, there was a sense that we would report it and not be part of it. That's playing games. Your choice is not to go. If you go, you are in a different world.

The issue of recognition of complicity emerges again in the work of Jan van der Merwe. In the Johannesburg and Pretoria showings, Van der Merwe exhibited *Chair and Jacket, Clothes Horse* and *Soldier's Bed* (1998). All three works are life-size renditions of military furniture crafted out of scraps of rusted tin. *Soldier's Bed* consists of a metal army issue bed made up with blanket and pillow of metal scraps. A helmet of rusted tin is placed on the pillow. This bed offers little comfort (see Fig. 18).

Figure 18: Jan van der Merwe, Soldier's Bed (1998). With permission of the artist.

The obsessive laboriousness of the technique is reminiscent of trench art fashioned by soldiers enduring long periods of waiting – either in POW camps or in the field between bouts of action. In its broadest sense trench art is a category 'that incorporates any object made by any person from any material, as long as both are associated in time or space with armed conflict or its consequences'.[37] But Van der Merwe never saw armed conflict, other than the battle for *hearts and minds*. He joined the Permanent Force of the SADF and spent four years working as an artist in the propaganda department, designing posters and exhibitions that were intended to entice young black recruits into the army. Van der Merwe writes that 'it is with hindsight that we get a full perspective on the system that structured our lives while we were growing up . . . I was caught up in a system into which I was born. My personal survival . . . overshadowed my awareness of political events . . .' He adds, 'with my present knowledge and awareness of past events in our country, I would not have wanted to participate in the propaganda machine of the SADF'.[38]

Works such as *Chair and Jacket*, *Clothes Horse* and *Soldier's Bed*, are Van der Merwe's way of dealing with this new perspective and the feelings generated by it. 'I have not put a name to it, but guilt, disillusionment and a desire to come to terms with everything is part of it,' he notes.[39]

The narratives of Richards and Van der Merwe are confessional and self-conscious, revealing of what Richards describes as the 'disfiguring memories, torn truths and equivocal embarrassments'[40] of their complicity.

Kendell Geers, who had worked on the exhibitions in Johannesburg, Pretoria and Antwerp, in contrast, is at pains to disassociate himself from any complicity. He states in the film *Gele Uanga* that while 'my brother ran to the army, I ran from it . . . I was part of the End Conscription Campaign, which was lobbying and being very militarily involved in trying to stop the war in Angola . . .' The work that he exhibits at *Memórias* is an extract of a diary of an unnamed South African soldier fighting in Angola. In it the writer notes down attacks and reactions, deaths, reprimands, as well as the obsessive counting of days until the soldier can return home. The title of the work, *Blood Brother* (1998), refers to the fact that it is the diary of Geers' brother. Yet despite that familial connection, and the tense relationship that is surmised might have existed between the brothers – given that one *ran to the army* and the other *from it* – the work retains a sense of anonymity. The viewer is allowed no scope to second guess the position of the narrator towards the conflict, even less does it allow the viewer to approach Geers' own position. Apart from the title, it is a document at a distance, appropriated. It makes of the viewer an unwitting voyeur to a situation of violence that lacks the sound of the artists' own self-conscious voice.

That voice does emerge in the work of another artist who began to exhibit at *Memórias* in Johannesburg. Willem Boshoff showed blow-ups of pages of his *Bangboek* (1977–1981) of which the opening line is, following the artist: 'This is an analysis and an account of pressing matters carefully considered while I was in the armed forces . . .'[41] The book is written in personal code, in phonetic English but with an Afrikaans title – all devices intended to thwart decipherment. The title of the book, *Bangboek,* can be translated as a pun on the words 'scary-pants' or as the 'book that is afraid'.

From the time of Boshoff's first call-up in 1973 he had been filling his diaries with contentions against military 'service'. He dwelt on religious arguments hoping that these would provide an adequate basis for exemption. In 1979 when he was called up for yet another camp he managed to persuade the parish minister, who doubled up as army chaplain, to allow him not to carry a rifle. He was put to administrative work and that camp saw him editing and re-writing all the subversive reservations from his earlier diaries. On a military typewriter and official army paper he produced an 86-page document against military 'service'.

Following this camp Boshoff prepared himself for the next confrontation with the SADF, in which he had decided he would refuse to wear uniform or obey orders. Assuming that this would result in a jail term, he designed a kind of spy-writing that would allow him to make notes in jail that could not be read by the authorities. To this end he rewrote his typewritten notes in cryptic code and the result was *Bangboek*. He explains the process as 'my own silent way of reinforcing loyalty to pacifist convictions, a secretly knitted armour against arguments I would encounter'.[42]

Encrypting his arguments in an indecipherable form meant that Boshoff denied the anticipated censor access to his arguments. Following the writer J. M. Coetzee, it is not so easy, once the writer is aware of the existence of the censor – or as in this case anticipates the presence of the censor – to exclude him entirely from the writing process. 'Working under censorship is like being intimate with someone who does not love you, with whom you want no intimacy, but who presses himself upon you.'[43] Coetzee argues that the contest with the censor assumes an importance in the inner life of the writer[44]. '[W]riter and censor [are] carried on waves of polemic toward identity or twinship.' In opposing the censor, the writer makes him- or herself available to, and intimate with, the very rhetoric that he or she opposes.[45] The writer becomes, in a sense, complicit with the system or discourse that he or she wishes to oppose.

The recognition of one's own complicity can be seen, in itself, as enabling. Literary theorist Mark Sanders argues that by affirming one's complicity and thereby assuming responsibility for that which is done in one's name, one is able to make the first step towards intellectual responsibility. To Sanders there can be no history of intellectual responsibility in apartheid South Africa, without a history of 'the troubling and enabling moment of complicity'.[46]

Scene 2: After-presences

A number of artists who participated in *Memórias* stress the connection between Christian religious rituals and the war. On the South African side of the border, artists – mostly Afrikaans-speaking – frequently mention the strong, even oppressive, influence of the Dutch Reformed Church (DRC) that encouraged them to go and fight. Boshoff tells how he tried to mobilise religious arguments against the call-up or the carrying of arms and yet the DRC, in whose doctrine he had been brought up, supported the military defence of apartheid ideology.[47] He persuades the DRC minister, who serves as an army chaplain, to exempt him from having to carry a rifle. In the Angolan diary extract that Geers transcribes onto the gallery wall, the anonymous soldier notes: 'We went to church (Sat) so we knew we would be going in tomorrow' – 'going in' referring to battle or an offensive. And Alvim piles up silver Christ figures, arms outstretched but without the cross to which the figure is usually nailed.

Exhibiting seven bibles in seven different South African languages, Abrie Fourie draws attention to the peculiar conflation of political and religious ideology in which he and many others in South Africa were raised. He notes that:

> [A]s a young white Afrikaner, I was raised to hold blindly to poisonous patriotism propagated by the apartheid era government. I did my compulsory national service (Angolan war), and spent Sunday church services sleeping under the pews in order to catch up with lost sleep, in short, subscribing to popular beliefs on a very superficial level but not veering out to confront or question them.[48]

Whereas the Bible is the iconic symbol in DRC communities, its parallel in importance in the Catholic imaginary is the figure of the crucified Christ. Apart from its presence in religious buildings of worship, the ubiquitous image of the Christ figure hangs above doorways in domestic Catholic settings and in the little chapels or shrines built along the roadside in many Catholic communities. Alvim's silver Christ figures in *Etranger* (1996–2000) are removed both from their crosses and any ritual setting and dumped, in large number, in a display fridge. Lacking their usual iconic status by this displacement, the figurines of Christ become truly abject. Whereas that abjectness once held the promise of redemption, the Christ figures in the fridge lack that signification.

It has been noted elsewhere that the First World War, hailed as the 'most modern of wars', triggered an *avalanche of the 'unmodern'*[49] and a marked interest in spiritualism. This involved not only religious but also secular spiritualism that explored the possible existence of human personality after death, and of communication with the newly dead. Alvim's work can be read as echoing related concerns, in the aftermath of war, with the lingering after-presences of the dead. His fetish-like objects seem to exist in intermediate spaces where the presences of those newly dead are trapped, their passing beyond somehow prevented. *El Hombre Solo* (1997) shows a white hospital bed with mutilated dolls suspended in its springs (see Fig. 19).

Figure 19: Fernando Alvim, El Hombre Solo (1997). Photo by Wendy Morris. Muhka 2000.

In the series *Difumbe* (1997–98) two-headed baby-dolls are suspended in liquid, attached to the wall behind plastic cupolas or set alight. In another work a plastic brain is caught in the metal coils of a mattress. The works speak of miscarriages of death. In the film *Blending Emotions*, over the image of transparent screens depicting the negative images of faces of people who died in the Angolan conflict,[50] the following words appear: 'It is the quality of the funeral that is the guarantee of rest. Without this the dead remain doomed to roam, souls in suffering, at the periphery of life . . .'

Alvim's objects are fetishes, objects invested with spiritual presence and subjected to ritual acts. The dolls get buried, birthed underground, trapped between two worlds, burnt. Like Garaicoa's work, his is a work of imaginative construction, but unlike Garaicoa who is attempting to (re) construct memory, Alvim seeks to conjure spiritual presence. He goes to great lengths not to explain his work or his attitude, adopting a poet's position of encoding, mystifying, and (re) investing the spiritual.

Act III: Autopsy

War museums seek to fix knowledge through the examination of the paraphernalia of war and, chiefly, from the vantage point of the victors. War memorials have the purpose of offering consolation – eternally, since they are designed with permanence in mind. Both are intended to draw the sting from death in war and to emphasise the meaningfulness of the sacrifice of those who fought and died. *Memórias Íntimas Marcas*, in contrast, in its transience as a project, its transnationalism and its multiple enactments of loss and intranslatability, and in its self-reflexivity, is the antithesis of a war memorial or museum.

Memórias sets out to install dialogue around a silenced war and it allows that dialogue to be hesitant, awkward and self-conscious. It turns out to be, in the words of Richards, a dialogue 'as much about weakness as about courage, as much about blindness as vision . . . as much about talking past each other as to each other . . . It is a dialogue of interruptions, outbursts, pauses; of silences and garrulity'.[51] *Memórias Íntimas Marcas* generates an open-ended and multivocal history, one that attempts, belatedly, to address the demands of the past.

Notes to Chapter Nine

1   S. Friedlander, *Probing the Limits of Representation: Nazism and the 'Final Solution'* (Cambridge: Harvard University Press, 1992), 3.

2   Friedlander is cited in J. Young, *At Memory's Edge: After-images of the Holocaust in Contemporary Art and Architecture* (New Haven: Yale University Press, 2000), 6.

3   The project *Memórias Íntimas Marcas* encompassed seven exhibitions (including the first in Cuito Cuanavale which Alvim describes as a kind of exhibition); the book *Autopsia & Desarquivos* containing five essays on the project; four editions of the exhibition catalogue, *Marcas News*; and two films, *Gele Uanga: War and Art of Elsewhere*, and *Zinganheca Kutzinga: Blending Emotions.* In this chapter the entire project is considered as one collaborative work.

4   Among the patrons of this project cited at the end of the third edition of *Marcas News* are: José Eduardo dos Santos (president of Angola), Jorge Sampaio (president of Portugal), Desmond Tutu (chairman of the Truth and Reconciliation Commission), Kofi Annan (Secretary-General of the United Nations).

5   P. M. Grobbelaar, retired Lieutenant-Colonel in the SADF and participant in Operation Savannah (1975) when the SADF entered Angola after independence, opened the first South African exhibition at the Castle of Good Hope in Cape Town, August 1997.

6   C. Richards, 'The Names That Escape Us', *Marcas News Europe* No. 4 (Antwerp: Sussuta Boé, 2000), 7.

7   Hirsch's notion of *postmemory* is discussed in Young, *At Memory's Edge*, 15, and in M. Sturken, 'Imaging Postmemory/Renegotiating History', in *Afterimage* (May–June 1999). Both refer to M. Hirsch, *Family Frames: Photography, Narrative, and Postmemory* (Cambridge: Harvard University Press, 1997).

8   *Zinganheca Kutzinga: Blending Emotions. A story told by a leg, a mine and a prosthesis.* A film by Fernando Alvim. Producer, Sussuta Boé (2001); *Gele Uanga: War and Art of Elsewhere.* A film faction by Fernando Alvim and Valérie van Nitsen. Producer, Sussuta Boé (2001).

9   Back cover of *Gele Uanga*.

10 C. Richards, *'Deflagration or Difumbe?'*, *Marcas News 3rd ed.* (Johannesburg, 1998), 19.

11 This conspiracy of silence finds its echo in the anti-colonial war in Angola in the 1970s when Portuguese conscripts were sent to fight the MPLA. The Portuguese writer and ex-conscript, António Lobo Antunes, writes in *Os Cus de Judas* ('The Arsehole of the Universe') of a sign in the officers' mess in Calambata that read in huge letters: *It is forbidden to say there is a war on* (É proibido dizer que ha guerra), in I. Moutinho, 'Gestures of Reconciliation: Three novels of Colonial War', *Mots Pluriels*, 13 (April 2000) :4–10.

12   Richards, '*Deflagration or Difumbe?*', 19.

13   Richards, 'The Names That Escape Us', 6.

14   D. M. Tutu, *No Future Without Forgiveness* (Johannesburg: Random House, 1999), 188–9.

15   C. Kellner, Interview with Brigitte Mabandla, *Marcas News* 3rd ed., 6

16   M. Taussig, *Defacement: Public Secrecy and the Labor of the Negative* (Stanford: Stanford University Press, 1999), 5 cited in J. Peffer, 'Animal Bodies/Absent Bodies: Disfigurement in Art After Soweto', *Third Text* 17, 1 (2003):71–83.

17   O. Hernández, 'Pincers to Remove Schrapnel: Notes for the Victim's Philosophy', in *Autopsia & Desarquivo* (Brussels: Sussuta Boé, 1999), 209. 'Pincers to Remove Schrapnel' is an exploration in words of the issues with which Alvim, Garaicoa and Younge grapple in Cuito. The searching narrative and poetic singularity of the text make it integral to any reading of the *Memórias Íntimas Marcas* project.

18   *Instrument to dissolve memory* was also drawn onto a wall of the Castle of Good Hope.

19   From an interview with Fernando Alvim by Christian Hanussek. Published as *Memórias Íntimas Marcas*, in *Springerin*, Vol. X, 2 (Summer 2004).

20   Ibid.

21   C. Garaicoa, *Marcas News* 3rd ed., 5.

22   O. Hernández, *Marcas News* 3rd ed., 5.

23   Personal correspondence with Gavin Younge.

24   Younge, in the film *Zinganheca Kutzinga: Blending Emotions.*

25   M. Dionisio, 'Omelette with Rum', *Marcas News* 3rd ed., 4.

26   A *laager* is a defensive ring into which ox-wagons were placed to fend off possible attack during the Afrikaners' *Great Trek* in early South African history.

27   Richards, in the film *Gele Uanga.*

28   Hernández, 'Pincers to Remove Schrapnel', 206.

29   Interview with Brigitte Mabandla by Clive Kellner, *Marcas News* 3rd ed., 6.

30   Garaicoa, in the film *Gele Uanga.*

31   Hernández, 'Pincers to Remove Schrapnel', 204.

32   Ibid. 203.

33   Ibid.

34   I. Rogoff, *Terra Infirma: Geography's Visual Culture* (London: Routledge, 2000), 4.

35   Richards, 'The Names That Escape Us', 7.

36   C. Richards, Fault Lines conference, 4 July 1996. Cited by J. Law, 'Performing on a Fault Line: The making(s) of a South African spy novel and other stories', in *Para-Sites, A Casebook Against Cynical Reason*, ed. G. Marcas (Chicago: University of Chicago Press, 2000), 181.

37   N. Saunders, *Trench Art: The Trench Art Collection of the In Flanders Fields Museum.* (Brugge: Van de Wiele, 2004), 4.

38   J. van der Merwe, *Marcas News Europe* No. 4, 16.

39   Ibid.

40   Richards, 'The Names That Escape Us', 5.

41   W. Boshoff, *Marcas News Europe* No. 4, 34.

42   Ibid.

43   J. M. Coetzee, *Giving Offense: Essays on Censorship* (Chicago: University of Chicago Press, 1999), 38.

44   Ibid. 10

45   Ibid. 18

46   M. Sanders, *Complicities: The Intellectual and Apartheid* (Durham: Duke University Press, 2002), 18.

47   Boshoff, in the film *Gele Uanga.*

48   A. Fourie, *Marcas News* 3rd ed., 12.

49   J. Winter, *Sites of Memory, Sites of Mourning* (Cambridge: Cambridge University Press, 1995).

50   This is, I think, a work by Colin Richards, but I can find no accreditation.

51   Richards, 'The Names That Escape Us', 4

Chapter 10

'Documents of Life': South African Soldiers' Narratives of the Border War

Karen Batley

Military and historical accounts of the Border War largely ignore the personal experiences of the thousands of participants in these events. That is true of all the soldiers who fought in Namibia/Angola, including South African soldiers. This chapter will confine itself to the poetry and prose written by some of these soldier–authors. These so-called 'documents of life'[1] are invaluable for investigating and understanding the meaning of individual experiences in the Border War. Until we read the documents, the individuals remain, as one of them said, 'just a boy in uniform, and just a number' (L. v. W.).[2] But in their writing these soldiers assert their right to record their stories.

This chapter demonstrates the therapeutic value of personal writing, as it allows for the expression of trauma that could not be negotiated at the time of the experience described. Writing 'documents of life' or talking about such events should be viewed as an act of catharsis, of retrospectively making sense of experiences that were not necessarily understood when they occurred.

Aliens in a hostile land

One way of reading the writings of soldiers is to view them as the authors' own efforts to interpret what had happened to them. One writer illustrates this principle clearly when he tries to understand the relation of the self to the landscape of South West Africa (renamed Namibia after independence). He says:

> We were rounded up, escorted to Waterkloof Airbase, jammed into transport planes (civilian markings) and headed for places unknown. Three hours later the tail opened and dumped us in the middle of the whitest hell any of us had ever seen.
> White as in Quartzite. Hell as in Hot . . . (D. B.)

This description of troops being transported for deployment in the so-called 'operational area' suggests their dehumanisation. The tail of the aircraft opens rather like a cargo truck, emphasising the vast impersonality of the war machine. It appears to 'dump' its human load unaided, making the passengers feel, perhaps, that they were worthless or expendable. The troops might not be cannon fodder, but they were treated no better than cattle.[3] The writer does not specify who exactly issues the orders. The writer's use of the passive voice in 'we were rounded up . . . and jammed . . .', creates the impression that the troops were passive subjects. And given that their destination is not specified in the phrase 'places unknown', this further hints at the sense of helplessness felt by the soldiers. The parenthetic reference to 'civilian markings' introduces a rather sinister sub-text of secrecy and subterfuge into the passage.[4]

If external human agency is strangely absent in his account of the Flossie's landing, the writer is acutely aware of the Namibian landscape. The heat and glare are expressed poetically in terms of 'Quartzite' and 'Hell'. Another writer, similarly trying to convey the effects of heat and glare, uses the image of 'Mr Spikes the sun', who was 'as hot as hell each day' (D. L.). This initially has a comic effect, but closer consideration suggests that the expression is also meant to convey the sun's ability to inflict discomfort and pain, which adds to the destructive potential of the landscape and the war in general.

Clearly some of the soldiers saw themselves as aliens in the Namibian landscape. The following poem, written from the viewpoint of an inhabitant of the territory, imparts the writer's awareness that he is not welcome. The message is conveyed in a language he does not understand, so his grasp of meaning in this case is interior, a moral recognition:

> This foreign land
> where a white boy
> on white sand
> listens
> to the clicking tongue
> of a foreign people
> saying
> Bwana, go home . . . (J. U.)

The land and its peoples might be 'foreign' to the soldier but he is actually the alien. Despite the dignified and deferential tone of the local population, the verse conveys a sense of unease at the latent hostility to the South African Defence Force (SADF) presence in Namibia.

The landscape was dotted with the detritus of war that signposted the immanence of death. This included a dreadful visual 'artefact' that greeted the newcomer to the 61 Mechanised Unit's base camp. This camp was, at first glance, pleasant, with 'a swimming pool, a library . . . an aviary full of finches and local bird life . . . a sort of low-grade institutional holiday camp'. But this first impression was deceptive.

> The only jarring note is a Ratel that was hit and burnt out during Operation Smokeshell in 1979. The steel has actually melted in some places and it's been painted silver. The passengers' rifles have melted and become part of the machine. Their barrels look like spaghetti. The RPG7 round that killed it came through the driver's window and then the vehicle burned. The engine block looks like a piece of cheese that's been left in the sun. Eleven people died in the thing and it gives everyone the creeps.

> Nineteen-year-olds find evidence of their own mortality hard to accept and the burnt-out hulk never made me realise that this could be a dangerous business. That came later. (E. W.)

The writer is attempting to reinterpret this warning which he did not heed at the time. He gives a very human reason for not doing so – he was 19 and unable to grasp his own mortality. The melted steel and silver paint gave the Ratel a macabre appearance, which the writer tries to explain in terms of familiar culinary images like spaghetti and cheese. In using the phrase 'killed it', he seems to be endowing both the vehicle and the weapon with life. The horrific power of the RPG7 round actually cooked the rifles as easily as if they had been spaghetti, melting them into the vehicle. He does not mention the 11 occupants other than to state their number and the fact that they died. Unwilling or unable to admit the nature of the scenario, the rifles serve as reminders that their owners died horrible deaths.

In an environment regarded as hostile, nervous troops were likely to shoot first and ask questions later. Not only innocent civilians but wildlife and domesticated animals were often killed by trigger-happy troops. A poem by an ex-soldier describes what seems to have been a very common border incident, potentially tragic, but ultimately humorous, exemplifying John Dewey's maxim that '[things] . . . are what they are experienced as':[5]

> Contact!
> Or should one say slaughter?
> A hundred guns spit death
> A movement in a bush.
> A tracker jumps into a Ratel,
> Gun hanging around him,
> Watching his aide.

The poet gives details of the panic, while 'helicopters dart about' and 'anticipation arrives knocking on our Ratel'. After a good build-up of suspense, the poet asks, 'Could it be true?

Did we get one?' The first question expresses a wish to kill the enemy in order to meet the requirements of the body count that served as a measure of military success. The use of the impersonal term 'one' in the second question is significant in its failure to indicate a human being.[6] He continues:

> Death!
> He lies in the bush,
> Head, body, flank all riddled.
> He has no arms – (guns or limbs) –
> He is a beast. He is dead.
> A donkey startled by an army,
> A casualty of war. (S. B.)

The writer tries to come to terms with a number of things facing the border troop. One is nervous tension, when taut feelings mean instant reaction. Another is the absurdity of an experience common to the Border War, when the victim of the (one-sided) fire-fight turns out to be a donkey. The description of the donkey's wounds, evidence of the troops' over-reaction, depicts what would have happened had it really been the human enemy.

The faceless/unknown enemy

For South African soldiers on the 'Border', the human enemy assumed various forms. The People's Liberation Army of Namibia (PLAN, the armed wing of the South West Africa People's Organization (SWAPO)) cadres were an unknown and unpredictable enemy. In the first stanza of his poem 'The enemy is near', the writer suggests the pervasive danger and the lurking presence of the enemy:

> It is night,
> An evil night.
> Stars glint in an acne sky
> Strange sounds eat the air . . .
> The full moon gloats . . .
> I see [with] icy stark clarity
> That churns my stomach.
> What is it?
> The enemy is near. (W. S.)

The indications of some impending danger and of the enemy's presence were implied in the words 'evil', 'glint', 'gloats' and 'icy'. Images like 'the full moon gloats' and 'stars glint' hint that even the forces of nature are in the enemy ranks. The writer's sense of the presence of the enemy is instinctive, but he writes about it again in much more concrete terms in the poem 'Ambush':

Now you will discover,

featureless man,

what it's like to die.

I am

just waiting

to kill you,

just waiting

for you . . .[7]

You have

not a chance

as I lie here

in the dark.

Will it be you?

Or you, perhaps,

faceless entity,

who dies first?

I have the choice –

Why?

Because I hold the rifle.

Ah, you have one too.

But – at what will you shoot?

You cannot see me

as I lie here

in the dark.

You will walk past,

Wary, but unsuspecting

into my trap,

my ambush.

Yes, you will die

as I lie here

in the dark. (W. S.)

The writer describes himself lying in wait in the killing ground for an enemy who is 'featureless' and 'faceless', nothing but an 'entity'. He understands with great clarity that he himself could die in the ambush, and this is what the poem is really about. It is full of questions, the important one being 'Will it be you?' He really means 'Will it be me?', but he must present himself as the aggressor in order to maintain his courage. The darkness suggests both literal darkness and the uncertainty of how the ambush will turn out. However, he regards the cover of darkness as his real advantage, reasoning that the upright, approaching enemy will be a visible target. Despite the writer's acknowledgment of his own mortality, he attempts to suppress his fear by striking a note of self-assurance in the final stanza.

When young and inexperienced South African troops realised that they faced an even more formidable and unfamiliar enemy in the form of Cuban soldiers, they evinced fear and trepidation. Many were intimidated by the reputation of these experienced communist warriors which, deserved or not, had preceded them. The South Africans would also have been influenced in their reaction by the powerful anti-communist government propaganda associated with the concept of the *totale aanslag*.[8] The unknown enemy was thought to be massing in numbers, as another writer points out:

> We sat all alone and waited for 2 000–3 000 Cubans, all 125 of us. I used to sleep badly. A dog from a kraal about 2 km north of us used to come around every night and look for food. I would be sleeping and actually heard the dog walking in the sand 3 km away! You became so hypersensitive to sounds, movements, etc. you can't believe it. I used to wake up at 12, 3 and 5 every morning. SWAPO usually revs between 12 and 3 in the morning around full moon. Full moon is a good time for dying. (P. B.)

This soldier seeks to understand his feelings of being hopelessly outnumbered by the Cubans. The overwhelming odds fill him with fear. Yet his first sentence has a mock-humorous, rueful tone that appears to subvert the soldier's preoccupation with the fears that haunt him. His heightened awareness of his surroundings is a result of his senses being aroused by the adrenalin rush that accompanies his fear. Under these circumstances, it is not difficult to imagine that the sounds of a marauding dog some distance from the base will alert the soldier when it disturbs the silence of the bush in the dead of night. For the dense bush provided not only cover, but camouflage for enemy soldiers.

The account mentions another mode of sonic assault produced by the enemy. 'SWAPO usually revs between 12 and 3 in the morning' is an understated comment on the psychological warfare waged by this adversary. 'Revs' took the form of mortar attacks launched by the enemy, frequently from across the border. Apart from threatening the soldiers' lives and devastating the landscape by creating craters in the soil and ripping trees apart, they were also intended to disturb the South Africans' sleep and to shatter their nerves. When such attacks occurred during full moon the light provided exposure of the destruction wrought while affording maximum visibility for a stealthy approach by the enemy. The eeriness is accentuated by the fact that the 'rev' occurs between 12 and 3 a.m. – a time when people feel most vulnerable. With his statement that '[f]ull moon is a good time for dying', the soldier means in the primary sense that he (and his compatriots) were most likely to be killed then, while at a deeper, mythic level there is a mystery, a life-death significance associated with the full moon. This is a dark piece of writing that is only slightly leavened by the faint hint of humour suggested by the fact that it is the dog rather than the Cubans or SWAPO that gives the soldier the jitters.

Sometimes the enemy is not envisaged as being human at all. One writer depicts death as an immense supernatural struggle, as in the death of this unwitting sentry:

> Endless vigil
> lone sentry
> staring
> without purpose –
> when Satan and God
> clashed
> in a duel of death –
> and you went home
> in
> a Jiffy bag. [9] (J. U.)

Death appears to have come from nowhere during the sentry's monotonous, endless watch. In considering how and why a sentry should have been killed, the writer portrays the death as part of an immense, universal battle between two powerful symbolic figures, God and Satan, who represent the forces of good and evil. He is a hapless victim, an unwitting cosmic puppet in a struggle that Satan wins. Then the dead sentry 'goes home' in a Jiffy bag, which reduces him to the level of refuse. In the great scheme of things little value it attached to a single human life.

Into Angola: Crossing the thin red line

South African soldiers recount their experiences of waging war in Angola in the knowledge that it constituted a transgression of national boundaries and violated international rules of warfare. The crossing of the border also had metaphorical dimensions. This much is implicit in the statement:

> There is an invisible line that stretches somewhere across the Namibian/Angolan border, which, in army terminology, is called the 'red line' or 'danger line'. . . It is difficult to explain the concept of this line, but for a soldier it does fit somewhere on the risk/reward equation of life. When one crosses the line the risk of death increases, and so does the

reward of danger pay and the glory of a medal. This invisible danger line has a private place in a soldier's mind . . . (C. P.)

Stories from Angola convey the idea that crossing this invisible line into foreign territory where the soldiers' lives are more at risk than ever before; a risk which is both physical and psychological. As if to demonstrate this, the writer describes his first impression:

> Every now and then a Casspir came from the opposite direction carrying troops from 32 Battalion. They waved *pangas* and wore bandannas on their heads.

The irregular soldiers of 32 Battalion, who enjoyed a reputation for utter ruthlessness, seem to emerge from Angola heralding that country's strangeness, its 'otherness', suggesting the unknown. And their appearance would seem to suggest that they would not have been out of place on the set of the film *The Deer Hunter* (1979). It must have been a somewhat daunting prospect for any unit whose task it was to replace them. They are rather like Joseph Campbell's mythic heroes,[10] who, to have their mettle tested, undergo the various trials awaiting them.

There may not be a demarcated border, but there is a border post: 'a building pockmarked with shell craters from previous barrages, with the broken letters ANGOLA written across the front'.

The writer slowly constructs a picture of this other, apart place they have entered. His choice of language offers clues as to what he is trying to understand about this border post. In his use of the words 'pockmarked', 'craters' and 'broken', he obviously intends creating an image of destruction and dereliction. He adopts a poetic style, which, together with the Portuguese name, adds to the sense of foreignness of the place:

> We arrived at our first town. Ghost town. Wreckage everywhere. Shops and houses cratered with bombs. We passed through silently. That night we reached Xongongo (Villa Rocadas in Portuguese). Xongongo . . . now served as the furthest mechanised South African base in Angola. There was a mixed contingent of recces, parabats and some 32 soldiers.[11]

The reference to 'the furthest South African base' suggests that the troops were approaching some metaphorical heart of darkness.[12] The writer's attention to detail shows us how carefully he must have observed his surroundings. The carefully chosen language alone bears this out. The 'ghost town', Villa Rocadas, is traversed in silence, effectively captured in his memory, itself a place of silence. Villa Rocadas is a place of dislocation and confusion, with relics of its past life scattered in the streets:

We see pamphlets littering the streets, the propaganda of previous days. An article from Red China about world communism. An East German perspective on the racist Pretoria regime. Some Swedish[13] sardine tins. A leaflet with a skull and crossbones dropped by the SAAF [South African Air Force] before Operation Protea, warning residents to evacuate. A poem in Portuguese dedicated to a SWAPO freedom fighter. The poem touches me and I snatch it into my pocket. Further away, a massive pit of discarded drugs. Mounds of syringes and thousands of ampoules containing sinister drugs apparently used to prop up the last defending army fighters. A little further, a trench with a pile of human bones and a human skull. I take the skull. I leave it on a little rock near my 'grave'. Later one of the guys sees my skull and cracks, crushing it in a fit of rage. We sleep on our backs in our private 'graves' at night, eyes pointed at the stars, death guns pointed north.

This is a sordid scene, where the outside world has intruded as some sort of visual 'Babel'. The place is pervaded by the hideous presence (and probably stench) of death. The writer's choice of the word 'sinister' is a key to the passage. The skull and crossbones, the human skull in the trench, and the image of the troops' trenches as 'graves' tell him that death is immanent in its ugliest form. His placing of the skull near his own 'grave' indicates that he is trying to understand the possibility of his own death in this strange territory, while his companion's reaction, 'cracking' emotionally and then crushing the relic, reveals the ever-present threat of a mad loss of control. And the reference to 'death guns' in the final sentence of the passage suggests a nightly ritual of G5 cannons dispensing death and destruction.[14] Earlier this writer refers to these 'great phallic symbols of death . . . firing their salute into the setting son' (C.P.).

Angola was the place where direct, violent contact with the enemy occurred, not only in large battles like Cuito Cuanavale, but in smaller engagements. A significant incident took place at Calueque Dam, where 12 soldiers were killed in an attack by Cuban MiGs that left a huge gap in the bridge, and occasioned this disturbing document:[15]

> *Gat in 'n brug*
> *Gat in die grond*
>
> *Stukke vleis oor die grond versprei*
> *Stadig probeer ons die stukke vleis*
> *Aanmekaar sit om 'n prentjie van*
> *Herinnering te skep.*
>
> *Is dit reg om te redeneer oor die dood?*
> *Is die dood van twaalf onskuldige soldate die moeite werd?*

Dis moeilik om die prentjie te visualeer.
Dis moeilik om dit te aanvaar.

'n Trommel vol.
Al wat oorgebly het.

Gelukkig was dit gou.
Daar was geen pyn

'n Trommel vol dood. (P. de W.)

This harrowing poem captures the writer's struggle to reconstruct an integrated picture of the event. The opening image, '*Gat in 'n brug/Gat in die grond*', depicts the gaping, physical hole in the bridge and intimates that the ground represents a fissure in the writer's life. There are no bodies, only *stukke vleis* (pieces of meat) scattered over the ground.

It is possible to interpret the writer's experience of picking up body parts at two levels. First, as the group slowly begins the awful task, they find themselves trying to reconstruct a picture through memory. Are they reconstructing these images simply for purposes of identification or are they striving to recall what these dead soldiers looked like? The questions the writer asks himself are deeply disturbing: Is it right to speculate on the reasons for these deaths? Is the death of 12 innocent soldiers worth it? Worth what? He repeats the phrase ' *'n Trommel vol*' – a trunk full of the body parts of 12 people who were there one instant and gone the next. That, for him, is the major image of Calueque. Second, the repetition of ' *'n Trommel vol dood*' in the final line of the poem indicates that he has never integrated the memory, the picture he tried to visualise while gathering body parts. The shattered remains of 12 soldiers have left the writer a shattered human being. These lines articulate the notion that there can be no accurate remembering, no complete picture. Everything he remembers is fragmentary.

The loss of life of a buddy invariable evoked sensitive and empathetic responses. This is expressed in the lines of the following poem:
Too young to die –
we stood and watched
too shocked to cry.
The bright and spreading stain
of oozing life
fell drop for drop
into the hot Angolan dust. (D. W.)

There is great compassion in this brief poem. The poet does not convey this death in terms of injuries or wounds sustained by the soldier, but in the image of drops of blood falling 'into the hot Angolan dust'. The writer, numb with shock at the time of the incident, has preserved in his memory the startling image of 'oozing life', which, in his mind's eye, is a spreading blood stain metaphorically connecting the dead soldier with the foreign territory. The body might have been repatriated, but the soldier's life essence remains in foreign soil.

Returning home, looking back

In the writing that reminisces about the experience of war, mention is often made of the concept of the divided soul. An interviewee remarked: 'You've got two souls, an army soul and this one', that is, the one that returns to civilian life. This suggests that, despite the horrors of the battlefield, he sometimes longed to be back in the war zone. Perhaps he missed the adrenalin rush, or perhaps civilian life seemed dull after the intensity of the war. Conceptualising this in terms of having two souls is a way of making sense of inhabiting two worlds. It is also suggests that the psychic fragmentation caused by the war meant that the soldier could never be really whole again.

For some veterans, flashbacks to the war seem more real than the experiences of civilian life. In one letter, a soldier mentions being mortared for long periods while he and his compatriots felt 'like sitting ducks'. This experience appears to have caused shell-shock and impaired his ability to distinguish between the past and the present. He describes protracted flashbacks to Angola, sometimes lasting for three hours. What he says about emerging from one flashback when '[a]ll the time I was back there in Angola' is both poignant and pathetic: 'I woke up three hours later and the first thing I looked for was my snake. Ag, but old Dief was still back there on some once-was airfield in Angola. The day we came back to the States, [16] Dief vanished while we were having our last bush church meeting' (D. R.).

This writer cannot differentiate between his two worlds, so concrete and vivid is his Angolan experience. But it is a 'once-was', lost world, even though it remains real to him. It is populated by the snake, *Dief* (Thief), who vanished the day the writer left Angola. For the writer the vanished snake symbolically represents his own personal departure from the operational area. The air of resignation in expression '*Ag*' signifies the realisation of his sorrow at leaving behind a life that evokes a mixture of pathos and nostalgia.

While the Cubans inhabit one writer's post-war dreams: 'The dreams are always on the same theme. I lie in my trench, shooting at the Cubans. They come closer, shooting all the time. I shoot and shoot and they don't die . . . I wake up just before they kill me' (P. D.), another soldier-poet describes in vivid terms the experience of 'returning' to the battle field in his flashbacks:

When the rolling thunder creeps closer
salvo for salvo
and the exploding shells of lightning
burn up the darkening sky,
the shadow of some nameless fear
grabs hold of me
and takes me back
a thousand miles
and many months.

They're ranging in, those long-range guns,
bracketing me with invisible shrapnel
hitting home every time –
the crash of thunder and lightning
shakes me up
and I lie on my bed crying,
wondering why nobody else
can hear the guns. (D. W.)

The poet is evidently aware that his patterns of behaviour are symptomatic of post-traumatic stress disorder (PTSD) and are likely to trigger episodes of dysfunctionality. Nonetheless, he is unable to prevent these symptoms from overcoming him. He understands that his flashbacks involve 'going back' in time and space and knows the exact moment when the journey will start. The first crash of thunder becomes a salvo and the first flash of lightning an exploding shell. The horrifying feeling that the guns are closing in on him, 'hitting home every time', is so real that he wonders why 'nobody else can hear the guns'. While he knows logically why this cannot be the case and he recognises that the flashback will pass, he is still assailed by loneliness, terror and confusion for as long as it lasts. While his poetry articulates the vividness of his experience, the ex-soldier tries to make sense of it in his prose. Here he tries to explain the reasons for the flashbacks:

If it happened again and had to be done over, I would have to do it again, albeit with a heavy heart and filled with fear. I have lost something 'up there' and cannot find it here back home . . . I often think back to those days in SWA/Angola. On a bad day I feel an intense longing and aching for those times, in spite of what happened . . . In some perverse way I sometimes wish the war was still going on . . . I'm obviously very confused, with the past pursuing me and the present not measuring up to the past. I have looked at my uniform hanging desolately unused in my cupboard, and I often nearly put it on. Maybe I still will. (D. W.)

In spite of his confusion, his account shows an amazing clarity of perception as to the nature and cause of his maladies. His comment that he 'lost something' in SWA/Angola suggests that part of him remains behind even after he attempts to adjust to life at home. His subconscious yearning to return to the war zone, of being pulled in two directions, is apparent in the image of his 'uniform hanging desolately unused' in his cupboard. While he resists the impulse to put the uniform on, the story resists closure. To give in to the impulse would put an end to the equivocation, thereby acknowledging that his pursuer, the past, has caught up with him. The story demonstrates the deep pathology caused by the war to sensitive, intelligent individuals who struggle in vain for the rest of their lives to integrate their conflicting emotions.

A disturbing poem in Afrikaans tells of the same longing to return to the war zone:

> *Ek mis*
> *Dae van saamwees*
> *Dae van plesier*
> *Dae van eensaamwees*
> *Dae van dood.* (P. de W.) [17]

At first glance this seems to be an uncomplicated expression of longing for things like companionship, fun, even loneliness. However, the last line, '*Dae van dood*' (days of death) strikes a discordant note. That this verse was written by the same soldier who wrote the harrowing poem about the Calueque Dam incident cited above, might explain the strange twist to his words. Why should he long for the days of death? He himself probably could not answer that question, but he is able to acknowledge the fractured nature of his looking back at the complex mix of war experiences that makes ordinary life seem dull by comparison. '*Ek mis*' (I long for . . .) refers, then, to the intense nature of the experience that this writer feels he is unlikely to find again: the thrill and fear of living close to the edge.

Generally, the documents that express regret, longing and sadness are expressive of the nostalgia that often accompanies the memories of military experience. Very often the regret is initiated by a reminder of some kind, as in this statement:

> It seems so long ago that I was a soldier, but there are times when a sight or some smell on the wind brings it all back in a crash. Diesel burning, dust and smoking rubber, the stink of choppers, or hot kerosene in the wind, gun oil burning off the Browning machine guns after a thousand rounds have been fired, the hot brass of the expended cartridge cases. The smell of explosives and dust and sand and blood and men lying in their trenches, gutted by explosives, bloated by the sun and attended by flies . . . Then it passes and it seems as if it all happened to someone else. In a way it did, but you are the one who carries it with you, a secret burden that is very difficult to share. (E. W.)

It is said that the sense of smell produces the most evocative memories and reminders of the past. This is obviously the case with this writer. He copes with the overwhelming nostalgia by saying it seems to have happened to someone else. In admitting as much, he is probably telling the truth. He *was* someone else then. The crucial point, though, is made in the final sentence: 'You are the one who carries it with you, a secret burden that is very difficult to share'. Memories remain and must be continually negotiated in the present.

In memoriam: Tributes to friends and fallen comrades

Friendships forged in the experience of war exhibit a type of closeness that civilians who have never been in combat may not readily understand. This camaraderie stems from the intensity of sharing the life-death experience that is difficult to capture in words. Still, such stories can be viewed as self-contained narratives that constitute a key component of the genre of war literature: the hero or protagonist's journey through life as a rite of passage.[18] Such epic stories form part of an ancient literary tradition that renders them almost archetypal. They are exemplified by classical works such as Virgil's *Aeneid,* in which the relationship of Nisus and Euryalus typifies (male) friendships formed in adverse circumstances.[19] Similar stories have been related by American soldiers in Vietnam where the loss of close friends proved so devastating that the surviving soldier could seldom remember the names and faces of other people in his unit.[20] And the operation of a 'buddy system' amongst South African soldiers during the Border War meant that soldiers formed close friendships which often outlasted the war. Not surprisingly, the loss of friends in battle could be devastating for those who survived.

There are many stories of deep and enduring friendship ending tragically in battle. One survivor of an attack on a Ratel in which his unit was travelling describes his best friend's death as follows:

> As I entered the ambulance, but before I was laid down, with a sense of detachment I saw the thick black column of smoke rising from Andre's funeral pyre and realised that I would never see him again. It didn't strike me at the time that he was dead, just that I would never enjoy good times and bad times with him again. (D. B.)

With the image of the 'funeral pyre', this writer is unconsciously expressing the picture of the burning Ratel in classical terms, relating it to images in Virgil's *Aeneid.*[21]

Although the nature of the work of medics routinely brought them into contact with maimed and wounded bodies, as well as dead and dying soldiers, they were not necessarily spared the trauma. Indeed, the loss of life could have a personal impact on them. A medic describes packing bodies burnt beyond recognition after a helicopter crash. When the list of the dead is announced, it includes the name of his best friend. He realises that he has packed the body without realising who it was, and remarks: 'That was my friend that I packed there, and that hurt' (D.C.). The same writer cites a case where a soldier killed his closest friend in error:

> This particular troop pulled himself over the Buffel. As he got on, he put his rifle down on the Buffel to pull himself up properly and the shots went off. He shot his friend sitting in front of him. And the most horrible thing about it was that his friend said, 'Oh God, no, not me', and died like that. (D.C.)

Accidental deaths were fairly frequent in the SADF's 'operational area'. And this matter-of-fact third person narrative does not begin to communicate the tragedy of this scene. Nor does it reflect on the guilt that the soldier who caused the needless loss of life would have experienced. In fact, accidents were sometimes responsible for multiple deaths: 'There were black days, there really were. One day there was a grenade explosion at Oshivello when about thirteen Lance Corporals were killed and about twenty-seven of them injured.'

However these soldiers met their deaths, they became a statistic of war. But for the medic who penned these lines it was a 'black day': tragic, terrible, infinitely worse than other days. He remembers this day as significant not only on account of the scale of the loss but precisely because the deceased were more than mere numbers, ranks and names; they were individuals who had family and friends.

One story of an unusual friendship could be construed as comic if it were not so tragic:

> One day I began a relationship with a fellow-being on the Border – a Southwest desert gecko. She was pure white, with scales on her body. Later I realised that she was pregnant – that's how I knew she was female. She was my best friend on the Border. She was <u>tiny</u> when I found her amongst my tent bags on the ground, but she soon grew large. I tamed her by stroking her head and body. Anyone else would have found her hideous, so I kept her absolutely secret.
>
> And then one evening, just before I returned to the States, I came upon her in front of the Ops room, where she lay pregnant and dying near my tent. It broke me more than all the death I had seen in the war. I will never forget it – it will never leave me. I kept her warm in my bed, and the next day I buried the ugly, swollen creature next to my tent. I think a bit of my soul went into her grave with her. (G. S.)

This story is arresting because of the honesty with which it is told and for what it reveals of the author's self-discovery. First, he views himself and the gecko in a growing relationship which serves as a substitute for human company. That there is compassion in his view of the gecko is clear in the use of the underlined word '<u>tiny</u>'. There is also recognition that someone or something does not have to be beautiful to be loved, as others could think of the object of his love as 'hideous' or 'ugly'. The gecko's function as companion means that her death is akin to the loss of a human friend.

The writer reveals great depths of compassion and tenderness in this writing, which he probably could not have done at the time given the macho culture prevailing in the army. The hurt that he must have felt is implied with great economy of language, in the statements 'she lay pregnant and dying near my tent' and 'I kept her warm in my bed'. His understanding of the meaning of the incident for his life as a whole is obvious from his statement, 'I will never forget it – it will never leave me'. He interprets this fact for himself in an unusually profound, perceptive way: 'I think a bit of my soul went into her grave with her'.

The idea of the friend as the 'second self', who takes something from the other's being when he dies, emerges as a recurrent motif in narratives of the Border War. The writer of one letter confessed: 'The name I gave you is not my own, but a friend's, who's dead. I'd like it that way. Half of his body is still back there. Our surnames were the same' (D. R.). The reader is alerted to the existence of separate identities that are consciously reconfigured as one. This has parallels with the concept found in the story of the gecko. While the first soldier takes a dying gecko into his bed and leaves something of himself behind with her in her grave, the second soldier tries to deal with the loss of his friend by taking on the first name of someone whose surname he shared. In this way, he attempts to take the dead friend into his own being so as to share his essence. His statement 'I'd like it that way' indicates that he is doing this consciously although he might not be aware that he is dealing with the idea of the 'second self'.

Apart from tributes, a soldier's death could trigger responses like anger and cynicism. Hatred of hypocritical civilians and rage directed in cutting language at the army and the church are mingled with a strange tenderness towards the dead soldier in the following poem. It is called 'Cuito Cuanavale: for Gary, 1987'.

> My boyfriend on the border
> she used to say,
> and smile (appropriately) – late-night-Saturday-disco-high
> when the time was ripe for sentiment.
> His father
> through miles and miles and miles of cordoned pathos
> would drip memories of Tobruk into his brandy
> as he dragged himself

melodramatic and maudlin
through the corpulent years.
And his mother and Pat Carr
were at one with the love
that crucifies itself between the armour
of the Southern Cross[22]
although she would halt in her giving
when the stories exploded in her chiffon living room
from his mouth.
Scrolls in his memory
Fort Klapperkop in his eyes
tears behind the cannon
and a sermon packed with lies.
And all this time he lay
womb warmthed in the curve of the Angolan earth
with a hole in his head in which
the starmoondarkness and veld stood vigil
without even as much as a simple letter
to tell them
the uncensored bloody truth. (R. W.)

The writer clearly despises the soldier's parents for their double standards: the father who is a veteran of the Desert War drowns in the nostalgia of his own war-time stories, but has no stomach or time for those of his son, and the mother who shuts herself off from her son's stories because she regards them as a personal affront on her own middle-class, patriotic values. The suggestion of attack is implicit in the reference to stories 'exploding' from her son's mouth. The writer's use of 'chiffon' to describe the conventional, respectable living room conveys this mother's shallow, frivolous values.

The military funeral does not escape the writer's disdain and scorn either. All the conventional images and practices of the occasion are revealed as hypocritical and hollow. The scrolls and the memorial are meaningless, the 'tears behind the cannon' on the gun carriage seem banal, and the sermon obviously referenced apartheid ideology in order to justify the SADF incursion into Angola. This was in line with many mainstream churches that uncritically supported the war and sought to invoke God's name so as to sanctify the state's sacrifice of its young men, most of whom were conscripts. By indicting what he sees as the three pillars of support for the war, namely the church, the army and the civilian population, the writer seems to suggest that Gary is a victim of the war in more than one sense of the word.

The final section of the poem is ambiguous, perhaps deliberately so, implying that Gary is still lying dead in Angola while the funeral is taking place in South Africa. The reader could entertain the awful suspicion that Gary's body is lost in Angola and is not actually in the coffin. On the other hand, the artificiality and emptiness of the funeral are contrasted with the maternal qualities of the Angolan earth, where Gary is nurtured and watched over by natural forces. Death is cold, but Gary, at one with maternal nature, is 'womb warmthed'. There is the suggestion in this image that the earth is, in fact, more maternal and loving than Gary's real mother.

So what is the author's 'uncensored bloody truth'? Is it the realisation that the letters written to parents by the army upon the death of their sons are seldom honest about how and why they die? Is it the perception that dying for one's country is anything but glorious? There is no doubt that the writer is appalled by the shameful hypocrisy resorted to by the state in vindicating its war against its enemies. The subversive, sub-textual suggestion of this 'document of life' is that individuals and social institutions find it more comfortable to live with lies than truth.

Conclusion

It is possible that the act of writing their narratives gave the soldier-authors some sense of reconstructing what had happened to them so that they could approach wholeness or self-healing. However, in certain instances, as in the case of the writer of the poem on Calueque Dam, this could not be done physically or psychologically. Perhaps the act of writing personal life narratives was cathartic, but if this principle is understood in its most accurate sense, catharsis was not for the soldier-authors, but rather for their audience, who ought to experience the events re-enacted in these documents as a vicarious purgation. But if (white) South African society is not willing to confront the truth, if the audience does not desire this catharsis, the writers narrate to no purpose, and are left unfulfilled and fragmented. They needed, and still need, a receptive audience for their documents of life, which is why one of them wrote in a letter, 'Please talk to us' (L. v. W.). He meant, of course: 'Please listen.'[23]

Following the SADF withdrawal from Angola/Namibia, it seems that not a great deal of listening was done by South African society at large. Civilians did not, for various reasons, want to hear 'Border stories', which tended consequently to be shared with other ex-combatants. One was told: 'Go and sit at Fort Klapperkop[24] . . . among the names of all those people who died on the Border . . . because we're sick and tired of it.' If this was the case in South Africa in the early 1990s, it was also true of the US. Jonathon Shay noted similar rejections of Vietnam veterans by the American public.[25] He found that most civilians actually did not want to hear stories of trauma and victimhood, and tended to forget them even when confronted with their truth. But such personal narratives deserve to be told and heard so that society can learn what was done in its name.

Notes to Chapter Ten

1   A term used by the sociologist Ken Plummer in his book *Documents of Life: An Introduction to the Problems and Literature of a Humanistic Method* (London: George Allen and Unwin, 1983).

2   When this material was collected, some contributors opted for anonymity. In view of the sensitive nature of much of this writing, I decided to respect this, and to use their initials for reference.

3   Another writer spoke of being 'taken in white, low-bed trucks, like a bunch of cattle, northwards to Oshivello'.

4   The same effect was described by a Portuguese man from Luanda, who described white planes without any markings at all that would land at Luanda airport. Despite the absence of markings, he said, everybody knew they were South African.

5   Plummer, *Documents of Life*, 55.

6   In all wars, armies tend to de-humanise the enemy, probably as a coping mechanism.

7   This poem is long in the original, and space precludes quoting all of it. I have selected stanzas so that the sense is, hopefully, not lost.

8   The onslaught of communism that was said to be threatening civilisation in Africa.

9   A well-known brand of plastic rubbish bags which came to stand for the body bags used by the army.

10 J. Campbell, *The Hero With a Thousand Faces* (London: Fontana Press, 1993).

11 It is important for our understanding of this passage to realise who these soldiers were. In fact, they were the 'elite' of the army, 'wild', 'mad' renegades, largely a law unto themselves. 32 Battalion was, in the main, Portuguese-speaking, and its members were known in Portuguese as *Os Terriveis*, the 'Terrible Ones'. Their origins were varied. As well as Portuguese Angolans, there were British, Rhodesian, and even Australian mercenaries. The parabats were often referred to amongst the troops as the 'glory boys' on account of their dangerous contacts in the bush and the elite nature of their training, while it was the job of the recces to reconnoitre, undertaking hazardous expeditions in Angola.

12 The idea of the 'heart of darkness' did not apply just to the sense of evil pervading the Angolan bush, but within the soldiers themselves. As one of them said during an interview, 'Survival will stop at nothing. I don't think I really reached that last stage. That's like something out of The *Lord of the Flies*. But we were getting so close to that – it was horrifying' (K. C.). A reference with even more resonance is to Captain Willard's journey up the imaginary Nung River to the Cambodian highlands in Francis Ford Coppola's film *Apocalypse Now* (1979) which is partly inspired by Joseph Conrad's novella, *The Heart of Darkness*.

13 Another writer recalled finding, at a deserted base, some Swedish condensed milk tins that said, 'To SWAPO with love from Abba'.

14 These were the G5 cannons, which were fired northwards every night. Earlier, this writer calls them 'great phallic symbols of death . . . firing their salute to the sinking red sun'.

15 Translation:
Hole in a bridge
Hole in the ground.

Pieces of meat scattered all over the ground.
Slowly we try to put the pieces together
To construct a picture that we can remember.

Is it right to argue about death?

Is the death of twelve innocent soldiers worth it?

It's difficult to visualise that picture.
Acceptance is difficult.

A trunk full,
That's all that's left.

Fortunately it was quick
And painless.

A trunk full of death.

16   Troop term for South Africa, adopted from America's Vietnam War culture.

17   Translation:
     I long for
     Days of companionship
     Days of pleasure
     Days of loneliness
     Days of death.

18   A point made by Thomas van Nortwick in *Somewhere I Have Never Travelled* (New York: Oxford University Press, 1996), 155.

19   So close was their friendship that when Nisus disappeared during an episode of the war, Euryalus returned to look for him, and they died together. I was told of one soldier in Angola, who, after his friend was killed in a contact, returned, perhaps to check, found him still dying on a pile of bodies, and stayed with him until he did die.

20   J. Shay, *Achilles in Vietnam: Combat Trauma and the Undoing of Character* (New York: Simon and Schuster, 1995), 44.

21   An instance in the *Aeneid* that comes immediately to mind as a comparison is Aeneas' departure from Carthage, when he looks back from his vessel at the city and sees the smoke rising from his lover, Dido's, funeral pyre after her suicide.

22   A charity organisation that helped families of soldiers named for the constellation of stars.

23   Vietnam veterans always told their therapists, 'Listen! Just listen!' Cf. Shay, *Achilles in Vietnam*, 189.

24   Erected in Pretoria following the Jameson Raid of 1895/6, used for military purposes and later for ammunition services, it became a museum in 1960. There is a monument in the form of an advancing infantry soldier with his rifle, at the foot of which are granite slabs containing the names of the SADF soldiers and national servicemen who have died since 1961.

25   Shay, *Achilles in Vietnam*.

Chapter 11

Savimbi's War: Illusions and Realities

Elaine Windrich

South Africa was able to carry out a secret war in Angola for more than a decade because it had the support of the United States (US) for its policy of countering the 'communist onslaught' in the southern African region. Also an essential element of this policy was Jonas Savimbi's National Union for the Total Independence of Angola (UNITA) movement, which provided Pretoria with a proxy army of expendable foot soldiers (thus sparing the white conscripts), a potential successor to the Popular Movement for the Liberation of Angola (MPLA) rulers in Luanda and tangible evidence for a 'plausible denial' that the South African Defence Force (SADF) was intervening in the war in Angola. UNITA was vital for the Americans as well, since they required a surrogate army to challenge an African government supported by the Soviet Union and Cuba. In this role, however, UNITA had to be seen not as puppets of a 'pariah regime' condemned by the international community, but as African nationalist 'freedom fighters'. As such, they would serve the same purpose as the other rebel movements opposing left-wing governments in the Third World which also received US support.

The US's tacit alliance with South Africa was very much a product of the Cold War, as was UNITA's participation in the project. This was certainly the case during the presidency of Ronald Reagan (1981–88), which coincided with the leadership of the hawkish P. W. Botha and the establishment of the 'national security state' in South Africa. But it had also been the case a decade earlier, when Secretary of State Henry Kissinger (in the Nixon–Ford administrations) had authorised a covert invasion of Angola on the eve of that country's independence from Portugal to prevent the MPLA from coming to power because it was receiving military aid from the Soviet Union. Since the South African government shared this aim (promoted by Botha at the defence ministry) and was determined to prevent the South West Africa People's Organization (SWAPO) rebels it was fighting against in Namibia from gaining a military ally in Angola, the decision to intervene was approved. As a result, the SADF was deployed to spearhead an invasion force including the UNITA and the rival National Front for the Liberation of Angola (FNLA) troops it had trained for that purpose. Although the SADF came perilously close to capturing Luanda, it was driven back to the Namibian border by the large-scale Cuban military intervention, with

Soviet logistical support, to rescue the beleaguered MPLA. Defeat was also in store on the political front, with the defection of South Africa's American ally in the midst of the allegedly 'covert operation'. Following the revelation in the US media that America had collaborated with the apartheid regime to destroy an independent African government, the US Congress rejected Kissinger's appeal for additional funds to hire more mercenaries to win the war. Instead, it enacted new legislation (the Clark Amendment) to prevent any future US intervention on the side of any party in Angola.[1] However, the long-term effect of this abortive operation was not resignation to the inevitable, but the memory of humiliation and the determination to avenge it. Thus the US and South Africa would be brought together once again in the 1980s, in a re-enactment of the Kissinger effort, although this time, with the Reagan administration committed to 'winning' the Cold War, they were in for the long haul.

Since South Africa's strategy of combating 'Soviet and proxy forces' by destabilising its 'Marxist' neighbours coincided with Savimbi's determination to pursue the war despite the decimation of his troops by the MPLA/Cuban armies, the alliance between the two former partners was soon renewed. And eventually (as a South African 'military analyst' put it) 'Savimbi's war and Pretoria's became so intertwined that the one could not be separated from the other'.[2] The first priority in this partnership was to establish a safe and secure base for a revitalised UNITA. Thus 'Jamba' was founded in the south-east corner of Angola ('the end of the world', as the Portuguese referred to their colonial hunting ground) which could be protected by the South African base just across the border in Namibia. From there, Savimbi could be briefed by liaison officers from the SADF who would arrange for the training and arming of UNITA's soldiers and the planning of military operations. The SADF also contracted 'front' companies to supply goods and services to both the troops and the civilian supporters. Together they engaged in contraband trade in ivory, timber and other valuable resources for mutual enrichment and to defray the costs of the war.[3]

On the propaganda front, with a view to 'winning of hearts and minds' both at home and abroad, South Africa provided for the transport of influential visitors to Jamba – journalists and politicians who came for the press conferences and interviews with Savimbi and other UNITA leaders. Also an important part of the propaganda war was UNITA's clandestine radio station – the Voice of the Resistance of the Black Cockerel (VRBC or VORGAN) – which began broadcasting from South Africa in 1979 and was later installed at Jamba, allegedly with the covert assistance of the US Central Intelligence Agency (CIA). With a 'Voice' from Jamba, and also a news service known as Kwacha UNITA Press (KUP), Savimbi would be able to recruit new followers, appeal for external support, vilify the MPLA government and extol the virtues of UNITA and its military prowess.[4]

The propagandists

While the SADF was building up UNITA as a credible military force, and escalating the cross-border operations which also benefited the rebels, in the US the South African lobby was working to promote the country's image. Heading the campaign was Pretoria's embassy in Washington, which was assisted by various satellite agencies (dealing with trade, investment, tourism, etc.) and the 'front' organisations set up by the Information Department which had survived the 'Muldergate' scandal (of 1978) revealing their excesses. Their strategy was to establish ties with sympathetic conservative groups such as the Heritage Foundation, the Conservative Caucus, the World Anti-Communist League and the Christian fundamentalists, especially those led by television evangelist Pat Robertson and the Reverend Jerry Falwell of the Moral Majority. Also targeted were influential right-wing politicians, including William Casey (Reagan's CIA director) and John Sears (Reagan's campaign manager), who had served as lobbyists for South Africa as well, and the media magnate John McGoff, who was charged with buying a newspaper for Pretoria's propaganda purposes. Although McGoff repeatedly failed to do so, much the same purpose was achieved with the establishment of the *Washington Times* by the Reverend Sun Myung Moon of the Unification Church (the so-called 'Moonies'), with South African support for the project. Since the newspaper became a steady source of pro-South African propaganda (and also favoured UNITA), the investment appears to have been well repaid.[5]

UNITA benefited considerably from this campaign, particularly when its role in resisting the 'communist onslaught' was featured in the propaganda. According to one of the providers, the business-oriented South Africa Foundation (SAF), as a result of its 'informative publications' the debate on the Angolan war had been considerably enhanced and a large number of respected individuals in the US now had 'a relatively clear understanding of the situation in southern Africa'.[6] Savimbi's role in that war was also praised, crediting him with having achieved 'the most prestigious thing to which an insurgent leader can aspire: a liberated zone', presumably meaning the area 'liberated' and protected by the SADF.[7] Another source of this propaganda was the International Freedom Foundation (IFF), which had offices in Europe as well as South Africa and the US. IFF chairman Jack Abramoff staged an extravagant media display at Jamba in 1985 to establish a 'Democratic International' linking UNITA with other 'freedom fighters' supported by the US, such as the Contras in Nicaragua. He later produced a commercial film called 'The Red Scorpion', featuring Savimbi as the heroic anti-Communist guerrilla, which was made in Namibia with the co-operation of the SADF.[8] But the main source for IFF propaganda was the vast array of publications (such as the *Southern African Freedom Review* and the *IFF Bulletin*) which were widely distributed by its branch offices at home and overseas.

Like their South African counterparts, Savimbi's American supporters also relied upon conservative political organisations and think tanks to raise public awareness of the rebel cause. Although most of the pro-UNITA propaganda appeared in right-wing publications with a strident anti-Communist slant (e.g., the *National Review*, *American Spectator*, *Commentary* and *Human Events*), some of the mainstream press began to take an interest in UNITA's struggle for survival and recognition, and also its potential as a Cold War ally. Such an interest was occasionally expressed in the syndicated columns of William Safire and the Rowland Evans-Robert Novak partnership, and in reports from journalists who had interviewed Savimbi and other UNITA leaders at their base camps in Angola. A typical example of the latter was a *Newsweek* report on Savimbi's first publicised visit to the US (in 1979) by Arnaud de Borchgrave, a future editor of the *Washington Times*. To obtain the maximum publicity for the forthcoming visit, he described in great detail how he personally delivered the invitation from the sponsors of the visit (the conservative human rights monitor Freedom House), interviewed Savimbi at a 'secret destination' in Angola and then accompanied him to the US.[9]

Although Savimbi's visit to the US produced no official recognition from a Carter administration committed to majority rule in southern Africa and sanctions against Pretoria's Rhodesian ally, his appeal for 'understanding' did result in the establishment of ties with the conservative lobby groups and their media that were to play such an important role in promoting UNITA's image during the 1980s. Their influence soon became evident when Ronald Reagan, as a presidential candidate, pledged that he would provide military aid to UNITA's 'freedom fighters', even though African issues were low on the campaign agenda. He renewed that pledge two months after taking office. And before that year was out Savimbi was once more in Washington, this time with the official recognition that UNITA was 'a legitimate political force in Angola' and the informal assurance that ways and means would be found to by-pass the Clark Amendment by channelling funds to UNITA through 'friendly' third countries.[10]

Diplomacy and war

With the 'Reagan Doctrine' committing the US to supporting insurgencies against left-wing governments in the Third World, UNITA was assured of continued US backing for its war against the MPLA government. But even greater gains were in store for South Africa under a parallel policy of 'constructive engagement', which in practice enabled the SADF to wage an undeclared war in Angola and 'linked' Pretoria's illegal occupation of Namibia to the withdrawal of the Cuban troops protecting Angola from South African attack. The architect of this policy was Chester Crocker, Assistant Secretary of State for Africa and one of the few conservative Africanists in the academic community. As such, he had been appointed to serve in the administrations of Nixon, Ford and Reagan. Since neither President Reagan nor Secretary of State George Shultz had much interest in or knowledge of Africa, Crocker was given a free hand to 'engage' the South Africans and their UNITA allies throughout his (record) eight-year term of office.

Crocker's main concern (which he had previewed in the Council on Foreign Relations' influential *Foreign Affairs* journal just before his appointment in 1981 and was to justify in a 500-page book thereafter) was 'countering Soviet-Cuban adventurism' in southern Africa, which coincided neatly with Pretoria's strategy for the 'total onslaught'. To achieve this purpose, he wrote, 'the proper course was to recognize publicly the legitimacy of UNITA's struggle and maintain pressure for Cuban withdrawal while pursuing an internationally acceptable settlement in Namibia'.[11] For South Africa, such an offer was irresistible because it consisted of all carrots and no sticks. While UNITA was encouraged to pursue its war against the MPLA government, and the SADF (Crocker's 'lobby of modernizing patriots') was allowed to continue its bombardment and occupation of Angola, no meaningful pressure was exerted upon the South African government either to withdraw from Namibia or to halt the destabilisation of its neighbours. Although Crocker may have cautioned the South Africans to exercise some restraint, on the grounds that they were using the cover of their special relationship with the US to pursue an aggressive policy of air strikes and raids, his strategy still depended heavily on South Africa as 'one of the anvils of our diplomacy' and on UNITA as 'the most potent organisation in Angola'.[12] Furthermore, with the assurance that the US would oppose any United Nations initiative directed against the South African government for its invasions of Angola, it was able to continue its aggression with impunity, as it was able to prolong its illegal occupation of Namibia, now 'linked' to a parallel Cuban withdrawal.

However, despite the appearance of a united front against the 'communist onslaught', the reality was that the three-way alliance was soon riven with mutual suspicion and mistrust. Crocker admitted as much in his memoirs, when he wrote that, 'as the wars hotted up in 1983, Washington was the object of growing distrust' and 'our relations with South Africa and UNITA became so ambivalent and strained'.[13] But this was hardly surprising, considering the differences in their long-term objectives. Thus the Angolan war offered South Africa a road to restore its military prestige and even the possibility, with its UNITA ally, of reversing the MPLA victory of 1975. For the US, however, this policy of 'covert' intervention in Angola was not intended to turn the tide of battle, but only to 'raise the price of battle' for the Angolans and the Cubans while also enhancing UNITA's military effectiveness as well as its international standing. In effect, by 'reinforcing the internal stalemate' (America's Cold War strategy of 'bleeding the enemy dry'), the US could 'help destroy Angolan, Cuban and Soviet illusions of a military victory over UNITA'.[14]

For Pretoria, however, determined to maintain its image as a regional superpower, this was not enough. The securocrats who determined policy during the Botha years regarded the American efforts to broker a peace settlement as an inadequate response to the 'total onslaught' threatening the region. Nevertheless, they seized upon the US offer of 'linkage' as a means of delaying the concessions on Namibian independence and, over the next several years, went through the motions of negotiations to comply with Crocker's rules of 'engagement'. At the same time, however, they continued to step up their invasions of Angola, destroying much of the infrastructure and economy of the southern and eastern provinces as well as the alleged military targets and SWAPO bases, which made a peace settlement impossible. In addition, despite the agreement for SADF withdrawal from Angola brokered by Crocker in Lusaka in 1984, South Africa simultaneously sent a high-level mission to Jamba to assure 'an increasingly alarmed Savimbi' that it would never 'leave him in the lurch'.[15]

However, as the war escalated during the mid-1980s it became evident that South Africa could not afford to fight a large-scale war in Angola on its own (as even the pro-government *Citizen* warned) 'just as it could not go it alone in 1975, when South African forces could have taken Angola if the United States had not pulled the rug from under them'.[16] Consequently, after a major SADF operation to save UNITA from annihilation in September 1985, the government immediately dispatched a mission to Washington to speed up the aid promised to Savimbi in order to replace the military equipment expended in turning back the MPLA offensive. Although the 'covert' aid to UNITA soon followed (with the repeal of the Clark Amendment, $15 million was allocated for Stinger anti-aircraft missiles), South Africa continued to bear a large share of the burden. However, when an even larger SADF commitment was required to rescue UNITA from a 'final' MPLA offensive in 1987, the cost of doing so, in terms of manpower and material losses, was to be one of the main factors in suing for peace. Yet another factor was the increasingly tense relationship with the US as a result of the economic sanctions imposed upon South Africa by its ally in the war in Angola. Although Crocker had opposed the sanctions as a threat to his policy of 'constructive engagement', a bipartisan US Congress overrode a veto by President Reagan to approve the Anti-Apartheid Legislation. Nevertheless, it was indeed ironic that the same Congress had also approved military aid for South Africa's UNITA ally, which would be sharing the Stinger missiles forbidden to the SADF by the US sanctions.

As the third party in the alliance, UNITA was often caught up in the conflicting game plans of its senior partners, while resenting their inability, or perhaps unwillingness, to comply with Savimbi's objectives. Nevertheless, UNITA was an indispensable part of the alliance and contributed 90% of the SADF's infantry (according to chief of staff General Jannie Geldenhuys)[17]. UNITA also provided the Americans with a potent force to pressure the MPLA government for a negotiated settlement, especially after the establishment of the Kamina base in Zaire to channel US military aid directly to UNITA. In fact, both partners were determined to keep UNITA 'on side', which was evident from the continual assurances and reassurances to Savimbi by both Crocker and Foreign Minister Pik Botha, often in competition with each other in their pledges of loyalty and fidelity. According to Crocker, Botha even went so far as to warn him that he could recommend nothing to his government without first getting the reaction of

Savimbi.[18] But Crocker himself was no less solicitous in appeasing the UNITA leader, whom he credited with having 'a world-class strategic mind' because he had 'grasped our emphasis on Namibia and Cuban withdrawal from Angola'.[19] At each of their many meetings in Africa over the years, when Savimbi's mind had allegedly been 'poisoned by misinformation, lies and distortions deliberately placed with him by opponents of our strategy', Crocker would be obliged to rebuild mutual confidence or restore the relationship or reiterate US support.[20] While the alleged poisoning of Savimbi's mind was sometimes attributed to prior briefings by P.W. Botha and his ministerial colleagues, more often it was blamed on the UNITA lobby in Washington which held Crocker responsible for the fact that Savimbi was not yet in power in Luanda.

Savimbi also had his differences with South Africa, in particular over their respective share of fighting the war, 'winning' the battles and paying the costs. These differences were most starkly revealed during the major confrontations with the MPLA forces in 1985 and 1987, when Savimbi would release UNITA's version of the 'victories' to a press conference at Jamba and a ministry of defence spokesman would publicly refute it, albeit politely and deferentially. Since South Africa was fighting a secret war in Angola, concealed as operations against SWAPO bases or 'hot pursuit' of SWAPO 'terrorists', UNITA was left with a virtual monopoly of the military communiqués relating to the conflict. By 1985, however, the SADF's intervention was on such a large scale, involving the deployment of air power and long-range artillery, that its presence could no longer be denied with any degree of credibility. Consequently, on 20 September, the Defence Minister, General Magnus Malan, admitted for the first time that the SADF had intervened in support of Savimbi's beleaguered forces, insisting that the MPLA offensive to destroy UNITA was a threat to South Africa's regional security.[21] But despite Malan's admission, reversing years of denial of military support for UNITA, Savimbi told a press conference at Jamba that same day that no South African troops were fighting on his side and that UNITA alone was confronting a massive MPLA offensive allegedly directed by Soviet military officers.[22] However, even Fred Bridgland (Savimbi's 'official' biographer) had to admit that it was an open secret among the diplomatic and journalistic communities in Pretoria that the South African Air Force had intervened on UNITA's behalf at Mavinga and the SADF's 32nd Battalion (Portuguese-speaking black mercenaries led by white officers) had been there on the ground.[23]

With the increasing isolation of South Africa as a result of US sanctions and the international community's condemnation of its internal repression and regional aggression, 'deniability' of its intervention in the war in Angola had become largely irrelevant. General Malan conceded as much after the MPLA offensive in 1987, when he admitted that the SADF had once again intervened in Angola to save UNITA from defeat, the reason this time being that 'Savimbi cherished the same values as those held by South Africa' and that if his forces were destroyed, southern Africa would be 'on the brink of an abyss'.[24] At the same time, however, Savimbi was telling the journalists assembled at Jamba that with American military support UNITA had won the most important victory since the war began in 1975. While expressing surprise that the SADF was trying to take credit for UNITA's military successes, he warned that UNITA could not accept 'contradictory and counter-productive statements, even from its allies'.[25]

Differences also arose over sharing the costs of the war, particularly after Savimbi became the recipient of large sums of US aid which, unlike the South African contribution, did not have to be repaid in cash or in goods and services. While it was not unusual for Savimbi to engage in sharp public exchanges with SADF spokesmen on such matters, his outburst about the cost of the war during the crucial battle over Cuito Cuanavale in March 1988 provoked a crisis which had to be quickly resolved if they were to preserve their alliance. The issue arose over the publication of Savimbi's complaints about South Africa in an interview with *Paris-Match* which was reproduced (in English translation) in the Argus Group of newspapers. The essence of the message was that while South Africa had agreed to help UNITA, it was not at any price. Although UNITA had diamonds, timber and ivory to sell, it was still not enough to meet its obligations, even with the offer of credit. In a vivid description of his grievances, he related that during the key battle at Lomba River (in 1987), when the South Africans were showering 2 000–3 000 shells and bombs on their opponents every night, they listed the cost of everything UNITA owed them and, at the end of the offensive, presented the bill.[26] Although Savimbi neither denied nor withdrew his remarks in the *Paris-Match* interview, his hurried meeting in Cape Town with General Malan to clarify the misunderstanding ended up with both of them attacking the messenger. They dismissed the reports in the Argus Press as '99 per cent false' (Savimbi) and 'a pack of lies contradicting the style and philosophy of Dr [sic] Savimbi' (Malan).[27]

While this crisis had been surmounted at the expense of a third party scapegoat, the grounds for disagreement remained unresolved. Even as the government was renewing its pledges of loyalty to UNITA and support for its cause, relying upon the South African Broadcasting Corporation (SABC) and the Afrikaner press to convey the message, it was putting out diplomatic feelers to Moscow for a political settlement that would fall far short of Savimbi's ultimate objectives. The person chosen for this role was General Malan, hitherto regarded as the arch anti-Communist hawk who had been in favour of installing UNITA in power since the abortive attempt to do so in 1975. Now, however, he was proposing to accept the new reality (as *Die Vaderland* put it) that no political solution was possible in southern Africa without the co-operation of the Soviet Union.[28] Therefore, he was offering an exchange of guarantees that neither side would attempt to impose its own choice of government in Luanda: i.e., Pretoria would not strive for the establishment of a pro-South African government provided that Moscow did not insist upon a pro-Russian one. Instead a future government in Luanda, given the reality of East-

West tension, would have to be a non-aligned and neutral one, and this would be an outcome that South Africa was prepared to live with.[29] Within a matter of weeks, South Africa would be at the negotiating table, taking up the proposals offered by Crocker eight years earlier. While UNITA would not be a participant, according to a senior foreign ministry spokesman, its 'presence' would be there because it had brought about 'the necessary climate for talks'.[30]

The media

The image of Savimbi as a 'freedom fighter', put forward by South African propagandists and conservative political organisations allied with the Reagan White House, could not have been publicly conveyed without the collaboration of the media. After the abortive US intervention in 1975, the war in Angola had been of little concern to most American journalists and their audiences. But once Savimbi had been recruited by the Reagan administration as an ally in the war against 'communism', the media began to cover the conflict in the Cold War context set by the US and South African governments. UNITA also played a part in this campaign to attract favourable media coverage of its side of the war, using the 'Free Angola Information Service' established by its supporters for this purpose. It also had the services of a public relations agency (Black, Manafort, Stone & Kelly), linked to the Reagan White House, which had unique access to the media to promote Savimbi's image as an anti-Communist guerrilla.

Through these contacts with the media, UNITA was able to attract a considerable number of journalists to visit Jamba. One of the early recruits was the *Washington Post*'s managing editor, Richard Harwood, who arrived at UNITA headquarters in the company of fellow journalist (and Savimbi supporter) Fred Bridgland. Although Harwood admitted (in a seven-part series on the front page of his newspaper) that he was neither an expert on Africa nor Savimbi, and had 'no definite knowledge about the rights and wrongs of the war', he was nevertheless convinced that UNITA was 'a strong and viable option to the Marxism in Luanda'. He was also convinced, on the basis of Savimbi's denials, that South Africa was not providing the rebels with weapons, training or joint military operations.[31] But Harwood's observations were not unusual among the American journalists visiting Jamba, since most of them also knew little about the war in Angola or Savimbi's role in it. This was evident from the similarity of their reports, based almost entirely on the information provided by UNITA, which they were unable or unwilling to confirm. A typical example was UNITA's claim to control one-third of the countryside. What 'control' meant, however, was never defined in a sparsely populated region (Portugal's 'end of the world') believed to contain less than five per cent of the total population. As a visiting South African journalist described it, 'any army that invaded that lush, strangely deserted bush wouldn't know what to do with it'.[32] Another frequent claim concerned UNITA's alleged military successes, such as capturing a village or a town, or killing an inflated number of MPLA, Cuban or Russian soldiers. In reality, however, much of the captured territory had been turned over to UNITA by the SADF, the Cubans were mostly in the north to defend the oil production, the Russian advisers operated well behind the battle lines, and the 'body count' largely consisted of Angolan civilians.

While the South African journalists who reported from Jamba were subjected to the same propaganda as their American counterparts, they also had to contend with legislation which stringently regulated what they could reveal about the Border War. In addition to the usual prohibition of reporting on troop movements, the Defence Act also banned the reporting of 'any statement, comment or rumour (concerning the SADF and its allies) calculated to prejudice or embarrass the government in its foreign relations or to alarm or depress members of the public'.[33] With these 'onerous press curbs' as Brian Pottinger of the *Sunday Times* complained, the official information on the war made available to journalists amounted to a pattern of 'subterfuge, elliptic statements by the SADF Public Relations' Directorate, and a barrage of counter-bombast whenever questions of destabilisation were raised'.[34] However, censorship was not always an issue so far as coverage of Savimbi and UNITA was concerned. According to one critic (and a sympathetic one at that), the media in South Africa – from the state-controlled SABC to the Afrikaner- and most of the English-language press – 'championed the cause of UNITA in Angola'.[35]

Such a commitment was not lost on the UNITA leader, who was so confident of the support of the South African press that he asked *Sunday Times* editor Tertius Myburgh, a self-confessed 'friend and admirer of Jonas Savimbi', to invite all the other editors to Jamba so that they could 'see for themselves'. As a result of Myburgh's initiative, some 20 of his colleagues from around the country opted for 'a fascinating time with Savimbi for a day and a half'.[36] While the visit was undoubtedly a propaganda triumph for Savimbi, who had most of South Africa's editors captive visitors at his headquarters in the bush to hear him speak and see his forces on the parade ground, it also provided plenty of ammunition for the critics. Savimbi may have been 'intelligent and articulate', as Anthony Heard of the *Cape Times* conceded, but he was 'pro-Western only for tactical reasons' and was 'fighting a dirty war with dirty means', including the downing of airliners, the taking of hostages and the denuding of the countryside of teak and ivory to finance his war.[37] Another editor, Harvey Tyson of *The Star*, also wary of what was presented to them at Jamba by 'a slick and exceedingly charming illusionist', expressed considerable doubt about the imagery of Savimbi's 'giant Robin Hood camp in the forest, fighting off the might of Cuba and Russia with little more than the big guns and tanks his guerrillas captured from a careless enemy' when it was generally known that the equipment had been captured by the SADF and handed over to UNITA.[38] But the most obvious of all the impressions was the sheer scale of South African involvement. According to Allister Sparks of the *Rand Daily Mail*, reporters visiting Jamba 'saw Pretoria's imprint everywhere, from industrial lathes in the vehicle workshop to drugs and surgical instruments in a well-equipped hospital to soft drinks, cigarettes and even South African wines'. And, of course, 'the oil to keep Savimbi's troops mobile'. However, he concluded, 'in the end the effort failed', as it had in 1975.[39]

Conclusion: Who won?

Although 'we did' was the stock reply from all of the contestants, the fact that they accepted peace negotiations with an enemy that had not yet surrendered indicated that this was a war without victors or vanquished. Nevertheless, the proclamation of victory did offer an exit strategy which enabled the external forces to cut their losses while maintaining their prestige. The SADF could claim to have avenged its humiliating defeat in 1975 by imposing its power in Namibia and Angola for more than a decade (although to no good, or even logical, purpose) and the Cubans, along with their Soviet allies, could claim that their heavy investment in securing the MPLA government in Luanda had been rewarded by the final retreat of the SADF from Angola. In effect (as Stephen Ellis has written), the South Africans had been 'out-fought and out-thought' in the final stage of the war, but not wanting to admit failure, they claimed it publicly as a victory.[40]

As for South Africa's UNITA allies, they too claimed victory in retreat, despite sustaining thousands of casualties (many of them run over by fleeing SADF tanks) because Savimbi had survived annihilation to fight another day. While the MPLA could also claim victory, in halting the assault on Cuito Cuanavale and in seeing off the SADF occupation of Angolan territory, victory would not bring peace to the country so long as Savimbi was determined to continue his quest for power, as he was for another 14 years and at the cost of another half-a-million lives. The US also proclaimed victory, for helping to create a stalemate by arming UNITA, thereby ensuring that all of the contestants would accept peace negotiations as the only alternative to continuing an unwinnable war. Or, as their SADF allies had put it, their war had made peace possible,[41] although not for the people of Angola.

Notes to Chapter Eleven

1   For Kissinger's version, see his *Years of Renewal* (London: Weidenfeld and Nicolson, 1999), chapters 26, 29.

2   W. Steenkamp, *South Africa's Border War 1966–1989* (Gibraltar: Ashanti, 1989), 254.

3   See J. Breytenbach, *Eden's Exile* (Cape Town: Queillerie, 1997).

4   See E. Windrich, 'The Laboratory of Hate: The Role of Clandestine Radio in the Angolan War', *International Journal of Cultural Studies* 3, 2 (2000):206–18.

5   See Windrich, 'South Africa's Propaganda War', *Africa Today* 36, 1 (1989):51–60.

6   *South Africa Foundation News*, February 1976.

7   *South Africa Foundation Review*, January 1983.

8   'Savimbi Goes to Hollywood', *Africa Report*, March–April 1988, 5–6. Abramoff was later indicted on charges of fraud and conspiracy for bribing US Congressmen in exchange for favours for his clients.

9   'Savimbi Asks for Help', *Newsweek*, 12 November 1979, 68.

10 F. Bridgland, *Jonas Savimbi: Key to Africa* (Edinburgh: Mainstream Publishing, 1986), 342.

11 C. Crocker, *High Noon in southern Africa* (New York: W.W. Norton, 1992), 64.

12 Ibid. 174–5.

13 Ibid. 170.

14 Ibid. 462–3.

15 B. Pottinger, *The Imperial Presidency: P.W. Botha the First Ten Years* (Johannesburg: Southern Book Publishers, 1988), 220.

16 Editorial, *The Citizen*, 25 September 1985.

17 F. Bridgland, *The War for Africa: Twelve Months That Transformed a Continent* (Gibraltar: Ashanti, 1990), 372.

18 Crocker, *High Noon in southern Africa*, 229.

19 Ibid. 174.

20 Ibid. 120.

21 SAPA, Foreign Broadcasting Information Service (FBIS), MEA, *Daily Report*, 23 September 1985, U5.

22 A. Cowell, 'Rebel Chief Says Angola Is Pressing Largest Attack in the 10-Year War', *New York Times*, 22 September 1985.

23 Bridgland, *Jonas Savimbi*, 445.

24 SAPA, FBIS, *Daily Report*, 12 November 1987.

25 M. Parks, 'Angolan Rebels Claim Biggest Victory Yet', *Los Angeles Times*, 13 November 1987.

26 *The Star* (Johannesburg), 16 March 1988.

27 FBIS, *Daily Report*, AFR-88-049, 14 March 1988.

28 FBIS, *Daily Report*, AFR-88-038, 26 February 1988.

29 Press statement, quoted in Pottinger, *The Imperial Presidency*, 388.

30 G. Babb, BBC *Summary of World Broadcasts*, MEA/0142, 2 May 1988.

31 'Angola: A Distant War', *Washington Post*, 19–25 July 1981.

32 H. Tyson, *Editors Under Fire* (Sandton: Random House, 1993), 180.

33 Quoted in Tyson, *Editors Under Fire*, 177.

34 Pottinger, *The Imperial Presidency*, 217.

35 D. Geldenhuys, *The Diplomacy of Isolation: South African Foreign Policy Making* (New York: St. Martin's Press, 1984), 185.

36 Quoted in J. Mervis, *The Fourth Estate* (Johannesburg: Jonathan Ball, 1989), 485–6.

37 A. Heard, *Cape of Storms* (Fayetteville: University of Arkansas Press, 1990), 158–9.

38 Tyson, *Editors Under Fire*, 179–81.

39 A. Sparks, *The Mind of South Africa* (New York: Knopf, 1990), 313.

40 S. Ellis, *Comrades Against Apartheid* (London: James Currey, 1992), 186–7.

41 J. Geldenhuys, *A General's Story: From an Era of War and Peace* (Johannesburg: Jonathan Ball, 1995), 228.

Chapter 12

Countdown to Cuito Cuanavale: Cuba's Angolan Campaign

Edgar J. Dosman[1]

As researchers access previously sealed documents, certain of the many unresolved questions regarding Cuba's remarkable role in Africa – dramatic in Angola and the 1987–88 South West African regional crisis – are being addressed with authority. Piero Gleijeses' recent work, for example, has set aside for good the notion that Cuba was Moscow's proxy in Africa.[2] Similarly, there are now few major unresolved controversies regarding the political and military aspects of Cuba's *Operation Carlota* from its planning stage to the withdrawal of the South African Defence Force (SADF) from Angola in March 1976. Researching the 1980s, of course, presents greater difficulties as archival gaps multiply, but some themes are being clarified. While Chester Crocker's (the then Assistant Secretary of State for Africa) memoir of regional negotiations under Ronald Reagan's two administrations, *High Noon in southern Africa: Making Peace in a Rough Neighborhood*, remains unchallenged, even he grudgingly acknowledges Cuba's success in halting the SADF advance at Cuito Cuanavale, and thereby facilitating the eventual peace accords in New York.[3] Cuban strategy during the crucial 1987–88 confrontation requires extensive research, however, beyond the available publications on Cuito Cuanavale or the official and detailed accounts from Havana. Thus the present chapter will attempt to contribute to this literature by utilising hitherto unavailable archival materials, particularly from the UN Contact Group and Central Committee records in Havana, to dissect its evolution, operationalisation and impact.[4] The discussion will close by addressing the blend of principle versus pragmatism underlying Fidel Castro's decision-making at this stage of Cuba's long and torturous Angolan campaign.

Cuba's dilemma after Angola's defeat on the Lomba

By mid-1987 Angolan President José Eduardo dos Santos faced his most important decision since taking office nearly a decade earlier.[5] Encouraged by the Soviet Military Mission, he approved *Salute to October*, a new Popular Armed Forces for the Liberation of Africa (FAPLA) offensive to begin 13 July 1987, the day Crocker arrived in Luanda to resume negotiations on the future of southern Africa. Angola hoped to strengthen its position at the negotiating table using a combined 'fight and negotiate' strategy. After 1983, as the southern African war gathered intensity and technological sophistication, the Soviets were able to impose their concepts, based on large-scale armoured offensives to engage and destroy enemy forces. *Second Congress*, a previous offensive in 1985 (on which *Salute to October* was modelled) had utterly failed; both *Second Congress* and *Salute to October* were vigorously opposed by Cuba, which refused to participate.[6] But convinced that new mobile air-defence units would neutralise South African air power, Dos Santos approved a campaign which risked the best units of FAPLA and placed the survival of the Popular Movement for the Liberation of Angola (MPLA) itself in question. Why take such a risk? Because Angola was desperate, and the potential gains of victory in *Salute to October* were as incalculable as the risks of defeat. In this operation FAPLA would strike out from Cuito Cuanavale, cross the Lomba River and capture the Union for the Total Independence of Angola (UNITA) strongholds of Mavinga and Jamba, throwing Savimbi and the UNITA forces back into Namibia while restoring government control over national boundaries. While Savimbi would lose credibility after this military blow, the MPLA could henceforth deal with South Africa and the Americans from a position of strength. Aware of its high risks in alienating Cuba, however, Dos Santos agreed to visit Castro in Havana on 31 July to brief him personally on his meetings with Crocker and the progress of *Salute to October*.

Since *Operation Carlota* a decade earlier, Cuban dreams – of a potentially-rich socialist ally in south-western Africa, of a victory which would ignite an irresistible momentum for Namibian independence led by Sam Nujoma's South West Africa People's Organization (SWAPO), and a Third World triumph shaking the foundations of apartheid itself in Pretoria – lay in wreckage. The MPLA's victory in 1976 had been followed by increasingly serious challenges, including border clashes with Zaire, a deep and savage assault by a revitalised SADF at Cassinga, and the renewal of civil war led by Savimbi and UNITA, supported by South Africa and its allies.[7] When in difficulty, Angola turned to Cuba and Cuba agreed to help. Documents from the period demonstrate beyond all doubt that Agostinho Neto, before his death in 1979, appealed to Castro who agreed to shelve their agreement on a phased withdrawal of Cuban troops from Angola given serious deficiencies in FAPLA.[8] By retaining the Cuban Mission in Angola (MMCA), Cuba became permanently enmeshed in southern Africa and Castro accepted a fateful risk for his beloved army, the Revolutionary Armed Forces of Cuba (FAR).

Shortly thereafter the election of Ronald Reagan as US President and the continuing deterioration of the security situation in Angola transformed danger into imminent threat. Apartheid South Africa, welcomed into the US fold as a bulwark of Western values against Black African 'terrorism' and its Cuban defenders, could occupy southern Angola in a large-scale invasion in 1981 behind Washington's diplomatic cover and consolidate its control in Namibia. Both South Africa and the US supported UNITA's campaign to replace the MPLA. Now seriously trapped in Angola, Cuba reinforced its Military Mission in 1981 and again in 1983 to prevent an MPLA collapse, reorganising it into the ATN and ATS (northern and southern force groups) with a combined troop strength of 40 000. The ATN guarded Cabinda and the capital and their linkages with ports and interior cities; the ATS formed a 600 km defensive perimeter 250 km north of Namibia extending from Namibe on the coast to Menongue on the east against deeper SADF penetration. Scattered in garrisons throughout a country twice the size of France, the Cuban forces were so purely defensive that the SADF never bothered to install air defence systems at the Angolan–Namibian border. The ATS in the South and ATN in the North defended major urban areas and bridges and guided convoys through the mined transportation corridors; their doctors and nurses provided an acceptable national health service; Cuban soldiers guarded US oil installations in northern Angola to safeguard export-earnings for the national economy. But they were defensive forces, without the equipment to counter-attack, essentially hostage to South Africa which controlled both the military tempo of the war from its bases in Namibia, and the pace of regional negotiations since Washington adopted 'constructive engagement' linking SADF withdrawal from Namibia with Cuban withdrawal from Angola.

The July meeting encapsulated all the dreams and frustrations of Cuban–Angolan relations. President José Eduardo dos Santos and the MPLA were moving toward the West. Angola had negotiated the Lusaka Accords in 1984 without consulting Cuba; now, in mid-1987 it was renewing US mediation (despite the ultimate insult of Reagan having initiated direct military support for UNITA), inviting Crocker to Luanda against the backdrop of *Operation Salute to October*. Castro was livid; he suspected that, in spite of Cuba's tremendous contribution to the continued survival of the MPLA government, it was about to be sidelined diplomatically. The cost of Cuba's military and social support for Angola since 1975 had been enormous; the minimally acceptable condition for full withdrawal was an agreement freely negotiated with Havana as a full partner in which South African forces would withdraw from Angola and Namibia within the full implementation of United Nations Security Resolution (UNSCR) 435. Anything else would be humiliation and surrender – impossible for Cuba to consider.

Meanwhile Dos Santos was expansive and confident: his 'fight and negotiate' strategy seemed to be going well. *Salute to October* was advancing with minimal opposition; international anti-apartheid opinion was strong, and the upcoming talks with the US looked promising. For his part, Castro was adamant that Cuba not be frozen out of the discussions with Crocker. Dos Santos responded ambiguously, then eventually made a commitment in their final meeting: the two governments reaffirmed an earlier Angolan–Cuban undertaking from Neto's time that bilateral US–Angolan talks would take place on 'strictly bilateral questions' such as US aid to UNITA; on all other issues which in any way affected Cuban troops in Angola, Cuba had the right of direct participation. Castro appeared to have received the commitment he demanded, and the meeting ended cordially.

Still nervous, however, he sent Jorge Risquet, his chief African advisor, to Luanda in early September 1987, prior to the resumption of US–Angolan negotiations on 8–9 September. Risquet was alarmed. In a note to President Castro on 4 September, he expressed his fear that Angola would not live up to his commitment to Castro on including Cuba in discussions with the US, and urged the strongest possible message to the Angolans. Days later the Angolan–US negotiations confirmed Cuban fears: Crocker insisted that the meeting not include the Cubans, and the Angolans caved in without much protest and in bad faith. Risquet was left in the corridor while Crocker and the Angolan team debated the future of the Cuban Military Mission behind closed doors – even though the Cuban delegation was connected to the discussions *on-line*.[9] Castro prepared a formal diplomatic note to Dos Santos, which Risquet read to him on 12 September. In it Castro began by saying that 'you are sovereign and can decide when our troops are no longer necessary', but reminded him as well that:

> Cuba is also a sovereign country and is free to decide its own schedule for the fastest possible, total and definitive withdrawal of its troops to prevent humiliating deals behind our back with the blood of our youth . . . More than a thousand of our best sons have been killed; hundreds of thousands of Cuban soldiers have preserved your security . . . Cuba, for itself and also for all the socialist and progressive forces of the world, will never be excluded from making its own history for a third time. First, the Cuban liberation army of Mambi Vencedor was excluded from the Paris Accords of 1900 after the defeat of Spain – the US took over Cuba directly from the Spanish army. Second, during the 1962 Cuban missile crisis, the US talked only to the owner of the missiles, not the owner of the territory of Cuba. Now, at the crucial moment of the war for Angola and Namibia, it appears that the US wants to negotiate with the owner of the territory of Angola – yourself, José Eduardo – but not the owner of the missiles – namely us. We shall not let history repeat itself a third time.[10]

Dos Santos sat through all this in silence. *Salute to October* continued to unfold successfully. But South Africa's *Operation Modular* was unleashed two days later on 14 September; instead of victory, the Angolan army suffered a humiliating defeat at the Lomba River at the hands of the SADF and its ally UNITA. The accounts of this battle are sufficiently complete, with only the main points requiring repetition: the failure of the Soviet SAM-8s to counter South African airpower; SADF penetration of FAPLA intelligence; the wiping out of FAPLA's best-equipped and best-trained units, notably the 47 Brigade and GT 2 Task Force among other units; and the consequent retreat of the remaining mauled FAPLA units with their 63 Soviet advisers back to Cuito Cuanavale – itself encircled and its airport closed by SADF G-5 and G-6 artillery.[11]

Pretoria was now openly leading the war in Angola rather than merely supporting UNITA. SADF units were deep inside the country and General Malan visited his troops there to demonstrate that they intended to stay. In fact, the SADF drew up military plans for two new Operations, *Hooper* and *Packer*, to build on *Modular's* success, with the purpose of moving on Cuito Cuanavale and destroying the FAPLA brigades which had escaped the Lomba, and then moving north to threaten the main garrison of Menongue. To the west the SADF gained approval for four 1988 operations: *Hilti I* and *II*; *Excite*; *Fulton*, and *Florentum*, with the overall objective of replicating the results on the Lomba River by rolling up FAPLA forces in the strategic Cunene province.[12] Militarily these four SADF operations would complete the eviction of FAPLA from the south, but they also fit into a broader military and political strategy against Angola and Namibia. Pretoria viewed a change in regime in Angola, with UNITA replacing the MPLA, as a vital safeguard for its interests in southern Africa.

Success required breaking Angola's defence structure and isolating Luanda from the garrisons in the Central Highlands and 3 Military District in eastern Angola. After success on the Lomba, therefore, South Africa and UNITA were in a position to achieve this objective – which had only been narrowly averted in 1983.[13] At Cuito Cuanavale FAPLA's remaining heavy units were isolated by road and air from the re-supply bases at Menongue, while UNITA had sufficient manpower and supplies to take Munhango and the provincial capital of Luena, cutting Angola in half. In short Menongue itself and the entire Namibe–Lubango–Menongue Line were threatened by the loss of Cuito Cuanavale and the Central Highlands.

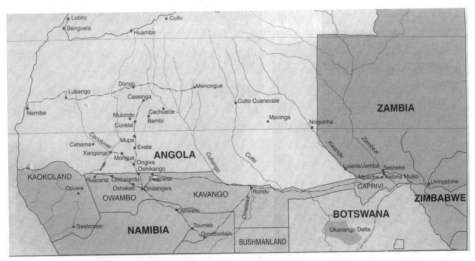

Figure 20: Map of Angola and Northern Namibia

The future of Namibia was also at stake, as a harassed Dos Santos confided to Castro. P. W. Botha wrote to Dos Santos on 5 November suggesting a deal in direct talks between the two countries, cutting out both the US and Cuba in what he termed an 'African solution': the MPLA accepting the Pretoria-guided Transitional Government in Windhoek as a 'Namibian entity' gradually evolving toward statehood within a version of UNSCR 435. Dos Santos also received another message, this time from the Transitional Government itself, repeating Botha's proposal and asking his help in designing a new independence strategy for Namibia which excluded 'terrorists' such as Nujoma. 'Democratic' SWAPO and other acceptable political forces in Namibia should be invited for talks, along with the MPLA and Pretoria; suitable recognition for this 'made-in-Africa' solution should be obtained from neighbouring governments; and a bilateral agreement should be signed between Angola and the Transitional Government on the future of the Calueque–Ruacana hydroelectric and irrigation complex on the border. The South West African Territorial Force (SWATF), however, would remain its army.[14] Reduced to a client state, and without the Cubans ('the bottom line'), and if it behaved, Angola could expect a benevolent future from South Africa. In such a new regional system the SWATF, *Koevoet* and the Ethnic Battalions (particularly 31 and 32) would provide a complete security guarantee against the People's Liberation Army of Namibia (PLAN) 'terrorists'. Therefore some sort of Pretoria-guided independence for Namibia, perhaps even a suitably-modified UNSCR 435, might be foreseen, as long as South African interests were satisfied and intolerable UN demands (such as the return of the Walvis Bay enclave) shelved.

Not just Havana, but also the Contact Group countries understood the reasons for renewed South African confidence: the military victory on the Lomba had created a favourable climate for its goals in the border war. On 26 October 1987 a Contact Group Secret Foreign Intelligence Report concluded that the South African attack 'had reaffirmed its position as a key player'. Titled *Angola: Coming to a Head*, it predicted that 'Angola could shortly become the focus of substantial international attention' following the South African–UNITA victory: Angola and the West are moving toward an accommodation,' it concluded, foreseeing a desperate Dos Santos with no option but to come to terms with the new realities. R. G. Evans, senior advisor to South African Foreign Minister 'Pik' Botha, spelled out four days later that these 'strengthened peace overtures' implied 'the need to get rid of the Cubans'. He was hopeful. 'Even before the recent offensive there were signs that the doves were gaining strength within the Luanda regime,' he noted, 'and the devastating defeat could not but strengthen these influences.'[15] As Pretoria's swagger toward its weak neighbours returned with decisive victory in southern Angola, the war-weary Frontline States looked more and more like its pliant buffer states, pressuring Angola to try to resolve the southern Africa crisis with Pretoria under US mediation. Mozambique had been reduced to a wasteland. Zimbabwe was under attack; threatened by internal conflict and economic pressure from Pretoria, Kenneth Kaunda had lost control of western Zambia to the SADF and UNITA and was sufficiently traumatised by the South African victory in Angola to postpone a meeting of the Frontline States for fear of retaliation. International pressure against South African apartheid decreased visibly in late 1987, according to Western diplomatic sources. US Ambassador Niles reported in Ottawa that 'South African restrictions on foreign media coverage in that country had been effective in lowering the profile of South Africa as an issue for public political debate in the USA, and that Congressional debate on this issue reflected this impact, with the result that prospects for new legislative sanctions remained far from certain'.[16]

The truth was that no Western government in 1987 could imagine an early alternative to P. W. Botha and his apartheid regime, given the position of South Africa after Angola's defeat: there was no countervailing military force to dislodge it from Angola, much less Namibia. According to Margaret Thatcher, the idea that Nelson Mandela could become President of South Africa was 'dreaming in cuckoo-land'. Germany and Japan were firmly opposed to economic sanctions against South Africa. As these larger powers wavered, so the smaller began to hedge their bets. The Canadian government, which in 1985–86 had taken a lead role in sanctions against South Africa, retreated from its position. Apartheid was not raised as an issue at the 1987 annual meeting of the G-7 nations. Increasingly, it seemed, the black uprising of 1986 was coming under Pretoria's control. Nujoma's SWAPO entered a wave of internal repression and dissension as South African intelligence penetrated the movement. Above all super-power relations were realigning, giving South Africa greater flexibility – if not necessarily affection. Reagan praised the 'heroes on the Lomba'; Crocker reassured South Africa that US support for an UNSCR 602 on 25 November demanding that it withdraw its forces from Angola did not involve a call for sanctions or assistance to Angola; and US Secretary of State George Schultz openly pondered a new approach in which UNSCR 435, until now accepted as the inviolable basis for a settlement, might have to be adjusted to new circumstances: 'We should not take as given now operational plans made a decade ago,' he noted.[17] As for Gorbachev, despite the embarrassment of its advisers trapped in Cuito Cuanavale and another 70 in Luena threatened by a UNITA attack, the progress of bilateral talks with the US ruled out a Soviet rescue operation for Dos Santos. In short, P. W. Botha had regained the initiative in the border war. On 11 November, Angola's Independence Day, Botha sent another message to the Angola leader by flying into Jamba for victory celebrations with Savimbi. It was an ostentatious display of South African power. Although unloved, Pretoria had outsmarted and outfought its antagonists: it was – like it or not – the essential power in Africa, strong enough to confront international opinion with a *fait accompli*: to exploit the extraordinary victory on the Lomba and force a regional settlement with Angola on its terms.

It was a grim ending to a military catastrophe; on 25 October, when the Angolan head of state officially terminated *Salute to October*, the entire southern African military picture had changed. Dos Santos' 'fight and talk' strategy had utterly failed and his Soviet advisors were discredited. The defeat of *Salute to October*, the crisis of morale in Luanda, and the evident South African triumphalism jeopardised the future of Angola. The loss of FAPLA's remaining heavy brigades, now surrounded in Cuito Cuanavale, would complete the disaster. There was nowhere else to turn but to Castro: just as Neto had successfully appealed for help in November 1975, Dos Santos had twice – in 1981 and again in 1983 – requested urgent military help from Havana. Despite Lusaka and the recent tension, he now went back to Castro for more, knowing that, in this extraordinary relationship, Cuba always came through in the end.

Cuba's global strategy

Cuban military leaders had anticipated the disaster of *Salute to October* from the beginning and realised that a military reverse of this magnitude endangered the entire Angolan–Cuban defence structure throughout the country.[18] President Dos Santos' appeals for assistance to Cuba began with the 2 October collapse of FAPLA 47 Brigade and GT2. Cuban pilots were needed immediately to cover the battered FAPLA brigades retreating from Mavinga to Cuito Cuanavale and to keep South African forces and artillery off balance as far as possible with bombing missions. Castro put all available warplanes in Angola to this purpose and on 27 October two Cuban pilots were shot down and captured by UNITA, taken to Jamba as prize exhibits and put on display. Cuban patrols also began operating south of the Namibe–Lubango–Menongue Line in support of FAPLA with hit-and- run attacks on enemy forces, but they were not adequate to stem the mounting panic in the Angolan forces. But with the ever-grimmer military reports in October and early November, a major decision on shoring up FAPLA could no longer be avoided. On 14 November, after P. W. Botha confronted world public opinion by appearing in Jamba, Castro decided to reinforce the MMCA with a tank brigade, an infantry Tactical Group and Cuba's only regiment of SAM-8s. But this was only a stop-gap measure. Havana had to prepare for the worst: the situation in Angola was likely to deteriorate further in the next two months, perhaps spiral out of control altogether. The problem was not just Cuito Cuanavale. FAPLA's *Operation Salute to October* had required stripping troops, spare parts and supplies from around the country for the advance on Mavinga, and neglecting other garrisons as the FAPLA General Staff concentrated its attention on the south. By November many FAPLA garrisons had not received food, munitions, supplies, recruits or visits of inspection for months, and those that remained were scattered and vulnerable, from Cuito Cuanavale to Cabinda in the far north. Many were shadow units at only 30–50% strength.[19]

The following day, 15 November, Castro summoned his inner circle of advisors including Raul Castro, Jorge Risquet, Army Chief of the General Staff Ulises Rosales del Toro, and other senior military chiefs as required to consider the implications of South Africa's victory at the Lomba and develop a coordinated military–diplomatic strategy for Angola and southern Africa. The meeting lasted through the night. Cuban military had not been able to penetrate SADF intelligence, despite training ten officers in Afrikaans, but the last 12 years of war had yielded valuable lessons in dealing with South African intentions after *Operation Modular*.[20] In 1976, in the aftermath of the victory of *Operation Carlota*, Pretoria had rebuilt the South African Defence Force, UNITA had been re-supplied and the war resumed, leading to Cassinga and the following ten years of destabilisation. Castro was determined not to let this happen again. *Operation Carlota* had revealed the apartheid regime's inability to absorb white casualties: as soon as the military tide had turned in 1976, the SADF was recalled across the Namibian border, and the SADF had never challenged major Cuban garrisons on the Namibe–Lubango– Menongue Line. But its bombing of Cangamba in 1983 signalled its support of UNITA's attempt to seize control of the Central Highlands. Finally, in terms of negotiation outcomes, 1976 offered an important political lesson: the SADF military had ignited an upsurge of ANC resistance within South Africa and a wave of international support. Now in 1987 a similar defeat would have an even greater impact considering the weak foundations of the Botha regime gambling for victory in the border war.

By the morning of 16 November Castro had decided to risk everything for a global solution, not just rescuing the FAPLA forces at Cuito Cuanavale and resisting UNITA's assaults in the Central Highlands and Eastern Angola, but also transforming the military situation on the ground in Angola and creating the conditions for a negotiated settlement anchored in the independence of Namibia and the end of aggression against Angola. The package of military objectives began with the defence of Cuito Cuanavale as a first priority to strengthen the morale and resistance of Angola, followed by the strategic denial of western Angola to the SADF by expelling it from Angolan territory in the west, and finally achieving sufficient air dominance and land power to pose a credible threat to South African forces and installations in northern Namibia. If Dos Santos' all-out gamble with *Salute to October* had failed, *Operation XXXI Anniversary* was an even more audacious bid to reverse the military momentum and achieve an honourable exit through a deliberate and bold confrontation with South Africa itself. It was a decision which changed the war. In launching *Operation XXXI Anniversary*, the Cuban leader committed a whole new army to Angola supported by his best pilots, latest war planes, armoured columns and air defence – even at the risk of denuding Cuba's home arsenal. In practice it meant taking over war strategy from FAPLA and its Soviet advisors.

The plan envisaged two coordinated fronts: a defensive plan for Cuito Cuanavale would repel further SADF and UNITA assaults, tying down these enemy units and safeguarding the Namibe–Lubango–Menongue Line, while strengthening as far as possible the main garrisons of the Central Highlands. Meanwhile *Operation XXXI Anniversary* would sweep down to the Namibian border in a massive offensive which would replicate *Operation Carlota* by pushing the SADF out of Angola, and maintaining pressure on the SADF and South Africa economic assets in Namibia. *Operation XXXI Anniversary* would therefore confront Pretoria with a choice: either accept negotiations and the independence of Namibia based on a strict interpretation of UNSCR 435, or face a bloody and uncertain war on equal terms.

Operation XXXI Anniversary would give Cuban forces air superiority over Angola, denying its air space to the once dominant South African Air Force. Apart from the tightest mobile air-defence system in African history, the Cuban offensive also included a new airport at Cahama for MIG-23s as well as upgrading the Xangongo facility close to the Namibian border. Bolstered against SADF counterattacks, they would provide a capability for deep air strikes into Namibia. If Pretoria chose to fight, its bases in Namibia would be open to attack, and to demonstrate escalation dominance at the border the Cuban leadership was prepared to bomb the Ruacana–Cunene hydroelectric and irrigation complex should South Africa or other powers doubt its resolve or credibility. Should this signalling fail, however, Cuba prepared *Operation Orange* to make good its threat of taking the war to the SADF in Namibia for another round of persuasion. However, a negotiated settlement was overwhelmingly the goal of Cuba's 16 November global strategy: if South Africa accepted UNSCR 435 as drafted in 1978 and the other conditions, it would agree to a flexible timetable for the full withdrawal of the MMCA from Angola.

Between 16 and 21 November Defence Minister Raul Castro and the Cuban General Staff developed the operational plans for the sea- and air-lift of Cuban forces to Angola, mobilising troops and equipment for 17 ships. In the first stage, a ship was loaded every night to escape US air surveillance, and 28 flights were made carrying troops and specialised equipment. Each ship was fitted with anti-submarine missiles in the event of South African attack; two were fitted with ASW grenade launchers. Angolan ports were given additional air defence as the ships arrived between 11 and 20 December. The second stage of the operation began on 17 December, expanding the Cuban contingent with three more Tactical Groups, a squadron of MIG-23s, four AN-26 transports, two more Pechora air defence regiments, two tank battalions, and radar equipment. Along with the 9 sailings, 26 additional flights were devoted to *Operation XXXI Anniversary* in this phase; the last ship would arrive in Angola on 25 August 1988, bringing the MMCA to a total strength of approximately 54 000. Top of the line equipment included 340 T-62 tanks and armoured cars, 433 IGLA shoulder-held AA missiles, 340 heavy artillery and AA canon, 790 trucks, a squadron of MIG-23 and 4 Antonov-26 transports, 15 661 tons of munitions and spare parts apart from communication and radar equipment.

For Cuba the stakes of mounting *Operation XXXI Anniversary* were enormous: it had to succeed because it was the only way out of the Angolan impasse. Besides the dangers of military setbacks – and Western analysts were unanimous in predicting the fall of Cuito Cuanavale – Havana confronted the immediate problem of dealing with the US and Moscow. Determined to underline the actual record of decision-making, the Cuban leadership has released key documents on Soviet–Cuban relations since 1976, and in particular on the 1987–88 years.[21]

An 'inform but not consult' strategy toward both superpowers was followed by Cuba after its 16 November decision. This involved a delay of eight days in informing Moscow until the first batch of nine ships for phase one were at sea and Gorbachev confronted a *fait accompli*, and then riding out Soviet warnings and criticisms until the success of Cuban arms in Angola gradually changed the mood in Moscow and arms shipments for some, but not all, Cuban requests, resumed. While Gleijeses compares this Cuban–Soviet action–reaction in 1987–88 to *Operation Carlota* in 1976, it also parallels the crisis of 1983, where Cuba in effect shamed the Soviet High Command into a major re-supply operation in Angola. But more archival material is required from Soviet sources to complete this analysis.

Few relationships were as complex as the Cuban–Soviet dynamic, always laced with complexity and multiple channels with an undertow of resentment and betrayal as well as closeness and solidarity. By late 1987 the Soviet leadership was evolving rapidly; the internal struggle over southern African regional policy was probably more complex than so far indicated. Yuri Pavlov, a Shevardnadze recruit in the Latin American Division of the Soviet Foreign Ministry who opposed the special Cuban–Soviet link, was aghast when informed of the Cuban arms build-up. The last thing he wanted was an independent Cuban initiative in a regional conflict which might undermine the imminent Soviet withdrawal from Afghanistan as well as forthcoming bilateral talks between Gorbachev and Reagan to finalise an Inter-mediate Range Nuclear Force (INF) treaty. While it seems clear that Cuba, not the Soviet Union, had the lead role in war and peace in this theatre during 1987–88 to the New York Accords, Castro was under no illusion regarding the sea-change occurring in Moscow. On 14 January, for example, he noted 'the terrible pressure from the Soviet Union on the other side of the world', and earlier, on 7 December, when the superpower INF treaty was announced and coincidentally Risquet provided the details of *Operation XXXI Anniversary* to Soviet Party Secretary Yegor Ligachev at the 1987 Congress of the French Communist Party.[22]

The more serious danger of exposure came from the US, but an adequate clarification of their responses will have to await the declassification of Defence, CIA and other documents. Havana was preoccupied with the threat posed by South African missile ships against which the approaching vessels carrying Cuban men and arms were vulnerable; Washington, it was feared, would pass on any intelligence to South Africa.[23] The operation coincided with scheduled military manoeuvres throughout the island, which provided some cover, particularly in the areas near ports where radio codes were controlled to conceal the operation. It appears, however, that *Operation XXXI Anniversary* unloaded a formidable strike force in Angola before Washington understood its scope and significance. The best hypothesis is that CIA and Defence Intelligence analytic capacity during the Reagan period had been sufficiently damaged by its ideological mindset of dismissing Cuba as a 'terrorist state' to rule out Castro's audacity of shipping a new conventional army to Africa.

The defence of Cuito Cuanavale

Cuito Cuanavale had to be held at all costs, and the condition of the FAPLA defenders was much worse than their actual numbers in uniform would suggest. Apart from a morale problem which involved the risk of breaking and running under fire, they had lost much of their equipment, with only 13 tanks scattered among the three brigades, and some of these out of service with motor problems and split cables. Over 30% of FAPLA's weapons were useless without repair facilities and FAPLA lacked skilled personnel to repair its damaged artillery. Infantry were down to their last clips of ammunition and lacked medical supplies. The defence of Cuito Cuanavale required munitions and supplies in large quantity, but in contrast with the SADF, which could simply truck supplies up from Mavinga, where its C-130s were landing around the clock, Cuito was cut off from its main garrison town of Menongue by SADF–UNITA guerrillas, as well as by air after South African artillery closed the Cuito airport. Re-supplying the eight brigades trapped in Cuito required regaining control of the Menongue–Cuito road.

SADF strategy aimed to exploit the overall weakness of FAPLA after its defeat on the Lomba by coordinating operations with UNITA. Not only the south, but also the core areas of the east, and Munhango and Cuemba in the Central Highlands, were threatened. While the SADF maintained pressure on FAPLA at Cuito Cuanavale and the south, and drew Angolan reinforcements to the southern front, UNITA would move northwards into the thinly defended and vulnerable east, central and north regions to score the breakthrough that had eluded it since 1983. Together they would multiply attacks on these targets, drawing FAPLA into battles on its terms, and cutting them up until UNITA controlled the Central Highlands and eastern Angola with the SADF dominating the south after the defeat of Cuito Cuanavale. The Angolan government would then govern little more than Luanda, and would have to sue for peace from a position of weakness. For their part the Cuban garrisons on the Namibe–Lubango–Menongue line would be exposed to assault from both north and south.

In the last week of December, the strategic town of Munhango on the Benguela Railway, and Savimbi's hometown, fell to UNITA forces using heavy equipment captured from FAPLA at the Lomba. Following on this victory, UNITA destroyed the bridge over the Kwanza River and moved on FAPLA forces at Cuemba with up to 14 battalions being drawn up from its southern bases for this key battle. If successful at Cuemba, UNITA would take complete control of a north–south corridor to the Lunda diamond areas and their US-supplied bases in Zaire, needing only the destruction of the main bridges on the Malanje–Saurimo–Luena road to isolate the entire eastern region. It was Dos Santos' bleakest New Year's Day. On 2 January 1988, he sent a personal letter to Castro requesting more military aid to stem the UNITA offensive, asking him to release special forces, artillerymen and specialists from Cuito Cuanavale to stem the military crisis of the Central Highlands. The MMCA should 'discard its role as a deterrent force, converting it from now on to one of intervention, above all in areas where the SADF is operating', to prevent the isolation of Luanda from the rest of the country, ensure the safety of Luena, and preserve MPLA control over eastern Angola.[24]

Castro refused to dilute scarce military resources, replying that they must concentrate defence forces at key points rather than disperse them around isolated outposts. The loss of the latter could later be corrected without lasting damage, but the loss of Cuito Cuanavale, facing imminent SADF attack, would be fatal for FAPLA and Cuba's global strategy. The SADF had to fail against allied defences at Cuito – to 'break its teeth' in Castro's metaphor, so that the *Operation* could be unleashed towards the Namibian border for the 'knock-out blow' in the western war theatre.[25] It was, in short, the strategic pivot of the campaign. In fact *Operation XXXI Anniversary* was moving ahead well: the deployment of the Second Army across the Atlantic had been remarkably successful and the Tactical Groups for the offensive were being formed up in their bases protected from South African bombers by SAM-8s. But all this would be wasted, and Cuba would be a global laughing-stock, if the SADF broke through at Cuito Cuanavale.

The defence of Cuito Cuanavale was inherently complex because the town and airstrip were situated on the west bank of the Cuito River, which required a defence perimeter on the eastern bank to prevent its control by enemy fire. Cuba's two top generals, Leopoldo Cintra Fria ('Polo') head of the newly-formed southern Lubango Command, and Arnaldo Ochoa who headed the Cuban Military Mission in Luanda, had arrived in Cuito on 9 December with an advance team of 166 men. There was only one bridge across the river, and it could not handle heavy vehicles or tanks. On the eastern bank FAPLA 21, 25 and 59 BIM were spread out in defensive positions up to 20 km from the Cuito River to guard the town against an attack from Mavinga. To the west of the river FAPLA had positioned 13 BDA and 66 and 36 BIL, along with an artillery group and 12 tanks; as on the eastern bank, these forces were spread out over a large area, and vulnerable to a concentrated attack. The result was that the SADF and UNITA had the choice of battlefield, with FAPLA 21, 25 and 59 BIM across the river as the logical first target since their defeat would break the defences of Cuito Cuanavale.

The SADF assault began at 07:00 on 13 January, with heavy shelling of the bridge and the three FAPLA brigades on the eastern side of the river, and a successful South African bombing mission against the 21 FAPLA command post 19 km from Cuito. These attacks were repeated at 11:00 and 12:00 against 21 BIR and 59 BIM, supported by SADF ground attacks led by tanks and armoured cars supported by mortar and artillery fire. By 15:00 the SADF had penetrated FAPLA's defences between the 21 and 59 brigades, sending the entire 21 BIR into flight toward a defensive line 5 km from the bridge: the brigade simply stopped fighting and ran. The FAPLA defenders counterattacked with 11 tanks unsupported by infantry in a disastrous failure: seven were lost with all their crews. Clouds and rain prevented effective Cuban or Angolan air support from Menongue. In the confusion 59 BIM held, but just. When the SADF broke off the battle at 22:00 it had been at the point of success. UNITA actually announced the capture of Cuito. Next morning FAPLA could mount no counter-offensive, cowering instead in its trenches and hoping the SADF would not resume the attack. 'This shouldn't have happened,' Castro cabled Ochoa. Why did 21 BIR just stop fighting and take to their heels with huge casualties, leaving the SADF and UNITA in its command post? Where were the rest? On 16 January only 300 of its soldiers could be located. The near-debacle was painful: Cuito Cuanavale would have fallen if the SADF had attacked from the south as well as east of the river, and if Dos Santos had lost three brigades in a day he might well have capitulated and accepted a negotiated outcome on Pretoria's terms.

Cuba moved quickly to shore up Cuito's defences. On 15 January Castro ordered a Cuban Tactical Group to be formed for Cuito Cuanavale from their Tank Brigade at Menongue as a reserve force to strengthen FAPLA defences on the western bank should the SADF attack from the south. Another and heavier Cuban Tactical Group with 31 tanks and corresponding armour, artillery and AA fire-power was to be stationed at Longa, mid-way between Cuito Cuanavale and Menongue, to support the re-supply convoys, but also as a backup force to be available should the enemy once again attack Cuito Cuanavale. Polo arrived to take over the defence and raise the morale of FAPLA troops: mine-laying, trenches, bunkers to protect against the long-range SADF G-6 artillery were stepped up; the artillery groups were reorganised, and a special Cuban reserve of seven tanks and infantry was positioned across the bridge on the eastern bank to prevent another outbreak of panic in FAPLA ranks. Ammunition was replenished; patrolling increased; and stepped-up MIG-23 missions harassed the enemy. At the same time Castro refused to weaken the southern advance aiming straight for South African vital interests in Namibia, which was now only weeks away, by transferring elite troops or the newest T-62 tanks to Cuito.

The main weakness of Cuito's garrison was the dispersal of FAPLA's three brigades on the eastern bank which had allowed the SADF to drive between and around their defences on 13 January. They were too far away from the west bank of the river to be covered by its artillery, but just far enough to he threatened by envelopment should the SADF get behind their rearguard. The positions were not selected for any strategic reason; rather, they were haphazard choices in the retreat from the Lomba. Immediately after the 13 January attack Castro asked Ochoa to reorganise these FAPLA brigades and their artillery group into a more compact and solid bridgehead, a much smaller defence system on the eastern bank anchored by a fully-equipped and reinforced 25 FAPLA, the best of Angola's brigades. Yet by 26 January nothing had happened. 'I don't understand what's going on in Cuito,' Castro complained to Ochoa. 'Who has the lead role?' He was increasingly worried by the dispersal of forces which meant that neither the western nor eastern bank defences could be really secure. He was surprised by the SADF delay in re-launching its assault. 'The enemy isn't acting in his interests,' he said, 'which is to attack the 59 and 25 brigade rearguards.' He became more and more insistent as time passed, but by mid-February the new defence perimeter at Cuito had still not been built.[26]

The 14 February SADF assault on Cuito Cuanavale began with a commando attack on the Menongue airport to neutralise Cuban air support, while SADF regular units (61 Mechanized Battalion and 4 SAI) and UNITA battalions again attacked FAPLA's three brigades on the eastern bank of the Cuito to separate FAPLA's 21 and 59 brigades, and then envelop and destroy them. The cloudy weather favoured South Africa: it achieved surprise, and Cuban and Angolan pilots were unable to fly until the afternoon. The SADF ground attack on Cuito nearly succeeded, breaking the defences of FAPLA's 21 and 59 brigades and capturing the latter's command post. The 21 Brigade, reassembled after its defeat on 13 January, again broke. With the 59 Brigade in full retreat, and SADF artillery shelling and four Mirage attacks weakening the remaining 25 Brigade, FAPLA faced the imminent danger of losing the bridgehead with 4 000 troops and all their equipment.

When the situation became critical the reserve tank force of T-55s, with two Cubans in each as commander and gunner, moved forward to counter-attack the SADF and provide the cover for an orderly withdrawal of 59 and 25 brigades toward the main garrison in the west. Cuban pilots flew 30 missions despite the poor weather in a desperate attempt to contain the SADF attack. Without this counter-attack it would have broken through and taken the bridge. When South African forces broke off at 18:00 they had scored one of their major victories of the war, but the strategic objective of destroying the defences on the eastern bank at Cuito had again eluded them. But seven of the eight Cuban-led T-55 tanks were destroyed with their crews. Castro was angry and demanded details of the disaster from Ochoa. He commended the heroism of the tank crews which probably saved Cuito, and acknowledged the skill and professionalism of the enemy. In a letter to Dos Santos he urged him not to negotiate with South Africa or agree to a cease-fire after the defeat on 14 February; FAPLA was in imminent danger should the SADF follow up immediately and renew its assault on Cuito, but it was the wrong time to negotiate and would be interpreted as weakness or an act of desperation which would encourage the enemy. 'The only way to deal with South Africa,' he wrote, 'is from a position of strength, nothing else will work.'[27]

Castro now demanded immediate action to create a viable bridgehead across the river: a 30 km square area, the Tumpo Triangle, to be defended by FAPLA's 25 Brigade behind the growing artillery power of the allied army on the western bank. Such a bridgehead could not be outflanked as FAPLA had been on 13 January and again on 14 February, and FAPLA's defences to the south could now be strengthened by the units brought across the bridge from the eastern bank. The two attacks had demonstrated the superiority of South Africa's Oliphant main battle-tank relative to FAPLA's T-55: mine-fields in front of the bridgehead were needed to pin them down and blunt the next SADF assault.

By 24 February the new bridgehead had been prepared, and just in time for an SADF assault the next day; during the ten-day interval after 14 February, South Africa could have changed the war by attacking Cuito Cuanavale, but its prospects had changed. Although the SADF again achieved surprise on the morning of 25 February, and sent a forward unit of FAPLA in flight without a shot, South African and UNITA units, including 230 men of 32 Buffalo Battalion and Mike Muller's 61 Mechanized Battalion, discovered a changed battlefield situation. They were pinned down for nine hours by the most effective artillery barrage of the war, while MIG-23s swarmed overhead. UNITA infantry were cut down by the defending garrison's heavy machine guns and rockets; disorganised and without the protection of Oliphant tanks and Ratel armoured cars they lost effectiveness, often targeting the SADF rather than FAPLA. SADF tanks and armour got stuck in the protecting minefield until late afternoon; with darkness about to fall, and its main mission still not begun, the SADF withdrew without a follow-on attack that night. For once FAPLA casualties were minimal and morale soared. A happier Castro congratulated Ochoa for the new defence system. 'Here we are calmer and happier. We have overcome serious risks.' Much remained to be done to turn Cuito Cuanavale on both banks into an impregnable fortress, but the SADF had been thrown back without having reached the FAPLA line, and the worst was over.

On 29 February, however, the SADF tried again in another attack again led by the 61 Mechanized Battalion with the 4 SAI in reserve. Col. Pat McLaughlin planned the attack for the night of Monday, 29 February to continue on Tuesday to take advantage of the SADF's night-fighting capability. A night attack would also curtail Cuban-FAPLA air activity so that South African artillery could support the assault by bombarding the Tumpo Triangle. Coming from the north with two Oliphant tank squadrons, heavy armour and two UNITA battalions as the main infantry, the SADF had assembled a credible force for the attack. But it also ran into problems 3 km before the FAPLA line, and again withdrew claiming equipment failures, but not before the exposed UNITA soldiers had again taken heavy casualties.

The SADF now set Wednesday, 23 March as the next date for a final ground assault on Cuito Cuanavale. To buck up morale, Savimbi, along with South African and US officers, visited SADF/UNITA forces in the theatre for a much-needed pep-talk. But each day of delay strengthened the defenders at their expense. Castro was cautiously optimistic after reviewing the overall military situation with Cuban Chief of Staff Ulises Rosales del Toro on the evening of 7 March. Cuban and Angolan forces had full control of the Menongue—Cuito–Cuanavale road; troops and munitions could now be brought in as required. All of Africa was watching for the next attack; psychologically Cuito Cuanavale was already a major victory over the SADF. Pretoria had 'broken its teeth', Castro predicted, confident that the allies would prevail after the numerous near-disasters since the Lomba. The dangers that remained were 1 000 times less than before. 'What we really want,' Castro concluded, 'is that they [the SADF] stay there [in Cuito Cuanavale] while we head down in the other direction.'

The SADF launched its most ambitious assault on Cuito Cuanavale on Wednesday, 23 March beginning at 06:15, following the same northern route as on 29 February. Like the earlier attacks, its objective was to wipe out FAPLA on the east bank, occupy the Tumpo Triangle and blow up the bridge once and for all. But while *Operation Packer* had luck with the cloudy weather (which limited Cuban air support from Menongue to one ineffectual mission), this time it confronted stronger Cuito defences. Its minefields were 80% complete with FAPLA 25 Brigade protected by a 5,4 km front with 1 319 anti-tank and 4 108 anti-personnel mines designed in combinations to steer the approaching SADF armoured columns into fire zones. Unable to penetrate the mine-fields, while FAPLA's heavy weapons from both banks of the Cuito River repaid them for their 13 January and 14 February defeats, they stalled and finally abandoned three Oliphant tanks. The once-feared G-5s and G-6s caused few casualties among the well-dug-in FAPLA defenders buoyed up by adequate equipment and the smell of victory. The re-supply problem from Menongue had also been resolved: convoys to Cuito Cuanavale arrived in 12–14 hours to supply FAPLA's needs, particularly its heavy BM-21, D-30 and C-130 field artillery. 1 813 shells and rockets were fired at the SADF and UNITA forces stuck in the mine-fields on 23 March, while tank fire, smaller cannon, machine-guns and smaller weapons hammered the exposed infantry all day. UNITA was no longer reliable; only 200 out of 700 soldiers showed up for one of the five participating battalions. By 16:00 it was over: *Operation Packer* was a complete failure.

The events of 23 March laid to final rest a long tradition of South African colonial warfare and would be the last major armoured battle for the SADF.[28] The changing military balance was also quickly reflected in regional politics: Kenneth Kaunda called a meeting of the Frontline States (which had not met since October) for 24 March. Resistance was galvanised within Namibia and South Africa, re-kindling in turn the international anti-apartheid campaign. Cuito Cuanavale became an international symbol of resistance and a destination for journalists to experience first-hand incoming SADF G-5 and G-6 artillery rounds on the town and garrison. Elsewhere in Angola UNITA's earlier dramatic military gains dissipated. On 14 March FAPLA invited foreign journalists to Bie Province to demonstrate the regaining of control of the Central Highlands and the imminent recapture of Munhango.

Meanwhile *Operation XXXI Anniversary* had been under way since 3 March and was meeting little South African resistance. The Cubans observed the SADF in apparent strategic confusion, maintaining a major force in Cuito Cuanavale when the far more dangerous Cuban offensive toward Namibia was already under way. 'They act as if there is nothing going on in the west,' Castro noted, 'as if they don't understand our movements in the direction of Calueque.' In addition to the sea-lift of the Second Army, Cuba had transferred its newest armoured units elsewhere in Angola to the southern front to add maximum force to the *Operation*.. At its height the southern offensive included 450 battle tanks (T-62 and T-55) and 200 armoured cars, 60 MIG-23s, 10 SAM-8 batteries and 16 groups of Pechora AA missiles, 500 IGLA shoulder-held AA missiles, 200 heavy artillery pieces, 200 AA artillery mounted by 15 Tactical Groups with 27 000 Cuban troops, 10 000 FAPLA and 2 000 SWAPO. An entirely new situation was unfolding in the border war. South Africa had lost air cover over southern Angola and northern Namibia; it was powerless to stop Cuba's armoured advance to the border of Namibia. FAPLA and SWAPO's PLAN were partners in the offensive, energised by the success of the military advance. Pretoria finally had a real war on its hands, and the diplomatic stalemate bedevilling the region for the past decade suddenly lifted.

Conclusion: Principle and pragmatism

Beyond achieving an honourable exit from Angola, Cuba's global strategy also contributed decisively to the liberation of southern Africa. While scholarly claims to this effect are not new, access to previously closed archives document permit conclusive evidence in support of Castro's achievement, and much more detailed study of process in Cuban foreign policy formation.[29] It is clear, for example, that the diplomatic revolution in southern Africa after FAPLA's defeat on the Lomba, which reversed Crocker's logic of 'constructive engagement', correlates precisely with the evolution of Cuba's war diplomacy. The hostile and dismissive US attitude toward Cuba and Angola during 1987 had scarcely improved by the end of January 1988. In fact, a meeting in Luanda on 28 January featured a temper tantrum from a petulant Crocker. In contrast, when the Cuban–Angolan–US negotiators met in their next session on 17–18 March – when defences at Cuito Cuanavale had held and FAPLA and the Cubans awaited the SADF confidently – talks were suddenly serious and positive.[30] With Cuba firmly in control of the military situation and the SADF about to be expelled from Angola, the US delegation adopted Cuba's four-part agenda for a global solution in south-western Africa: the unconditional South African military withdrawal from Angola; the cessation of South African aggression against Angola including its aid for UNITA; the approval without modification of UNSCR 435; and the total withdrawal of Cuban forces from Angola within a negotiated timetable and UN verification.[31] But changing minds in Pretoria required the shock of a changed military balance; by the London Conference on May 2–4, Cuban and allied forces were sweeping the SADF out of south-western Angola. 'We have to be ready to stay there another year if necessary,' Castro noted a week before the London meeting. 'We want a solution, but not just any agreement.' But even that shock – that Cuba could and would punch as hard as necessary to achieve a global solution in southern Africa – did not register fully until clashes culminated in Cuba's bombing of the Ruacana–Calueque complex on June 27.[32]

London confirmed a *de facto* alliance between the US and Cuba as the two key players driving the peace process in southern Africa. In March both had come to the conclusion that neither the Angolan Government nor Pretoria had the cohesion or diplomatic skills to lead such a complicated diplomatic effort. Tough work lay ahead, much of it technical, related to drafting and verification, which required qualified professionals at the diplomatic and military levels. Cuba could provide these for the joint Cuban-Angola team, and the US team would have to pull and drag along South Africa. Thus Cuba and the US, with the experts and later military representatives playing as important a role as the diplomats and politicians, shepherded Angola and South Africa along to the 22 December 1988 New York Accords. The Soviet Union was essentially a bystander, while the UN Contact Group – dormant for a decade – realised that the success of Cuban arms had rescued it from oblivion: it would now oversee the transition to independence in Namibia after all.

Crocker's depiction of the struggle for peace in southern Africa, as largely his personal achievement over great odds, ranks as one of diplomatic history's greatest ironies: only Cuba's military challenge to South African aggression after the Lomba provided him with the diplomatic opening required to rescue his reputation after the disaster of 'constructive engagement'. While it would be an error to minimise the US contribution during 1988 in achieving the New York Accords – it alone had the resources to lead a global southern African peace process – Cuba's role as the creative and driving force behind regional conflict resolution in south-western Africa in the climactic 1987–88 phase cries out for recognition. After the New York Accords, isolated after the end of the Cold War, and suffering the self-inflicted wound of the Arnaldo Ochoa crisis, Cuba was dispensable: Nelson Mandela excepted, Western leaders minimised Castro's role.[33]

Cuba escaped the fate of the US in Vietnam or the Soviet Union in Afghanistan by an exceptionally skilful concentration and coordination of military and diplomatic assets between 16 November 1987, when the Cuban military build-up was decided upon, and the New York Accords eventuated. The effort consumed the attention of its leaders; elaborate preparation and scenario-building exercises preceded the key diplomatic and military initiatives. The flexibility and search for compromise demonstrated in these talks fit poorly with the popular caricature of a leadership blinded by revolutionary idealism. Some trademark Castro characteristics are apparent – autonomy; internationalism; the dismissal of financial considerations (cost-sharing of the military build-up was not discussed among the Cubans during their November 1987 meeting); above all the insistence on a principled withdrawal.[34] But Cuba's global strategy in 1987–88 also revealed the outer limit of principle for Castro's ideological bottom line did not extend beyond feasible objectives: Angolan territorial integrity; Namibian independence; and Cuban honour and independence. Beyond this, the pragmatic core of the Cuban leadership became apparent, particularly towards Angola. While US aid to UNITA was a core issue for Angola, and while Cuba urged Dos Santos to hold firm with Crocker, Havana concluded logically that Angola would have to settle this matter separately with the US. Cuba also withdrew Cuban aid workers as its departing soldiers left them unprotected targets for UNITA's guerrillas, terminating a historic partnership in support of the MPLA. Both were painful decisions, based on the recognition that Cuba could do no more in Angola. Cuban–MPLA relations since 1976 had become a kind of Siamese twin, their fates joined organically through triumph and disappointment. This stage was now over. As Angola–Cuba–US negotiations resumed in 1988, Crocker repeated Washington's intention to provide arms to UNITA notwithstanding an international agreement on the other outstanding items, ensuring that the civil war and the destruction of Angola would continue until Savimbi was eventually isolated and neutralised. While Namibia and South Africa benefited enormously from the New York Accords, therefore, the Angolan nightmare intensified after Cuba's full military and civilian withdrawal. Cuito Cuanavale and *Operation XXXI Anniversary* are therefore the bitter-sweet symbols of the Cuban chapter in southern African history, unrepentantly cherished by Castro as the Revolution's finest hour.

Notes to Chapter Twelve

1   I wish to extend particular thanks to Jorge Risquet, Fidel Castro's chief adviser on Africa and Member of the Politbureau, for his vital support in this research project, as well as the other officers, officials and scholars in Pretoria, Luanda, Washington, Havana and Moscow who generously contributed their time and expertise. The Department of Foreign Affairs in Ottawa assisted my work immeasurably by facilitating access to the UN Contact Group files.

2   P. Gleijeses, 'Moscow's Proxy? Cuba and Africa 1975–1988', *Journal of Cold War Studies*, Vol. 8, No. 2, (Spring 2006), 3–51.

3   C. A. Crocker, *High Noon in southern Africa: Making Peace in a Rough Neighborhood* (New York: W.W. Norton, 1992).

4   Cuban sources include the Ministry of Defence (MINFAR), military intelligence (CIDFAR), correspondence and cables between Cuban and Angolan leaders and Havana and the Cuban Military Mission (copied to the Lubango command under General Leopoldo Cintra Frias after 6 December 1987, transcripts of senior consultative meetings chaired by Fidel Castro and the peace negotiations, and other internal papers. Like the files of the UN Contact Group, access requires permission until they are declassified. The translations are the author's.

5   Jose Eduardo dos Santos was chosen by the MPLA to succeed Agostinho Neto after his premature death in 1979.

6   CIDFAR, *Comportamiento de la participacion (aerea) cubana en la operacion* 'Saludando Octubre', 14 July to 20 August 1988 contains a devastating critique of Soviet-Angolan strategy. See endnote 27 for further details.

7   The considerable literature and growing literature on Angola cannot be reviewed in full here. For Cuba and Angola see Gleijeses' path-breaking book *Conflicting Missions: Havana, Washington and Africa, 1959–1976* (Chapel Hill: University of North Carolina Press, 2002), and E. George, *The Cuban Intervention in Angola, 1965–91: From Che Guevara to Cuito Cuanavale* (London: Frank Cass, 2005).

8   Compare Gleijeses, 'Moscow's Proxy?', 18–21.

9   Behind 'bambolinas', Risquet called it, in his colourful language.

10   Note from Fidel Castro to Jose Eduardo dos Santos, 12 September 1987.

11   Including FAPLA 16 Brigade which collapsed with all its equipment at the source of the Chambinga and Hube rivers. MINFAR, Extracto del resumen de la maniobra *XXXI Aniversario del Desembarco del Granma*, 1988.

12   With the possibility of settling UNITA permanently in strategic areas in southern Angola to consolidate South African control over Namibia. See C. Legum, *The Battlegrounds of southern Africa* (New York: Africana Publishing Company, 1988). Information on the four SADF operations proposed for western Angola was derived from SADF field commanders.

13   The military emergency facing Angola in 1983 and its impact on the already complex Angolan–Cuban–Soviet relationship requires detailed analysis.

14   The two letters were so hot that José Eduardo dos Santos locked them in his office, unwilling even to consult his Political Bureau without further soundings.

15   United Nations, 'Angola: Coming to a Head', UN Contact Group Foreign Intelligence Report, 26 October 1987.

16   'Meeting between US Ambassador Niles and the Secretary of State External Affairs, Ottawa, 13 May 1988'. Ambassador Niles specifically mentioned Representative Howard Volpe's proposed disinvestments Bill.

17   Cable from the US Secretary of State to US Embassy in Pretoria, 5 December 1987, quoted in Gleijeses, 'Moscow's Proxy?', 37.

18   The next sections rely on a synthesis of MINFAR and CIDFAR documents as well as South African and other Western accounts, so that individual items will not be referenced. For military historians, *Existencia del armamento y tecnica de las FAR en la RPA* (Angola), 19 November 1988 gives a complete inventory of Cuba's military equipment in the campaign.

19   CIDFAR, *Cronologia de las principales actividades de la Maniobra XXXI Aniversario*, 1988.

20   Central Committee, *Acta sobre la reunion de analysis de la situacion politica en el cono sur de Africa*, Havana, 20 June 1986.

21   Gleijeses, 'Moscow's Proxy?', 37–40 in particular.

22   Compare Gleijeses' account, 'Moscow's Proxy?', 37.

23   Risquet briefed the Angolan President and N'Dalu on the operation on 23 November, who mistakenly hinted at the build-up to the Mozambique press. South African intelligence knew something was up, but like Washington, Pretoria failed to grasp the scale of Cuba's strategy.

24   Note from José Eduardo dos Santos to Fidel Castro, 2 January 1988.

25   Note from Fidel Castro to José Eduardo dos Santos, 4 January 1988. Castro saw the hand of the Soviet Military Mission behind the Angolan President's letter – 'Practically dictated by the Soviets,' he complained. 'Once again they have created serious problems for us and almost impossible obstacles which are the consequences of their scatter-brained advice to the Angolans in this war.' After 16 November 1987 Cuba had insisted on daily meetings of a trilateral Operations Centre (CDO) comprising the Angolan Minister of Defence and the Cuban and Soviet Military Missions to prevent separate Angolan–Soviet deals.

26   Notes from Fidel Castro to Arnaldo Ochoa, 15 and 21 February 1988. 'This could really have been a disaster,' he mused on 15 March.

27   Note from Fidel Castro to José Eduardo dos Santos, 18 February 1988.

28   However Cuba's casualties were heavy, with 20 killed or missing-in-action in Cuito Cuanavale; 140 Cubans died in the first four months of 1988, with illness, accidents and 'friendly-fire' incidents, particularly the accidental loss of an aircraft well behind the lines with 26 officers and men on April 27, accounting for most of the casualties. SADF claims of inflicting major losses on advancing Cuban forces (at Tchipa, for example) are false.

29   The detailed analysis of 1987–88 war diplomacy lies outside the scope of this chapter; a forthcoming book is designed to address this theme.

30   Compare E. George, *The Cuban Intervention in Angola, 1965–1991*, Chapter 10; W. Breytenbach, 'Cuito Cuanavale Revisited: Same Outcomes, Different Consequences', *Africa Insight*, Vol. 27, no. 1 (1997), 54–62; and Gleijeses, 'Moscow's Proxy?', 40–3.

31   The Cuban leadership prepared 15 scenarios for military withdrawal before the London Conference, May 2–4, with 26 months at the low end, indicating its flexibility so long as SC 435 was achieved untainted, and the SADF levered out of Namibia and away from UNITA.

32   CPP, *Anotaciones concretas del Comandante en Jefe que quiaran la actuacion de la delegacion cubana a las convercasiones el Londres*, 22–23 April 1988.

33   General Arnaldo Ochoa, Head of Cuba's Military Mission in Angola in 1987–88, and a Hero of the Revolution was tried, convicted and executed for corruption in 1989.

34   Note that all Cuban soldiers participating in *Operation XXXI Anniversary* were given the option of withdrawing; only 7% decided against. Compare Gleijeses, 'Moscow's Proxy', 43–51 for an insightful analysis of the controversy surrounding Cuban motivations in Africa.

Chapter 13

'Oh Shucks, Here Comes UNTAG!': Peace-keeping as Adventure in Namibia

Robert J. Gordon

The Adventure, according to the foremost theorist on these matters, Georg Simmel, is largely experiential fantasy, others and ours, packaged as time away from ordinary life Rereading Simmel, the reader is struck by how his view of the Adventure creating an 'exclave' is similar to Victor Turner's notions of anti-structure, liminality and communitas.[1] Most studies of adventure have focused on individual adventures, and this chapter suggests that the notion can be extended by incorporating the Turnerian dimension. Transitions, as Turner showed, are situations of uncertainty and danger in which a person moves to a new status. Conventional analyses of Adventures see them as entailing a distinctive structural movement, either spatially and/or socially, in which the adventurer has to deal with a challenging element of unpredictability, risk and danger, all of which combine to create a 'Time Out' from the operation of the daily humdrum of society (with the challenging element of danger).

Perhaps a better sense of what is meant can be gained from looking at the roots of the word. Adventure is derived from the Latin *ad*, meaning 'toward' and *venire*, meaning 'coming'. An adventure then has that tingling air of expectancy of something about to happen. This tingling is also coupled to an awareness of danger or fear, no matter how dominant or niggling.

It was this aura of expectancy that is intrinsic to the experience of adventure that was so blatant among the personnel of the United Nations Transitional Assistance Group (UNTAG) who were overseeing the transition of the de facto South African colony of South West Africa to the independent country of Namibia. Given that UNTAG literally and figuratively assisted in the change of status of South West Africa to Namibia, the participants clearly served as ritual elements designed to facilitate this transformation. Adventure is very much a staged performance.[2] The ways adventures are performed do not merely reflect views of reality, but also create and confirm them.

In 1989, after about a decade of international negotiation against a background of constant low intensity guerrilla warfare against the South African Defence Force (SADF) by the South West Africa People's Organization (SWAPO), the first United Nations (UN) 'multi-functional peacekeeping' exercise took place. About 9 000 members, mostly troops, of UNTAG arrived in Namibia, one of the world's most sparsely populated countries, with a population of about 1,5 million, to keep the peace and to organise 'Free and Fair Elections' as part of Namibia's transition from disputed territory to an independent democratic state. In undertaking this task UNTAG faced many challenges, including resettling some 41 000 refugees, organising elections where illiteracy was estimated by the UN to range from 60–80%,[3] removing all discriminatory legislation and monitoring the police in an effort to prevent harassment, especially by police 'irregulars' (known locally as *Koevoet* or 'Crowbar' in English). During this transition, I was recruited by the UN as a consultant to make recommendations concerning how the Apartheid Second Tier Authorities should be replaced. It is on these experiences, coupled to a reading of UNTAG memoirs and reminiscences, that this chapter is based.

Most UNTAG personnel saw themselves as having, and were seen by Namibians to be having, an Adventure. Could it be that how they defined and acted upon the situation contributed to making UNTAG the success it was proclaimed to be? This adventurous attitude, indeed it resembled a temporary *weltanschauung*, was in sharp contrast to the departing South African military who might initially have been sucked into the notion of duty as adventure, but certainly not by the late eighties. Like UNTAG, the SADF troops were largely male, younger, uniformed and had travelled away from home for their 'tour of duty', yet clearly except for a few individuals, the majority did not see their sojourn in Namibia as an adventure. This was despite the fact that structurally it was a situation containing unknown dangers and risks and an eventual return 'home'. Given structural similarities between them, it is important to ask, why the UNTAG experience was defined as an adventure and a 'success', while the SADF engagement was largely seen as neither an adventure nor a success. How can this difference be accounted for and is there any relationship between 'adventure' and 'success' in peacekeeping? This is no idle question. Indeed, Demobilisation, Re-integration Programmes (DRPs) are now one of the 'hot areas' of development practice by the World Bank and other donor agencies. One of the cases frequently invoked as a success of such transitions is that of Namibia.[4] Recently Lise Howard has argued that the critical factor was not so much the consent of the warring parties and the strong Security Council interests, as that UNTAG were able to adapt to the needs of the post-war environment.[5] How exactly were they adaptable and might not this be part of the adventure?

The South African Defence Force in Namibia

During the 1980s the SADF deployed some 7 000 troops, mostly conscripts, in the more populated north in what was known as the 'Operational Area'. This is the area where the South African regime had been fighting a low-intensity war against SWAPO guerrillas who were seeking independence for Namibia. From a white (South African) point of view it was a frontier, not only culturally and symbolically, but a state perimeter area as well since it skirted the Namibian-Angolan border[6] – the frontier between what was then seen as Black Africa and White Africa. It clearly had the characteristics of a liminal situation. As one white soldier said:

> The guys were saying that it was freedom up there you could get away from the basics of disciplined structures of the force at the time, you could go up there, there was freedom, there was more money, they were having a good time.

Such a situation was promoted by an overwhelming sense that people in the 'States' (as South Africa was called) 'just didn't care, they didn't know what we were really doing' 'up there'.[7]

In 1985 a small independent South African magazine appropriately named *Frontline*[8] decided to do something about this ignorance and published a story, 'Ends of the Rifle', which dealt with the border experiences of a young, white, South African national serviceman. The tenor of the story is clear:

> When I was up there I felt nothing . . . You look at terrs [insurgents] as stupid. He doesn't know what he's doing. He doesn't know what's right and wrong . . . You don't think of him as a human being . . . They go to extremes. That's stupid. You can't see them as people . . . There was a lot of rape. We had some low guys with us.

> Some of those guys you couldn't understand . . . Also, when you're there you're *sommer* (just) fighting, you aren't thinking about what you're fighting about . . . Mainly the *ous* (chaps) don't bother about prisoners. If you take a prisoner you have to go through a whole procedure, filling in forms and that. So you say he was shot in contact. Maybe you don't say anything.[9]

In this geographical expanse the normal rules of society (and 'civilized warfare') did not apply. Both prominent politicians and lowly soldiers publicly claimed that if they were attacked 'no rules apply at all . . . We will use all means at our disposal, whatever they may be'.[10] In this zone a new lexicon came into play based, rather intriguingly, on a vocabulary developed by Americans in Vietnam. This zone was populated by people who are the obverse of normal society. Recognising SWAPO was easy said the *Frontline* troopie: 'If you see a big, healthy looking, male you know he's a Swapo. Only the Swapos eat well enough to look like that – apart from the Ministers . . . and they're Swapos anyway . . . If he had soft feet that would prove it beyond doubt . . .' Similarly, while white women were seen to be non-active combatants, loyal, upright, moral and supportive societal exemplars, black women in the combat zone were the antithesis. The official *Ethnology Manual of the South African Defence Force* gave the following advice to young servicemen:

> Direct contact with Bantu women should be avoided, while <u>social contact should be</u> <u>ABSOLUTELY FORBIDDEN AND PREVENTED.</u> The comings and going of the Bantu woman should, however, be closely observed for the following reasons: 1: She provides food and is the 'beast of burden'. It will most probably be her duty to provide the insurgent camp with food and beer . . . and she may even carry the heavier automatic weapons, as happened in Angola. 2: She incites the men to successful military action by arousing them sexually before a battle, taking part in the 'Washing of the Spear', a ceremony based on a party where sexual intercourse takes place. 3: Experience has shown that the Bantu will take advantage of the 'weakness' of the whites not to treat women roughly by pushing them to the front in political riots . . .[11]

In this scorpion dance the chief protagonists were not of this world. The *Frontline* troopie claimed, 'terrs are all on drugs – morphine and heroin (That's one way you can recognize a Swapo. You see the needle marks in his arms)', but goes on to admit that 'some *ous* [guys] would get morphine from the medics, but most of us were just on dagga [marijuana]'. Even experienced pundits attributed extra-human, animal-like qualities to the enemy. As one explained: 'Some of these terrorists are able to walk two or three kilometers [sic] at a stretch *on their toes* in order to confuse security forces. The imprint left in the sand is almost indistinguishable from animal tracks.'[12] Nothing could be taken for granted in this theatre, not even the audience. Again, the *Frontline* troopie:

> The guy who is lost is the guy in the middle. He can't win. SWAPO comes and says who do you believe, us or South Africa? So he says you, but SWAPO doesn't believe him so they hit him. Then we come and we say who do you believe, us or SWAPO, so he says you, but we don't believe him so we hit him . . . We had two cases where the guy says he believes SWAPO. So we wipe him out. He's a terrorist sympathiser.

A South African officer commented: 'The Ovambo tribesman is very stoic and fatalistic. Simple killing does not have the impact on tribal members as does, say, cutting off arms and legs or noses and ears and then forcing the victim's wife to fry and eat the flesh.'[13]

And then there was *Koevoet*, auxiliary police recruited from local people or 'turned' SWAPOs, who lived a life of their own on the perimeter of the social order and who operated almost by their own laws. They were paid large bounties for every SWAPO terrorist they 'brought in Dead or Alive' and would wear t-shirts proclaiming 'Killing is our Business, and Business is Good'. *Koevoet* was generally despised by both the local population and the SADF troopies. Plainly, except for a small minority who thought that they were fighting to preserve the West from the onslaughts of communism and black domination, most South African soldiers felt that that they were there against their will. Moreover, reading the numerous accounts and memoirs of service in the operational area it is clear that despite the SADF's Winning Hearts and Minds (WHAM) policy, the SADF was generally not welcomed by the local population.

The Blue Berets in Namibia

UNTAG was also distinctive. The military wore blue berets and scarves while civilians had blue UN armbands. Their vehicles were all painted white and featured 'UN' prominently painted on the side. They also clearly sensed an element of danger, that was reinforced at the start of UNTAG operations when, on the day before the cease-fire was to be implemented, the SADF engaged SWAPO in a bloodbath, alleging that SWAPO was trying to move troops into a strategic position prior to the 1 April cease-fire. By 5 April, more than 260 SWAPO combatants and 30 security forces had died in the heaviest fighting of the 23 year-long war.[14] This nearly scuttled the mission. One UNTAG officer, Col. Mwarania, of the Kenya Battalion, or Kenbatt, described the Kenyan reaction as they prepared to embark for Namibia:

> It was not a reaction precipitated by fear, but the unpredictability of plunging into the unknown, the first step in a make or break situation. It may last a few seconds at most, then the normal flamboyant and easygoing manner wills itself over the doubts lingering in the soldier's minds, and all is over. Only then is such a soldier ready to fight and fight hard, for, though death hangs as a possibility in the periphery of his subconscious it loses its sharp fangs . . . (Once) reconciled to the new situation the troops jested on how they would go about their UNTAG duties. They saw themselves as acting as buffer to the flying bullets and missiles between the warring SWAPO and South Africans by standing in between and stopping the flying missiles with their own bodies. They laughed at the incredulity of the whole idea.[15]

UNTAG military activities consisted largely of patrols, flag marches, and participating in the many national day celebrations of the numerous countries participating in UNTAG. Kenbatt, for example, was constantly called to parade for visiting foreign dignitaries and celebrated two national holidays, *Madaraka* and *Jamhuri* that attracted many spectators and guests and featured 'traditional' dancing, sports and choirs as well as the inevitable parade. Civilian members of UNTAG, backed up by a slick multi-media campaign, engaged in a constant flurry of voter education which entailed visiting churches, schools and numerous public civic events.

UNTAG, in contrast to the SADF, was generally welcomed in the Operational Area. Indeed, some observers felt that UNTAG members were treated as 'The Liberators'.[16] It was in the south, the area where most white and black people opposed to SWAPO resided, that the UNTAG peacekeepers picked up some mute and occasionally active resistance, but this was largely attributed to the fact that they were black people, in contrast to the Malaysian and Finnish troops stationed in the north. Indeed, black UNTAG members commonly feared that they would be subject to apartheid, and in cases where this did surface, UNTAG swiftly took redressive action.

Reactionary white people constantly accused Kenbatt of being in cahoots with SWAPO. Their chronicler believed that hostility from sections of the Namibian community was endemic. Stories of black UNTAG members being refused service at country hotels were common. Accusations and other intimidating mechanisms had become the order of the day. For the Kenyans, 'danger was always lurking in the *veld*, in houses and along lonely streets'[17] and reached its climax with the bombings of the UNTAG offices in Outjo, a small white town.

Most UNTAG personnel were volunteers, and apart from the high salaries such secondment brought, they were drawn to their assignment by a sense of history, duty and adventure. In the years preceding the transition, South Africa's policy of apartheid had been a constant *idée fixe* at the UN especially among the Afro-Asian bloc. Many of the volunteers from Third World countries stressed this, especially those coming from the Caribbean, who saw this as an opportunity to return to their ancestral continent and assist in the end of apartheid. They also believed that the eyes of the world were upon them (as emphasised by the presence of an extremely large press corps) and made them feel that they were participating in an important historical event. This notion is transparent in their accounts, memoirs, and even in the kitschy doggerel published in the UNTAG house journal.

The extensive media coverage which preceded the operation meant that most UNTAG personnel had strong preconceived ideas about what to expect, namely an oppressed black majority; and most accounts continued to present simplified versions of the present and past, namely that local black people were still badly discriminated against in terms of salaries and living conditions, and that six o'clock curfews still pertained for black people in the urban areas. Urban legends of white settler atrocities were also common. Similarly, in the Swiss UNTAG contingent's reminiscences, the standard clichés about apartheid persisted in their descriptions of the social landscape, this, despite being chosen because of their expert knowledge of southern Africa. Black people' claims to inequalities and injustice were readily accepted at face value, despite the fact that the apartheid structure had been radically liberalised and transformed in the decade preceding the Transition. It appears that UNTAG personnel had mixed success in making friends with locals, either black or white, but all claimed that they had made good friends with UNTAG members from other countries. The Swiss, who served mostly in the settler-dominated south, were most impressed by the landscape. A railway station reminded one Swiss of a scene out of *High Noon* and references to Western movies and the 'Wild West' were a frequent theme.[18] This was 'Picture Book Africa' to them.

Similarly, in the black-dominated north, Jamaican Angelinna Griffin, in charge of the Oshikuku District Centre in Owambo, epitomised the spirit of most UNTAG officials. Arriving at her posting in the early afternoon she hoisted the UN flag – at first upside down. 'I want you to share the pride I feel that the UN is here in this little corner of the earth and that I am here to offer the best that I can in its name. There were half a dozen boys helping me put up that flag and cheering as it [went] up.' Her prime task was voter registration, a challenge that UNTAG took up 'ready to brave the unknown'. She initially stayed at the local Mission station that was 'built like the Old West'. Indeed the 'Wild' or 'Old' West was to be a constant descriptive metaphor employed by black and white UNTAG members. The gratitude of the returnees was so heartfelt that it made her 'big sacrifice for being here so insignificant'. Certainly the local people treated the UNTAG operation with more than due respect and several observers noted that they dressed up in their Sunday best just to register to vote.

Personnel from the Caribbean were particularly eloquent about why and what they were doing: they were returning to the land of their ancestors and felt at home 'as the people of Africa shared one common ancestry'. So strong was this common ancestry that some of them felt that communication was not a problem – despite not sharing a common language – because the people were so friendly and welcomed them in their own way: 'The satisfaction and fulfillment derived from these simple acts (of smiling and greeting) is not easy to describe and will not be forgotten.'[19] The friendliness of the 'sun-baked faces' many felt was the mission's key to success. Time and again UNTAG personnel, at least those serving in the dangerous north, were impressed by the friendliness of the local people as epitomised by their smiling, waving and greetings.

Others were not so sure. Thus Peter Burke, an Irish policeman stationed in the North claimed:

> It took a while for the people to have confidence in us, but the real turning point came when we got our own UN Casspirs. The Casspir was the most intimidating vehicle I've ever seen, not only the size and the colour, but the design of the whole thing . . . To see the big white UN Casspir driving around, that really sent the people a different message. Before that we couldn't keep up with the SWAPO teams, but after that, we could follow them anywhere. Then the people began to realize that there was really a change taking place, and that the UN was there for a reason.[20]

Reflecting on his experiences, Major Zareen Khan Khatak of Pakistan observed that: 'During my six months in Owamboland, I was particularly struck by the constant state of festivity prevailing all around. People appeared drunk on the notion of independence. I am sure they know their responsibilities too. Creating a nation is far easier than building one!'[21]

Most UNTAG personnel fondly recalled the good times they had, especially with fellow UNTAG workmates, during the various national celebrations. As an international bonding exercise it was an unqualified success. UNTAG was unique in that it was the first UN operation in which female personnel played a large role. Colonel Krish Mehra, the deputy commander of the Indian contingent, was concerned about the way UN personnel of different sexes greeted each other with 'the three kiss syndrome' and the attractions and dangers of 'playing'. But he concluded that when in Rome one should do as the Romans do and engage in the various nightly escapades and visits to the thriving restaurants and night clubs in the larger towns. 'Fun parties', he noted, were ubiquitous and frequently entailed weekend trips to resorts. He added that no one in the UN ever said 'No'.[22]

Host reaction to UNTAG

Interviewing Namibians ten years after the event, the first reaction on being asked what was most memorable about UNTAG was 'UNTAG BABIES'. This response is in sharp contrast to UNDP officials who deny that many illegitimate babies were born out of UNTAG liaisons, based on the naïve claim that few mothers came to them seeking assistance.[23] But this ignores the culture of local sexual practices and strategies for seeking support. Even today, when visiting Windhoek, the capital city, locals will point out houses which supposedly served as bordellos during the Transition. Given the relatively high salaries UNTAG personnel were paid, many local women and men saw this as an opportunity to obtain money. That there were many amorous relationships between UNTAG members and locals is clear from folklore, cartoons and court records. From senior officials to the lowest soldiers engaged in love affairs. There were jokes about middle-class white people having to unplug their phones and take them with them to prevent their domestics from calling their lovers in Finland or wherever. It is interesting to note that Simmel regarded the love affair as the ultimate example of an adventure. Indeed, the only adventurer he mentions by name is Casanova. Licentiousness is a common characteristic of tourists and soldiers abroad. Mwarania, a chronicler of the Kenbatt, raved about the nightlife:

> A night at 'Club Thriller' in Windhoek's Katutura township, or one of the many night-spots was quite an experience. The music was good, the beer was plenty and the beautiful girls were willing to gyrate their delicate bodies to the rhythm of music. It was not impossible to witness UNTAG personnel immersed in the merry-making to ease up the pressures of the day and just feel good.[24]

Indeed a close reading of the Kenbatt chronicles and those of journalists suggests that most assaults on Kenbatt personnel were not by reactionary racist white people, but aggrieved black people, and that the root of the conflict was sex and drunkenness in shebeens, the black–run unlicensed taverns.[25]

After initial apprehension, in which urban legends readily circulated among white Namibians, such as that UNTAG's bias was shown in the fact that the condoms issued to their personnel were coloured red, blue and green, the SWAPO colours,[26] most white Namibians greeted UNTAG's presence with humour. Jokes abounded about the 'White West' (in reference to the white vehicles they drove). Stealing UNTAG number-plates became a favourite past time of white youths to the extent that UNTAG personnel were forced to paint the numbers onto their vehicles. Some locals would also paint an 'F' in front of the UN vehicle logo. Indeed, one of the local movie hits was the South African comedian Leon Schuster's still-popular *Oh Shucks, Here Comes UNTAG* released in 1990 shortly after Independence and just after UNTAG had left. It portrays UNTAG as being a bunch of naïve foreigners being taken for a number of rides by locals, both white and black. It ends with the Afrikaner Hero having impersonated a number of local people, including a Herero woman, and making out with the blonde UNTAG medical officer. Of course this was not how UNTAG personnel saw themselves.

While a minority of local black people were apprehensive about UNTAG, most black people, especially in the former Operational Area of Owambo, welcomed UNTAG, in some cases with considerable passion. In an important sense local people were also having an adventurous time. An adventurer is, apart from one who seeks adventure, someone who is ready to take risks for personal gain (*Oxford Shorter Dictionary*); 'a person who hopes to gain wealth or high social position by dishonest, dangerous or sexually immoral means' (*Longman Dictionary of Contemporary English*) and finally 'a soldier of fortune, one who engages in risky commercial enterprises for profit, one who lives by his wits' (*Concise Oxford Dictionary*). But clearly here the line between risk and opportunism is problematic. Risk undermines trust relations and one of the features of Namibian society that has struck a number of observers is precisely its lack of trust. Clearly the transitional situation was one in which the whole populace was thrust into massively increased opportunities for adventure.

Undoubtedly white people' apprehension was moderated by the economic benefits they derived from the sudden influx of a large number of relatively big-spenders. UNTAG personnel filled the hotels and restaurants and chased up property prices beyond the wildest expectations of speculators. Prices of hotel accommodation more than doubled within a few weeks. UNTAG's presence also created new employment nodes, especially in the Private Security Industry for Diplomats, Development Workers and other affluent foreigners who sought protection. But it also had a devastating impact as people had to cope with a huge influx of returnees. Practically every house in Katutura, the sprawling black township outside Windhoek, had a backyard squatter, and single mothers became increasingly dependent upon part-time domestic work with unscrupulous landlords not being averse to extracting sexual favours. Meanwhile, with the high unemployment rate, crime sky rocketed as well. Not only did UNTAG members' bulging wallets attract youth gangs, but violent and sexual crimes escalated, exacerbated by the fact that the colonial police were not trained to deal with such forms of criminality. A journalist who lived there reminisced how self-preservation became a priority epitomised by residents increasingly ignoring victims of crime. 'Armed criminal gangs, motivated by joblessness, the lack of an effective police force, and a feeling that independence meant you could do what you liked-also roamed the region, stealing, looting and intimidating the population. But the full-scale rebellion feared by so many never materialized.'[27] Indeed, 'the once amicable, all-embracing township was becoming a jungle. Instead of the ubiquitous *braais* (barbeques) they were replaced by clubs which deprived many of the youth of the chance to socialize and mix with people of all backgrounds'. *Braais* were not only broken up now by gangs, but the emergence of 'Clubs' catering to UNTAG also undermined *braais* economically, so that many households and young women found it easier to simply raise income by getting UNTAG 'sugar-daddies'.

On the uniqueness of adventure

So what is the explanation for why the South African troops and personnel, who were in the same place and of the same broad demographic profile and education as the UNTAG personnel, did not generally see their experiences as an adventure while the latter did? It is clear that imagination played an important part in both perceptions. In reality, only a small number of SADF troops actually had 'contact' with the enemy, but their officers exaggerated the enemy presence to motivate their troops and to keep up their interest. Most writers of accounts and memoirs emphasise that they had lots of time to think and their thoughts were largely concentrated on what they would do once they got back to the 'States', typically girls and get-rich schemes.[28]

Perhaps part of the answer lies in the element of flirting with danger, to use the Simmelian metaphor. Unlike UNTAG personnel, the South African troopies did not blatantly engage in sex. By all unofficial and popular accounts, UNTAG members were notorious for their sexual liaisons. By contrast, except for the occasional rape, the records seem to suggest that the South Africans rarely engaged in local sexual liaisons.[29] A number of conditions would reinforce such behaviour. The South Africans came from a state where the strict apartheid legal system had until recently defined interracial sex as a criminal offence. One of the key arguments made for the abolition of the so-called 'Immorality Act' was not that it discriminated, but that the stigma attached to white people convicted under the act was such that some committed suicide. Even after 'racial discrimination' was legally abolished, there were social and cultural pressures that mitigated against such sexual liaisons as the *SADF Ethnology Manual* cited above illustrated so well.

But there were other factors as well. Adventures achieve much of their value by being unique. There is a curious dialectic at work. Once an Adventure has been had, it is never exactly replicable. It is no accident that alpinists have their eyes firmly set on unconquered peaks and explorers gaze lovingly at the blank spots on a map. UNTAG personnel were clearly aware that they were witnessing what they took to be an important and unique event in world history. The South African troopies, on the other hand, were aware that they might have to replicate their experience at the next military camp they attended. This raises perhaps the most significant difference between the SADF and UNTAG. The former were largely conscripts – they had no choice – while all the UNTAG personnel were there voluntarily. I would suggest that intrinsic to defining an experience as an adventure is the notion of a wilful individual decision to allow accidental events to take place. Another corollary is that in an adventure, as opposed to a misadventure, there has to be an expectation, no matter how minimal, of a positive outcome. This positive outcome is exemplified in a successful homecoming or re-incorporation into the adventurer's home society. Indeed, I would suggest that some of the principal reasons for embarking on a journey into the relative unknown are rooted in the homecoming, for this gives the ultimate justification for undertaking the journey. For adventurers, participating in an adventure is a way of demonstrating to others who they are and what they believe in. It is a status placing activity.[30] UNTAG members saw themselves and were portrayed as such by the mass media as 'Agents of Virtue' and there was a distinct tone of melodrama about how they went about their business. For them peacekeeping was theatre. An important component of contemporary adventure is the prospect of talking about it. Most UNTAG members were exceptional in their home society, after all, they felt they were part of 'making History', unlike the conscripted South African troopies who, at least in their white social circles, were clearly unexceptional. Their experiences lacked 'scarcity value'. Most important of all, when they went home, they were not treated as heroes or as someone who had had an adventure, and this led crucially to their negative definition because adventure tales are pre-eminently about successful adventures. It is only now, like Vietnam vets, that former South African troopies are starting to discuss their experiences.[31] UNTAG personnel could brag about their sexual conquests and adventures to their peers, while the South African troopies, if they did have sexual adventures, suffered the burden of not being able to brag about them.

Karl Schiebe suggests that adventure is central to the construction and development of life stories and that life stories are the major supports for human identities that are of course constantly evolving.[32] People require adventure in order for satisfactory life stories to be constructed and maintained even if vicariously in fantasy. The need to tell others about yourself is perceived in Western society as a mechanism of individuation whereas, paradoxically, as Foucault observed, it is a mechanism of socialisation and subordination. Confessions and similar literary productions like adventures, he would argue, do not mystify but rather establish authoritative 'regimes of truth'. Confessions of the 'border literature genre' and adventure tales create the space within which human types (the terrorist, the animal and bestial) can be located and treated, and the rules of proper confessional and adventure discourse systematically preclude alternative classificatory schema.[33] But adventures and tales thereof are also searched for what they reveal of 'character'. Indeed the *raison d'être* of many youth organisations is to have an adventurous slant, precisely to develop 'character'. 'Character' in the bourgeois world, as Erving Goffman would put it, [34] includes a complex of observations and characteristics (in the proper sense of the word!) such as the ability to stand correct and steady in the face of sudden pressures.

There is another factor that also played a role in adventure. The German cultural critic Hans Magnus Enzensberger has pointed out that the sense of adventure is intrinsic to the romantic ideology of tourism and that nowadays the global elite/bourgeoisie see it as a human right to distance themselves as far as possible from their own 'civilization'. Paradoxically, the destination has to be both accessible and inaccessible, distant from civilisation yet comfortable, dangerous yet safe.[35] The logistics structure of UNTAG clearly suggests that these conditions were fulfilled in Namibia.

But how important was this glow of adventure for the success of the UNTAG operation? David Lush, a young British journalist, offers a unique perspective on the Transition. Unlike most of the UNTAG personnel and the scores of visiting journalists, he lived in the sprawling township of Katutura, and associated with the local black people. The picture he paints from this vantage point is significantly different from the comfortable UNTAG self-image which was sustained by the visiting tarmac-bound journalists. UNTAG personnel settled 'into their new surroundings in a manner not too dissimilar to a horde of holiday makers'.[36] For all their talk of patrolling, UNTAG's presence was largely in the cities:

> In the bars, the UNTAGs continued to fall off their stools and brawl with the locals. In fact, everywhere you turned there seemed to be someone in uniform wearing a blue beret. (Yet) Throughout the 2 000 km I traveled during my trip to the war zone, I saw just three UNTAGs; one at Oshivelo (a control post) and two in a Kombi turning into Ondangwa airbase. So much for the peacemakers . . .[37]

Lush presents a devastating picture of how the notorious para-police, *Koevoet*, would simply ignore the UNTAG monitors and openly display their contempt for them, and how the Police would, when needed, simply ignore the UNTAG monitors and wade into strikers, while tolerating riots by the pro-South African political groups.[38] Even after the deployment of UNTAG in Owambo, the South African forces, and *Koevoet* in particular, could still hunt down (alleged) SWAPO guerrillas in what one diplomat described as a 'licensed turkey shoot' wiping out several hundred valuable SWAPO cadres. Indeed, Lush provides powerful evidence that when faced with a riot or a massive conflict, UNTAG was totally ineffective. UNTAG's role, he seems to suggest, was largely ceremonial. The only power UNTAG seemed to have was when the United Nations Special Representative threatened to suspend the Transitional Process. Indeed, UNTAG personnel could not have known or related to most of the populace because most Namibians, and certainly those in the 'War Zone', hardly spoke English, (the lingua franca of UNTAG personnel). For communications most UNTAG personnel had to depend upon interpreters, who were generally in short supply, and had in some cases formerly worked for the SADF. Nor could they appreciate the nature of 'Terror', especially its spectral element or the subtle acts of intimidation that occurred in everyday interactions. UNTAG personnel could not know, for example, that certain known policemen were present at public gatherings dressed in ordinary clothes, or that individuals might have been ambiguously threatened with the abduction of their children or the 'mistaken' destruction of their crops and houses, or that all the weapons surrendered on demobilisation had in fact been accounted for. In short, they could not get to the underneath of life in a seemingly tranquil sun-drenched scene.

In retrospect, there seem to have been two structural factors that contributed far more to the success of UNTAG which the literature on the Transition has largely ignored. The first is that the coffers of the South African State were being drained and international bankers were calling in their loans. Economically, South Africa could not no longer afford the war and really had no alternative but to bow out gracefully. Second, far more important in ensuring that the Transition worked was not UNTAG per se but the myriad of international (mostly) white observers who descended upon the Territory to observe and offer advice. These were the people who pushed beyond the tarmac to the outermost nooks of Namibia and threatened to unleash the politics of embarrassment upon the South Africans. Unfortunately no exact figures exist concerning their numbers, but most observers agree that they were substantial. Certainly judging from oral evidence and some written accounts,[39] they were sometimes in danger, but always accorded high status by local people, a situation largely attributable to what Paulette Goudge calls the 'whiteness of power'.[40] Race played an important if unacknowledged role in both the discourses and practices of power during this transition. Race, especially in apartheid-ridden southern Africa, was part of the still pervasive discourse of superiority and inferiority.

To be sure, UNTAG was lulled into a sense of adventure by a number of factors, not least the friendliness of the natives. Having talked it up as an Adventure they could do nothing but treat it as such. Adventures must be recounted after the fact if they are to be treated as adventures, but unlike adventures of yore, UNTAG's adventures only proclaim what everybody already knows. The visual world of advertising and propaganda both for and against apartheid shaped how they framed their accounts. Adventures pretend to provide relief from the world of commodities by escaping from the everyday, but ironically it is the trademark of the adventure that plays the decisive role in calculating its value. The effort of UNTAG lay in confirming the make-believe as the authentic. In the final analysis the key condition for an adventure in Simmel's sense, that notion of the freedom of the 'Exclave' is sadly missing. It was never really an Adventure as much as a Tour of Duty because if things got bad they could leave.

But the narratives generated by UNTAG are important beyond what they tell us about Adventure. The 11-month UNTAG exercise, which ended as planned, and on schedule with Independence on 19 March 1990, only cost some $383.5 million, far less than the original request of $700 million.[41] It also enjoyed widespread support, with more than 50 countries providing personnel. Despite having an authorised upper limit of 7 500 military, at its peak it consisted of 4 493 at all ranks, 1 500 civilian police, and just under 2 000 international and local staff. Specifically for the elections, the mission was strengthened by some 1 000 additional international personnel. During its operations UNTAG suffered only 10 fatalities, mostly the result of road accidents. By these counts alone it is easy to see why the UNTAG operation was heralded as a success by senior UN officials and this set the tone for later assessments of the Operation.

Conclusion

UNTAG's task was to assist in transforming a zone of fear and insecurity into a culture of tolerance. Of course creating a civil society takes much longer than a year. Writing the constitution and supervising the elections were the easy part. Scholarly assessments of UNTAG read like many 'development' documents, so well critiqued by Jim Ferguson and Emery Roe:[42] narratives based on unquestioned assumptions which develop their own momentum and ignore context and reality. Thus the World Bank study on DRPs, which compared Namibia, Uganda and Ethiopia, pays surprisingly little attention to 'External Assistance' and then only to discuss strategies and timelines, purpose of support and coordination.[43] Like most UNTAG personnel, the World Bank authors claimed to have found the local people abysmally ignorant, supposedly because they had suffered from a long period of social and cultural isolation.[44] There was little 'real' information in the Territory and thus information had to be regenerated. They also ignored the role of NGOs and the role of the world economic system. Perhaps precisely because they were so concerned to portray UNTAG as an Adventure of heroic proportions.[45]

Christopher Hope, in his satirical novel *Darkest England,* captures the UN and South African dynamics and outcomes well, and far better than I could, when he has his narrator muse:

Africa is not so much a place as an *Adventure,* which they made up as they went along. And truth was never allowed to interfere with the pleasures of certainty. This wise policy ensured their progress in Africa for generations, their ideas so firmly fixed that no subsequent experience was allowed to disturb them. How else does one explain how they succeeded so well and saw so little?[46]

Notes to Chapter Thirteen

1   G. Simmel, 'The Adventure', in *Georg Simmel: On Individuality and Social forms*, ed. D. Levine (Chicago: University of Chicago Press, 1971); V. Turner, *The Ritual Process* (Ithaca: Cornell University Press, 1974).

2   D. MacCannell, *The Tourist: A New Theory of the Leisure Class* (New York: Schocken Books, 1989).

3   A. Griffith, *Conflict and Resolution: Peace-building Through the Ballot Box in Zimbabwe, Namibia and Cambodia* (Oxford: New Cherwell Press, 1998), 157.

4   See, for example, N. Colletta, M. Kostner and I. Wiederhofer, *The Transition from War to Peace in Sub-Saharan Africa* (Washington DC: World Bank, 1996); M. Goulding, *Peacemonger* (London: John Murray, 2002); R. Hearn, *UN Peacekeeping in Action: The Namibian Experience* (Commack, NY: Nova Science Publishers, 1999); Griffith, *Conflict and Resolution.*

5   L. M. Howard, 'UN Peace Implementation in Namibia: The Causes of Success', *International Peacekeeping* 9, 1 (2002), 99–132.

6   This area, which contained over half of Namibia's population, had never been an area of white settlement for a variety of demographic and geographic reasons.

7   W. Verwoerd, 'Oorlog, Trauma en die WVK', in *De Helende Kracht van Literatuur*, ed. C. van der Merwe and R. Wolfswinkel (Haarlem: In de Knipscheer, 2002), 23–4.

8   Founded by liberal maverick Denis Beckett in 1979.

9   Anon., 'Ends of the Rifle', *Frontline* (August 1985), 54.

10 *Weekly Mail*, 2 Sept. 1988.

11 South African Defence Force (SADF). *Ethnology Manual.* Cyclostyled, 1977. This section is largely derived from R. Gordon, 'Marginalia on "Grensliteratuur": Or How/Why is Terror Culturally Constructed in Northern Namibia?', *Critical Arts*, 5, 3 (1991), 79–95.

12 A. J. Venter, 'Chipping Away at SWAPO', *Soldier of Fortune Magazine*, (January 1983):51.

13 R. Brown, *Soldier of Fortune* (New York: Exeter House, 1986), 53.

14 D. Lush, *Last Steps to Uhuru* (Windhoek: New Namibia Books, 1993), 147.

15 B. Mwarania, *Kenya Battalion in Namibia* (Nakuru: Media Document Supplies Mwarania, 1999), 46.

16 Henning Melber, Personal comment, 24 October 2003.

17 Mwarania, *Kenya Battalion*, 68.

18 See for example, Anon., *Untag in Namibia* (Windhoek: Untag, 1990) and Anon., *Namibia en Route* (Bern: Eda., 1990).

19 Anon., *Untag Journal.* n.d., n.p.

20 Anon., *Untag in Namibia.*

21 *UNTAG Journal* (1990), 33.

22 *UNTAG Journal* 2 (1990), 21.

23 Hearn, *UN Peacekeeping in Action.*

24   Mwarania, *Kenya Battalion*, 64. He also reported that even before departing from Kenya many young men on their last home leave, hurriedly 'took wives' supposedly on the grounds that nobody knew what to expect in Namibia; Mwarania, *Kenya Battalion*, 45.

25   Lush, *Last Steps*; Mwarania, *Kenya Battalion*, 65, 68, 94.

26   Lush, *Last Steps*; B. Harlech-Jones, *A New Thing?* (Windhoek: EIN, 1997).

27   Lush, *Last Steps*, 212, 260.

28   A. Feinstein, *In Conflict* (Windhoek: New Namibia Books, 1999); A. Strachan, 'Die "Werklikheid" van die Grens', in *De Helende Kracht van Literatuur*, ed. C. van der Merwe and R. Wolfswinkel (Haarlem: In de Knipscheer, 2002).

29   Barry Fowler, ed. *Pro Patria* (Halifax: Sentinel Projects 1995), 32.

30   C. Rojek, *Leisure and Culture* (New York: St Martins Press, 2000), 37.

31   R. Andrew, *Buried in the Sky* (Sandton: Penguin, 2002); Fowler, *Pro Patria*; B. Fowler, *Grensvegter?* (Halifax: Sentinel Projects, 1996); C. van der Merwe and R. Wolfswinkel, eds. *Telling Wounds*. Proceedings of the conference held at the University of Cape Town, 3–5 July 2002 (Cape Town, 2003).

32   K. Schiebe, 'Self-Narratives and Adventure', in *Narrative Psychology*, ed. T. R. Sarbin, (New York: Praeger, 1986).

33   M. Hepworth and B. Turner, *Confession* (New York: Routledge, 1982), 89.

34   E. Goffman, *Interaction Ritual* (New York: Doubleday, 1968), 214–25.

35   H. M. Enzensberger, 'A Theory of Tourism', *New German Critique*, 68 (1958/1997), 127.

36   Lush, *Last Steps*, 138.

37   Ibid., 154.

38   Ibid., 229.

39   B. Carton, 'Unfinished Exorcism: The Legacy of Apartheid in Democratic southern Africa', *Social Justice*, 27 (2000), 116–27.

40   P. Goudge, *The Whiteness of Power* (London: Lawrence and Wishart, 2003).

41   United Nations, *The Blue Helmets* (New York: United Nations, 1990), 445.

42   J. Ferguson, *The Anti-politics Machine* (Cape Town: David Philip, 1992); E. Roe, 'Except Africa: Postscript to a Special Section on Development Narratives', *World Development*, 23, 6 (1995), 1065–9.

43   Colletta et al., *The Transition*, 60.

44   These figures, Henning Melber (personal communication, 24 October 2003) points out, illustrate the double standards so characteristic of this era. No one bothered to base any of these guesstimates on sound empirical assessments. As it turned out, Namibia's literacy rates were very much higher, much to the embarrassment of the current regime which tried to market the country to Aid agencies as a less developed country.

45   Indeed after UNTAG most UN operations appear to have been much more problematic due to a variety of factors including manipulation by more powerful countries by threatened withholding of funds and a chronic lack of resources. L. Polman, *We Did Nothing: Why the Truth Doesn't Always Come out When the UN Goes in* (London: Viking, 2003).

46   C. Hope, *In Darkest Africa* (Macmillan: London, 1996), 62.

Chapter 14

The Road Back: Psycho-social Strains of Transition for South Africa's Ex-combatants

Sasha Gear[1]

Before South Africa's first democratic election in 1994, thousands of South Africans were members of armed formations and participants in violent conflict. Today most former soldiers have disappeared from the public eye. But how do their previous roles as combatants impact on their current lives and what challenges does this impact pose for individuals, communities and societies emerging from violent conflict?

Societies in transition are faced with unenviable challenges on economic, psycho-social and political fronts as they grapple with the violence of the past, attempt to build transformed institutions, repair damaged relationships, and develop economically. In the resulting struggles that involve not simply re-construction, but engaging with and attempting to transform ways of thinking, relating and securing income that have been generated through conflict, the intertwined issues of reconciliation, victim empowerment and justice become paramount. Ex-combatants' proximity to the preceding conflict, and the shifts required of them with the 'outbreak of peace'[2] can be considered to represent at the individual level the complex transition facing the society as a whole.

This chapter focuses on some of the key psycho-social experiences, demands and challenges that numerous of South Africa's former soldiers are encountering. These represent the convergence of past experiences with the usually daunting process of moving into the 'post-conflict' era and negotiating the changes this requires of them. For many ex-combatants it necessitates departure and demobilisation from the military, and then building a civilian life. Some will find this relatively smooth, but for others it will be intensely difficult and alienating. Commonalities may emerge across this diversity, but the vast range of experiences, and differing intensities with which they may be felt, requires recognition. In exploring some of these ex-combatants' experiences of the psycho-social strains of war and peace, this chapter draws predominantly on existing knowledge gleaned in relation to the more vulnerable former soldiers in these transitional dynamics.

The violent conflicts of South Africa's recent history saw people drawn into numerous armed formations, and different situations within these, giving rise to a vast and varied ex-combatant population. Very broadly, this can be divided into the former fighters of the liberation movement made up of, amongst others, the African National Congress (ANC) and Pan Africanist Congress (PAC) and those of the apartheid state. Each of these expansive categories contained a host of subdivisions, which in turn informed a wide range of experiences. The experiences of white, male conscripts meeting the requirements of their compulsory military service, contrast, for example, with those of 'recces' – elite members of the reconnaissance commandos in the Special Forces of the apartheid state. Similarly, in the ranks of the liberation movement, the workings of the ANC's military wing, Umkhonto we Sizwe (MK) and the PAC's Azanian Peoples Liberation Army (APLA) – both armies that were forced to operate mainly from exile – departed significantly from the involvement of the relatively small groupings of mostly young people variously linked to political organisations who fought on the streets of their neighbourhoods in the townships of South Africa in self-protection and defence units.[3] The intrusion of South Africa's war into neighbouring countries also saw the emergence of many non-South African combatants who served in full, or in part, the interests of the South African Defence Force (SADF) and the apartheid state, thus prefiguring another grouping of South Africa's ex-combatants.[4]

While retrospectively, South Africa's ex-combatant population is broadly framed into the two main groupings of state versus liberation forces, defining 'ex-combatants' is contested terrain. This is not surprising given the size and diversity of the population who participated in the conflict. That both the apartheid government and the liberation movement sought to mobilise the entire population in furthering their war interests (as is frequently the case in civil wars) adds to the complexity involved in attempts to clearly distinguish combatants from 'non-combatants'.[5] Indeed, definitions may/should be adapted for the purposes they are employed. While not typically regarded as 'soldiers', the former South African Police (SAP) provides an obvious example of a grouping central to the war efforts of the apartheid government. Under the auspices of 'total strategy', the SAP was not only given primary responsibility for internal operations against the liberation movement and its allies,[6] but was also active in furthering counter-insurgency in neighbouring countries.[7] In the post-conflict era, many of its former members will be facing similar challenges to their SADF counterparts.

Definitions of precisely who constitute the 'real ex-combatants' are contested even amongst the former fighters themselves. Processes involving former soldiers in the 'post-conflict' era often also accentuate, or give rise to, such conflicts as definitions become linked to access to limited resources, opportunities and the construction of collective memory. One example of this has been the formal programme (that began in 1994) of integrating various former armed forces into the new South African National Defence Force (SANDF). Tensions have been reported for instance, between MK members who spent a long time in exile, and others who were locally based in self-defence structures.[8] At the same time, large numbers of people who consider themselves to be ex-combatants have been excluded from the process altogether.[9]

The term 'ex-combatant', in some countries (e.g., Mozambique) is associated specifically with liberation fighters. Similarly, 'military veteran' has at times, been used to refer to only those from the more formal military structures. While many South African ex-combatants apparently prefer to be known as 'veterans', 'ex-combatant' is used in this chapter inclusively, and to point beyond the formalised militaries.[10] In the recent context of highly publicised land-grabs by 'war-veterans' in neighbouring Zimbabwe, the term 'ex-combatant' is also employed for its arguably greater neutrality.

The considerable diversity of combatant experiences informs a similar breadth of experiences among former soldiers today. Some have made the transition to the new South Africa with relative ease and opportunity, as is evident in the prominent positions many former liberation fighters hold in both government and the private sector. Numerous others, however, are finding it more difficult as they attempt to build new lives for themselves, and negotiate civilian society where they face obstacles that represent a complex mix of the impact of past experiences together with fundamental breaks in the ways they understand themselves and are understood by others.[11]

Traumatic trajectories and militarised identities

Soldiers regularly accumulate varied and numerous layers of traumatic experience through their armed histories. The ways in which people become combatants in the first place is pertinent here. Many South Africans took up arms in response to direct experiences of violent victimisation. This was a reason for many young people leaving the country to join liberation armies during the late 1970s and 1980s when they were exposed to the resistance-repressing excesses of the apartheid state. Other violent trajectories also propelled people into armed action. Examples include conflicts between liberation organisations (such as between elements in the student and youth arms of the ANC and PAC) as they vied for domination in their localities, and the SADF's forced recruitment of Namibian civilians. Indeed, the brutal and involuntary recruitment of combatants, frequently children, is reported from war zones around the globe.[12] Also relevant here is the practice of conscription. Whether processes of military conscription can in general be considered a crime of the state would no doubt be an issue of hot debate. But the apartheid era compulsory National Service demanded of all young, white men (predominantly teenagers) – who were also key beneficiaries of the system – has certainly been seen as such (fuelling some relatively rare shows of resistance in the white population, such as the End Conscription Campaign (ECC) – an organisation that was banned in 1988 because of its activism to abolish compulsory military service).[13]

In addition, certain kinds of criminality are typically embedded in political conflict, presenting dilemmas for efforts to clearly distinguish between 'political' and 'criminal' actions and violence.[14] Specific forms of violent victimisation (e.g., recruitment by abduction) underscore just one aspect of the interrelationship. Another common example, and one which has been reported by former MK members, is the sexual violation of female combatants by fellow male soldiers.[15] Other types of crime/abuse of power within armed formations are also not unusual: the treatment of liberation cadres who were suspected of being spies as well as the bizarre sexual medical experiments carried out on particular gay conscripts by officials in the SADF to name just a few.[16]

Despite the numerous possibilities for harm contained within military experience, militarised discourses have little room for the acknowledgement of victimisation and vulnerability, especially where soldiers are concerned. Certainly, many ex-combatants do not consider themselves as such – some denying even the potential for trauma within their ranks.[17] However, it was, after all, in relation to soldiers' experiences of war that the classification post-traumatic stress disorder (PTSD) was coined to explain the paradoxical symptoms presenting in numerous veterans of the Vietnam War. Symptoms include, amongst others, intrusive distressing recollections, difficulty with sleep and concentration, hyper vigilance, psychological numbing, an inability to trust, and an inability to experience enjoyment or care about the future.[18]

Potential sources of trauma for South Africa's ex-combatants occurred unevenly, are numerous and wide-ranging.[19] Amongst them are imprisonment, torture, 'turning processes' (recruitment into enemy ranks via brutalisation), security-force harassment of family members, harsh living conditions in exile, the accompanying culture of infiltration paranoia, and witnessing and participating in violent acts.

The denial in militarised discourses of soldiers' vulnerability as well as of the terrifying and confusing aspects of war is, in itself, a source of potential trauma and distress. These discourses are rarely if ever restricted to military structures, and are bolstered by the powerful discourses on gender (to which they are intimately connected). The distressing potential comes from the contradictory relationship between actual experience and idealised notions of soldiering and war: the impossibility of (consistently) living up to the demands these notions make of soldiers, unrealised expectations, and/or experiences that contradict these expectations.[20] Combat, for instance, 'that ultimate test of manliness' may be experienced 'as frightening, chaotic, and noisy rather than noble and heroic'.[21] In a similar vein, that combat is constructed as distinctly and intensely masculine fuels damaging 'tests of manliness' and also launches an offensive on women, generating additional sources of distress for female soldiers.[22] As one former MK cadre explained, 'We faced . . . rife harassment, sexual abuse, emotional abuse . . . Women were always sort of run over by men. Trying to find identity; that was the most traumatic, . . . there was no women's voice . . .'[23]

Importantly, trauma can result from the more 'ordinary' soldier experiences as well as direct combat and gross violations of human rights. Some conscripts, for example, find the dehumanisation of conventional military training, deeply distressing and brutalising.[24] The dehumanisation or 'breaking down' of troops is a central component of conventional military training (so as to make way for 're-building' them into those 'capable of killing or dying on command'),[25] which may in turn be enacted between trainees in a system 'designed to turn aggression onto one "failure" in the platoon – one guy that was not making it'. These patterns clearly inform numerous traumatic possibilities. The related detection of disquieting, alarming and contradictory impulses and processes such as the 'almost intoxicating desire to kill'[26] within the self represents one of many sources of confusion and stress.

Different experiences structure different layers and possibilities of trauma and distress, and the personal contexts in which ex-combatants encounter the effects of these will influence the impact. As Bronwyn Harris (after Ingrid Palmary) notes, 'identity feeds into and shapes the experience of particular types of violence during and after war. This has implications for the ways that trauma is processed, expressed and experienced by people, which can in turn affect the way that identity itself develops'.[27] In addition, combat is one of the stressors for which the rates of PTSD are comparatively variable.[28] The potential influence of socio-cultural and personal factors on traumatic stress can be seen in differences of PTS levels displayed between veterans of different wars and the impact of the nature of the conflict, individuals' beliefs regarding their involvement,[29] dominant societal perceptions of the conflict, and homecoming experiences and support.[30]

Geographical location can also influence how ex-combatants (and others) engage with trauma. For example, conflict in Africa has made new demands on understandings of trauma and healing, and the usefulness of conventional Western approaches and the applicability of PTSD to non-Western contexts has been questioned. Challenges include continuous (rather than exclusively 'post') traumatic exposure;[31] the ignored importance of collective meanings and cultural networks for healing processes in responses directed solely at the individual level;[32] and the extent to which current socio-economic hardships complicate the identification of and responses to conflict-related traumatic stress.[33] Questions have also been raised about the circumstances in which the perpetration of violence may be experienced as traumatic,[34] and the relation of this to reconciliation efforts;[35] this, as part of an attempt to promote conscious attention to the political and moral components of diagnostic practices.[36] In addition, the extreme levels of violence that often continue into 'post-conflict' societies have led to calls for re-conceptualising 'the notion of trauma [as] *itself* in transition. [This] is . . . crucial to developing a victim empowerment strategy that can accommodate complex trauma, 'new' victims and a context of consistent but changing patterns of violence.[37]

Changing relations and 'post-conflict' conflict

Undoubtedly, the extent of violent crime that is a feature of contemporary South Africa has particular significance for ex-combatants' reintegration experiences. This is both from the perspective of ongoing sources of trauma, and because of its import for ex-combatants' shifting understandings and experiences of self (as they move from combatant to ex-combatant).

Ex-combatants' oft-changed relationship with agencies of security and defence mediates their current experiences of victimisation and/or their fear of this,[38] and for some, also complicates their interactions with the state security structures. One facet of this is the commonly expressed frustration at the feeling that, while the former fighters' own roles as part and parcel of policing and defence structures have been removed, in the past they did – and would still be able to do – a better job of meeting the country's security requirements. Moreover, many have been refused entry into current structures – which instead frequently treat them as threats.[39] The intertwining of past notions of crime and politics is deeply implicated here, and continues to play out in transmuting patterns of violence and conflict. This can take on a racial tone. Certain ex–SADF soldiers perceive themselves as 'whites' to be the targets of an undeclared continuation of the conflict being fought by 'blacks' in the form of violent crime.[40] In turn, some (amongst those in more precarious conditions)[41] register crime as but one component of a broader drive to exclude white males from the new South Africa. In other sets of relations, former MK members and SADF soldiers complain of police harassment as a consequence of their previous roles.[42] And internally based former liberation fighters in particular localities state that their ex-combatant status renders them more likely targets of violence than other South Africans.[43] The feeling of being systematically 'disarmed' is also powerful and unwelcome amongst many ex-combatants irrespective of their previous affiliation. Groups from across former forces carry the sense that they are being marginalised and victimised in current societal processes.[44]

These dynamics underscore the complexity of 'post-conflict' relations. National processes aimed at demilitarisation, reconciliation and transformation are unable to engage with the multi-layered and localised aspects and impact of violent conflict. At the same time, these wider processes can themselves give rise to tension and conflict. Both the Truth and Reconciliation Commission (TRC) and the establishment of the SANDF, for example, feature in former soldiers' explanations of new tensions within former armed hierarchies.[45] The most vividly expressed of these is a sense of having been deserted by former leaders in these processes – processes which have contributed to making particular sense of the past and to structuring access to scarce opportunities. As a result, they have also shaped a politics of exclusion and marginalisation.

Reconciling past and present: Amnesia, stigma and silence

Echoing post-war experiences elsewhere, many South African ex-combatants articulate a sense of betrayal in relation to the state, their former leaders and their present communities. Many feel badly let down by those who urged them into action and inspired their lives as soldiers. After they have won, I am nothing anymore . . . We are spanners to fasten bolts, after the bolts have been fastened we are sidelined. (MK)

Former members of the liberation armies expected that a free South Africa would recognise the sacrifices they had made and provide for them. Instead, many face unemployment and consider themselves to have been discarded by their organisations. A former MK member laments:

> The disparities that exist now are not only between ourselves and our white counterparts but our comrades as well, that have become, overnight bourgeoisie, and they are driving flashy cars and sleeping in very expensive hotels; they fly over our heads. (MK)

A sense of betrayal often still exists amongst those economically better off, revolving around the abandonment of the very ideologies which framed their involvement. That the agencies responsible for entrenching these ideologies reached far beyond the security apparatus is underscored in one former SADF recce's outrage at his church:

> With the previous regime having made the ANC the enemy . . . you grow up with them the enemy, and then you get this change over and the church says – after 48 years! – 'We have been wrong, apartheid was wrong, it was a sin'. And you suddenly realise, well we're the indoctrinated ones, we're the brain-washed ones, not them. I asked the people at the church, 'Can one of you just tell me who will go to heaven, those who died before 1994 or those who died after 1994?' . . . The church taught what was right and what was wrong, and now . . . change[s] overnight . . . with the political system . . . Do you want to tell me that not one church leader received inspiration that they were on the wrong track until the new government came? . . . Those were the guys who've done me in the most, who've stolen the most from me. We lost our jobs. We lost our future. Everything that was stable for us is gone. All of a sudden all that we believed in is gone, and once your belief is gone, everything goes.

Soldiers from across the political spectrum note a collective amnesia in society. They feel that they as combatants, as well as the causes they fought for and the meanings through which these were understood, are now relics of something remote or forgotten. As one former MK cadre put it, 'Forgotten is an understatement, we have been wished away.'[46]

In contrast to the 'invisibleness' brought on by collective amnesia, some complain of derision and/or stigmatisation around negative stereotypes. This fuels feelings of exclusion. Some MK soldiers, for instance, report that they have become a laughing stock – that in light of their current socio-economic predicaments, people around them constantly point out to them the contradictions that their lives represent, ridiculing them as misdirected idealists who have wasted their lives. The sting is worsened when those doing the ridiculing are the same who in the past accused them of naivety in thinking that anything could come of their struggle, or did not themselves make particular sacrifices but are nevertheless beneficiaries of the new dispensation. This is part of a wider lack of acknowledgement from the beneficiaries of transition fuelling frustration on the part of ex-combatants. One former MK cadre notes:

> . . . after this is done, now they are fortunate. They have these qualifications and certificates. They're being roped in through affirmative action and all the other measures that are seeking to equate the scale. We welcome that, it's just that even today . . . they are not inclined to say, 'Lets swallow our pride and say, "But you see folks, when you did what you did, we said you wouldn't do it. But you did it," and "Thanks to you, we have this now. No-one will ever forget what you did. With my qualifications, I would have been a doormat of someone but today I can compete with who-ever. (MK)

Many ex-soldiers also consider their military backgrounds to count against them in the job market,[47] saying that they are stereotyped as volatile and untrustworthy.[48] For some, legislation outlawing mercenary activities exacerbates their economic marginalisation and the sense of being ostracised as one of the few opportunities to which they have easier access is criminalised.[49] Within a number of contexts, returning female ex-combatants often face particular issues of stigmatisation related to their erstwhile involvement in a traditionally male domain and the threat this poses to accepted gender roles.[50]

More broadly, ex-combatants regularly feel misunderstood by those around them.[51] This is compounded by the secrecy that shrouded their combatant pasts, and which has meant that much of their experience has never entered public knowledge and thus public memory. A former conscript explained, for example, how the news blackout surrounding the SADF's operations meant than many other South Africans had little clue their country was at war. The boys were just off to 'the border', a term which rendered the reality of war invisible:

You come home, 'Howzit up on the border? Is it *lekker*?' . . . Nobody even seemed to know there was a war going on . . . It was just like . . . 'Oh, that's nice, so and so is also there'!!!

Civilian South Africa's lack of knowledge and understanding of the nuts and bolts of its militarised past, contributes to mistrust, paranoia and a sense of insecurity on the part of many ex-combatants.[52] This has fundamental implications for ex-combatant transitions. Even close family and friends are commonly in the dark about what their soldier relatives have experienced.[53] One component of an explanation for this relates to trauma, of which common consequences are avoidance of its subject(s) and things associated with it, and the mistrust of others. Other reasons for the silence are the weighty threats that previously hung over soldiers and framed military secrecy. Those who were sworn to secrecy have not seen these threats revoked anywhere,[54] at the same time being in the 'habit' of secrecy and/or associating it with ethical and professional behaviour. Ex-combatants may have fears (of future victimisation) about as yet unrevealed knowledge they carry from their military experiences, and which others have interests in keeping hidden.[55] In a similar vein, layers of past abuse and betrayal (e.g., females abused at the hands of fellow male combatants) have mainly been excluded from contemporary constructions of recent history, and this silence will likely complicate current betrayals and loyalties and intensify alienation.

Even less 'inflammatory' knowledge is veiled by silence, contributing to former soldiers' frequent sense of being thoroughly alone in their histories and incomprehensible to contemporary society. In South Africa, the TRC has been the most extensive exercise in uncovering the violent past. But because of its particular mandate (and focus on gross violations of human rights) it too, has left the experiences of ordinary soldiers largely invisible. Furthermore, many ex-combatants from both sides registered TRC processes as yet another component of their betrayal.[56] SADF members, for example, saw their superiors abandoning 'foot soldiers' to 'carry the can for the generals',[57] and cadres of the liberation movements resented being called to account, in the face of rigorous legal and moral questioning, for their actions against the apartheid government. That the process also left former colleagues of theirs in prison has added to their anger.[58] The TRC has also contributed to a sense of loss: individuals felt that what they may have offered and experienced went unacknowledged, and soldiers were instead being 'defined' by the atrocities that became public knowledge in the TRC hearings.[59]

This process has been abetted by the lack of other initiatives to recognise soldiers' histories. In addition, the specific nature of the histories that *have* been captured (through the TRC, and neat narratives of heroism and noble anti-apartheid struggle) has arguably also served to stigmatise alternative and additional stories and knowledge even before they are revealed. Accordingly, the nature of the recorded histories can be seen as assisting in keeping alternative and additional knowledge hidden, at the same time as discrediting ex-combatants sense of their selves. So, for example, some ex-SADF conscripts' resentment that their 'good' SADF deeds (or valuable contributions) will never be appreciated is complicated by a discomfort at the expectation that it should be. Other ex-SADF members may struggle with recollections of the enjoyment and adventure experienced during national service (or parts of it), and experience feelings of shame and confusion layered into their particular alienation.[60] This is because it is not considered right to have enjoyed any part of the experience because of the stigma associated with anything done in the name of the SADF. And these guilty feelings coexist with other memories of experiences too terrible to tell.

Amongst their former enemies, dominant constructions of liberation histories will similarly contribute to alienation and the pressure not to share other things that were not 'supposed to happen'. For instance, an MK member and political prisoner complained of sexual abuse during his confinement:

> In there is the hell hole . . . only a few were able to say a[ny]thing about that . . . it
> embarrasses . . . A lot of comrades were so young and they were left to the hands of those
> gangsters [who] . . . abuse[d] them sexually . . . and all that . . . While I was there, the
> Boers left me openly for abuse . . . When I look at these [things], I think, God this was
> not suppose[d] to [have] happened . . .

If certain cadres were psychologically and physically abused in apartheid jails, other exiles lived with the boredom and frustration which stemmed from not being able to put into practice their training by returning to fight in South Africa. Others were traumatised on account of the suspicions with which they were regularly regarded within their own organisations, and the abuses that they suffered at the hands of their own comrades. Their self perceptions contrasted sharply with the heroicised images of freedom fighters prevalent in public discourse. The currency of such images exerted (and continues to exert) pressure on soldiers to refrain from sharing their vulnerabilities and conflicts as well as increasing expectations on them when they returned home.

Trials of transition

The difficulty of making sense of oneself in relation to changed roles and broader societal processes is a central feature of what could be termed 'transition stress' (bearing in mind that identity is always in the process of formation). Typically this involves a range of losses and pressures. A sense of loss frequently accompanies the questioning of the purpose on which much of a person's life has been based. A loss of community and camaraderie comes with the shift from a life framed around collectiveness to the type demanded in the individualistic and market-driven civilian world. Organisational support is replaced with remoteness and difficulty in accessing the structures that had up until that point shaped most experience. Bureaucracy, and perceived nepotism and expedience within these structures, contribute to a sense of marginalisation, and can feed ex-soldiers' anger and frustration. Related to this is the sudden void where before there was a highly regimented, hierarchical and only-too-clear framework organising most aspects of their life. Degrees of external ordering of combatants' lives will have differed substantially between the types of formations to which they belonged and the individual roles they performed in the military structures, but the experience of this loss is usually profound and disorientating. It can affect things as seemingly mundane as the necessity of learning how to open a bank account and use money in a cash economy – as it did for some former exiles. The ambit of daily responsibilities expected of former soldiers in civilian life is a dramatic departure from that required in their previous combatant lives.

For large numbers of ex-combatants there is the impact of the sudden change or loss of occupation and the accompanying loss of particular status in family and community life. Other consequence of these losses are intense pressures, such as the fundamental need to secure income, to build, re-establish and negotiate relationships and roles, as well as the often negative, or alternatively idealised, perceptions and expectations that others have of them.

These pressures and stresses regularly play out in the family.[61] The sense of alienation experienced by one MK ex-combatant, in relation to his relatives, and especially the younger generation, was acute. His explanation underscores how his unemployment together with the dismissal of his past, deny him any status in the present.

> People are forced to leave their homes [in] an effort to find peace in the heart. He runs away from the problems in the home, . . . his nephew looks down on him . . . [The nephew will say] 'Hey! Don't tell me anything you hobo. I was not there in your early days, stay away from me' . . . That is why there are a lot of shacks . . . The uncle is ridiculed. He has been trained as a soldier, but he is just an uncle. This is because of unemployment.

This feeling of lost status/identity is thoroughly gendered. Men's sense of masculinity regularly takes a severe hammering with the loss of a combatant role. Because notions of masculinity (as well as male sexuality) are so enmeshed in the construction of 'soldiers' and combat,[62] when the opportunity to enact masculinity through this role is denied, 'manhood' is perceived to be threatened. This is magnified in contexts of lost employment, which under any circumstances, tends to produce feeling of emasculation. An ex-MK combatant reflects:

> Your family looks up to the father, the father must make a plan so that we can eat before we go to bed. But you do not know where to make plans . . . [Your wife says to the children] 'Even your father cannot find something for you to eat' . . . You are still holding

a thought that you're head of the house, but you are unable to satisfy their needs. They don't understand.

The impact of transition stress complicates and becomes embroiled with trauma generated through combatant experiences. Of significance too, is that violence is not necessarily restricted to militarised pasts. Some former soldiers continue to encounter, be targeted, or fear being targeted in current dynamics of violence. Others share with broader society a fear of falling victim to the violent crime so prevalent in South Africa's transitional context. Additionally, though, their fear is refracted through their militarised pasts, rendering another substantial blow to their 'manhood'.[63] Where male identity has been built on defending/fighting for hearth and nation against a clear 'enemy', former soldiers are now confronted with relatively random and unpredictable violence, perceived, paradoxically, to be much closer to home (than during combat days). The loss of organisational support is hard felt here. Not only are they, unlike before, on their own in their attempts to protect their loved ones, but this is in the face of a violence that – unlike 'war' – is perceived as random and simultaneously as a creator of victims – as opposed to heroes and nobility. This sense of assaulted masculinity is evident across previous force allegiances and the fear/experience of violence, a bitter pill to swallow. Indeed it represents an opposing reality to that which they believed was the primary purpose of their armed action, whether this was protection of hearth and home, or alternatively gaining freedom from injustice and repression.[64]

At the same time, former soldiers may feature amongst the perpetrators of current violence. This link, however, which is too readily asserted even on the 'flimsiest of evidence',[65] tends to be the predominant 'lens' through which society views and interacts with former soldiers. The concern that ex-combatants represent a security threat typically drives the limited attention they receive in societies emerging from conflict (fuelling another facet of stigmatisation).[66]

The sparse information available indicates that unemployed former members of militarised structures can be vulnerable to being caught up in violent crime as a result of their skills and marginalisation. Whether or not 'ex-combatants' are over-represented in current criminal activity remains unknown, while the evidence which exists (from different geographic localities) suggests that where they are current perpetrators, violence most often occurs in the domestic sphere.[67] Transition stress and trauma are themselves drawn upon in explanation of/ justification for this violence. Ex-soldiers (and their relatives) from a range of South African former forces have spoken about outbursts of aggressive/violent behaviour in their homes directed at wives or girlfriends, both since being demobilised and during the period of conflict – with some former SADF conscripts, in particular, connecting their domestic violence to the multiple demobilisations that required adapting and re-adapting to civilian life *in between* periods of combat while simultaneously struggling with the psychological effects of recent combat experience.[68] Importantly, patterns of gendered, often sexualised or domestic violence should be recognised as continuing – if transmuting – out of war/conflict situations (rather than an exclusive phenomenon of transition).[69] Sexual violations, perpetrated by soldiers against enemy women provide regularly reported examples, and have been explained as the outcome of particular brands of militarised masculinities that fuse maleness, sexuality, military victory and aggression.[70] Moreover, as ex-combatants also regularly point out, numerous strains and processes *other than* militarised experience cause 'civvy' men they know to perpetrate domestic violence, while many of their former fellow combatants apparently do not do so at all.[71]

There can be little doubt that militarised identities, unresolved trauma, and personal transition are all potential ingredients for violence, and their roles in transmutations of conflict out of war into peacetime require careful investigation. But the simplistic linkage regularly made between ex-combatants and violence curtails informed consideration of this relationship, and prevents meaningful engagement with the varied and numerous challenges and hardships of war in 'peace'.

Neglected necessities: Psycho-social support, empowerment and multi-pronged strategies

While not all of South Africa's former soldiers suffer similarly in relation to trauma and transition – or some seemingly not at all – a range of significant burdens have been reported. These include unpredictable and disorientating tempers and aggression experienced as 'snapping' which sees the individual losing control and thrashing out. Some maintain that the propensity for such outbursts has intensified with the passing of time. The opposite has occurred for others, and/or they have developed strategies to pre-empt and manage them by removing themselves from tension-provoking situations, controlling alcohol consumption and not carrying weapons. A small minority have accessed trauma counselling.

Other reported manifestations of these ex-soldiers' distress include terrifying nightmares, flashbacks to combat experiences, and exaggerated startle responses. Some 'become loners',[72] avoid interaction with others, instead withdrawing into themselves and experiencing an inability to maintain personal relationships, trust or experience enjoyment. Levels of alcohol and drug abuse are purportedly high. That drug use was, for some, a coping strategy during the war is a facet of this, as is the impact of poverty and unemployment. At the extreme end of the self-destructive spectrum lies suicide, which both ex-SADF and MK soldiers maintain, is not uncommon amongst their former colleagues.[73]

The immense challenges faced by many former soldiers receive scant attention. Instead demobilisation programmes – the very programmes ostensibly designed to specifically ease transition to civilian life – have typically been (fairly superficial and) focused on the 'threat' posed by unemployed ex-combatants, which they seek to contain by providing minimal economic assistance (in the form of once-off gratuities and some vocational skills development training). South Africa's formal demobilisation process of (only) APLA and MK cadres was of this ilk,[74] and has been criticised on a number of counts, including its scope and the nature of the assistance offered.[75]

A key shortcoming of this and other initiatives has been the lack of attention paid to the various and complex psycho-social challenges the ex-soldiers encounter. This tends to result, at best, in the severe minimising of potential economic benefits or, at worst, the exacerbation of disillusionment, resentment and a sense of 'victimness' together with unchanged or disintegrating material circumstances. Indeed, the dire socio-economic situations facing numerous former fighters are becoming increasingly apparent.[76]

The lack of psycho-social support for ex-combatants is usually a continuation of what they could expect during combat days. As one put it, 'We don't know what debriefing is because we never had it!!'[77] An oft-cited source of ex-national service men's anger is the lack of such support from the SADF following combat, or in the numerous transitions the call-up and camp system necessitated. A conscript recalls:

> On Thursday [I was] holding a guy bleeding out his life all over my browns with my R5 [firearm] . . . hot after an ambush. Friday [I was] on a *flossie* back to *klaar out* and Monday driving to work. No support, no debriefing. Once you are *klaared* out they owe you nothing.

Of the 'final' transition to civilian life, a psychiatrist who periodically offered his assistance to MK cadres in exile, explained how the planned provision of psychiatric support to returning exiles was never realised, 'The fact is they have disappeared into South Africa and we suspect that they would be in need of help most of the time.'[78] This no doubt applies across the political spectrum, as well as beyond the bounds of ex-combatant groupings. In countries attempting to recover from war situations with so many pressing needs on socio-economic fronts, psycho-social care for ex-combatants is typically not afforded high priority. More generally, such services tend to be out of reach of most at the same time that there is lack of exposure regarding the potential value of such support (and of the consequences of trauma). Amongst former soldiers, well schooled in macho myth (and the denial of vulnerability it demands), resistance to such services, and fear of stigmatisation for seeking emotional/mental health assistance tends to be particularly strong (where any acknowledgment of traumatic stress would apparently amount to admission of having completely lost one's mind). Again, such perceptions are not helped by the frequent linkage of former soldiers to violence: the possibility of trauma in their ranks appears to receive public exposure mainly in reaction to violent (and sensational) events.

As a former recce put it, 'It's such a good story to say, "Here's another military guy that went cuckoo" . . .'[79] This adds another layer to stigmatisation via pathologising stereotype. It also reinforces the taboo around seeking assistance.[80]

One avenue of support is that amongst the soldiers themselves. Contrasting with vertical networks – more often than not broken down and sullied by 'betrayals' – horizontal bonds between friends from the military appear often to be strong. Many view these fellow soldiers as the only people who understand them. Such relationships, however, are difficult to maintain and a loss of camaraderie and unity amongst former colleagues is much lamented as individuals become preoccupied with trying to 'make it' in the civilian world. Moreover, while clearly 'army mates' are, in some cases, able to support each other through deeply personal trauma- and transition-related difficulties,[81] this is limited as delicate subjects and memories are apparently mostly avoided or mentioned only in passing.[82] In addition, as a former MK soldier has noted, sharing experiences can feed a sense of despair and hopelessness 'as they talk and talk and nothing changes'.[83]

More broadly, individuals and organisations grappling with ex-combatant issues are calling for holistic approaches, ones that incorporate, for example, healing and relationship building/ mending components into the more conventional economic interventions (focused on the provision of 'hard skills'). At the same time, this makes demands for new and creative models of working with mental health and trauma that similarly take into account past, present and changing social, economic and political components to ex-soldiers' personal transitions as well as their dual victim-perpetrator experiences. Some organisations (local non-governmental, community-based organisations and church structures) have implemented promising initiatives in this vein with positive effects for many of those involved. Amongst others, these include, memorialisation projects, psycho-social support components to skills training programmes, networking for economic, educational, and benefit opportunities, as well as striving for a clearer picture of the scope and situations of the former-soldier population. Initiatives are sometimes related to energies amongst ex-combatants themselves who have sought to assist and support fellow former soldiers (e.g., via establishing therapeutic support groups, reconciliation processes and skills development programmes). Overall, however, and notwithstanding the immense value of such contributions, a lack of resources regularly makes it difficult if not impossible to sustain and evaluate such models. Engagement with the issue remains ad hoc, severely under-resourced and under-coordinated; and support mechanisms are absent or sporadic and often inadequate.

Conclusion

More and more ex-combatants are emerging across the continent and the world. They are expected to reintegrate into society and leave their militarised identities behind. Usually, this reintegration is into a hostile environment of transitional relations beset with daunting social, economic and political challenges. While ex-combatants' transitional situations vary dramatically in terms of the levels of support available to them (social, economic and political), rarely are they or the people around them equipped for the equally complex personal transitions demanded of the soldiers. Rather, too often, changing and new patterns of exclusion, marginalisation, and victimisation are generated – a danger that is arguably exacerbated when for the most part ex-combatants are 'wished away' by the rest of society, and focused upon only in so far as they are feared as security threats.

Conversely, placing issues of psycho-social wellbeing firmly on the ex-combatant agenda would go a long way to meaningfully support them in their efforts to build positive 'post-conflict' identities (and thus also make inroads into the demilitarisation of South Africa). At the same time, victim-empowerment strategies need to be developed that can take account of this complexity. Ultimately, this is about foregrounding the context of both personal and societal transition. As such, strategies need to cohere with reconciliation initiatives and the objectives of transformation, human security and justice – for example, by balancing the needs of other marginalised groupings and victims (sometimes the direct victims of ex-combatants). Moreover, the potential inter-changeability of victim–offender roles is seldom as vividly embodied as it is by numerous ex-combatant groupings, and in this, they demand innovative approaches that can accommodate the temporally shifting and layered nature of victim–offender dynamics (where they are/may be victims and perpetrators of the past, and in the present and the future). While ex-combatants experience these dynamics to differing degrees (some barely at all), they continue to produce new requirements for reconciliation and healing.

Central to the challenge of building connections between ex-combatants and broader society, and supporting them in renegotiating their identity, is the recognition of their pasts. While society generally seems uninterested in uncovering these pasts, without at least some acknowledgement of ex-soldiers' histories, and a commitment to understanding how these continue to impact on individuals, ex-combatants' efforts to reconcile their militarised identities with their present realities will be severely undermined. As well as having specific consequences for ex-soldiers' reintegration, failure to engage will bring general consequences for reconciliation. Indeed, the situation of ex-combatants can be considered to represent the problems and possibilities inherent in the transition that society as a whole is experiencing.

Notes to Chapter Fourteen

1   This chapter is based on the work done in the Violence & Transition Project at the Centre for the Study of Violence and Reconciliation (CSVR). Funding from the International Development Research Centre made the project possible. Thanks to all those ex-combatants who, willing to share their stories, participated in the research. Thanks also to Bronwyn Harris, Piers Pigou, John Gear, Gary Baines, Amanda Dissel, David Bruce, Hugo van der Merwe, and Helen Hajiyiannis for editorial inputs.

2   S. Willet, 'Demilitarisation, Disarmament & Development in southern Africa', *Review of African Political Economy* 25, 77 (1998):419.

3   These structures differed considerably from each other with varying degrees of connection to political organisations. Those broadly associated with the liberation movements commonly engaged in combat with the SAP and others perceived as agents of the apartheid state

4   In addition to the SADF's reliance on proxy forces such as UNITA and RENAMO, its special indigenous units, including 31 and 32 Battalions, and the SAP's *Koevoet*, were integral components of apartheid's security apparatus. For example, 31 Battalion forcibly recruited large numbers of the few remaining !Kung and JU/Wasi (Namibian San People), and put them to war against their fellow country people.

5   The ANC's strategy of 'People's War' highlights the problem of a clear differentiation between 'combatants' and 'non-combatants' that 'rests on a precise demarcation of the battlefield' (*War and Society: The Militarisation of South Africa*, ed. J. Cock and L. Nathan (Cape Town and Johannesburg: David Philip, 1989), 2). Similarly the vast military network developed by the state, including various 'civilian' military structures meant that white 'civil' society also became highly militarised and security-orientated.

6   G. Cawthra, *Brutal Force: The Apartheid War Machine* (London: International Defence and Aid Fund for southern Africa, 1986).

7   S. Ellis, 'The Historical Significance of South Africa's Third Force', *Journal of Southern African Studies* 24, 2 (1998):261–99; *Truth and Reconciliation Commission of South Africa (TRC) Report* Vol. 2 (Cape Town: Juta & Co., 1998).

8   S. Gear, *Wishing Us Away: Challenges Facing Ex-combatants in the 'New' South Africa*, Violence & Transition Series 8 (Braamfontein: CSVR, 2002).

9   More generally, problems experienced in the armed forces integration and related demobilisation process (for those who did not qualify or chose not to integrate into the SANDF) have been a source of frustration and disillusionment. Amongst other things, poor planning, bad communication, and a lack of coordination or monitoring dogged the processes.

10 H. van der Merwe and R. Smith, 'Ex-combatants as Peacebuilders: Opportunities and Challenges', in *Struggles in Peacetime* (Amsterdam: Netherlands Institute for southern Africa, 2006).

11 This chapter draws extensively on qualitative data gathered in focus groups and interviews with SADF and MK ex-combatants. These were conducted by the author for the Violence & Transition Project at the CSVR during 1999 and 2000. Supplementary SADF data was gathered through engagement with an English-medium Internet chat-line 'Army Talk'. See Introduction note 46.

12 T. Bennet, *Using Children in Armed Conflict: A Legitimate African Tradition?* ISS Monograph Series 32 (Pretoria: ISS, 1998), 31; M. Mausse and N. Daniel, *Child Soldiers in southern Africa*, ISS Monograph Series 37 (Pretoria: ISS, 1999), 11–12, 57; A. Veale and A. Stavrou, *Violence, Reconciliation and Identity: The Reintegration of Lord's Resistance Army Child Abductees in Northern Uganda*, ISS Monograph Series 92 (Pretoria: ISS, 2003), 10–11.

13 A conceptualisation of 'victims' of conscription arguably fits with the UN definition that incorporates victims of 'immoral abuse of power', where 'action or laws *should* be criminal but because of the immoral

nature of the government, they are not' (S. Garkawe, 'Modern Victimology: Its importance, Scope and Relationship with Criminology', *Acta Criminologica*, 14, 2 (2001):94). As Garkawe argues, South Africa's apartheid laws provided a prime example; and although he focuses on those that sought to directly regulate black South Africans, racially-based conscription was clearly the product of the 'crime against humanity' that was apartheid.

14   S. Ellis, 'The New Frontiers of Crime in South Africa', in *The Criminalisation of the State in Africa*, ed. J. Bayart, S. Ellis and B. Hibon (Oxford: James Curry, 1999); B. Harris, *Spaces of Violence, Places of Fear: Urban Conflict in Post-apartheid South Africa*. Paper presented to Foro Social Mundial Tematico, Cartagena, Colombia, 16–20 June (2003):1; G. Simpson, '"A Snake Gives Birth to a Snake": Politics and Crime in the Transition to Democracy in South Africa', in *Justice Gained? Crime and Crime Control in South Africa's Transition*, ed. B. Dixon, and E. van der Spuy (Cape Town: UCT Press, 2004).

15   L. Mashike and M. Mokalobe, 'Reintegration into Civilian Life: The Case of Former MK and APLA Combatants', *Track Two*, 12, no. 1& 2. (2003):20; D. Skinner, *Apartheid's Violent Legacy: A Report on Trauma in the Western Cape* (Western Cape: The Trauma Centre for Victims of Violence & Torture, 1998), 81.

16   *Mail & Guardian*, 'Mutilation by the Military', 28 July 2000; *Mail & Guardian*, 'Gay Coalition Wants Probe Into Levin', 18 August 2000.

17   Gear, *Wishing Us Away*, 95.

18   H. Hajiyiannis and N. Vienings, 'Arguing for the Inclusion of Trauma Counselling in Medical Health Insurance', CSVR occasional paper (1999).

19   Psychological problems may emerge only months or years after the initiating trauma and may also intensify with time. See D. Sandler, 'The Psychological Experiences of White Conscripts in the Black Townships', in *War and Society*, ed. Cock and Nathan; B. Shepard, 'Still in Shock: Treating the Aftermath of Trauma', *Times Literary Supplement*, 4–5 July 16, (1999).

20   See R. W. Eisenhart, 'You Can't Hack it Little Girl: A Discussion of the Covert Psychological Agenda of Modern Combat Training', *Journal of Social Issues* 31, 4 (1975):13–23; K. Jochelson, 'War, State and Society: Men, Masculinity and Militarism: Theorising Military Violence', Unpublished paper (1987); S. Gear, *Now That the War Is Over: Ex-combatants, Transition and the Question of Violence. A Literature Review*, Violence and Transition Series 9, CSVR report (2002).

21   L. Vetten, 'War and the Making of Men and Women', *Sunday Independent*, 16 August 1998.

22   While non-conventional military formations are typically more progressive in their attitude to women, and the presence of women in their ranks has been understood to deter sexual violence against enemy women during war (Arnett in *Against Our Will: Men, Women and Rape*, ed. S. Brownmiller (New York: Simon & Schuster, 1975)), intra-organisational sexual violence appears not to be uncommon. See P. Dewhirst, *Women's Experience of Trauma*, CSVR seminar report, 23 April 1998; Skinner, *Apartheid's Violent Legacy*, 81; *TRC Report*, Vol. 4, Chap. 10, para. 44–51; Gear, *Now That the War Is Over*, 108.

23   Skinner, *Apartheid's Violent Legacy*, 81.

24   J. Cock, *Colonels & Cadres: War and Gender in South Africa* (Cape Town: Oxford University Press, 1991); Gear, *Wishing Us Away*, 96.

25   Cock, *Colonels & Cadres*, 56. See also Jochelson, 'War, State and Society'.

26   Ex-SADF member cited in Gear, *Wishing Us Away*, 84.

27   B. Harris, *Between a Rock and a Hard Place: Violence, Transition and Democratization. A Consolidated Review of the Violence and Transition Project* CSVR (2006) after I. Palmary, 'Report narrative for VTP 2. Violence and Transition 2: Obstacles to and Opportunities for Democracy', *Final Report to the International Development Research Centre*, CSVR (2005).

28   Shepard, 'Still in Shock'.

29   L. Apteker and D. Stocklin, 'Children in Particularly Difficult Circumstances: A Cross-cultural Perspective', Unpublished paper (1995); *TRC Report*, Vol 5., ch 4.

30   Shepard, 'Still in Shock'; Z. Solomon, *Combat Stress Reaction: The Enduring Toll of War* (New York: Plenum Press, 1993); Gear, *Now That the War is Over*.

31   A. Honwana, 'The Collective Body: Challenging Western Concepts of Trauma and Healing', *Track Two*, 8, 1 (1999):30–35; G. Straker, F. Moosa and Sanctuaries Counselling Team, 'Post-traumatic Stress Disorder: A Reaction to State-supported Child Abuse and Neglect', in *Child Abuse & Neglect*, 12 (1988):48.

32   M. Chachiua, 'Demilitarisation of Post-conflict Societies: The case of Demobilization of Youth in Mozambique', Paper presented at the KATU Workshop on Youth for Conflict Prevention in southern Africa, Livingstone, Zambia, April 12–16 (1999); Honwana, 'The Collective Body', 33.

33   B. Hamber, 'The Burdens of Truth: An Evaluation of the Psychological Support Services and Initiatives Undertaken by the South African Truth and Reconciliation Commission', *American Imago*, 55; A. McKay, 'The Survivors of Apartheid and Political Violence in KwaZulu-Natal', in *Spirals of Suffering: Public Violence and Children*, ed. B. Rock (Pretoria: HSRC, 1997).

34   This became an issue at the TRC, for example, when apartheid agents responsible for numerous atrocities, litigiously employed the diagnosis of PTSD, claiming to be suffering from it (G. Eagle, 'The Political Conundrums of Post-traumatic Stress Disorder', in *Psychopathology and Social Prejudice*, ed. D. Hook and G. Eagle 75–91 (Cape Town: University of Cape Town Press, 2002), The TRC resultantly considered it indirectly, as an explanation for why perpetrators did not remember details. While commissioners did not generally appear sympathetic to such justifications, they ultimately seemed to be lenient when considering 'poor memory' in their decisions. Furthermore while the TRC recognised the trauma involved in combat (e.g. the conscript hearing) they did not have a clear analysis or strategy to engage with the ex-combatants who showed such symptoms (Hugo Van der Merwe, personal communication, 2006).

35   Eagle, 'The Political Conundrums of Post-traumatic Stress Disorder', 87; T. Abrahamsen and H. van der Merwe, *Reconciliation Through Amnesty? Amnesty Applicants' Views of the South African Truth and Reconciliation Commission* (Braamfontein: CSVR, 2005) http://www.csvr.org.za/papers/paptahv/.

36   Eagle, 'The Political Conundrums of Post-traumatic Stress Disorder', 85–9; M. A. Simpson, 'What Went Wrong? Diagnostic and Ethical Problems in Dealing with the Effects of Torture and Repression in South Africa', in *Beyond Trauma: Cultural and Societal Dynamics*, ed. R. J. Kleber, C. R Figley and B. Gersons (New York: Plenum Press, 1995), 187–212.

37   Harris, *Spaces of Violence*, 11.

38   This particularly applies to those no longer accommodated in these structures.

39   For accounts of some of these changing relations, see Gear, *Wishing Us Away*, 47–62; L. Khalane and M. Parlevliet, *Integration of Defence/Protection Formations (Militarised Youth) Into the Mainstream of Society* (Cape Town: Urban Monitoring and Awareness Committee (UMAC), 1998), 5–14, 16–18; P. Thulare, *Uniform Solution?: The Attempted Assimilation of Community Defence Units Into the South African Police Service* (Johannesburg: Centre for Policy Studies, 1997).

40   Gear, *Wishing Us Away,* 52.

41   The compulsory nature of apartheid-era conscription makes this 'category' especially diverse – indeed almost as much so as the entire white male population of a broad age-range. In relation to attitudinal variances detected amongst former conscript respondents see Gear, *Wishing Us Away*, 10, 15.

42   These ex-MK soldiers maintain this has been exacerbated by high profile cases of ex-combatant involvement in cash-in-transit heists – and allegations of this.

43   Complex relationships with police members together with a fledgling human rights based criminal justice system make these specific ex-combatants' interactions with contemporary crime particularly fraught, and variously situate them in a dynamic interplay of current relations of victimisation and perpetration

(including legitimate crime fighting, vigilantism and 'criminal' action as well as victimisation). See Gear, *Wishing Us Away*, 51–92.

44   See Gear, *Wishing Us Away*, 51–62.

45   Ibid. 24, 28, 111–16.

46   Ibid. 21

47   Mashike and Mokalobe, 'Reintegration into Civilian Life', 17.

48   Gear, *Wishing Us Away,* 43–4.

49   G. Lamb, 'From Military to Civilian Life: The Case of Retired Special Forces Operators', *Track Two.* 12, 1 & 2 (2003):37–60; Gear, *Wishing Us Away.*

50   M. Mokalobe, *Demobilisation and Re-integration of Ex-combatants in South Africa*, Group for Environmental Monitoring (1999):22; NGO Networking Service, 'Demobilisation and Reintegration Issues in the Horn of Africa', in *Dismissed: Demobilisation and Reintegration of Former Combatants in Africa*, ed. J. Cilliers (Halfway House: Institute for Defence Policy, 1996), 76.

51   Lamb, 'From Military to Civilian Life'; Gear, *Wishing Us Away.*

52   Gear, *Wishing Us Away*, 116; Mashike and Mokalobe, 'Reintegration into Civilian Life', 28.

53   Lamb, 'From Military to Civilian Life'; Gear, *Wishing Us Away.*

54   This was abundantly clear in the fieldwork drawn on for this chapter where attempts to organise focus groups of former conscripts who had served on the border, were derailed as planned participants repeatedly pulled out at the last minute on the grounds of the oaths that they had been required to sign at the time.

55   Gear, *Wishing Us Away*, 116.

56   Ex-combatants' involvement in the TRC occurred mainly through applications to the amnesty process. The process however did not contribute positively to their reintegration, and many were faced with the dilemma of whether or not to apply (Van der Merwe, forthcoming). While many experienced pressure from among their ranks not to participate, amnesty applicants also variously regarded it as biased, uncompassionate, additionally stigmatising, and distorting of their experiences (Y. Henry, 'A Space Where Healing Begins', 2000, http://www.trcresearch.org.za/papers99/henry.pdf/). Amnesty applications and armed force submissions were overwhelmingly (and ironically) from the ranks of the liberation armies and its allies, while the SADF submission refused to acknowledge its role in perpetrating human rights abuses both in and outside South Africa. 'Of the 256 members of the apartheid era security forces that applied for amnesty . . . only 31 had served in the SADF. In contrast, there were close to 1 000 applications for amnesty from members of the various armed structures aligned to the ANC' (D. Foster, P. Haupt and M. de Beer, *The Theatre of Violence: Narratives of Protagonists in the South African Conflict* (Cape Town: Institute for Justice and Reconciliation, 2005), 15–16). Relatively few made statements as victims, choosing to not categorise themselves in this way. A special and unique hearing on conscription provided some acknowledgment of the indoctrination and trauma suffered by conscripts and their families, but was treated with hostility by most ex-SADF officials.

57   Gear, *Wishing Us Away*, 111.

58   H. van der Merwe, Draft CSVR Overview for South Africa for 'Disarmament, Demobilization and Reintegration (DDR) and Transitional Justice'. A research project of the International Center for Transitional Justice (ICTJ) April 2006; S. Phakathi and H. van der Merwe, *Survivors' Perspective on the TRC Amnesty Process*, CSVR (2005).

59   Gear, *Wishing Us Away*, 112; Henry, *Where Healing Begins*, 168.

60   Thanks to discussion with Bronwyn Harris, 2006.

61   One dynamic in relation to former liberation fighters, is that their family members also often suffered severe hardship because of their military involvement, and contemplated 'liberation' with their own expectations, expectations that have since been dashed.

62 As one former conscript described his military training, 'they turned you from a mouse . . ., into a person, then into a man'.

63 Gear, *Wishing Us Away*, 51.

64 Ibid. 47–52.

65 P. Laurence, 'Scapegoats for the Country's Ills', *Focus Ten*, Helen Suzman Foundation. (April 1998):6.

66 Often with few skills beyond their military ones (a situation regularly exacerbated by disrupted educational backgrounds) the concern is that unemployed ex-combatants will become disaffected and turn to crime and/or threaten reconciliation and reconstruction efforts (P. Collier, 'Demobilisation and Insecurity in Ethiopia and Uganda; A Study in the Economics of the Transition from War to Peace', in *Dismissed: Demobilisation and Reintegration of Former Combatants in Africa*, ed. J. Cilliers (Halfway House: Institute for Defence Policy, 1996).

67 Y. Danieli, 'Intergenerational Legacies of Trauma in Police Families', in *Police Trauma: Psychological Aftermath of Civilian Combat*, ed. J. Violanti and D. Paton (Illinois, USA: Charles C. Thomas Publisher, 1999), 179; P. Muzaale, *Evaluation of the Second Phase of the Veterans Assistance Program: Final Summary Report* (The Republic of Uganda Veterans Assistance Programme, 1995), 10.

68 Gear, *Wishing Us Away*, 85.

69 That domestic violence may increase in war times is evidenced in some women's experiences at the hands of their SDU partners during the height of violence in Gauteng's East Rand in the early 1990s, as it is in testimony from certain former SADF conscripts (Gear, *Wishing Us Away*, 84, 88).

70 Cock, *Colonels & Cadres*, 8–62; Eisenhart, 'You Can't Hack it', 21–2; Gear, *Now That the War Is Over,* 125; Jochelson, 'War, State and Society'.

71 Gear, *Wishing Us Away*, 90.

72 Ibid. 98.

73 Ibid. 100.

74 It basically involved provision of a once-off gratuity payment and the opportunity to receive some vocational skills training.

75 Mashike and Mokalobe, 'Reintegration into Civilian Life', 3, 21–2; Gear, *Now That the War Is Over*, 61–8; Gear, *Wishing Us Away*, 23–30; T. Motumi and P. McKenzie, 'After the War: Demobilisation in South Africa', in *From Defence to Development: Redirecting Military Resources in South Africa*, ed. J. Cock and P. McKenzie (Cape Town and Johannesburg: David Philip, 1998), 194–202.

76 A 2003 study found the rate of unemployment amongst former MK and APLA cadres to be 66% – dramatically higher than the already alarmingly inflated national average (Mashike and Mokalobe, 'Reintegration into Civilian Life', 17).

77 Gear, *Wishing Us Away*.

78 Ibid. 97.

79 Ibid.

80 Despite this resistance (not exclusive to soldiers) anecdotal evidence suggests that where former soldiers have been exposed to (even minimal) psycho-education activities, the mere knowledge that what they experience are *normal* responses to traumatic incidents brings a sense of relief, but sometimes also anger when they are informed for the first time, especially when coupled with the fact that they were not supported and equipped with this knowledge during combatant days.

81 Gear, *Wishing Us Away*, 85.

82 Ibid. 14, 20 and 103. This 'limitation' is not surprising or unique in that most ex-combatants – and indeed civilians – have never participated in related services/skill developments initiatives.

83 Organisationally, individual branches of some veterans associations have expressed the desire for gaining skills to provide psycho-social support to their constituents, but associations are not generally equipped

to do so. Indeed many suffer from a wider lack of capacity, resources and strategy. Many of those derived from SADF units are more along the lines of 'social clubs' for interested participants, while a few offer some sort of welfare assistance to former soldiers/their families. The newer organisations of the former liberation armies battle with inadequate human and financial resources, constraining goals to link ex-combatants to work opportunities and other services. See Mashike and Mokalobe, 'Reintegration into Civilian Life' regarding non-statutory associations.

Chapter 15

South Africa in Namibia/Angola: The Truth and Reconciliation Commission's Account[1]

Christopher Saunders

Almost all of the now voluminous secondary literature on the Truth and Reconciliation Commission (TRC) is concerned with the Commission in relation to South Africa itself. In most of this literature there is no mention of the fact that the Promotion of National Unity and Reconciliation Act of 1995 charged the Commission with 'investigating and documenting gross human rights abuses committed 'within *or outside*' South Africa in the period 1960–94'.[2] The addition of 'outside' South Africa was a necessary injunction because what happened inside the country was intimately bound up with what happened in the rest of the region. But the regional context of the TRC's work has been given relatively little attention, especially by historians, and what the TRC's five-volume *Report*, handed to President Nelson Mandela in 1998, said about South African involvement in the region has been largely ignored.

While the TRC was asked to investigate aspects of South Africa's recent past, very few historians were involved in the Commission's work, and to date historians have shown more scepticism about the work of the Commission and the findings embodied in the *TRC Report* than concern to engage with what the *Report* found.[3] Most of the literature on the TRC since the *Report* appeared is concerned with such matters as truth versus justice, and philosophical and psychological aspects of the work and findings of the Commission. Few historians have begun the task of subjecting the *TRC Report* to sustained and detailed criticism,[4] and none have done so with regard to what the *TRC Report* said about what happened in countries in the region rather than in South Africa itself.

There are a number of reasons for this. Few historians are actively involved in researching and writing on the recent political history of the country, let alone that of the region. The *TRC Report* contains no index and few footnotes, and therefore few clues to the sources on which its statements are based. It only identifies its sources sporadically and haphazardly.[5] Access to the documentary material that the TRC collected, and to other relevant source material, remains difficult, and in some cases impossible. It is not known when historians will be able to gain access to the mass of documentation collected by the TRC's Research Department, or to the amnesty applications submitted to the Commission, which are part of the vast TRC archive now housed in the National Archives in Pretoria. Special permission has to be obtained to access any of this material. And there are problems accessing the material on the TRC website, because of the failure of the relevant authorities to keep the site updated. At the time of writing, the links to the so-called Caprivi hearings (see further below), which were broken when the site was transferred from the Commission to the Department of Justice, had not been restored.[6]

Though the TRC investigators used previously unknown documentary material on Namibia and Angola from as far afield as Havana, Cuba, and from the archives of the South African Defence Force (SADF), little that was new emerged in the *TRC Report*. What happened in the region was given very short shrift: of over 2 700 pages in the five volumes, only some 60 or so relate directly to what happened in Namibia and Angola. More was written, but that had to be cut down to fit the number of pages allocated for this section of the *TRC Report*.[7] Yet from what the Commission says, it is clear that it was fully aware of the importance of what happened in the two neighbouring countries. The *TRC Report* makes the key point that more people died as a result of apartheid crimes in the region outside South Africa than in the country itself.[8] Many of the most brutal apartheid atrocities occurred in Namibia, and the single most brutal atrocity occurred in southern Angola because of the presence there of Namibian refugees (see the section on the Cassinga massacre below). In southern Angola the apartheid state engaged in a war that in its final stages became semi-conventional in nature and involved thousands of deaths.[9]

Though the Commission was right to recognise that apartheid in South Africa cannot be understood without placing it in the context of the region as a whole, the *TRC Report* says little about the ways in which what happened in Namibia and Angola is interlinked with, and helps explain, what took place in South Africa itself. Much that South Africa did in Namibia anticipated what would happen in South Africa itself, from moving away from apartheid to the attempt to manipulate the result of the first democratic election.[10] A number of the leaders in *Koevoet*, the paramilitary police unit in northern Namibia, moved into the Vlakplaas death squads in South Africa, including, most notoriously, Eugene de Kock.[11] The impact of apartheid on the region clearly deserved much greater attention than the TRC accorded it.

The *TRC Report* mentions 'the enormity of the topic' and says: 'South Africa's occupation of South West Africa would merit a separate truth commission of its own'.[12] The Namibian government has consistently refused to organise such a commission, in part because it has not wanted the atrocities perpetrated in the South West Africa People's Organization (SWAPO) camps in Angola to come under public scrutiny, and because it would have no powers to bring South Africans before such a commission, and without their presence any such truth commission would inevitably be very one-sided.[13] There has been not even been a suggestion of a Truth Commission for what happened in southern Angola in the 1980s. In South Africa, victims were asked to testify to the TRC about their sufferings, and the victim hearings received major publicity and lay close to the heart of the TRC's work. A series of special hearings on particular aspects of the past were held, but few related in any way to Namibia/Angola. For the region, only a few particular atrocities were probed in detail, and the victims remained largely unheard, for there were no victim hearings as such for the region. The TRC was concerned only with gross human rights violations committed by the state and South Africans outside South Africa, and the *TRC Report* presents little more than a survey of South African aggression, with only a few aspects considered in any detail. What, then, can be learned from that survey, and from the few cases that the TRC did investigate? Did it select appropriate cases for special attention?

The TRC: Acts of commission and omission

What the *TRC Report* says about Namibia and Angola constitutes a useful summary of certain key events relating to South African involvement in those countries from the mid 1970s to the late 1980s. The criticism of excessive legalism that has been directed at some of the work of the Commission does not apply to this section of the *TRC Report*. It rightly makes the points that South Africa's rule of Namibia was illegal in international law – after the International Court of Justice had in 1971 declared its rule to be illegal, the United Nations Security Council (UNSC) had taken up the issue and supported that ruling – and was excessively brutal. It was also extremely damaging to the region as a whole, because it made possible, and provided the justification for, South African aggression into Zambia and Angola. If this has been forgotten in the public discourse, especially in South Africa itself, and if the *TRC Report*, by making these points, helps increase public awareness of them, it will have served a valuable purpose, but the document itself is hardly bed-time reading, and the promised short, popular version has not appeared in English.[14]

What the *TRC Report* says about Namibia/Angola mainly concerns the actions of the South African state. The relevant section of the second volume of the *TRC Report* is entitled 'The State Outside South Africa'. But later in that volume there is a quite separate section on the human rights violations committed in the African National Congress (ANC) camps in Angola, as if these were unrelated to the activities of the South African state. The *TRC Report* does not provide enough context in which to explain how the two were linked, nor does it explore the underlying reasons why crimes were committed in the ANC camps. Similarly, the South African state's actions in Namibia/Angola cannot be understood in isolation from what SWAPO was doing, yet there is no attempt to get to grips with this. It is now generally acknowledged that during the 1970s and the 1980s SWAPO presented a greater challenge to the security forces in Namibia than the South African state admitted at the time,[15] but the nature of that challenge is not investigated. That much of what is said about Namibia/Angola in the *TRC Report* is broad-brush was perhaps inevitable, given the limited space allocated to it, but the result is that the document does little more than synthesise parts of the relevant secondary literature, including what emerged in, say, the investigative work of the journalist Jacques Pauw in the late 1980s and early 1990s.[16] What is new is the level of detail, whether about what the SADF knew about Cassinga before the massacre, for example, or the structure of the Civil Co-operation Bureau (CCB), or the training given to different groups of armed men by the SADF in the remote Caprivi Strip in the far north-east of Namibia.

Why is the *TRC Report* not more revealing? I will first consider what it does say, rather than what it omits. What follows may seem nit-picking criticism, especially when the TRC itself, and those who worked for it, acknowledge that they did a less than perfect job. It is nevertheless important to point out the limitations in the *TRC Report* because it is likely to remain a major source for scholars in future. Some of the reasons why the *TRC Report* does not tell us more that is new about what happened in Namibia and Angola are generic in the sense that they apply to all its work. Others are specific to its work on countries outside South Africa or to what it says of Namibia/Angola in particular. I consider the generic reasons first.

Many of those who have written about the *TRC Report* have pointed to the short time the TRC was given in which to undertake its work: a mere two years. It was given an impossible mandate: to investigate gross human rights violations over a 34 year period, and in a number of countries, as well as to explain the context in which those human rights violations occurred. The TRC found, moreover, that great swathes of documentation relevant for its work had been destroyed, 44 tons in 1993 alone, including all the records of the CCB, consigned to the furnaces of the steel-works outside Pretoria.[17] The Commission spent time finding individuals accountable, while the *TRC Report* makes general arguments about, say, the role of race and the Cold War in helping to explain the brutality of the conflict. Inevitably, given the constraints under which it worked, the Commission's investigations could not be exhaustive. Not surprisingly, it chose to focus primarily on high profile individual cases and to adopt a narrow definition of 'gross human rights violations'. This meant, as Mahmood Mamdani and others have pointed out, that much of the routine brutality of apartheid rule was excluded from its enquiry.[18]

The five-volume *TRC Report* was written and published before some of the relevant amnesty hearings took place, in which new information about Namibia came out, information relating for example to the extent of the work of the CCB in destabilising Namibia in 1989. If the evidence given to the amnesty committee in 2000 by the assassin Ferdi Barnard is to be believed, this extended to a plot to bludgeon Maarti Ahtisaari, the UN Secretary' General's special representative, in a hotel in Keetmanshoop in southern Namibia with an axe.[19] The TRC's investigative work led to the trial of Dr Wouter Basson, head of the South African government's chemical and biological weapons' programme. It was only in that trial, in May 1999, that a horrifying revelation concerning South Africa's war in Namibia was made, when Johan Theron testified how he threw the bodies of captured and drugged SWAPO fighters from small planes into the Atlantic Ocean off the Namibian coast. That evidence has not been explored in court, for charges relating to it were dismissed in the trial of Basson, and Theron himself has not been tried.[20]

Some material relevant to the TRC's work was not made available to the Commission. Some of this was probably deliberately kept from it, such as the voluminous records of the SADF Military Intelligence section (MI), records which only came to light late in 2001, when the South African History Archive based at the University of the Witwatersrand took advantage of the new Promotion of Access to Information Act to ask whether such records existed. After that it was necessary to apply for access for them, and then a lengthy process of declassification had to take place, meaning that to date only a small portion has been opened to scholars.[21]

There are other, more specific reasons why the 'external' part of the TRC's work, of which Namibia/Angola forms the single most important part, was not more valuable. Those who appeared before the Commission – especially members of the former SADF – were able to refuse to talk about what they had done in Namibia/Angola on legal grounds, for they could say that they might be open for arrest and trial in those countries, which had not agreed to respect any amnesty granted in South Africa. Though the TRC tried to get the Namibian and other governments to accept its amnesty decisions, it failed in this, which is perhaps not surprising in the cases of Namibia and Angola, given the refusal of those governments to consider appointing a truth commission of their own. The failure to secure such agreements, however, robbed the TRC of much potentially valuable evidence. Only 13 of the well over 7 000 amnesty applications the TRC received related to incidents in Namibia/Angola; and these were mainly from members of the South African police. Only one submission related to a human rights violation.[22] The top brass of the former SADF were opposed to the TRC and obstructed its work by setting up a 'nodal point', which was supposed to facilitate co-operation with the TRC, but in fact served to frustrate its work, especially in relation to the war fought in northern Namibia and southern Angola.[23]

Even had more space been available, the *TRC Report* could not have provided a comprehensive account of the brutal South African occupation of Namibia, or of the major war, linked to a broader process of destabilisation, that South Africa was responsible for in Angola, or of the ANC's external operations. What the *TRC Report* says about South Africa's role in Namibia/Angola is inevitably highly selective. It does not even synthesise adequately the existing secondary literature on the occupation and the war, limited though that literature is. All I can do here is to point, first, to some things that the *TRC Report* did deal with, but which demand fuller consideration, and second, to some issues that it did not consider at all.

Assessing the TRC Report's findings

While the *TRC Report* mentions the vast scale of the violence perpetrated by South Africa in northern Namibia and southern Angola, it makes no satisfactory attempt to discuss it, and consequently no startlingly new revelations emerge. One of the problems about the *TRC Report*'s findings on the region is that they are based mostly on evidence from the state, not from victims or from the countries concerned, such as archival material relating to SWAPO or documentary evidence from the Angolan government. Though there are major problems with obtaining such material – the SWAPO archive is reported to be in Windhoek, but has not been made accessible to scholars, and if Angolan documentation were available, it would be in Portuguese – there is a vast amount of evidence that the TRC researchers did not tap. While the basic reason for the South African attacks on Angola is of course given in the *TRC Report* – South Africa's concern was to prolong its illegal occupation of Namibia – much of the context that would help to explain South African operations in Angola and their significance is missing because of the failure to exploit the records that are available, including the military records held in the Documentation Centre of the South African National Defence Force (SANDF) and the voluminous records of the Department of Foreign Affairs held in the Union Buildings, Pretoria.[24] Admittedly, this would have taken years to do.

In its account of atrocities committed by SADF members, the *TRC Report* concentrates on a relatively few cases of torture and extra-judicial killing, especially those carried out by members of *Koevoet*. Major episodes, such as the South African invasion of Angola in 1975, known to the SADF as Operation Savannah, are only covered briefly and obliquely. More is said on the results of Operation Savannah than on the Operation itself, perhaps because the Commission was neither able to access any files on it in the SADF archives, nor gain access to any Angolan data.[25] Neither of the two detailed published accounts of the invasion in Afrikaans is cited.[26] After mentioning 'the introduction of Cuban forces into Angola', the *TRC Report* goes on: 'The South African government's initial objective, therefore, was to prevent the MPLA from taking power at independence'.[27] This may suggest to the reader that the introduction of Cuban forces led to the South African invasion, when the reverse was the case, as has recently been confirmed in an exhaustive analysis by Piero Gleijeses.[28] The *TRC Report* then refers to events in the aftermath of the South African invasion:

> The movement of the forces of the South West African People's Organisation into bases in Angola was regarded as escalating the threat to South Africa's position in South West Africa. Aware that it would ultimately have to implement UN Resolution 435, the South African government was determined to weaken or cripple SWAPO's military capacity in preparation for the time when SWAPO would enter the electoral stakes inside South West Africa.[29]

UNSC Resolution 435 was not passed until September 1978, five months after the South African government had accepted the Western plan providing for an election under UN auspices in Namibia. Before that, if the South African government thought of SWAPO entering an election, it would have been an election under the constitution drawn up by the Turnhalle conference in Windhoek, and SWAPO never contemplated entering such an electoral contest. The *TRC Report*'s claim that not all South African forces withdrew from Angola in March 1976 is impossible to verify, as no source is given. It was widely reported at the time that all South African forces had withdrawn, and this was confirmed officially. [30]

Much attention is given in the *TRC Report* to the Cassinga massacre of 4 May 1978, in which over 600 residents of the camp in southern Angola were killed by the SADF forces that attacked it on that day. So much emphasis is placed on this event partly because it was the largest single case of gross human rights violations in the whole period that the Commission was concerned with, and partly because of the allegation that the casualties were unarmed civilians. It is also one case in which the TRC investigators found new material in the SADF archives. Presumably because of the TRC's inability to get the military to talk, however, no special hearing was held on the massacre. The new archival material helps to clarify the SADF motives for the raid, but the *TRC Report* does no more that confirm the assessment that others had reached in the face of the conflicting claims by SWAPO that it was purely a refugee camp, and by the SADF that it was a military base.[31] In fact it was both, for while the majority of the population in the camp were refugees, there was also a People's Liberation Army of Namibia (PLAN, the armed wing of SWAPO) force there, which engaged the incoming SADF troops in battle.[32] The *Report* accepts that the SADF did believe that they had sufficient evidence to show that Cassinga had an important military function, and that a primary objective of the raid was the capture or killing of Dimo Hamaambo, the commander of PLAN. He escaped before the raid took place. The *TRC Report* then cites evidence from the Cuban archives that 150 Cubans died when a Cuban force, based at Tchamutete, 16 km south of Cassinga, advanced to confront the South African paratroopers, and claims that this was the largest Cuban loss in its entire Angolan adventure from 1975–1991.[33] But more recent evidence from Havana is that only 16 Cubans died on that occasion, the first on which Cubans and Namibians died together.[34] The *TRC Report* accepts that no orders were given by the SADF officers in charge to kill already wounded people. This does not, of course, mean that such killing did not take place. It adds: 'The Commission also has evidence from the war in South West Africa that, on occasion, badly wounded SWAPO fighters were shot and not given medical treatment', but it does not tell us what that evidence is.[35] Nor does the *Report* add to the reader's knowledge of the significance of the massacre by exploring its wider context, relating it, say, to the even larger massacre perpetrated by the Rhodesian security forces against Zimbabwe African National Union guerrillas at a base in Mozambique some months earlier.[36]

The *TRC Report* continues with accounts of cross border raids into southern Angola. While some of this is well known to specialists, the document is able to draw upon State Security Council documents not previously accessible, as well as '*Aanvullende Dokumente*' (Supplementary Documents) held in the Documentation Centre of the SANDF. From these it concludes that Operation Protea, launched in 1980, 'probably caused more human suffering and physical damage than any other operation in the thirteen-year-long Angola war, resulting in violations of human rights on a vast scale'.[37] The *TRC Report* goes too far, however, when it speaks of de facto secession along with South African military occupation of southern Angola.[38] As it says, along with some 8 000 people who were killed in the various raids, there was an unknown number of civilian deaths, and massive destruction, but the question of reparation for Angola is not discussed, nor other consequences of South Africa's Angolan venture, in particular the development of the G5 and G6 artillery pieces, thanks to smuggled technology and expertise from Canada.[39] Over time, the SADF was sucked into ever greater involvement in southern Angola, from which by early 1988 it could not easily extricate itself. This was a major factor in the decision to agree to the implementation of UNSC Resolution 435, which meant South Africa withdrawing from Namibia. That withdrawal in turn helped to bring about the later negotiated settlement in South Africa itself.

At the Health Sector hearing held by the TRC, testimony was given on *Koevoet* and its role. That *Koevoet* had acted with extreme brutality was well known from a number of published accounts,[40] but Sean Callaghan's evidence added new detail. In early 1983, when the South African government was still denying any involvement in Angola, Callaghan was working as a doctor at Ongiva in northern Namibia. He wanted to repatriate a wounded person to 'the States' (i.e. South Africa),[41] but this was rejected by his superiors because they did not want the South African presence in Angola to come to international attention. The International Red Cross could therefore not be informed. Callaghan went on to recall that at the *Koevoet* camp next to Onamwani SWAPO guerrillas being kept in solitary confinement were offered jobs in *Koevoet* or in the police. If they accepted, they were no longer held as prisoners of war, and the Red Cross could not touch them. Callaghan wondered what happened to the hundreds who did not agree to change sides, and suggested that they may have been assassinated when *Koevoet* 'broke the UN cease-fire' in April 1989.[42] As already mentioned, it was only in the trial of Basson that details emerged of how SWAPO fighters were thrown into the Atlantic Ocean.[43]

Numerous people were assassinated in the course of South Africa's war in Namibia. However, the only assassination treated in any detail in the *TRC Report* is that of Anton Lubowski, the leading white member of SWAPO, which occurred in September 1989, after the war was over. Though the TRC held a public hearing on this assassination, the *TRC Report* merely confirms what was known from the inquest, and only adds a few details.[44] Other killings by members of the South African security forces are only mentioned in passing: the murder of Isaac Shifidi in Windhoek and of Jeannette Curtis Schoon and her daughter in Lubango by a letter-bomb in June 1984.[45] That the CCB contemplated killing Gwen Lister, the editor of the *Namibian* newspaper, Daniel Tjongerero and Hidipo Hamutenya of SWAPO in 1989 is also mentioned without further elaboration, as is the much earlier abduction of two Namibian political activists.[46] There is no mention of many other attacks, such as the raid on the SWAPO regional headquarters at Lubango by the South African Air force in 1979, or of numerous atrocities committed by members of SWAPO, including the assassination of the Herero leader Clemens Kapuuo in Windhoek in March 1978 and the planting of a bomb that exploded in the First National Bank in Oshakati in northern Namibia in 1988, killing 27 people.[47]

Nor does the *TRC Report* include material relating to Operation Victor. It was only in August 1997 that a TRC researcher conducted interviews with a former manager of the Namib Foundation, which oversaw this Operation, launched by the Security Branch to assist anti-SWAPO parties in Namibia in the run-up to the November 1989 election. These parties were given logistical support, training and media coverage. The operation had an initial budget of R25 million, and more was added later. In 1991, at the time of the so-called Inkathagate scandal, when South African government funding to Inkatha was revealed, the South African Foreign Minister, perhaps to distract attention from such funding, mentioned that the South African government had spent over R100 million on the anti-SWAPO parties. From his perspective the money had achieved its objective, of preventing SWAPO from obtaining a two-thirds majority in the Constituent Assembly, which meant that SWAPO had to bargain with others over the constitution for an independent Namibia.[48]

When the *TRC Report* tackles the human rights violations committed by the ANC in its Angolan military camps in the early 1980s, it draws heavily on the earlier enquiries conducted by the ANC itself – which Priscilla Hayner has described as truth commissions of a kind, but which are hardly objective sources – and on a 1992 *Report* by Amnesty International, as well as some interviews.[49] The *TRC Report* mentions that more ANC members died in the war against the Union for the Total Independence of Angola (UNITA) than from any other cause in Angola, but it does not investigate the conflict between the Angolan government and UNITA in any detail, nor explain why the ANC was fighting in an internal war in a country a long way from its objective, South Africa itself. The *TRC Report* merely says: 'The list of ANC members killed in exile reveals that considerably more MK combatants were killed in what are termed "UNITA ambushes" than by the SADF in combat. This was, indeed, the single largest cause of unnatural deaths amongst ANC members in exile.'[50] The *TRC Report* does not attempt to explore in any detail what happened to the hundreds of ANC exiles who died in Angola from causes ranging from 'accidents' to death in raids by UNITA. While in places, the *Report* is concerned with context, it gives the names of commanders of the different ANC camps in Angola, but adds nothing to help the reader understand the names, or their significance.[51]

There is considerable new information in the *TRC Report* on the training of various groups in the Caprivi. It tells that the first training-camp was established there by Major Swanepoel in the 1960s, and that Zambians were trained there in the 1970s and 1980s. The Zambian Foreign Minister claimed in 1981 that RENAMO forces were being trained at Camp Hippo.[52] None of this was known at the time, but the training of militia of Inkatha in the Caprivi became front-page news when the *Weekly Mail* broke the story in 1989. Though the trainees were officially to provide protection for Buthelezi and other Inkatha dignitaries, they returned to KwaZulu Natal and launched raids on Inkatha's enemies.[53] While the *TRC Report* had inevitably to be selective in what it could cover, it is not clear why it mentions, say, some of the military operations undertaken by the SADF into Zambia against SWAPO, [54] or Operation Silver, in which the SADF gave aid to UNITA because it was anti-SWAPO,[55] and ignores others.

Conclusion

The TRC left much unfinished business. This was less because it wanted to avoid opening cans of worms than because of its mandate and limited resources.[56] I have explored here only a small part of the useful, but flawed *TRC Report*. The work of the TRC as a whole is very much larger, and it is to be hoped that all the documentation it collected will one day become available. Though the *TRC Report* merely scratches the surface, it points the way to further work on the history of South Africa's involvement in Namibia and Angola, a history that retains its relevance in the present. Presumably because the victims of South African activities outside its borders were not South Africans, the TRC did not deal with the issue of reparation for the tens of thousands, if not millions, affected by gross human rights violations committed in Namibia and Angola. From a historian's perspective, the TRC process was of limited use, but it helped to show that much further research is needed before we have anything like a comprehensive and reliable account of South Africa's role in Namibia and Angola.

Notes to Chapter Fifteen

1   This is a revised version of a paper presented to the Canadian African Studies Association meeting in Toronto, May 2002. I thank Alan Jeeves for inviting me to participate on that occasion, and John Daniel, the main author of the section of the *TRC Report* dealing with the countries in the region beyond South Africa, for comments on the paper as delivered then.

2   *TRC Report*, Vol. 2, Chap. 2, para. 1 (hereafter 2/1/1). As of June 2006 there were 262 entries on the South African Truth and Reconciliation Commission in the Library catalogue of the University of Cape Town. Among the leading works by participants and observers are D. Tutu, *No Future Without Forgiving* (London: Rider, 1999); A. Boraine, *A Country Unmasked* (Cape Town: Oxford University Press, 2000); A. Krog, *Country of My Skull*, 2nd ed. (Johannesburg: Random House, 2002); W. Orr, *From Biko to Basson: Wendy Orr's Search for the Soul of South Africa as a Commissioner of the TRC* (Saxonwold: Contra Press, 2000); Z. Khoisan, *Jakaranda Time: An Investigator's View of South Africa's Truth and Reconciliation Commission* (Observatory: Garib Communications, 2001). Among the leading scholarly assessments are those by K. Christie, *The South African Truth Commission* (Basingstoke: Macmillan, 2000); W. James and L. van der Vijver, eds., *After the TRC: Reflections on Truth and Reconciliation in South Africa* (Cape Town: David Philip, 2000); M. Meredith, *Coming to Terms: South Africa's Search for Truth* (New York: Public Affairs, 1999); R. Rotberg and D. Thompson, eds. *Truth v. Justice: The Morality of Truth Commissions* (Princeton: Princeton University Press, 1999); D. Shea, *The South African Truth Commission: The Politics of Reconciliation* (Washington: United States Institute of Peace, 2000); E. Stanley, 'Evaluating the Truth and Reconciliation Commission', *Journal of Modern African Studies*, 39, 3 (2001); C. Villa-Vicencio and W. Verwoerd, eds. *Looking Back, Reaching Forward* (Cape Town: University of Cape Town Press, 2000); K. Wilson, *The Politics of Truth and Reconciliation in South Africa* (Cambridge: Cambridge University Press, 2001).

3   See C. Saunders, 'Historians and South Africa's Truth and Reconciliation Commission', *History Compass Journal*, 2005: www.history-compass.com. This scepticism arose in part from the idea that the TRC would not have time to undertake substantial historical research, without which there could be no significant progress in advancing the study of human rights violations in our recent past. Russell Ally was a historian by training; Madelaine Fullard and Nicky Rousseau of the University of the Western Cape's Department of History worked for the Research Department of the TRC.

4   An excellent example is P. Bonner and N. Nieftagodien, 'The Truth and Reconciliation Commission and the Pursuit of "Social Truth": The Case of Kathorus', in *Commissioning the Past*, ed. D. Posel and G. Simpson (Johannesburg: Wits University Press, 2002). Cf. also J. Cherry, 'Historical Truth: Something to Fight For', in Villa-Vicencio and Verwoerd, *Looking Back*.

5   The *TRC Report* did not always quote General Jannie Geldenhuys' *A General's Story: From an Era of War and Peace* (Johannesburg: Jonathan Ball, 1995) accurately (e.g. 2/2/58). This gave the former SADF generals an opportunity to score brownie points in evading the case that the *TRC Report* makes against them. See 'The Contact Bureau's Analysis of the TRC Report' (unpublished, Pretoria, 1999), esp. 18–19. (I thank Annette Seegers for giving me a copy of this.) The *TRC Report* draws upon the evidence of a few individuals (e.g. Mike Kuhn (2/1/68)) and a random set of sources (e.g. *X-Ray in southern Africa* (2/1/70) and *Apartheid Terrorism* (2/1/71)). Books such as Hooper's on *Koevoet*, cited below, or W. Minter, *Apartheid's Contras* (London: Zed Press, 1994) are not mentioned. Much of what is said about the ethnic units created to fight in southern Angola is known from books such as J. Breytenbach, *They Live By the Sword* (Alberton: Lemur, 1990), J. Breytenbach, *Eden's Exiles: One Soldier's Fight for Paradise* (Cape Town: Quellerie, 1997), J. Breytenbach, *The Buffalo Soldiers: The Story of South Africa's 32 Battalion, 1975–1993* (Alberton: Lemur, 2002).

6   See http://www.doj.gov.za/trc/index.html. When accessed in 2006, this site had last been updated in April 2003. It is in time to be transferred to the National Archives. For a time there was a better site, organised by a TRC staffer, www.struth.org.za, but that has long since disappeared. For the additional *Report* released in March 2003 see http://www.info.gov.za/otherdocs/2003/trc/ A more recent site is 'Traces of Truth. Documents relating to the South African Truth and Reconciliation Commission': http://truth.wwl.wits. ac.za/ but as of June 2006 that site had only one relevant collection on Namibia (on Operation Victor, for which see below), and none relating to Angola.

7   Information from John Daniel. I have not had access to what was not included in the *Report*.

8   *TRC Report*, 2/1/11 and cf. 2/2/5.

9   In the battle of Cuito Cuanavale in late 1987 and early 1988, thousands of Angolan government and UNITA troops were killed, and over 300 SWAPO fighters in northern Namibia in April 1989.

10   On the latter, see below. In 1978 some aspects of apartheid were removed, and then a one person, one vote election was held in December.

11   For details of his involvement, as deputy commander of *Koevoet*, see his autobiography, E. de Kock, *Long Night's Damage. Working for the Apartheid State* (Saxonwold: Contra, 1998). Dirk Coetzee also moved from northern Namibia to head Vlakplaas.

12   *TRC Report*, 2/2/75.

13   J. Saul and C. Leys, 'Lubango and After: "Forgotten History" as Politics in Contemporary Namibia', *Journal of Southern African Studies*, 29, 2 (2003); S. Nujoma, *Where Others Wavered* (London: Panaf Books, 2001); L. Dobell, 'Silence in Context: Truth and/or Reconciliation in Namibia', *Journal of Southern African Studies*, 23, 2 (June 1997). On the atrocities see especially *Breaking the Wall of Silence Movement, A Report to the Namibian People. Historical Account of the Swapo Spy-drama* (Windhoek: Breaking the Wall of Silence Movement, 1997) and J. Hunter's chapter in this volume.

14   The only short version to appear did so in German.

15   For the actions of the People's Army of Namibia (PLAN) see Nujoma, *Where Others Wavered,* and especially, O. Namakalu, *Armed Liberation Struggle. Some Accounts of PLAN's Combat Operations* (Windhoek: Gamsberg Macmillan, 2004). For the South African side, see various books by P. Stiff, especially *The Covert War. Koevoet Operations Namibia 1979–1989* (Alberton: Galago Books, 2004).

16   J. Pauw, *In the Heart of the Whore: The Story of Apartheid's Death Squads* (Halfway House: Southern, 1991); *Into the Heart of Darkness. Confessions of Apartheid's Assassins* (Johannesburg: Jonathan Ball, 1997).

17   V. Harris, '"They Should Have Destroyed More": The Destruction of Public Records by the South African State in the Final Years of Apartheid, 1990–1994', *Transformation,* 42 (2000); *TRC Report*, 1/8 and 5/6/105.

18   See, for example, M. Mamdani, 'Reconciliation Without Justice', *Southern African Review of Books*, November/December 1996; M. Mamdani, in *Crises and Reconstruction – African Perspectives*, ed. C. Leys and M. Mamdani (Uppsala: Nordic Africa Institute, 1997); M. Mamdani, 'The Truth According to the TRC', in *The Politics of Memory – Truth, Healing and Social Justice*, ed. I. Amadiume and A. An-Na'im (London: Zed Books, 2000).

19   *The Namibian*, 29 September 2000. Barnard was subsequently convicted and sentenced for the killing of Wits academic David Webster.

20   On Basson see especially M. Burger and C. Gould, *Secrets and Lies. Wouter Basson and South Africa's Chemical and Biological Weapons Programme* (Cape Town: Zebra Press, 2002). A second trial of Basson became possible in 2005 when the South African Constitutional Court ruled that the first trial had been flawed, and that Judge Willie Hartzenburg had been wrong to dismiss what had happened outside South Africa, but the National Prosecuting Authority declined to put Basson on trial again. It is not known, for

example, on whose orders Theron was acting, or whether this practice was taken over from the Argentina case, where some of those who 'disappeared' were dropped into the Atlantic.

21 See the South African History archive website at http://www.wits.ac.za/saha/programmes_foip_07.htm Photocopies of these records are now housed in the SAHA archive at Wits (B1).

22 *TRC Report*, 2/1/76. In 2000 South Africa's highest court confirmed, in an appeal by two South Africans seeking to avoid extradition to Namibia for offences committed in that country in the run-up to the 1989 election, that the TRC's Amnesty Committee had never had the right to grant amnesty for offences committed outside South Africa: Stopforth v Minister of Justice and others: Veenendal v Minister of Justice and others: *South African Law Reports*, 2000 (1) SA 113 (SCA).

23 See 'The Contact Bureau's Analysis of the TRC Report', p. 6 and n.1.

24 On these see S. Onslow, 'Research Report on the South African Archives', *Cold War History*, 5, 3 (2005).

25 *TRC Report*, 2/1/89–90, 2/2/15.

26 F. du Toit Spies, *Operasie Savannah* (Pretoria: Suid-Afrikaanse Weermag, 1989); S. du Preez, *Avontuur in Angola: Die verhaal van Suid-Afrika se Soldate in Angola, 1975–1976* (Pretoria: Van Schaik, 1989).

27 *TRC Report*, 2/2/11.

28 P. Gleijeses, *Conflicting Missions. Havana, Washington and Africa* (Chapel Hill: University of North Carolina Press, 2002).

29 *TRC Report* 2/2/12.

30 Ibid. 2/2/17.

31 Ibid. 2/1/10; 2/2/20.

32 For example, J. Heywood, *The Cassinga Event: An Investigation of the Records* (Windhoek: National Archives, 1994).

33 *TRC Report* 2/2/36.

34 Personal information from Piero Gleijeses, Washington, 2005. Edward George says 'at least sixty Cubans were killed': E. George, *The Cuban Intervention in Angola, 1965–1991. From Che Guevara to Cuito Cuanavale* (London: Frank Cass, 2005), 134.

35 *TRC Report*, 2/2/47.

36 Cf. R. Reid Daly, *Selous Scouts: Top Secret War*, 2nd ed. (Alberton: Lemur, 1982).

37 *TRC Report*, 2/2/61: OD 1968 no. 20.

38 *TRC Report*, e.g. 2/2/58.

39 L. Freeman, *The Ambiguous Champion: Canada and South Africa in the Trudeau and Mulroney Years* (Toronto: University of Toronto Press, 1997). The G5 and G6 guns were developed as a response to the Stalin Organs that the Cubans and Angolans had used against the South Africans in 1975–76. It was once thought that South Africa developed nuclear weapons because of the Cuban presence in Angola, but documents in the South African History Archive, made available under the Promotion of Access to Information Act, make clear that the nuclear weapons programme was started by Prime Minister Vorster before the arrival of the Cubans in Angola in late 1975.

40 See, for example, the chapter on *Koevoet* in *The Devils Are Among Us: The War for Namibia*, ed. D. Herbstein and J. Evenson (London: Zed Press, 1989) and J. Hooper's two books: *Koevoet* (Johannesburg: Southern, 1988) and *Beneath the Visiting Moon: Images of Combat in southern Africa* (Lexington, Mass.: Lexington Books, 1990).

41 Because of the analogy with Vietnam, Namibia could be abbreviated to 'Nam' and so linked to Vietnam. Within months of the war fought by the US in Vietnam ending, the South African war in Namibia became more intense, and involved an invasion of Angola. South Africa's adventure in Angola became, in a sense, its own Vietnam, though South African losses there were proportionately small compared to those of the

US in Vietnam. On the analogy cf. G. Baines, 'South Africa's Vietnam? Literary History and Cultural Memory of the Border War', *South African Historical Journal*, 49 (November 2003).

42   In late 2005 a number of mass graves were uncovered in northern Namibia. These were the graves of the over 300 PLAN fighters killed in early April 1989 when they were attacked by South African and Namibian security forces because a cease-fire was supposed to be in place and it appeared that the PLAN fighters were violating it. SWAPO claimed that they were merely seeking to have bases in the north recognised by the UN.

43   See note 20 above.

44   For example, the desire to prevent a SWAPO victory led the CCB into action before it was ready, derailed its timetable: *TRC Report*, 2/2/141–57. The CCB and the way it was organised are given considerable attention in the *TRC Report*: see 2/2/377–418.

45   *TRC Report*, 2/2/245-6 and photograph opposite p. 41.

46   *TRC Report*, 2/2/329, 2/2/407.

47   That Kapuuo was assassinated by a PLAN unit seems confirmed by the report of the assassination mission, found by the SADF at Cassinga. But cf. J. B. Gewald, 'Who killed Clemens Kapuuo?' *Journal of Southern African Studies*, 30, 3 (September 2004).

48   For information on Operation Victor see the Traces of Truth website mentioned in note 7 above.

49   *Report of the Commission of Enquiry into Complaints by former African National Congress Prisoners and Detainees* (Skweyiya Commission Report 1992, available at www.anc.org.za/ancdocs/misc/skweyiyareport.html; Amnesty International, South Africa, 'Torture, Ill Treatment and Executions in African National Congress Camps', 1992; P. Hayner, *Unspeakable Truths: Confronting State Terror and Atrocity* (New York: Routledge, 2001).

50   *TRC Report*, 2/2/199.

51   See especially *TRC Report*, 2/4/Appendix.

52   *TRC Report*, 2/1/55, 2/1/67, 2/1/72, 2/1/158.

53   Cf. C. Merrett and C. Saunders, 'The Weekly Mail', in *The Resistance Press in South Africa*, ed. L. Switzer and M. Adhikari (Athens and Ohio: Ohio University Press, 2003).

54   *TRC Report*, 2/1/159. SWAPO retaliated for the Cassinga Massacre by attacking the South African base at Katima Mulilo in the Caprivi in August 1978. In response to that, the SADF launched attacks into Zambia, and led the Zambian government to withdraw support from SWAPO, which then concentrated its military activities in Angola. The Caprivi was then no longer a major theatre of war. Cf. *TRC Report*, 2/2/160.

55   The South Africa aim is said to have been the 'elimination of SWAPO as a realistic threat': *TRC Report*, 2/2/198.

56   Cf. T. Bell and D. Ntsebeza, *Unfinished Business. South Africa, Apartheid and Truth* (South Africa: Redworks, 2001).

Chapter 16

Remaking Our Histories: The Liberation War in Postcolonial Namibian Writing

Heike Becker

If I am lost, if my past is lost amongst historical events over which I have no control, who then shall make or remake my history? (Ellen Namhila, *The Price of Freedom*)

In this chapter, I read three published narratives of the liberation war in Owambo that assume the perspective of ordinary residents of the former war-zone. This sets them apart from the bulk of pre- and post-independence Namibian writing about the liberation struggle whose protagonists tend to be prominent political figures and/or participants in the armed struggle.

My interest in these texts is primarily that of engaging them as a narrative mode of memory-making in postcolonial Namibia. I investigate whether these written narratives may provide the reader with as yet largely unexplored routes of access to the archive of memory of the liberation war and its social formation in postcolonial Namibia. I ask, further, whether the reading of written narratives that assume the perspective of civilians during the war has the potential to disrupt the dominant narrative of the liberation war in postcolonial Namibia, namely that the 'South West Africa People's Organization (SWAPO) brought us freedom through the barrel of the gun'. This central tenet of postcolonial Namibia's master narrative has been coupled with the assumption that the non-combatant population of Owambo were mainly victims, but not agents during the war. Like all narratives of agency, the founding myth of postcolonial Namibia legitimises the existing power relations in that country.[1] As an anthropologist, I remain sceptical of the official archive that records the experience of the powerful and I am particularly interested in making accessible views that exist alongside, and perhaps run counter to, those elaborated in power discourses. My reading of postcolonial Namibian writing, thus, is guided by my interest in history as the representation and exploration of how the past is constructed and contested.[2] I am particularly concerned with how the texts I discuss relate to the multiple ways in which experience is filed in the social archive of postcolonial Namibia and how they connect with the ways in which it is transmitted.

This reading, while attempting to do justice to the stories of the past, pays special attention to these texts as 'acts of transfer that make remembering in common possible'.[3] In his seminal study of social memory, Paul Connerton singles out commemorative ceremonies and bodily practices as salient acts of transpersonal and transgenerational transfer; yet, there are numerous other spatial, visual and narrative modes through which we can access the mediated archive of memory.[4] My approach to reading the literary texts in question, thus, defines fictional and autobiographical writing as a technology through which memory is articulated, and a practice of memory work, which for Annette Kuhn is 'an active practice of remembering which takes an inquiring attitude toward the past and the activity of its reconstruction through memory'.[5]

The texts I engage with have several things in common: All of them were authored by women, and more specifically by women whose mother tongue is one of the closely related northern Namibian languages, collectively known as OshiWambo. All three texts were written in English, however, and published in post-1990 Namibia by the, now defunct, local publishing house, New Namibia Books.[6] On the other hand, they vary enormously in format and authorship. The first set of texts form the core of the first anthology of Namibian women's writing, which was published in the country. *Coming On Strong* was edited by two feminist Namibian activists and intellectuals, Margie Orford and Nepeti Nicanor, both then working at New Namibia Books as an editor and a publisher respectively. The 15 short texts collected were written by Owambo women as part of their class work when they participated in the mid-1990s in an adult education English class in northern Namibia. The other two publications I discuss in this chapter were authored by academically trained writers with fluency in English. The texts themselves fit into more conventional literary genres; Kaleni Hiyalwa's *Meekulu's Children* is one of very few English novels set in Owambo, while Ellen Namhila's *The Price of Freedom* falls within the autobiographical genre.[7]

Producing memory

There is no remembering without forgetting. As Johannes Fabian has argued recently, forgetting as an act should preoccupy students of memory more than forgotten content; thus, making it possible to think remembering and forgetting together.[8] Following Fabian's argument, I show in this chapter that the silences in the narrative texts under investigation speak as loud as, if not louder than, the words punctuating them and that this may be of special significance in the social and political silence that shrouds the experience of the civilian population in the former war-zone in northern Namibia.

In March 1998, a group of men were discussing their feelings about Namibia, the political situation, and democracy in the country over a few snacks and cool drinks at the Anamulenge Roman Catholic Mission[9] in the rural, western Owambo district of Ombalantu. For more than an hour they happily listed, for the researcher's benefit, the numerous changes for the better that had taken place since the country's day of independence eight years earlier, naming peace and stability, freedom of movement, and access to better schooling and health care, among others. Then, suddenly, one elderly man broke the amiable atmosphere with an angry comment:

> The problem is that they 'empower' [in English] only those of us that went across the borders into exile. But the fact that we remained here does not mean that we did not help to liberate the land. We gave them food, shelter and information to prevent floggings and imprisonment. If our cries were to be weighed up, they would probably weigh more than theirs.[10]

This single moment sparked off my intense curiosity. Had I listened without hearing? For several years I had been constantly in and out of Owambo where I conducted research on a variety of issues, mostly of an applied nature, and ran adult education programmes. Occasionally, people spoke about 'the war', always emphasising their suffering caused by the atrocities of the *Boers*,[11] never saying much about their own deeds and actions, though. The old man's comment suddenly made me realise that I only ever had heard narratives of victimhood in informal conversations as much as in the national public discourse. Had I not heard them, or were there really no narratives of agency to supplement the dominant representations of victimhood? And if there were indeed no audible narratives of local agency, why had they remained muted?

The invisibility, and inaudibility, of the local people's agency during the war appears to be conspicuously in line with the Namibian nationalist master narrative. The official public history discourse emphasises the role played by the armed liberation politicians from exile. The part played by the civilian population during the liberation war is, at best, an attenuation of the dominant discourse. Namibia's official narrative, its ritual political calendar and monumentalisation, celebrate heroism cast in stone, which has found its most potent symbol in the national Heroes' Acre on the outskirts of Windhoek. The Heroes' Acre, to honour the 'fallen heroes and heroines', was completed in 2002. Since then the SWAPO leadership has made it the centre stage of many national political rituals to commemorate the official milestones of the liberation struggle, such as Heroes' Day (26 August) and Cassinga Day (4 May).[12] Agency in the liberation war, thus, is located – in stone as in quasi-official publications such as President Sam Nujoma's autobiographical tome[13] – in discourses of national liberation that legitimate and authorise the power of the postcolonial elite as the sole, heroic liberators from apartheid and colonialism.

Unlike in South Africa, there have been no official physical or cultural and social spaces left for ceremonies of mourning in Namibia. These would have provided 'a primary expression of symbolic reparation', as C. Rassool, L. Witz, and G. Minkley [14] have described this function of the process provided by the Truth and Reconciliation Commission (TRC). Namibia has not seen a process that would have given space for investigating and openly discussing the legacy of the country's past under apartheid and colonialism. At Independence in 1990, the SWAPO government adopted a *Policy of National Reconciliation*, which centres on an approach of 'forget and forgive'. Officially sanctioned forgetting, indeed, has been the cornerstone of this policy, partly, as critics have argued, because SWAPO feared a public examination of the recent past that would force the former liberation organisation, now the country's ruling party, to account for human rights violations that occurred within the organisation in exile.[15] The untainted official narrative emphasises that 'SWAPO brought us liberation through the armed struggle'; the detention, torture, and the death of hundreds of the organisation's members in exile are portrayed as an unavoidable side effect of the war against apartheid colonialism. In Namibia, the postcolonial, post-apartheid era has given short shrift to previously silenced voices and thereby denied them what Richard Werbner has famously called 'rights of recountability'[16], which is the right to make a citizen's memory known and acknowledged in the public sphere.

Producing narrative

Over the past decade or so, southern African studies have seen a wave of attention given to forms of individual and collective memories, which is inextricably intertwined with the TRC. As a locus of public remembrance, the TRC, has been subject to much critical scrutiny.[17] Notwithstanding the rampant criticism, there can be no doubt that in the aftermath of the TRC, the public telling of personal memory narratives has become a widely accepted form of personal and social catharsis in South Africa. Characteristically, witnessing the TRC process has in itself been subjected to 'telling'.[18] The TRC process has also encouraged a substantial number of autobiographical and fictional literary texts, which are not only concerned with the violence of the anti-apartheid struggle and the apartheid state's machinery of repression, but also take up the topic of daily life under apartheid. As writer and literary critic Njabulo Ndebele has argued, due to the proliferation of oral and written forms of telling (hi)stories, it has become possible to reconstruct identities in the process of public and semi-public remembering.[19] Ndebele argues, further, that these forms of public remembrance embrace liberating moments. He writes: 'The passage of time which brought forth our freedom has given legitimacy and authority to previously silenced voices.'[20] Hence, he emphasises that the attention increasingly directed at forms of narrative remembrance has made audible and visible those whose lives had previously played themselves out in the margins of society. The phenomenon of telling (hi)stories has given a voice to the subalterns (to borrow Gayatri Spivak's term), to the lowest echelons of society, who otherwise would have remained as invisible to the postcolonial elites as they were to those of the colonial era.[21]

I do not necessarily agree with Ndebele's optimistic appraisal; the potential usurpation of personal narratives and their subordination to political agendas needs much more critical scrutiny, as various critics have emphasised. Notwithstanding the need for a more cautious perspective, I take up Ndebele's suggestion that the 'triumph of the narrative' has broadened the canon of audible voices in postcolonial, post-apartheid South African society.

Namibia has not seen a comparable triumph of the narrative. It appears that the culture of silence in the official public discourse has also inhibited the production of written narratives of the liberation struggle in Namibia. Even 15 years after the end of colonialism and apartheid in Namibia, there is at best a faint anticipation of a postcolonial Namibian literature that would work through memories of the almost 25 years of the liberation war or of daily life under apartheid colonialism.[22]

War is frightening: Women's narratives from Owambo

Memories of violence of Owambo residents who had lived through the war in northern Namibia were published in 1996 as a collection of 15 brief essays that appeared in the first locally-published collection of Namibian women's poetry and short stories, under the title *Coming on strong. Writing by Namibian Women.* These brief essays provide interesting indicators of the multiple forms of audibility and inaudibility in the construction of social memory in northern Namibia.

The above-mentioned texts describe the moments of the war that had become traumatic memory for them: beatings by soldiers of the South African Defence Force (SADF) and *Koevoet*[23] when they suspected that rural residents refused to disclose the whereabouts of People's Liberation Army of Namibia (PLAN) combatants in the area, or because they simply did not know about the 'terrs' ('terrorists'), as the SWAPO fighters were generally referred to by the South African occupation forces and their allies. The women recounted that their houses were burnt down and that women were severely beaten because the 'security forces' suspected them of having prepared food for the guerrillas. They also narrate some extremely violent incidents. For instance, Hildegard Shilongo remembers how soldiers entered the village centre and indiscriminately shot and killed local residents – including her elderly mother-in-law. In most of the stories that they tell, the women themselves or close relatives were hurt, injured, maimed or killed. These personal testimonies of suffering are remarkable. The background of the authors as ordinary, semi-educated women from rural Owambo makes them even more special. And only one author chose to remain anonymous.

In their published form, these texts are open for public scrutiny. Yet there can be no doubt that in the prevailing Namibian culture of silence events of the liberation war experienced and remembered by ordinary civilians have been absent from the public discourse. While the accounts are not mediated through any academic, journalistic or literary narrator, they come across as highly restrained voices. They speak of the pain and suffering that was inflicted on individuals and communities in the war-zone as a matter of fact; it is only by their, mostly very brief, comments and conclusions that the trauma of the years of everyday violence they experienced at the hands of the 'security forces' becomes readily apparent

Most of the women conclude their accounts of terrifying events by emphasising that the memories of violence and war will stay with them:

> I won't forget it in my life. (Klaudia Osisia)
> That was the worst day of my life I will not forget it. (Valeria Nampila)
> I cannot forget this time. (Pelagia Gottfried)
> I cannot forget that year. (Angelina Kashweka)
> I shall never forget that day. (Faustina Endjala)
> It was an unforgettable day for me. (Anonymous)

Among them is one highly articulate voice. Eufemia Uutoni writes:

> War is frightening and amazing for all people. War does not have peace for old people and young people. It changes the idea of the nation when it comes in their country. It makes the people unhappy and nervous. The people do not like to hear the war . . . In the time of the war, the people do not know what they can do. They forget their work that they will do on the next day. The soldiers kill the people without sin and burn their houses. It is better to hear than to see.

This thoughtful woman reflects on the nature of war and the pain of witnessing violence in times of war. She notes the possible consequences of the aftermath of war where those who have lived through the violence cannot simply go back to the situation as it was before. I have not been able to trace the authors who were included in Orford and Nicanor's collection, but it may well be that Uutoni was involved in educative activities that would identify her as a peasant intellectual, in the sense which Steven Feierman has used the term.[24] The roles played by such individuals in the rural communities of Owambo during the war and in postcolonial local memory work and identity formation is indeed remarkable, especially where it goes against the grain of officially sanctioned memorialisation. Their often ostensibly simple actions may indeed disrupt an otherwise seamless performance of memory. For instance, I think of the black mourning attire worn by an elderly peasant intellectual on the occasion of a Cassinga Day commemoration in the Oshikango area in May 2004 which stood out in stark contrast to that of the official delegates and speakers adorned in SWAPO colours. The impression was heightened by the setting of the poorly maintained grave of a fallen PLAN soldier in the rural location.

In the context of nationalist violence in Sri Lanka, E. Valentine Daniel has argued that, 'words are symbols that, even at the edges, pull one toward culture's centre. Deeds even when culturally centred – "habitus" notwithstanding – threaten to push against culture's limits'.[25] According to Daniel, words pull the speaker toward the centre of what, despite all their misgivings about the term, anthropologists continue to call 'culture': the ways in which people make sense of the world around them. I argue, however, that words may also threaten the margins of experience and memory. Memories of violence and trauma may be specific instances where 'telling', language and oral history may *not* assist the processes of explanation and healing. Depending on historical contexts, people may not *perceive* words to be helpful in pulling together shattered fragments. Thus, the silences in oral and written texts may at times speak louder than the words punctuating them. Forgetting is party to the practice of remaining silent. My discussion of silence expands Fabian's poignant analogy of forgetting and secrets:

> Secrets are not things un-known but things known or performed in a special way; secrecy is not the absence of communication but a certain kind of communication. Secret things – the content of myths and doctrines, certain ritual performances and their paraphernalia (places, masks, dances) – may in fact be common knowledge but that does not affect their secret status as long as a community keeps to rules that acknowledge secrecy as one form of communication, one cultural practice, among others.[26]

If applied to the northern Namibian women's stories in Orford and Nicanor's collection, Fabian's insightful observation allows for fresh perspectives on the silences in these texts, which pertain to both the authors' own bodily integrity and agency and to the integrity of the postcolonial Namibian body politic. Their silences are not about things (events, experience) unknown, but about the narrative performance of memory in a special way, as the following discussion shows.

It strikes me that the threat of sexual violence and rape is strangely absent, only one anonymous text goes as far as narrating an incident where o*makakunya* ('bloodsuckers'; the term refers to local young men who had joined the South African 'security forces') expressed an intent to rape the author, but she recounts that they were called off by a superior before the act could be committed. In the light of the high incidence of acts of sexual violence that were reported in the 1980s in some Namibian print media and by international aid and solidarity organisations,[27] these silences are indeed startling. They may be grounded in prevailing silences around local constructions of sexual and bodily violations. When I conducted research on sexual and gender-based violence in Owambo in the 1990s, I observed that rural women in northern Namibia found it often incredibly difficult to reveal such harm inflicted upon them outside the spaces of family and local community.[28] *Writing* about the experience of sexual violence, hence, becomes even harder; it demands that the survivor/narrator use an unfamiliar form of telling an unknown, anonymous audience. Under such circumstances, the narrative may not have the effect of catharsis; it may not help to reintegrate the fragmented body and self. On the contrary, words and telling may in this instance – in the current form of writing at least – push towards the cultural margins of women's lives, become undesirable and frightening deeds, as Daniel suggested.

Another silence pertains to agency. Only one of the women claims a sense of political agency. This absence is striking as it stands out against public and published knowledge. Even before independence, publications such as Denis Herbstein and John Evenson's *The Devils Are Among Us*[29] and pro-SWAPO media of the time, such as *The Namibian*, recorded substantial active support for the SWAPO guerrillas among Owambo residents. Yet, Pelagia Gottfried alone reveals her active support of the armed struggle for liberation. She narrates an incident where she and her young daughter outwitted the 'security forces':

> On June 26, 1984, an 'outside soldier' [i.e., a SWAPO guerrilla fighter], named Naftalie, came to my house. It was between 4:00 and 5:00 p.m. Together, we discussed about the ideas for the war.
>
> I brought him beans to eat. In our tradition, beans are good for the soldier. Beans have luck.
>
> Meanwhile, as we talked, he heard the 'casperi'[30] when they came. He climbed up a tree as quickly as possible. It was the 'casperi'. Naftalie started to escape into the forest. In front of him there were three 'casperi'.
>
> In my house, my daughter, Elizabeth, said to me: 'Let us sing.' She began to sing a church song. At this time, she was three years old. We began to sing. By this time, there were nine 'casperi' blocking one 'outside soldier'. They were *Koevoet*, the dangerous soldiers.
>
> Meanwhile, we heard a voice say, 'Kill him.' The other voice said, 'I don't see him.' They saw him, but they were afraid of him. At midnight, the 'outside soldier' came to our house to get his things. He told us all that happened.

But otherwise civilians' and particularly women's active contributions to the struggle for liberation are absent from these essays. Why is this so? If Connerton's argument that the way in which the official historical narrative is constructed can profoundly shape a social group's memory and identity is correct, [31] this may help to explain the neglect of the contributions of the civilian population to the official nationalist historical narrative, although their sufferings have received a certain, albeit limited, recognition.[32] The memories of those who lived through the war in Owambo may thus have been and continue to be reshaped by the hegemonic public discourse – at least, those memories that a marginalised section of the population feel safe to tell.

Connerton's argument may also provide a clue to the understanding of another striking silence. The texts generally appear to go to great lengths to externalise painful memories. The women invariably depict *omakakunya* as outsiders. While some of the accounts reveal that in many instances the perpetrators of war-time violence were black, they are regularly presented as outsiders to the war-zone. Two of the texts literally describe the perpetrators as 'South Africans', that is, as foreigners who had come from another country, and left when Namibia won her independence: 'Up to now, I don't like *Omakakunya*. When they came from South Africa to stay here in Namibia, I was angry at them' (Ria Kakelo).

But now, Namibia has won and Namibia is free. Now the South African soldiers went back to Cape Town, to their motherland. The Namibians stayed with their motherland in Namibia (Atanasia Kakelo).

The characterisation of *omakakunya* as South Africans is in obvious contradiction to the historical facts. Furthermore, it is well known among the local population of the former war-zone that a substantial number of young Owambo men were recruited into the 'security forces', especially in the 1980s. SADF 101 Battalion, based at Ondangwa, was largely made up of local recruits (under the command of white officers), and so was the notorious counter-insurgency unit, *Koevoet*.[33] The recruitment of young Owambo men as mercenaries that pitted them against their own brothers and sisters who fought for PLAN is an acknowledged part of the official Namibian historical narrative. At times, the need for a 'no tell' policy of national reconciliation has explicitly referred to this. The country's first Prime Minister, Hage Geingob, argued in 1992 that the policy was aimed at healing the wounds created by hatred between black people and white people, as well as between and amongst families: 'Many of you will recall that it is not unusual for one person from a family to be a member of *Koevoet* and the other a fighter with the liberation movement.'[34]

Several of the authors in Orford and Nicanor's collection opted for narrative strategies to remake the past in the light of the national reconciliation policy adopted by the SWAPO government. The strategies of forgetting are crucial in this context. They are contradicted by other statements though, which demonstrate that local residents such as Anna Iipinge may have opted for forgiveness along the lines of the official public discourse, but also felt the need to emphasise that the notion of forgetting is unrealistic. She thus positions herself in opposition to the state and the ruling party's official public history narrative with its popular trope that only 'forgive and forget' can prevent the re-opening of old wounds. Iipinge writes: 'That was the time of war. We will forgive their trespasses, but we won't forget what they did.'

Why then are the past acts of violence committed by local *omakakunya* omitted from the women's narratives? The authors, who positioned themselves as victims and witnesses of war-time violence, as did many others among the Owambo residents I interviewed during the course of fieldwork, obviously felt uncomfortable to narrate stories that shared social space with perpetrators of that violence. Occasionally, the pain erupts. This may be the case especially as many among the former Owambo members of the colonial 'security forces' have had great difficulties in adjusting to civilian life. Some former Owambo soldiers still pose a threat of violence and disturbance to their families, communities – and to themselves, as there is apparently a great tendency to suicidal acts amongst them.[35] Some informants also reported that some families at least have been reluctant to reintegrate former '*koevoets*', which is the generally used local term by which all the local recruits in the former 'security forces' are known, irrespective of whether they were actually members of this unit or fought in other South African or South West African units.[36] To accept that the painful memories also include violence perpetrated by brothers and neighbours may weigh too heavily upon people who daily have to cope with the current social and structural crisis involving poverty, gender-based violence, and the HIV/AIDS scourge.

A literary tale of war and survival from northern Namibia

The written testimonies by local women who lived through the war in Owambo and the discussion of the words and silences comprising these narratives provide occasion for a deeper understanding of the making of local memories. I have shown how these memories, represented in literary format, are extensively mediated through the Namibian postcolonial master narrative. The following section considers a very different text.

Namibian writer Kaleni Hiyalwa's first novel, *Meekulu's Children*, depicts the lives of the *ovakalimo,* the 'stayers', those Owambo residents who lived through the war at home. This slim novel of just over 100 pages differs in many respects from the personal narratives I have discussed above. Hiyalwa is a published poet and short-story writer. In *Meekulu's Children* she has chosen the literary form of a novel to present histories and memories of the Namibian liberation war. Her novel is the first imaginary literary account of the war; it is neither a piece of autobiographical writing, nor a literary narrative that draws directly on the author's own lived experience.[37] Hiyalwa was born in Oukwanyama, the part of Owambo where the novel is set, but left for exile at a young age, before the onset of the fiercest phase of the war from the late 1970s onwards, which she depicts in her novel. She was educated in Zambia, Cameroon and Ghana and worked as a teacher in a Namibian expatriate school in Angola.[38] It was the exile experience rather than the immediate experience of war and oppression at 'home' that prompted her writing. At the launch of *Meekulu's Children* in Windhoek in May 2000, Hiyalwa recalled:

> I used to write poems to chase away exile loneliness and the longing to see my mother and family. Through poems, I also wanted to express my longing to belong – to belong to a country or nation of my own. I wrote to express my pride and dignity that seemed to dwindle away whenever I was in the midst of people who only considered me as a refugee; a notion that at times broke my self-esteem and self-confidence to be who I had wanted to be. My writings helped me to live and be very much alive. I would dash into my corner and write to relieve myself from anger and tears, – praying for peace and freedom for my country so that I, like other people in the world, would live to be recognized as a human being and not just as a refugee. It was through writing poems that I ripped off sadness from my heart and dark cloud from my soul. This was because, in homes far away from sweet home Namibia, I sometimes had felt out of place and isolated. It was more painful when, as it was in my case, one didn't know whether time might come to return home. Home indeed! – Where your parents lived but you didn't know whether they were alive or dead. But they neither knew whether their children were alive or dead. This situation had shaped my writing and the choice of my themes.[39]

Hiyalwa's experience is reflected in *Meekulu's Children* as the absence of those of *Meekulu's* (Oshikwanyama: grandmother) own (grand)children and the many 'children' of her community who had gone into exile and return at the end of the story. Even though they are absent for most of the story, they still are a stark presence. Yet, the book's main theme is the liberation war lived 'inside'.

The story unfolds through the eyes of Ketja, a young girl who grows up in the 1970s and 1980s in a village on the Angolan border. In the novel's opening chapter, nine-year-old Ketja comes home from school to find her parents murdered at their homestead. The year is 1976. They are the first war victims in the fictitious village of Elombe. Ketja's brother and sister, Kamati and Estela, have disappeared, and for a long time no one knows what has happened to them. Ketja's life is shattered, but the nurturing spirit of her grandmother helps her to survive. The first few years prove difficult, but gradually some sense of normality returns to her life. Ketja and her grandmother are poor, but they work hard to grow *omahangu* (millet; the local staple), and the neighbours help out. Together they attend church. Ketja excels at the village school under the tree. As she grows up, the young girl experiences some of the typical emotional turmoil of adolescence.

But as Ketja comes of age, so does the intensity of the war. Increasingly, the *ovakalimo* suffer at the hands of the colonial apartheid forces, known as *eembulu* and *omakakunya*. Hiyalwa details incidents of how in their attempt at terrorising and intimidating the population, army casspir vehicles destroy the residents' fields and houses. Hiyalwa's teenage protagonist relates the fear and powerlessness she felt the day she had to face the forces of destruction:

> They were a convoy of about five vehicles. They smashed Meekulu's crops. When I came to my senses that I could be in danger, it was too late. The five Casspir trucks were approaching from different sides and had put me in the middle . . .

> I looked at the giant ugly monsters with huge wheels that did not match the wheels of any other vehicle. I had no more life in me at the sight of the huge things. Their height and shape sent my soul above and left my body with nothing but dry vessels . . .

> I was just an ant below those wheels and whenever I attempted to run away from the scene, one of them would speed to turn me back . . .

> It was only one second before I would greet the Holy Ghost . . . There was no time to think. I rolled quickly into the deep wheel tracks that the white man's devil left on the ground. Meekulu's crop field was no more than a cemetery. The crops we had worked so hard to produce were all smashed down.[40]

In the 1980s such incidents became an ever-threatening imposition on the lives of rural Owambo residents, particularly in those areas along the Angolan border. Yet, 'the white man's devil' was not the only force that left deep scars on the local landscape. *Eendume do momufitu*, the 'children of the forest' as Hiyalwa's people of Elombe call the PLAN fighters, otherwise more commonly referred to in Owambo as *ovamati*, (OshiKwanyama: '(our) boys')[41], also pose a threat to the equanimity of the community. Ketja's grandmother and other adults in the village support the combatants with food, shelter and information. The fighters are regarded as the people's 'children'. And yet, they also instil fear. They are 'mysterious things', said to be able to become invisible because they have been boiled in a pot when crossing the border into Angola. Hiyalwa depicts the sympathies that most villagers have with the fighters as they originate in most instances from Owambo, and many of the local residents themselves have sons and daughters who have gone across the border and may return as fighters.[42] And she also dwells on the ambiguous feelings aroused by *eendume do momufitu*. It is more than fear of the ever-present possibility of the *Boers'* retaliation. Too many things remain inexplicable. Hiyalwa shows the difficulties the villagers have in making sense of the bewildering changes brought about by the war. The people of Elombe are caught between loyalty to older cultural beliefs and allegiance to the war for liberation.

Ketja's *Meekulu* contemplates, 'the world is no longer the world it used to be, my child. It is now full of strange things'.[43]

In Hiyalwa's writing, the war is mediated through the bodies, souls, and minds of those who were caught up within it. Hiyalwa's earlier short story, *The Baby's Baby* (anthologised in Orford and Nicanor's anthology),[44] had graphically drawn on the experience of exiled youngsters like herself who found themselves suddenly on their own in a strange country. Navigating the landscapes of exile and home has become a major theme in recent Owambo women's literature in English.[45] Without ever leaving the confines of the war zone, *Meekulu's Children* navigate them as well. The children of Ketja's grandmother are all these young people from Owambo who had left for exile, and in intervals return in the course of the war as somewhat mystical fighters. These include her own grandchildren, Ketja's brother and sister who were taken to Angola by PLAN soldiers who found them – mere children – after their parents' murder.

At the launch of *Meekulu's Children*, Hiyalwa said that her main motivation in writing the novel had been to pay tribute to the people and their culture that had come under threat in the war zone. However, she also expressed the conviction that it would be wrong to focus solely on the liberation war as the people's defining experience.

> I wrote this story in order to bring out the history of the people who were caught up in war, those who lived under siege, people who had to be divided and hate each other because of a war – a war they had never provoked – but their crime was because they lived on the land, their own.

> In this book, I wanted to speak about people's culture. The culture, – people's way of life, that formed their pride and dignity but which had to be disrupted and destroyed by war. Instead, the people's culture, of which Meekulu is the symbol, had died and faded away, because during the war nothing could be heard except stories about war and death and destruction of property . . .

> However, we should remember that war stories are not the only memories that we have. We should also remember that before the war and colonialism, we had a life; and that life needs to be told and recorded especially when people who can relate to us those issues orally, are still alive. We, as a people, have lived that life, and we must be proud to talk about it.[46]

Hiyalwa's endeavours to remind her readers that, before the war and the imposition of colonialism in Owambo, people had a way of life. This becomes apparent in her depiction of the ambiguous personal and collective development of Ketja, *Meekulu*, and the people of Elombe. The *Boers'* atrocities provide a relentless tale of suffering and grief. However, Ketja's story is also one of resilience and strength, of hope and survival that rely, to an extent, on pre-existing cultural norms and beliefs and social practices that were reconfigured through the war. This perspective makes *Meekulu's Children* a powerful historical narrative as it tells the story of those who lived through the war in northern Namibia, and who today so often feel forgotten, from the inside. The slim novel is certainly not a straightforward, nationalist account of the war. As a piece of imaginary writing, it does not directly question the master narrative. However, in addressing issues such as the actions of civilians during the war and the ambivalent feelings *ovakalimo* had towards the SWAPO combatants, it breaks some of the silences that prevail in both Namibian public history, as well as the common themes of personal narratives which are mediated through the official discourse.

Remembering and telling history from the inside out

In *The Price of Freedom,* Ellen Namhila writes primarily a history of the Namibian exile experience. Only the first chapters of her autobiography are set in Owambo during the 1970s. Despite its focus on exile, however, Namhila's book is important for my discussion of how stories of the liberation war may disrupt the seamless master narrative because, unlike most other autobiographies of former SWAPO exiles, it transcends the personal reminiscence of political history.[47] Namhila pushes the bounds of the history of the liberation struggle from exile beyond its reconstruction as the heroic, nationalist memorialisation that has been cast in stone in the National Heroes' Acre, or as told in the 476 pages of Nujoma's book.

Namhila's book disrupts the heroic narrative because she remembers the political as personal and confers a central place to personal aspirations and wishes. Most significantly, perhaps, she narrates her memories in such a way that the personal experiences stand on their own. In Namhila's writing, memories of life in the northern Namibian war-zone and in exile emerge from the inside out; this is in distinct contrast to those autobiographies, where the political context invariably frames even the most intimate personal memories. Sarah Nuttall's comments on South African struggle autobiographies also fit most of the Namibian autobiographical texts. Nuttall observed, with special respect to Nelson Mandela's autobiography, *Long Walk to Freedom,* that, the political appears to set the framework for personal remembering and that, 'memory is seen as proceeding less from the inside out, structured by an internal set of needs and desires, as from the outside in. Structured in this way, the individual or private self is vulnerable to being ignored, or seen as "unpolitical"'.[48]

The Price of Freedom breaks with this narrative format. Namhila does not claim to have written a definitive history of the Namibian exile mediated through her experience. Instead, she speaks of the doubts that beset her reflections and memories. In the book's opening chapters, she frankly depicts her flight into exile as the consequence of a loss of personal security rather than as a politically conscious decision. Namhila was still some months short of her thirteenth birthday when she left the war zone in northern Namibia for Angola in April 1976. Twenty years later she reflected on why she as a girl of such a young age left home for an unknown destination abroad. She describes her first traumatic encounter with the South African occupation forces at the age of ten when the police used brutal force while arresting Ellen's uncle, in whose house she lived at the time:

> First they set their dogs on him. This scene was such a terror that I still have nightmares. As soon as the dogs stopped biting and pulling, the police dragged him out of our homestead and drove away with him. Two days later he was returned home beaten half dead and the whole body swollen . . . I could not bear the scene of my uncle's body lying helplessly on the floor, a man who was my protector, provider and security. Now he could not even feed himself.[49]

She reflects upon how the daily experience of violence impinged increasingly on the intimate lives of families and local communities and, particularly, how many children felt a frightening loss of security in a situation where adults could no longer provide protection and guidance. Namhila remembers that this was one of the main factors that drove youngsters like her into exile:

> We lived in constant fear and we started wondering who would be next. What was most frightening was that teachers and parents did not want to talk about these things with their children out of fear for their own lives. Some adults thought that if they answered our questions they would encourage us to get involved in social and political problems, Unfortunately they achieved the opposite effect, because it was partly this unexplained brutality that forced most of us to look for answers and seek for alternatives by going into exile.

> As a child I always felt secure in the presence of adults – parents or teachers. It terrified me to realize that adults were no longer a source of security. I did not like to live in fear, surrounded by people who posed this fear threat to me. So I decided to leave the country.[50]

Unlike other writers of struggle autobiographies, Namhila also reflects upon her return from exile which brought about new conflicts and identity crises at homecoming, a time that she, like most exiles, had imagined would bring closure. Instead, the return meant a new form of exile that embodied the disillusioned hopes and aspirations of a liberated society. She remembers most vividly that there was no trace of the communitarian spirit of the 'camps' where most Namibian exiles had lived in Zambia and Angola. This experience was replaced by the challenges of a situation where many of the returnees had to adjust to the demands of an ordinary civilian life for the first time in their lives. The situation was aggravated by the high, completely unrealistic expectations that many of their *ovakalimo* families had of the returnees. These were the realities of life in postcolonial Namibia. The refugees came home to a considerably changed political, social and cultural landscape. Namibia had become another country, while the journeys of exile had transformed those who now returned. Namhila describes the recognition that dawned upon her after her return, 'hearing people talk about going back home was like waking from a wonderful dream . . . [but] . . . a lot had happened to me and to Namibia since I had left. I would not just be able to continue from where I had left off and pretend that I had never been away'.[51]

There is no sense of closure. Namhila questions her citizenship and identity, when she writes that, 'my heart tells me that I am home because Namibia was my place of birth, even though I do not have the feel of home. This is the conflict of identity my brain is going through now, now that I am at home and at the same time I am not because my picture of home is different'.[52] In the process of negotiating her fragmented identity, remembering and writing her own history has become significant. Namhila describes her writing as an attempt to come to terms with the identity crisis of a returnee and to retrieve the lost memories of childhood without negating the fragmentations of the exile experience that continue to influence her personal life like that of the imagined community of the nation.[53]

Conclusion

I now return to the opening question posed by Namhila, 'Who . . . shall make or remake my history?',[54] and present some conclusions on the part played by written narratives in the remaking of history and identities in postcolonial Namibia. I begin by expanding Namhila's question, and ask, 'Who – and *what* – shall remake history?'

Allen Feldman, drawing on his work in violence-ravaged Northern Ireland, has argued that language has the power to construct historical narrative and embodied memory. He writes, 'In oral history, the body fragmented is reassembled, and this act, the weaving of a new body through language, as much as any act of violence testifies to the emergence of political agency.'[55] My discussion of Namhila's and, to a lesser extent, Hiyalwa's texts, has shown that it is not only in oral history that this reconstruction of the violated self, and the emergence of political agency, occurs. In written texts as well, new selves can be created to counter the devastating effects of war and violence. Both authors attempt the deconstruction and reconstruction of lives and identities during the war and its aftermath. The acts of remembering and writing create order and structure in the shared experience, however chaotic and fragmented it may appear. I have shown how Hiyalwa's fiction and Namhila's autobiographical writing have disrupted the postcolonial state's master narrative through breaking the silences surrounding the agency of the local population in Owambo during the war, and by allowing ambivalences to creep into their narratives.

While these hidden moments of social memory command a strong presence in the novelist's imaginary and the autobiographical writer's critical reflection, they are largely absent from the written narratives of ordinary women from the former war zone. I have shown that their brief texts perform remembering and forgetting in a way that by and large follows the tenets of the postcolonial state's historical narrative. The contents of their silences – the actions of local PLAN cadres as much as those of local mercenaries (*omakakunya*) – are in fact common knowledge, but they remain shrouded in silence as one form of remembering/forgetting, among others. I have shown that their silences are not about things unknown, but that they constitute a certain type of narrative performance of memory; that silence serves as a form of communication and social practice, similar to Fabian's elaborations of secrecy as cultural practice.[56]

The significance of silence for the construction of social memory raises questions about the adequacy of the written form, and indeed of any narrative form, in making accessible memories that exist alongside, and perhaps run counter to, those elaborated in power discourses in postcolonial Namibia. Literary and autobiographical texts authored by reflective writers such as Hiyalwa and Namhila subtly contest the triumphalist master narrative, but thus far they have not been very influential as acts of transfer in the constitution of social memory in postcolonial Namibia. My recent ethnographic and oral history explorations of how the past is constructed and contested in contemporary Owambo indicate, however, that repositories of memory, which differ from the highly restrained victim narratives, largely void of agency, that emerge in the texts written by rural Owambo women, do exist. My research suggests that performances of memory, which are rich in personal detail of ordinary people's agency and which have found expression in forms of local commemoration and mapping of war memories, exist in the former northern Namibian war zone.[57] Whereas the narrative performance of memory, to all appearance, still follows closely the official narrative, this popular form of memorialisation suggests the existence of much more complex and fragmented forms of liberation war memory in Owambo.

Notes to Chapter Sixteen

1   H. Becker, 'Sites of Violence & Memory: Mapping the Namibian Liberation War'. Paper presented at the 5th Northeast Workshop on Southern African Studies. Burlington, Vermont, 5–7 September 2003.

2   This has been the predominant approach in much of the recent research on nationalist memory, and countermemories in the African, and especially Southern African, postcolony (cf., for instance, the chapters of R. Werbner's edited volume under the apt title, *Memory and the Postcolony. African Anthropology and the Critique of Power* (London: Zed Books, 1998).

3   P. Connerton, *How Societies Remember* (Cambridge: Cambridge University Press, 1989), 39.

4   My research of memories of war and violence in northern Namibia has taken me along multiple routes of access to the social archive of memory, moving from the documentary archives to oral history, to landscapes of physical memorialisation, to political ritual, visuality, and, last but not least, to fiction and autobiographical writing. I gratefully acknowledge the funding provided by the UWC Arts Faculty research fund and the Wenner-Gren Foundation for Anthropological Research, which have made possible research in Owambo in 2001 and 2002–2004 respectively.

5   A. Kuhn, 'A Journey Through Memory', in *Memory and Methodology*, ed. S. Radstone (Oxford: Berg, 2000), 186; cited in M. Hirsch and V. Smith, 'Feminism and Cultural Memory: An introduction', *Signs: Journal of Women in Culture and Society* 28(1), Autumn 2002, 8.

6   *New Namibia Books*, founded by Jane Katjavivi, the British-born wife of the University of Namibia's first Vice-Chancellor, was a remarkable effort of providing a space for the development of a new Namibian literature and, particularly, of postcolonial literary and autobiographical writing that recounted war memories and thus helped to remake the northern Namibian recent past. In addition to publications by Namibian authors on the war experience, the Windhoek-based company also published Anthony Feinstein's *In Conflict*, the diary of a young medical officer in the SADF based in northern Namibia in 1983. Unfortunately, the enterprise could not be sustained financially and was incorporated into the larger Gamsberg MacMillan publishing house in 2000.

7   Liberation struggle autobiographies constitute a fairly proliferate literary genre in Namibian writing. However, Namhila's text is exceptional, as I shall suggest elsewhere in this chapter.

8   J. Fabian, 'Forgetful Remembering: A Colonial Life in the Congo', *Africa* 73, 4 (2003):490–1.

9   In the politically correct terminology of contemporary Namibia, the mission stations of the various Christian denominations are officially labelled 'centres'; however, the local referent in northern Namibia characteristically has remained 'mission'.

10   H. Becker and P. Bruhns, *Sa xu-I ge a sa. What Is Yours Is Yours. Popular Perceptions of Political Institutions in Namibia* (Windhoek: National Democratic Institute for International Affairs (NDI), 1998), 40.

11   In Owambo, *Boers (eembulu* in the OshiWambo languages*)* is the common referent for the South African occupation forces, as well as for white South Africans more generally.

12   Heroes Day marks the start of the armed liberation struggle on 26 August 1966 when the first armed contact between SWAPO guerrilla fighters and the South African forces took place at Ongulumbashe in western Owambo. Cassinga Day commemorates the SADF's raid on the SWAPO refugee and military training camp at Cassinga in southern Angola on 4 May 1978, where hundreds of Namibian exiles died.

13   S. Nujoma, *Where Others Wavered. The Autobiography of Sam Nujoma* (London: Panaf Books, 2001).

14   C. Rassool, L. Witz, and G. Minkley, 'Burying and Memorialising the Body of Truth: The TRC and National Heritage', in *After the TRC: Reflections on Truth and Reconciliation in South Africa*, ed. W. James and L. van de Vijver (Cape Town: David Philip, 2000), 126.

15   See for example, J. S. Saul and C. Leys, 'Lubango and After: "Forgotten History" as Politics in Contemporary Namibia'. *Journal of Southern African Studies* 29, 2 (2003): 333–53.

16   R. Werbner, 'Beyond Oblivion: Confronting Memory Crisis', in *Memory and the Postcolony. African Anthropology and the Critique of Power*, 1.

17   Some of the TRC's critics have pointed out that the Commission focused on the human rights violations that were committed by the apartheid state's 'security' forces but omitted the everyday violence of life under apartheid. They argue, thus, that the TRC process did not contribute much to the documentation of the southern African region's contemporary history. (See, for instance, C. Bundy, 'The Beast of the Past: History and the TRC', in *After the TRC*, ed. James and Van de Vijver). Other commentators have drawn

attention to the fact that the TRC's public hearings tended to (de facto) exclude certain sections of the population on political or social grounds. Fiona Ross, for instance, found in her ethnographic study (partly based on extensive fieldwork in Worcester in the Western Cape) that many young women anti-apartheid activists of the 1980s were reluctant to testify at the Commission's hearings because of the perception that the TRC would present them as victims, rather than as active agents of change (F. C. Ross, *Bearing Witness: Women and the Truth and Reconciliation Commission in South Africa* (London: Pluto Press, 2003)).

18   See, especially, the partly fictionalised prose narrative by poet and journalist Antjie Krog who accompanied the TRC hearings for the Commission's first two years as a reporter for the national radio services (A. Krog, *Country of My Skull* (Johannesburg: Random House, 1998)). The TRC-induced political economy of traumatic storytelling has been critically discussed in Chris Colvin's insightful doctoral thesis (C. J. Colvin, 'Performing the Signs of Injury: Critical Perspectives on Traumatic Storytelling after Apartheid', PhD thesis, University of Virginia, 2004).

19   N. Ndebele, 'Memory, Metaphor, and the Triumph of Narrative', in *Negotiating the Past. The Making of Memory in South Africa*, ed. S. Nuttall and C. Coetzee (Cape Town: Oxford University Press, 1998), 27.

20   Ibid. 20.

21   G. Spivak, 'Can the Subaltern Speak?' in *In Other Worlds: Essays in Cultural Politics* (London: Routledge, 1988).

22   Notable exceptions include Kaleni Hiyalwa's short stories, and her novel *Meekulu's Children* (2000), which is discussed in this chapter. Two other novels that deal with liberation war-related themes were written while their authors were still in exile, Ndeutala Hishongwa's *Marrying Apartheid* (1986) and Helmut Angula's *The Two Thousand Days of Haimbodi ya Haufiku* (1990). The body of liberation struggle autobiographies is considerably larger, although, apart from Namhila's, very few of the autobiographical texts of former exiles and guerrilla fighters recall *personal* memories of the liberation war. Partial exceptions include H. Shityuwete, *Never Follow The Wolf: The Autobiography of a Namibian Freedom Fighter* (London: Kliptown Books, 1990), J. Ya Otto, *Battlefront Namibia: An Autobiography* (Harare: Zimbabwe Publishing House, 1982) and, particularly, M. Shamena and E. Shamena, *Wir Kinder Namibias: Eine Lebensgeschichte* (Erlangen: Verlag der Evang.-Lutherischen Mission, 1984), while former President Nujoma's *Where Others Wavered*, although sub-titled 'the autobiography of Sam Nujoma' mentions hardly anything of a personal nature.

23   From 1980, newly-formed Namibianised units, such as the ethnic battalions of the supposedly independent South West Africa Territorial Force (SWATF*)*, and the counterinsurgency unit known as *Koevoet* (Afrikaans for 'crowbar') fought alongside the SADF and paramilitary South African police in northern Namibia. *Koevoet*, made up of locally-recruited young black men under the command of white officers, became synonymous with the terror local people were subjected to during the decade before independence.

24   S. Feierman, *Peasant Intellectuals. Anthropology and History in Tanzania* (Madison: University of Wisconsin Press, 1990).

25   E. V. Daniel, *Charred Lullabies: Chapters in an Anthropology of Violence* (Princeton, NJ: Princeton University Press, 1996), 199.

26   Fabian, 'Forgetful Remembering', 491.

27   See, e.g., D. Herbstein and J. Evenson, *The Devils Are Among Us. The War for Namibia* (London: Zed Books, 1989); B. König, *Namibia. The Ravages of War* (London: International Defence and Aid Fund for southern Africa, 1983); *The Namibian* 1985–1989 passim,

28   H. Becker and P. Claassen, *Violence Against Women and Children: Community Attitudes and Practices* (Windhoek: Report prepared for the Women and Law Committee of the Law Reform and Development Commission of the Republic of Namibia, 1996).

29   Herbstein and Evenson, *The Devils Are Among Us.*

30   Casspirs, armoured trucks, which in the 1980s were deployed by the SADF in Owambo as well as South African townships.

31   Connerton, *How Societies Remember.*

32   Former President Sam Nujoma's published autobiography, for instance, recounts some of the better-known 'atrocities', which the 'security forces' committed against the civilian population (Nujoma, *Where Others Wavered,* 326–8; 357), but makes no mention of the local residents' agency.

33   In addition, the 1980s saw young black men from the southern and central parts of Namibia conscripted into the SWATF. Young men from northern Namibia were not subject to conscription, presumably because of the Owambos' known general allegiance to SWAPO.

34   As quoted by Saul and Leys in 'Lubango and After', 336.

35   Interview with Rev. Josephat Shangala; Okahao, 4 July 2001.

36   Interview with Erastus Shamena; Ongwediva, 3 July 2001.

37   *The Two Thousand Days of Haimbodi Ya Haufiku* by Helmut Angula, first published in a German edition in 1986, is an example of a 'novel' about the Namibian liberation struggle, which does not move far beyond a thinly disguised piece of autobiography.

38   At the time of the novel's publication in 2000, Hiyalwa lived in Windhoek and was employed by the *Ministry of Women Affairs and Child Welfare.*

39   K. Hiyalwa, 'Remarks by Kaleni Hiyalwa at the launch of *Meekulu's Children*', 17 May 2000, Windhoek.

40   K. Hiyalwa, *Meekulu's Children* (Windhoek: New Namibia Books, 2000), 77–8.

41   Despite the gendered referent, a substantial number of PLAN guerrillas were young women, although only very few Owambo residents remember having ever encountered female fighters during the war. It appears that women rarely participated in combat in Namibia but were mostly deployed on the Angolan side of the border.

42   It was rare, however, for PLAN combatants to be deployed in their immediate home areas; while some residents in the border area east of Oshikango, where I conducted several months of field research in 2004, said that they occasionally identified a guerrilla as a known young man. No one I spoke to remembered having seen a neighbour's son among the 'boys'.

43   Hiyalwa, *Meekulu's Children,* 30.

44   M. Orford and N. Nicanor, eds. *Coming on Strong. Writing by Namibian Women* (Windhoek: New Namibia Books, 1996), 55–67.

45   M. Orford and H. Becker, 'Homes and Exiles: Owambo Women's Literature', in *Contested Landscapes. Landscapes of Movement and Exile*, ed. B. Bender and M. Winer (Oxford: Berg, 2001).

46   Hiyalwa, 'Remarks by Kaleni Hiyalwa'.

47   This chapter is not the place to discuss another body of Namibian autobiographical writing, which has been produced by former SWAPO exiles who were expelled from the liberation organisation or left it on their own account during the various moments of conflict within SWAPO in exile. These autobiographical texts, like those of SWAPO stalwarts, subordinate questions of personal experience and agency to a political narrative, although theirs tell of upheaval, rather than triumph. (See, e.g., K. P. Nathanael, *A Journey to Exile: The Story of a Namibian Freedom Fighter* (Aberystwyth: Sosiumi Press, 2002).)

48   S. Nuttall, 'Telling "Free" Stories? Memory and Democracy in South African Autobiography Since 1994', in *Negotiating the Past. The Making of Memory in South Africa,* ed. S. Nuttall and C. Coetzee (Cape Town: Oxford University Press, 1998), 77.

49   E. N. Namhila, *The Price of Freedom* (Windhoek: New Namibia Books), 28.

50   Ibid. 31.

51   Ibid. 97–8.

52   Ibid. 198.

53   B. Anderson, *Imagined Communities. Reflections on the Origin and Spread of Nationalism* (London: Verso, 1983).

54   Namhila, *The Price of Freedom*, 199.

55   A. Feldman, *Formations of Violence: The Narrative of the Body and Political Terror in Northern Ireland* (Chicago: The University of Chicago Press, 1991), 10.

56   Fabian, 'Forgetful Remembering', 491.

57   See Becker, 'Sites of Violence & Memory'.

Chapter 17

No Man's Land of Time: Reflections on the
Politics of Memory and Forgetting in Namibia

Justine Hunter

In Namibia, the simultaneous processes of decolonisation and democratisation took place in the form of controlled change, based on political compromises needed for a peaceful settlement. Amnesty laws of an unconditional nature were passed as part and parcel of a proclaimed policy of national reconciliation. In spite of international recommendations, the general amnesty did not meet conditions such as a public debate and disclosure preceding the enactment of amnesty laws nor did the process involve as much reparation and truth-seeking as possible. The issue of dealing with atrocities committed by both sides during the liberation war was dealt with by evading a formal search for truth and justice, and no lustration legislation was passed. On the contrary, the Namibian constitution provided that any person who held an office before independence should continue to do so. This policy of national reconciliation, though, has been a mixed blessing.

In this chapter I intend to explore the politics of memory and forgetting in Namibia since independence. First, I will provide an overview of war atrocities committed during the liberation war by both sides and attempt to shed light on the political circumstances under which they took place. Second, I will evaluate the historiography of the war of national liberation in order to determine whether the truth about matters such as the identity of those responsible for killing those discovered in undocumented mass graves in northern Namibia can be known. Third, I will examine the parameters of public discourse since independence: whether or not national reconciliation is government policy, its compatibility with international recommendations, and the substance of parliamentary debates, as well as the findings of international committees of inquiry. Then I will raise the question as to how and why a wall of silence has been erected by the ruling South West Africa People's Organization (SWAPO), and what strictures have been imposed on the highly politicised debate about detainees. Thereafter, I will examine the extent to which the buried memory of Namibia's armed liberation struggle (1966–1989) amongst society's marginalised groups contests the official version of historical events. Finally, I conclude the chapter with a suggestion of how Namibia can find a way forward.

Namibia's violent heritage: Human rights abuses and atrocities

The warfare between South African occupation forces and Namibian freedom fighters was concentrated in that country's northern regions. South African forces pursued a dual-track strategy to defeat SWAPO's liberation army: military engagement and a hearts-mind-campaign aimed at winning 'the support of the population, their approval, sympathy and active participation'.[1] The South African Defence Force (SADF) Chief of Staff (1985–90), General Jannie Geldenhuys expressed a wish to avoid a war of white occupiers against black guerrillas. He reckoned that Namibians should begin 'fighting their own battles' against the 'communist threat'.[2] The so-called security forces in Namibia effectively became a parallel command structure to the SADF in different uniforms. The 'Namibianisation' of the war enabled the SADF to create a quasi-independent territorial force and police force that employed conscription and financial incentives to recruit the local population.[3] Although the liberation movement could be sure of the loyalty and support of the majority of the civilian population, even the notorious counter-insurgency police unit known as *Koevoet* recruited around 90% of its numbers from amongst the young male population of Owamboland.[4] This gave the lie to its slogan that 'Every Wambo was a SWAPO'.

During the so-called Bush War, the front lines ran straight through villages, communities and families. Ordinary people living in Namibia's northern rural areas were caught in the middle of the conflict bearing out an African proverb that says: 'when elephants fight, it is the grass that suffers'.[5] It soon became clear that 'both forces were using the population to inform them of the whereabouts of the other force'.[6] South African counter-insurgency units employed 'terror' tactics to gather information from the Namibian population in order to track People's Liberation Army of Namibia (PLAN) guerrillas. During interrogation and torture sessions in detention, some captured freedom fighters were 'turned' to become members of the South African security forces. *Koevoet* committed numerous atrocities among civilians, creating an atmosphere of fear and distrust. For instance, the massacre in Oshikuku village in northern Namibia became synonymous with *Koevoet*'s reputation for brutality and mercilessness. Simultaneously, reports of human rights violations committed against alleged spies who appeared to have infiltrated the liberation movement in exile were exposed. This led to a cycle of claims and counter-claims of atrocities by the warring parties.

Across Namibian borders in neighbouring states, the exiled wing of SWAPO commanded its liberation army and was also responsible for thousands of civilian refugees. The Namibianisation of the war, as well as the devastating South African air attacks on military/refugee camps in Angola and Zambia, furthered the firm belief that enemy agents had joined the ranks of the liberation movement. Accounts generally allude to four phases of self-inflicted violence by SWAPO in exile: the Kongwa Crisis in the 1960s, the Party Crisis in the 1970s, the Muyongo Crisis and the Spy Drama, both in the 1980s. During the course of the Spy Drama, suspects were arrested, interrogated, tortured, and detained in the dungeons of Lubango in Angola. As independence approached, approximately 150 detainees were released and returned to Namibia. Many were simply left behind in the dungeons, and approximately 2 000 Namibians are still unaccounted for.[7] It is crucial to distinguish between two detainees' groups: on the one hand, well-known political dissidents among the leadership of SWAPO in exile and, on the other hand, thousands of exiled Namibians, among them many SWAPO Youth League (SYL) and PLAN members who had been detained in Zambia's notorious Mboroma camp in the 1970s and the dungeons of Lubango in Angola in the 1980s.

Explanations for human rights abuses in SWAPO's camps remain partial as evidence is restricted to victims' testimonies. Besides the suspicion of enemy agent infiltration, various additional factors seem to have contributed to the eruption of violence: anti-intellectualism, generation gaps, power struggles, autocratic structures, ethnic rivalries, military defeats, diplomatic impasses, distrust between the liberation army and the political leadership and between the internal and external wings of SWAPO, as well as the wheelings and dealings of security agencies in the East and West.

The first casualty of war is truth

The current state of research on gross human rights abuses committed during the armed liberation era[8] attests to the aphorism that the first casualty of war is truth. A record of South Africa's criminal regime in Namibia reveals that the countries' recent histories are so interwoven that it will prove difficult to disentangle them.[9] With regard to the warfare waged by the SADF and the Namibian territorial forces, accounts have been written by pro-South African war correspondents,[10] retired generals,[11] and undercover agents.[12] In many cases, war atrocities have been mythologised as heroism, pious patriotism and military romanticism. Various documents published by international solidarity and anti-apartheid movements,[13] as well as the liberation movement itself,[14] provide crucial information provided that the historical and political conditions are carefully scrutinised and ideological orientations are taken into consideration. Recalling experiences that were shared in one way or the other by thousands of Namibians and South Africans in those years, autobiographies of those who joined the struggle in exile and those who resisted at home, as well as former South African recruits,[15] provide different perspectives on the conflict. The report of the South African Truth and Reconciliation Commission (TRC) includes only a limited chapter on human rights abuses and war atrocities committed in neighbouring countries. The Namibian government's rejection of cooperation, its amnesty legislation, and the fact that the TRC laid emphasis on human rights violations committed in South Africa rather than beyond its borders, means that discovery procedures have been limited. Nevertheless, the TRC dealt with events such as the South African air attack on the SWAPO camp in Cassinga, Angola, and the role of *Koevoet*, as well as the assassination of lawyer Anton Lubowski.[16] But a veil of silence still hangs over much of what transpired in Namibia during the South African occupation.

Recently, the monumental trial against the former head of South Africa's biological and chemical warfare programme,[17] Wouter Basson, revealed valuable information about South Africa's strategies and the fate of hundreds of missing freedom fighters.[18] In April 2002, the verdict of not guilty revealed the consequences of the Namibian general amnesty, as well as reiterating how high-ranking South Africans politicians, officials and military personnel had avoided prosecution for human rights violations. Nevertheless, in September 2005, South Africa's Constitutional Court surprisingly ruled that Basson might be prosecuted on charges that were quashed when his trial in the Pretoria High Court started almost six years ago, including a charge relating to the alleged killing of as many as 200 captured SWAPO cadres whose bodies were thrown from an aeroplane into the Atlantic Ocean. The Constitutional Court considered 'the extreme gravity' of the charges Basson faced, as well as the need to take account of South Africa's obligations to uphold principles of international humanitarian law.[19] On the grounds that nobody should face criminal charges twice for the same offence in South Africa, the National Prosecuting Authority dismissed the Constitutional Court's decision in October 2005.[20] Recently, the South African Institute for Justice and Reconciliation stated that prosecuting crimes of apartheid is going to be 'a very delicate balancing process' and Namibia's most senior prosecutor added that 'prosecutions need to be considered within the process of national unity and national reconciliation'.[21]

It has been taken for granted that the ruthless South African security forces, including their Namibian collaborators, were responsible for the vast majority of political crimes that occurred in the country. As a result, numerous allegations of human rights abuses committed within the ranks of the liberation movement across the borders in Zambia and Angola were disregarded by observers and activists at the time. Confidential correspondence between church leaders and international human rights organisations, as well as church umbrella bodies that date back to the mid-1970s and 1980s, provide the first written evidence of human rights abuses in exile.[22] For many years, refugee pastors and the Committee of Parents (CP) as well as the Parents' Committee of Namibia (PCN) that represented relatives of missing persons who were last seen in SWAPO facilities appealed to clerical leaders, church bodies and human rights activists in vain.[23] Claims of atrocities committed within the ranks of the liberation movement were met with a wall of silence on the part of perpetrators and bystanders. And on the part of commentators there was a lack of objective analysis that 'takes seriously the grim nature of SWAPO's enemy, South Africa's colonial regime in Namibia, and the nobility of SWAPO's cause, but that nonetheless surveys realistically SWAPO's own record'.[24] The assassination attempts on alleged collaborators, including henchmen, informers and public servants of South Africa's colonial administration in Namibia, have neither been officially solved nor properly discussed. Human rights abuses against suspected enemy agents who seemed to have infiltrated the liberation movement in exile are still unaccounted for. The high number of exiles unaccounted for attracted a significant amount of media attention as the founding elections approached. Eyewitness accounts of survivors produced a surge of newspaper articles and publications, broaching the issue either in a 'constructively critical'[25] or an 'unsympathetic' manner.[26] Although some of the 'unsympathetic' work has been discredited,[27] the bulk of findings cannot just be rejected.[28]

Two publications in the mid–1990s addressed SWAPO's record of human rights abuses. The first text was a work by reputable Canadian scholars, but which was not all that accessible to the general public and so the debate it engendered was confined to academic circles. Colin Leys and John Saul's *Namibia's Liberation Struggle: The Two-edged Sword* (1995) was an indictment of SWAPO's human rights record during the war of liberation and (to a lesser extent) the culture of silence it fostered since being in office.[29] But the real bombshell was the subsequent publication of the memoirs of German refugee pastor Siegfried Groth.[30] Respected for his personal contribution to the liberation struggle and the moral authority that he commanded as a Lutheran pastor, Groth's personal narrative invited reaction even if his criticisms were not new. Given the simple language of his text, his charges were understood by the wider Namibian public and, therefore, served as a lightning rod for a public debate. Select extracts from readers' letters published in the Namibian press reflect a range of responses to the English translation of Groth's memoirs in 1996:

> You, Groth, when you write your books, keep them to the church. Don't disappoint and spoil the peace for the Namibian people, please, please. We don't want the war anymore in the land of Namibia.[31]

> Mr Groth, you should have written two books opening all sides of the story . . . SWAPO was fighting for freedom and SWAPO was haunted by South African soldiers and *Koevoet* . . . SWAPO won the war and they didn't take revenge. Instead they asked for peace, forgiveness and to reconcile. Is that too much to ask?[32]

> First of all we want to know whether there was a competition between SA [South Africa] and SWAPO as to who would kill, torture or cause disappearance of Namibians . . . SWAPO was expected to raise high the banner of Basic Human Rights but badly failed the test.[33]

These mixed reactions brought as much heat as light to the debate. All in all, the controversy produced a sense of paralysing disbelief that SWAPO might have violated the very principles for which it has been recognised as defender.

The recent discovery of mass graves in Namibia's northern regions proved 'once again that truth is often the first casualty of war'.[34] The discovery of the graves, most of which apparently contain the remains of freedom fighters killed in April 1989, has revived allegations and rumours current at the time. It has been said that (the then) SWAPO President Sam Nujoma had sent approximately 1 600 armed cadres over the Angolan-Namibian border as a ceasefire was declared. Blaming the United Nations Transition Assistance Group (UNTAG) special commissioner Martti Ahtisaari who had recalled South African units from their bases to back up the police, Nujoma flatly denied that there had been an incursion.[35] Instead, he claimed that he had instructed armed guerrillas that were already in Namibia to regroup and prepare for demobilisation at UNTAG bases. At the time, observers speculated that Nujoma took a calculated risk to show SWAPO's military presence and to strengthen solidarity among the population with the elections approaching.[36] The discovery of mass graves recalled the so-called nine-day war, and the *Mail & Guardian* suggested that SWAPO wanted to get rid of potential troublemakers and the issue might turn out to be a 'Pandora's Box' in an emerging Namibia. The author asked rhetorically: 'Who might have a lot of uncomfortable und uncomplimentary things to say about their own leadership in the lead up to a period of triumphalist electioneering back on home soil geared to assuring Nujoma a clear run to the presidency?'[37]

According to the *Mail & Guardian*, 'amnesia [was] all around'. Geldenhuys, too, pointed a finger at Ahtisaari whose failure to control the situation allowed the South Africans to 'stick . . . their tongues out to world community' and 'teach [SWAPO] a final, useless lesson they [would] never forget'.[38] President Hifikepunye Pohamba urged Namibians who had been members of the South African security forces to come forward and provide information that would help the identification of bodies, while former president Nujoma again rejected any truth-seeking initiatives and referred to reconciliation as 'the Namibian way'.[39] But SWAPO had to make concessions towards the population in its political heartland, and had to help identify the human remains found in the war graves.[40] The point is, the identification of human remains found in mass graves should not be restricted to northern Namibia, but should be extended across the border to Angola where Namibians lie buried in anonymous graves in Cassinga, Oshatotwa and Lubango.

If the South African security forces tried to cover up their deeds by disposing of bodies in unmarked graves, the apartheid government also sought to cover its tracks by dispatching the paper trail left by its administration of Namibia. During the transitional phase, the outgoing South African authorities removed, and probably destroyed, incriminating evidence.[41] The disappearance of such records has been described by Charles Villa-Vicencio as 'perhaps the major violation of collective memory'.[42] This has made the safeguarding of privately owned documents and the conducting of interviews with the eyewitnesses even more essential and urgent. As with documents, oral testimonies constitute a problematic source of information. Traces of the Namibian past can be excavated from historical records and the personal memories of observers, bystanders, offenders and victims. But the real issue is how much light a divisive, violent past can withstand. For nations, especially emergent ones such as Namibia, depend 'on forging myths of unity and identity that allow a society to forget its founding crimes, its hidden injuries and divisions, its unhealed wounds. It must be true, for nations and for individuals, that we can stand only so much truth. But if too much truth is divisive, the question becomes, how much is enough'?[43]

Michael Ignatieff's question has a direct bearing on Namibia's decision to forego truth-seeking initiatives in favour of forgetting. Indeed, the political transition in Namibia has been shaped by the leitmotif *forgiving and forgetting* that is bound to the policy of national reconciliation.

The politics of national reconciliation

The process of dealing with systematic war crimes is a heavy burden on any new democracy. Namibia refrained from truth-seeking inquiries such as the commissions of investigation in Latin America and South Africa, and individual disclosure processes such as lustration and similar initiatives in Eastern Europe. Instead, Namibia decided on *national reconciliation*, an approach to conflict management which has been tried mainly in Africa. Closing the book on human rights violations from the past means that full disclosure is unlikely to be forthcoming and that closure is equally unlikely to be achieved. However, governments following this approach are often seen in a positive light, both by a large section of their own people and by public opinion abroad, as forgetting the past serves the nation-building project.[44] Yet, the Namibian government's reason for choosing not to initiate truth-seeking initiatives seems to hinge on the detainee issue which had the potential to embarrass high-ranking party officials.[45] Timothy Dauth argues that while South Africa's brutal heritage by far outweighs SWAPO's human rights abuses, 'it is SWAPO that currently has the most to lose'.[46] In the same vein, Warren Buford and Hugo van der Merwe state that certain political and social constraints that complicate the process influence the 'state of denial'.[47] Generally, politicians seem to be reluctant to embrace the idea of truth-seeking initiatives in instances in which they might stand to lose politically.

Namibia opted for a liberal constitution and institutions, such as the Office of the Ombudsman, that aim to ensure that human rights abuses do not recur in the future. The issue of dealing with atrocities committed during the liberation war by both sides, including gross human rights abuses such as torture, extra-judicial executions and disappearances, was thus dealt with by evading any formal search for truth and justice. In contrast to South Africa (that passed its Promotion of National Unity and Reconciliation Act in 1995), the Namibian government has to date refrained from defining the contents of the policy of national reconciliation that was introduced at independence.[48] Nevertheless, official statements by representatives of the ruling SWAPO Party leave no room for doubt that instruments of truth-seeking inquiries will not be established. Party officials such as then Prime Minister Hage Geingob mooted the possibility of civil war,[49] and of the necessity to focus on economic reconciliation in the form of development, growth and social justice in defence of their stance of letting bygones be bygones:

> Now, that many people have been hurt and disrupted by the war and the consequences of the war, we must now heal the consequences of the war. How do we do it? We say the only way is to forget the past, to forget what happened during the war . . . If you reopen that thing [the SWAPO detainee issue] many people think that they are just going to target SWAPO ex-detainees. We'll have to open that whole thing . . . The future of the whites here. Most of them were actually oppressors. They believed in apartheid . . . Now we should focus on economic reconciliation. If we could have our economy working, if people's stomachs are full, the pain they have been feeling because of the past will somehow disappear.[50]

However, the negotiated settlement demanded a political compromise between the old and the emerging elites that has been designed to control the process of social liberation, which originally had been part and parcel of SWAPO's vision. Defined along the lines of Christian ethics and morally supported by influential Christian communities, the policy of national reconciliation falls between two stools: on the one hand, it seeks the promotion of national unity and wishes to reverse structural conditions of racial discrimination and ethnic division while, on the other hand, it upholds the socio-economic status as a product of the political compromise and the desire to maintain political and economic stability. The *Windhoek Advertiser* defined national reconciliation in Namibia as 'a code word unlocking a civil religious ritual'.[51]

The Namibian approach to national reconciliation, including the renunciation of financial compensation and the general amnesty as an alternative route to retributive justice, has been the result of a negotiated settlement based on a compromise between moral imperatives and political realities. Thus, the blanket amnesty not only allowed bad apples to stay in the basket but also guaranteed a mutual standstill agreement. Burford and Van der Merwe refer to 'constant denial and a failure to apologise for wrongdoing from both SWAPO and the South Africans'.[52] The demand for truth-telling is also complicated by the political weakness of victims' groups and the lack of support from players in civil society such as the churches. Claims by victims other than SWAPO ex-detainees seem clearly to be overshadowed, for the fate of the inmates of Lubango's dungeons has monopolised the issue of dealing with the past in Namibia.[53] Without a doubt, the top-down approach to reconciliation that prioritises actions on the national level needs to be complemented by an inclusive bottom-up approach represented by grassroots, cultural and civil society initiatives and focusing on truth-seeking and healing procedures within widely acceptable guidelines. However, in the absence of opinion polls that would allow an assessment of public support for national reconciliation, SWAPO has been able to press ahead with its policy without public consultation. Thus, national reconciliation has trumped truth-telling initiatives under the SWAPO government.

The wall of silence

The construction of a wall of silence predated the end of Namibia's war of national liberation. Reports of international missions and committees that investigated wartime atrocities served no real purpose. In 1988, SWAPO invited a delegation of the Lutheran World Foundation (LWF) to visit its refugee camps in exile and, thereby, to refute any accusations of human rights abuses. The then General Secretary of the LWF unreservedly held that the allegations were part of South Africa's propaganda campaign.[54] As independence approached, the former General Secretary of the LWF, Gunnar Staalsett, explained that the church body had not been 'responsible for SWAPO' and that 'without SWAPO there would not be a liberated Namibia.[55] And Pastor Groth noted that it had been 'impossible' to discuss the human rights situation in international church bodies during the liberation era as the churches had been 'struck down by paralysis and sheer helplessness'.[56] Admitting misjudgements and an implicit trust in the liberation movement and Namibian church leaders, Bishop Heinz Joachim Held of the Evangelische Kirche in Deutschland (EKD), for instance, acknowledged 'inhibitions [and] helplessness in the face of obscure reports and insecurity considering undesirable political consequences'.[57]

As part of the political transition process, the implementation of UN Security Council Resolution 435 required the withdrawal of South Africa's military forces and the release of political prisoners on both sides. 'Even though both SWAPO and the South Africans released political prisoners, neither side accounted for those who disappeared or published information on the total number arrested and detained over the 23-year war.'[58]

Only 153 SWAPO detainees were released from exile, leading to claims that many more have been left behind in the dungeons. The United Nations responded to the repatriated ex-detainees and investigated whether Namibians were still kept imprisoned in Angola or Zambia. The United Nations Mission on Detainees (UNMD) which refrained from consulting former detainees who would undoubtedly be capable of locating mass graves,[59] returned empty-handed. After lengthy debates on the establishment of an all-party committee or a judicial commission, the first Namibian parliament commissioned the International Committee of the Red Cross (ICRC) with the task of investigating the fate of more than 2 000 missing Namibians. In 1993, the ICRC finalised its investigations and submitted its report. It stated that: 'The circumstances of death are not necessarily of concern to the ICRC . . . It is not in the province of the ICRC to dispute the validity of the replies provided by SWAPO.'[60]

According to the ICRC, it had submitted 2 161 queries to SWAPO, but that responses were forthcoming in only 556 cases. As a result, the committee had not been able to account for the plight of the missing. The report did little to break down the wall of silence.

A number of explanations for the wall of silence that surrounds the atrocities committed in the past are possible. First, household surveys suggest that people are preoccupied with daily burdens such as unemployment and the HIV/AIDS pandemic.[61] A second possible explanation is that SWAPO's strong political leadership must be regarded as a significant source of stability that unfortunately also translates into a blind faith in authority. A third possible explanation is that Namibian society is sharply divided along partisan lines that are inspired by both the struggle for liberation, post-independence political affiliation and civil society activism. The clear *us* (SWAPO) and *them* (critics) dichotomy has provoked 'a psychosis of fear' that permeates 'the entire Namibian society'.[62] Consequently, there seems to be no visible popular desire to institute truth-seeking initiatives in Namibia at this time, apart from a small number of victims and human rights groups whose claims have been persistently discounted by political brokers. Only a handful of civil society activists, mainly representing SWAPO's ex-detainees and sympathisers, unremittingly but without powers of self-assertion, recall the essential minimum demands of reconciliation processes such as healing the causes of distress,[63] and truth-telling, that would signal the transition to a more open and democratic political culture.[64] Victims of the liberation movement's human rights abuses have called repeatedly for a public investigation into their predicament. They believe that an apology from SWAPO and a public acknowledgement that they did not betray the struggle is due to them. They hope for the same measures that symbolically made reparation to an extensive number of victims of the South African forces. Moreover, many ex-detainees were well known SWAPO activists inside the country before they left for exile and, thus, regard themselves as having been victimised by both sides. Many also demand proper investigations into the fate of those still unaccounted for.

The detainee issue as political football

As national independence finally became a reality after 23 years of armed liberation struggle and complicated diplomatic negotiations, the detainee issue was regarded as a political liability for SWAPO. In fact, those who had survived the Lubango camp were despised as troublemakers that played straight into the hands of the anti-SWAPO alliance. Confronted with an opposition that turned the detainee issue into 'a club with which to batter the liberation movement during the election campaign',[65] individual party representatives such as Theo-Ben Gurirab, noticeably softened their tones:

> We have to come home and they have to come home – at the end of the day we will have to sit around the fire and take inventories: who is alive, who is dead, [and] how did it all happen? As a SWAPO leader, I will never defend the humiliation and suffering of torture. If the allegations are true, I apologize to the victims and to their parents and pledge to you now that the SWAPO leadership will take the necessary steps to bring those involved to book.[66]

Clearly, at this time it was difficult for the SWAPO leadership to find common ground on which to find a way forward. Claiming that the detainees' accusations had been one-sided, the former liberation movement tactically tried to postpone the debate. According to SWAPO, the detainee issue was 'not a political issue [and] not an electoral issue', and stressed that it opposed any commission of inquiry as SWAPO had structures to deal with their own members. It became clear that SWAPO expected 'families to deal with it' in the spirit 'of national reconciliation and healing of wounds.'[67] Thus it became apparent that the wall of silence would not be broken down from within the ruling party.

While SWAPO undoubtedly benefited from the legitimate claim to be the liberator, Franz Ansprenger is convinced that it paid for the revelations of the ex-detainees by missing a two-thirds majority in the 1989 elections,[68] thus ensuring that Namibia's democratic constitution was a document negotiated by all parties. Since independence, the former liberation movement has been ruling Namibia and has even managed to increase its dominance. In 1994, SWAPO achieved a two-thirds majority in the National Assembly elections for the first time. Legitimately reflecting voters' preference, Namibia's dominant party state is characterised by a distinct power imbalance between the ruling party and opposition parties. Notwithstanding SWAPO's constant gain and consolidation of political power, the detainee issue has cast a shadow over its leadership.

Parliamentary debates on human rights violations centred on the ruling party's record. From time to time, the desperate opposition used the detainee issue as an election campaign issue, and the ruling party, therefore, had no difficulties in dismissing the issue as a political football and blackmailing campaign. Before independence the right-wing organisations, who are little more than apologists for the South African colonial regime, had also climbed on the bandwagon and sought to obtain political mileage out of the adverse publicity the matter generated for SWAPO.

Between 1990 and 1996, the detainee issue was sidelined as international missions of inquiry ran out of steam. By way of compensation, individual members of small opposition parties demanded truth-seeking initiatives, particularly with regard to the numerous cases of disappearances, as a vital element in the pursuit of reconciliation. So, for instance, some former detainees had founded the Political Consultative Council (PCC) as a non-partisan pressure group,[69] and then established the Patriotic Unity Movement (PUM) that linked up with the alliance of opposition parties known as the United Democratic Front (UDF). As a Member of Parliament (MP), ex-detainee Eric Biwa provoked parliamentary debates on the so-called detainee issue from time to time until he resigned in 2003.[70] And SWAPO-ex-detainee Reinhart Kala Gertze, who recently took over the office of the General Secretary of the largest opposition party Congress of Democrats (CoD), has also attempted to place the 'forgotten war' on the national political agenda. But since SWAPO managed to wrest exclusive control of the parliamentary decision-making process, such efforts have met with little success.

While the SWAPO political leadership showed little interest in truth-seeking, there was also a lack of pressure from significant non-governmental actors. Factors that would enable the establishment of truth-seeking inquiries, such as strong public support, the presence of a vigorous and engaged civil society, and persistent international media attention, are absent. In contrast to some Latin American countries, where the churches together with strong human rights organisations have undertaken inquiries into past atrocities, the Namibian churches remain silent. Only civil society organisations such as the Legal Assistance Centre (LAC), the National Society for Human Rights (NSHR) and the Breaking the Wall of Silence Movement (BWS) lobbied for reconciliation measures based on truth telling and healing that was established in the atmosphere generated by the publication of Pastor Groth's memoirs.[71]

Given that the English translation of Groth's memoirs appeared six years after independence, when SWAPO's dominant political position was assured, the response to the publication was partially blunted. Dauth reckoned that: 'On the face of it, SWAPO was unlikely to have been damaged in the slightest by Groth's work had it not felt the need to react in such an extreme manner. Far more than the work's own content, it has been SWAPO's reaction to Wall of Silence that has provided cause of debate.'[72]

By means of bringing the author and the organiser of the book launch, theologian Christo Lombard, into disrepute, the SWAPO leadership tried to: quash the debate, maintain unity among its allies, diminish international attention and, last but not least, ensure the loyalty of its supporters. Groth's critique has been understood as an attack on the SWAPO leadership and has been interpreted as an unpatriotic assault against the liberation struggle and Namibia's independence.[73] It became clear that a challenge from within was what would disturb SWAPO most. In particular, the behaviour of the Council of Churches in Namibia (CCN) tipped the scales: the ruling party successfully prevented the umbrella body from implementing its reconciliation programme *Year of God's Grace* by pressurising loyal bishops to toe the party line and by identifying scapegoats among them. Nevertheless, the verbal attacks did not interfere with personal freedoms, and, in the course of the debate, a conciliatory atmosphere gained the upper hand.

Meanwhile, on Heroes' Day (26 August) 1996, the ruling party released the long-awaited but hurriedly compiled list of heroes and heroines who had lost their lives during the struggle for national liberation.[74] Known as the *Book of the Dead*, it proved controversial. Human rights groups at first welcomed SWAPO's contribution to help shed light on past events, but quickly identified numerous discrepancies and misleading information that 'left more questions than answers'.[75] SWAPO's promise to provide a second edition of the *Book of the Dead* that would address objections and complaints has not been forthcoming. Instead, the ruling party initiated a debate in the National Assembly, arguing that the report of the ICRC has proven that the accusations against SWAPO were no more than a red herring. Deflecting criticism back on opposition parties that had participated in South Africa's transitional government prior to independence, Prime Minister Geingob demanded that they, too, should be held accountable for past human rights abuses.[76] For their part, the opposition pleaded ignorance of any wrongdoing. Instead, they pinned the blame on South Africa's colonial forces: 'Now since you [SWAPO] have called us puppets, now how can you expect a puppet to report in the House when the boss is gone? The boss took all the papers, he was in charge, and the puppets have no papers to report on.'[77]

During the parliamentary debate, SWAPO MP, Nahas Angula, demanded the names of enemy agents that had been employed by South Africa in order to infiltrate the liberation movement in exile. He attempted to shed light on past events:

> Political dishonesty, betrayals, disloyalty to the struggle, leadership crisis, power struggles, tribalism, racism and the generations-divide from time to time surfaced their ugly heads . . . Lured by material benefit or under fear of torture, arrest or harassment some young Namibians allowed themselves to be used as spies and informers . . . Brother spied against brother, sister against sister, son against father and daughter against mother . . . When those suspected of working for the colonial racist regime started to drop names left, right and centre, implicating each other in the process the situation became complicated . . . In such situations possibilities exist of innocent people having been framed . . . To those innocent people who got caught in the crossfire, I want to say: 'Error is human [sic], forgiveness is divine'.[78]

There is no room for doubt that the liberation movement had been infiltrated by spies trained to recruit other enemy agents within SWAPO in order to destroy the movement from within. In a paranoid atmosphere, however, there was thought to be a spy behind every bush. Nonetheless, the heat of the moment does not explain the fact that approximately 2 000 detainees are still missing; some of whom were severely traumatised by torture and illness, and left behind in the dungeons of Lubango after the ceasefire. However, truth-seeking initiatives should not seek to identify perpetrators of atrocities by one party. In fact, both South Africa and SWAPO, were obviously embarrassed by violations of human rights in the past, and were 'pleased to have . . . a general amnesty'.[79] Despite a mutually accepted agreement to forget the past, it has not been possible to erase memory.

Memory in a divided society

Collective memory mirrors the collective identity of a people in a nation-state. Both remembering and forgetting shape a collective memory that is selective and strategically appropriated. A narrative is constructed to reinforce this sense of belonging to the emergent nation. In Namibia, common points of reference are the anti-colonial resistance and the founding of the state as a result of the liberation struggle. The foundational myth projects the unity of anti-colonial forces during the liberation struggle and endorses the nation-building process in the post-colony. Blurring the distinction between party, government and state, the liberation movement turned ruling party appropriates and defines collective memory. Public holidays and memorials such as the gigantic Heroes' Acre statue in Windhoek that honours the liberation struggle glorify SWAPO's veterans and heroes of the armed resistance against German colonial forces at the beginning of the last century. The victor forgets the casualties but remembers the sacrifices and the triumph of the armed liberation struggle and, consequently, immortalises heroes and heroines. Such selective remembering and memorialisation serves to legitimise the claim to political power. The politics of memory is not all inclusive for it distinguishes between 'insiders' and 'outsiders'. 'Insiders' clearly have a vested interest in their version of the past, as Heribert Adams and Kanya Adams recognise:

> Even if something is an obvious truth to any 'objective' outsider, it might be far from acceptable to an insider. For a member of the 'in-group' the belief in the wickedness of the other or the goodness of itself is not just a myth that can be unmasked. It is part of an identity, a daily reality to be lived by, a lens through which the world is interpreted and a tool to give meaning to life.[80]

'Outsiders' exist in Namibia precisely because it is not a homogenous, united society. These 'outsiders' might include those who have been detained by SWAPO on the strength of claims that they were enemy agents, or who have dissociated themselves from the ruling party after independence. They invariably resent the ruling party's monopolisation of the past and public memory and preserve their own buried memories. Richard Werbner holds that:

> Buried memory produces ... popular history in which the past is perceived to be unfinished, festering in the present – these are narratives which motivated the people to call again and again for a public resolution to their predicament. Subjected to buried memory, people do not so much forget as recognize – and often even more forcefully – that they have not been allowed to remember. Though not always obviously or immediately, such situations are potentially explosive, when people feel compelled to unbury the memory and reject their past submissions.[81]

So when sizeable groups within the same nation-state simultaneously attribute different interpretations to the same history, divided memories exist. They prevail because memory is tied to collective and institutional identity.[82] These memories exist in a twilight zone or a *no man's land of time* because the political elite and other stakeholders compete for hegemony. The politics of memory is a contest over whether dominant or buried memories prevail.

Conclusion

Since Namibia gained national independence in 1990, the young democracy has battled with a legacy of decades of foreign rule, apartheid and violent conflict. In many ways, Namibia's response to the post-conflict situation which it inherited deserves commendation. After decades of colonial rule and brutal conflict, peace is a delicate balancing process and should not be taken for granted. Accordingly, the fear of revisiting the past is based on concerns that the disclosures would lead to a witch-hunt and renewed strife, even bloodshed. The tragedy of human rights abuses committed by both the South African colonial regime and the liberation movement is that this legacy continues to shape the country's political culture. During the liberation struggle, the detainee issue was regarded as South African war propaganda, while it was treated as an election campaign issue by some of the opposition parties after independence. South Africa's strategy aimed at discrediting the liberation movement while SWAPO defended its human rights record. As a result, the international solidarity movement was hamstrung by a paralysing disbelief. The question remains whether human rights violations by perpetrators of apartheid oppression can be equated with those perpetrated in the struggle for liberation. This question highlights the problem of giving moral principles absolute value irrespective of the historical context.[83] Thus, it has been argued that South Africa's colonial rule cannot be equated with SWAPO's liberation struggle and, therefore, human rights abuses cannot be weighed up against each other. But in claiming the moral high ground, SWAPO is effectively downplaying its own human rights abuses by pointing a finger at South Africa charging that they 'did it too'.[84] Notwithstanding this dilemma, observers have been engaged in a yet unresolved discussion as to whether the human rights abuses were an aberration brought on by the exceptional circumstances of an armed conflict, or part of an authoritarian political culture within SWAPO. The latter might have serious implications for the ruling party in a democratic state, as SWAPO's intolerance of political dissent, especially within its own ranks, has raised its ugly head occasionally since independence.

In post-conflict societies, where the wounds are deep and both victims and offenders lost their voices in the face of inhuman and cruel war crimes, where the roles of victims and offenders alternated and moral standards were confused, coming to terms with the past could take decades. In comparison with other post-war generations around the world, Namibia's amnesia is anything but an exception to the rule. Nonetheless, numerous examples of national and international criminal prosecutions that are based upon obligations to uphold principles of international humanitarian law indicate that the victims' call for a public resolution of their predicament must not remain unheard. The expectation should not be that 'coming to terms with the past' will bring about consensus and a singular interpretation of past events. For contested history is preferable to the myth-making of official selective memory.[85] So a more reasonable goal should be a pragmatic approach that accepts the reality of a shared history and a common future. There is no doubt that a compromise is needed – one that recognises SWAPO's indisputable contribution to Namibia's independence and, at the same time, does justice to direct and indirect victims of human rights abuses on both sides of the conflict. Most importantly, Namibia has to create a sustainable human rights culture through training and education that reduces the possibility that violations will be repeated in the future. Thereby, Namibia must not necessarily replicate the South African or the Latin American models but should adopt an approach that fits its political history.

Notes to Chapter Seventeen

1   J. Geldenhuys cited in H. Hamann, *Days of the Generals. The Untold Story of South Africa's Apartheid Era Military Generals* (Cape Town: Zebra Press, 2001), 67.

2   Cited in S. Brown, 'Diplomacy by Other Means – SWAPO's Liberation War', in *Namibia's Liberation Struggle: The Two-edged Sword*, ed. C. Leys and J. S. Saul (London: James Currey, 1995), 28.

3   Not surprisingly, the compulsory military service was met by stiff opposition on the part of political activists and the churches, and caused a tide of refugees.

4   M. O. Hinz and N. G. Leuven-Lachinski, *Koevoet Versus the People of Namibia* (Utrecht: Working Group Cairos, 1989), 3; A. Feinstein, *In Conflict* (Windhoek: New Namibia Books, 1998), 16.

5   M. Schivute, *Go and Come Back Home* (Windhoek: Gamsberg Macmillan, 1997), 58.

6   K. Hiyalwa, *Meekulu's Children* (Windhoek: New Namibia Books, 2000), 67–8.

7   It has to been taken into consideration that SWAPO might not be responsible for all 'missing persons' that are listed on the records of the human rights groups. Some of the missing might have been among the victims of Wouter Basson's warfare programme or might have been 'turned' into *Koevoet* members after they had been captured and tortured by South African security forces. Others might be buried in the nameless mass graves in Cassinga or northern Namibia. Nevertheless, it is possible that the liberation movement might have sent potential 'troublemakers' that had been released from Mboroma camp or the Lubango dungeons on suicide missions. However, many people listed on the named records were last seen in SWAPO detention in exile.

8   The temporal limitation should not suggest that gross human rights abuses in Namibia have been restricted to the period of time 1966 until 1989. Furthermore, the focus on severe violations of human rights, say,

torture, extra-judicial executions and disappearances, does not intend to ignore systematic political and economic discrimination imposed by the apartheid regime.

9   D. Soggot, *Namibia. The Violent Heritage. The Untold Story of South Africa's Vietnam* (London: Rex Collings, 1986).

10   For example, W. Steenkamp, *Borderstrike! South Africa Into Angola* (Durban: Butterworths, 1983); W. Steenkamp, *South Africa's Border War, 1966–1989* (Gibraltar: Ashanti Publishing Limited, 1989); P. Stiff, *Nine Days of War: Namibia – Before, During, After* (Alberton: Galago Publishing, 1989); P. Stiff, *The Covert War. Koevoet Operations in Namibia 1979–1989* (Alberton: Galago Publishing, 2004); P. Stiff, *Warfare by Other Means. South Africa in the 1980s* (Alberton: Galago Publishing, 2000); J. Hooper, *Koevoet!* (Johannesburg: Southern Book Publishers, 1988.)

11   For example, J. Geldenhuys, *Die Wat Wen: 'n General se Storie uit 'n Era van Oorlog en Vrede.* (Pretoria: Van Schaik, 1993); J. Breytenbach, *The Buffalo Soldiers: The Story of South Africa's 21 Battalion 1975–1993* (Alberton: Galago Publishing, 2003).

12   For example, R. Labuschagne, *On South Africa's Secret Service. An Undercover Agent's Story* (Alberton: Galago Publishing, 2002); G. Winter, *Inside BOSS: South Africa's Secret Police. An Ex-spy's Dramatic and Shocking Expose* (Suffolk: Penguin Books, 1981).

13   For example, G. Cawthra, *Brutal Force. The Apartheid War Machine* (London: International Defence and Aid Fund, 1986).

14   For example, SWAPO, *To Be Born a Nation: The Liberation Struggle for Namibia* (London: Swapo of Namibia, 1981).

15   For example, C. Leys, and S. Brown, eds. *Histories of Namibia. Living Through the Liberation Struggle* (London: Merlin Press, 2005); S. Nujoma, *Where Others Wavered. The Autobiography of Sam Nujoma* (London: Panaf, 2001); E. Namhila, *The Price of Freedom* (Windhoek: New Namibia Books, 1997); A. Shipanga, *In Search of Freedom. The Andreas Shipanga Story as Told to Sue Armstrong* (Gibraltar: Ashanti Publishing, 1989); M. Shivute, *Go and Come Back Home* (Windhoek: Gamsberg Macmillan, 1997); H. Shityuwete, *Never Follow the Wolf: The Autobiography of a Namibian Freedom Fighter* (London: Kliptown Books, 1990); J. Ya-Otto, *Battlefront Namibia: An Autobiography* (Westport: Lawrence Hill, 1981); L. Engombe, *Kind Nr. 95. Meine Deutsch-Afrikanische Odyssee* (Berlin: Ullstein, 2004); K. P. Nathanael, *A Journey to Exile. The Story of a Namibian Freedom Fighter* (Aberystwyth: Sosiumi Press, 2002); A. Feinstein, *In Conflict* (Windhoek: New Namibia Books, 1998).

16   *Truth and Reconciliation Commission of South Africa Report*, Vol. 2 (Cape Town: TRC, 1998), ch. 2 'The State Outside South Africa Between 1960 and 1990', *passim*.

17   M. Burger and C. Gould, *Secrets and Lies. Wouter Basson and South Africa's Chemical and Biological Warfare Programme* (Cape Town: Zebra Press, 2002).

18   For two decades the whereabouts of captured freedom fighters have unsatisfactorily explained or simply ignored. See Cawthra, *Brutal Force*, 215; Amnesty International, *Namibia. The Human Rights Situation at Independence* (London: Amnesty International, 1990), 9.

19   *The Namibian*, 'Namibian charges come back to haunt "Dr Death"', 12 September 2005.

20   *The Namibian*, 'Dr Death is off the hook in South Africa', 24 October 2005.

21   *The Namibian*, 'SA walks tightrope trying apartheid killers', 3 February 2006.

22   Documentation and correspondence privately collected and archived by Salatiel Ailonga, Siegfried Groth, Christo Lombard and others.

23   Numerous notes, memos, and letters provide documentary evidence for the rejection of the claims offered by the PCN, the CP, and individual church representatives such as Salatiel Ailonga and Siegfried Groth.

24   C. Leys and J. Saul, 'Liberation Without Democracy? The Swapo Crisis of 1976', *Journal of Southern African Studies*, 20 (1994), 125.

25   For example, D. Herbstein and J. Evenson, *The Devils Are Among Us. The War for Namibia* (New Jersey: Zed Books, 1989).

26   For example, N. Basson and B. Motinga, *Call Them Spies* (Windhoek and Johannesburg: Africa Communications Project, 1989); Shipanga, *In Search of Freedom*.

27   For instance, Basson later admitted that he had been a South African spy. See D. Lush, *Last Steps to Uhuru* (Windhoek: New Namibia Books, 1993), 178.

28   T. Dauth, 'Review of Siegfried Groth's Namibia – the wall of silence: The dark days of the liberation struggle'. http://www.hartford-hwp.com/archives/37/054.html/.

29   C. Leys and J. Saul, eds. *Namibia's Liberation Struggle. The Two-edged Sword* (London and Athens: James Currey, 1995).

30   S. Groth, 'Namibische Passion. Tragik und Grösse der Namibischen Befreiungsbewegung' (Wuppertal: Peter Hammer Verlag, 1995).

31   *The Namibian*, 22 March 1996.

32   *The Namibian*, 12 April 1996.

33   *Windhoek Observer*, 13 April 1996.

34   *Mail & Guardian*, 'The elusive truth about Namibia's mass graves', 21 November 2005.

35   Nujoma, *Where Others Wavered*, 388, 396–8.

36   A. Harneit-Sievers, *Namibia. Wahlen zur Verfassunggebenden Versammlung 1989. Analyse und Dokumentation* (Hamburg: Institut für Afrika-Kunde, 1990), 8; F. Ansprenger, 'Die SWAPO als Regierungspartei, *Aus Politik und Zeitgeschichte* B8 (1990), 14; B. O'Linn, *Namibia. The Sacred Trust of Civilization. Ideal and Reality* (Windhoek: Gamsberg Macmillan, 2003), 334.

37   *Mail & Guardian*, 'A grave case of memory loss', 28 November 2006.

38   Ibid.

39   Cited in *The Namibian*, 'President in plea on mass grave', 14 November 2005.

40   Clues to the origins of the graves and those persons buried in them may be found in the Administrator General's files located in the Namibian National Archives, or SWAPO's own files which are to be housed at the SWAPO Archive and Research Centre currently being established at the party's headquarters (*Insight*, 2/2006, 'The truth will out – but when?'). But as confidential files are likely to remain closed for up to 25 years, testimonies of villagers that are able to locate war graves in the north of the country are indispensable to identifying the victims. The graves might bear testimony to South African security forces predilection for killing rather than holding POWs whom they considered 'terrorists'. South Africa did not ratify the 1977 protocol that extended the Geneva Convention to liberation struggles. Thus, the mass graves around former military bases may not only contain the human remains of those who crossed the border in 1989, but also of freedom fighters and civilians suspected of supporting the liberation movement that had been detained by the South African security forces during the war. Without doubt, the identification of victims and the establishment of causes of death should not be restricted to Namibia's north, but should include human remains buried in Angolan and Zambian soil.

41   In 1993, the National Intelligence Service (NIS) destroyed 44 tons of documents and microfiches. See Labuschagne, *On South Africa's Secret Service*, 249; C. Bundy, 'The Beast of the Past: History and the TRC', in *After the TRC: Reflections on Truth and Reconciliation in South Africa*, ed. W. James and L. van der Vijver (Cape Town: David Philip, 2000), 16. Following initial refusals, the records of South Africa's Administrator General (1977–90) and the South West African Territory Force (SWATF) have only recently been transferred to the Namibian National Archives in Windhoek (*Insight* 2/2006).

42   C. Villa-Vicencio. 'On the Limitations of Academic History', in *After the TRC*, ed. James and Van der Vijver, 25.

43   M. Ignatieff, *The Warrior's Honour: Ethnic War and the Modern Conscience* (Toronto: Henry Holt, 1998), 170.

44   D. Bronkhorst, 'Truth and Reconciliation. Obstacles and Opportunities for Human Rights' (Amsterdam: Amnesty International, 1995), 32–47.

45   P. Conway, 'Truth and Reconciliation: The Road not Taken in Namibia', *The Online Journal of Peace and Conflict Resolution*. http://www.trinstitute.org/ojpcr/5_1conway.htm/.

46   Dauth, 'Review of Siegfried Groth's Namibia'.

47   W. Buford and H. Van der Merwe, 'Reparations in southern Africa', *Cahiers D'études Africaines*, Vol. 44, 1–2 (2004).

48   SWAPO, *Resolution of the Central Committee of SWAPO Adopting the Policy of National Reconciliation* (23 May 1989), unpublished.

49   For details on the parameters of the debate subsequent to the launch of Pastor Groth's memories, see: Vereinigte Evangelische Mission, *Namibische Passion. Chronik einer Debatte. Mitarbeiter-Materialmappe.* Wuppertal: Vereinigte Evangelische Mission, 1997).

50   *I have seen (Nda Mona): Searching for Truth and Reconciliation in Namibia*, documentary produced by Richard Pakleppa (Namibia 1999).

51   *Windhoek Advertiser*, 'Namibia – The wall of silence (4)', 14 March 1996.

52   Buford and Van der Merwe, 'Reparations in southern Africa'.

53   Ibid.

54   Press release LWF, 14 April 1988, unpublished.

55   *Allgemeine Zeitung*, 16 February 1990 (Author's translation).

56   Cited in *Evangelischer Pressedienst* 1989, 14, (Author's translation).

57   Cited in Groth, *Namibische Passion,* 10 (Author's translation).

58   Buford and Van der Merwe, 'Reparations in southern Africa'.

59   *I have seen (Nda Mona)*.

60   ICRC, 'Missing Namibians', ICRC Final Report (Geneva 1993), unpublished.

61   The 2003 *Afrobarometer* poll surveyed public attitudes towards democracy, markets and civil society. When asked 'In your opinion, what are the most important problems facing the country that government should address?', many respondents indicated that 'Unemployment/Job creation' (72%) and 'HIV/AIDS' (28%) should receive most attention from the government. See C. Keulder, *Public Opinion and the Consolidation of Democracy in Namibia.* (Cape Town: Institute for Democracy in South Africa, 2002), 28; C. Keulder and T. Wiese, *Democracy without democrats? Results from the 2003 Afrobarometer Survey in Namibia* (Cape Town: Institute for Democracy in South Africa, 2003), 14.

62   'Ultimately it is more than a culture of silence – it is a lifestyle, the norm and acceptable political language . . . In a system where the state is the largest dispenser of material rewards, loyalty towards the one who controls the state's purse strings is essential' (J. Diescho, 'Government and Opposition in Post-independent Namibia: Perceptions and Performance', in *Building Democracy. Perceptions and Performance of Government and Opposition in Namibia*, ed. Namibia Institute for Democracy (Windhoek: Namibia Institute for Democracy, 1996), 16–17.

63   State-sponsored initiatives and church rehabilitation centres have solely been directed towards physically disabled veterans. Survivors of traumatic events that are suffering from Post-Traumatic Stress Disorder or related psychological conditions 'were urged to let sleeping dogs lie' (*New Era*, 16 – 18 May 1997).

64   As many factors, including the type of transition and socio-economic circumstances, influence reconciliation processes, there exists no model for the process that can apply to all. But international human rights organisations identify certain minimum requirements, such as the establishment of the truth and healing processes. Relevant literature gives a schematic overview of certain aspects of the reconciliation process. See, for example, International IDEA, *Reconciliation After Violent Conflict. Policy Summary* (Stockholm: International IDEA, 2004); Amnesty International, *Namibia. The Human Rights Situation at Independence*

(London: Amnesty International, 1990); J. P. Lederach, *Building Peace. Sustainable Reconciliation in Divided Societies* (Washington DC: United States Institute of Peace Press, 1998); D. Bronkhorst, *Truth and Reconciliation. Obstacles and Opportunities for Human Rights* (Amsterdam: Amnesty International, 1995).

65   Lush, *Last Steps to Uhuru*.

66   Cited in the *Times of Namibia*, 10 July 1989. After taking up his seat in parliament Theo-Ben Gurirab 'disassociated' himself from his campaign pledge. Republic of Namibia: Debates of the National Assembly, 1990, First Session, First Parliament, 21 March – 31 May 1990, Volume 1, unpublished.

67   Interview with Theo-Ben Gurirab, recorded by Rolf-Henning Hintze on 11 October 1989 (unpublished).

68   Ansprenger, 'Die SWAPO als Regierungspartei'.

69   The PCC aimed at bringing SWAPO's human rights violations to public attention, and at achieving the release of fellow detainees that have been left behind in Lubango's dungeons.

70   Another outspoken parliamentarian was Moses Katjiuongua of the National Patriotic Front (NPF), and later the Democratic Coalition of Namibia (DCN).

71   NSHR also intends lawsuits against the governments of SWAPO's former host countries Tanzania and Zambia that committed abuses against members of the liberation movement. See Buford and Van der Merwe, 'Reparations in southern Africa'.

72   Dauth, 'Review of Siegfried Groth's Namibia'.

73   Ibid.

74   A critical review was provided by the National Society for Human Rights, *Critical Analysis: SWAPO's Book of the Dead* (Windhoek 1996), unpublished.

75   *Windhoek Advertiser*, 19 September 1996, '"Book of the Dead": A massive cover-up'.

76   Republic of Namibia, Debates of the National Assembly, 1996, Third Session, Second Parliament, 17 September – 16 October 1996, Vol. II, unpublished.

77   Moses Katjiuongua in ibid.

78   Ibid.

79   C. Saunders, *From Apartheid to Democracy: Namibia and South Africa Compared* (Basel: Basler Afrika Bibliographien, 1998), 5.

80   H. Adam and K. Adam, 'The Politics of Memory in Divided Societies', in *After the TRC*, ed. James and Van de Vijver, 44.

81   R. Werbner, 'Beyond Oblivion: Confronting Memory Crisis', in *Memory and the Postcolony. African Anthropology and the Critique of Power,* ed. R. Werbner (London and New York: Zed Books, 1998), 9.

82   Adam and Adam, 'The Politics of Memory', 33, 44.

83   J. de Gruchy, 'The TRC and the Building of a Moral Culture', in *After the TRC*, ed. James and Van der Vijver.

84   Dicker in Buford and Van der Merwe, 'Reparations in southern Africa'.

85   Adam and Adam, 'The Politics of Memory', 37.

Select Bibliography

Military/Diplomatic/Political History

Abel, R. *White Resistance to the Military*. Johannesburg: Centre for Applied Legal Studies, 1996.

Addison, G. N. 'Censorship of the Press in South Africa During the Angolan War: A Case Study of News Manipulation and Suppression'. MA thesis, Rhodes University, 1980.

Alden, C. *Apartheid's Last Stand: The Rise and the Fall of the South African Security State*. Basingstoke: Macmillan, 1996.

Alexander, E. G. M. 'The Cassinga Raid'. MA thesis, University of South Africa, 2003.

Barber, J. and Barratt, J. *South Africa's Foreign Policy: The Search for Status and Security 1945–1988*. Johannesburg: Southern Books, 1990.

Barrell, H. *MK: The ANC's Armed Struggle*. Harmondsworth: Penguin, 1991.

Breytenbach, J. *They Live by the Sword*. Alberton: Lemur, 1990.

_____. *Eden's Exiles: One Soldier's Fight for Paradise*. Cape Town: Queillerie, 1997.

_____. *The Buffalo Soldiers: The Story of South Africa's 32 Battalion, 1975–1993*. Alberton: Lemur, 2002.

Bridgland, F. *Savimbi: A Key to Africa*. London: Coronet Books, 1988.

_____. *The War for Africa: Twelve Months That Transformed a Continent*. Gibraltar: Ashanti, 1990.

Brittain, V. *Hidden Lives, Hidden Deaths: South Africa's Crippling of a Continent*. London: Faber & Faber, 1988.

_____. *Death of Dignity: Angola's Civil War*. London: Pluto Press, 1998.

Burger, M. and Gould, C. *Secrets and Lies. Wouter Basson and South Africa's Chemical and Biological Weapons Programme*. Cape Town: Zebra Press, 2002.

Burgess, J. *The Great White Hoax: South Africa's International Propaganda Machine*. London: Africa Bureau, 1977.

Cawthra, G. *Brutal Force: The Apartheid War Machine*. London: IDAF, 1986.

Catholic Institute of International Relations. *Out of Step: War Resistance in South Africa*. London: CIIR, 1989.

Crocker, C. *High Noon in southern Africa*. New York: W.W. Norton, 1982.

Crocker, C., Hampson, F. O. and Aall, P., eds. *Grasping the Nettle: Analyzing Cases of Intractable Conflict*. Washington: United States Institute of Peace, 2005.

Deutschmann, D., ed. *Changing the History of Africa*. Melbourne: Ocean Press, 1989.

Dorbell, L. *SWAPO's Struggle for Namibia 1960–1991: War by Other Means*. Basel: P. Schletwein Publishing, 1998.

Davis, S. *Apartheid's Rebels: Inside South Africa's Hidden War*. Craighall: Ad. Donker, 1987.

De Kock, E. *Long Night's Damage. Working for the Apartheid State*. Saxonwold: Contra, 1998.

Du Pisani, A. *Beyond the Barracks: Reflections on the Role of the SADF in the Region*. Braamfontein: The South African Institute of International Affairs, 1988.

Du Preez, S. *Avontuur in Angola: Die Verhaal van Suid-Afrika se Soldate in Angola, 1975–1976*. Pretoria: Van Schaik, 1989.

Du Preez, S. and Spies F. J. *Operasie Savannah: Angola 1975–1976*. Pretoria: SA Weermag Direktoraat Openbare Betrekkinge, 1989.

Ellis, S. *Comrades against Apartheid*. London: James Currey, 1992.

Ellis, S. 'The Historical Significance of South Africa's Third Force'. *Journal of Southern African Studies* 24 (2) 1998:261–99.

Evans, M. and Phillips, M. 'Intensifying the Civil War: The Role of the South African Defence Force'. In *State, Resistance and Change in South Africa*, edited by P. Frankel, N. Pines and M. Swilling. Johannesburg: Southern Books, 1988.

Frankel, P. 'Race and Counter-Revolution: South Africa's Total Strategy'. *Journal of Commonwealth and Comparative Politics* 18 (3) 1980.

_____. *Pretoria's Praetorians: Civil-Military Relations in South Africa*. Cambridge: Cambridge University Press, 1984.

Frederickse, J. *South Africa: A Different Kind of War*. Johannesburg: Ravan Press, 1986.

George, E. *The Cuban Intervention in Angola, 1965–1991. From Che Guevara to Cuito Cuanavale*. London: Frank Cass, 2005.

Geldenhuys, D. *The Diplomacy of Isolation: South African Foreign Policy Making*. New York: St Martin's Press, 1984.

Gewald, J. B. 'Who killed Clemens Kapuuo?' *Journal of Southern African Studies*, 30 (3) 2004:559–76.

Gleijeses, P. *Conflicting Missions: Havana, Washington, Pretoria*. Alberton: Galago, 2003.

_____. 'Moscow's Proxy?' Cuba and Africa 1975–1988', *Journal of Cold War Studies* 8 (2) 2006:3–51.

Grundy, K. W. *The Militarization of South African Politics*. Oxford: Oxford University Press, 1988.

Guelke, A. *Rethinking the Rise and Fall of Apartheid*. Basingstoke: Palgrave Macmillan, 2005.

Guimarães, F.A. *The Origins of the Angolan Civil War: Foreign Intervention and Domestic Political Conflict*. Basingstoke: Macmillan, 2001.

Hallett, R. 'The South African Intervention in Angola 1975–76'. *African Affairs* 77 (1978):347–68.

Hamann, H. *Days of the Generals*. Cape Town: Zebra Press, 2001.

Hanlon, J. *Beggar Your Neighbours: Apartheid Power in southern Africa*. London: James Currey, 1986.

Harlech-Jones, B. *A New Thing? The Namibian Independence Process 1989–1990*. Windhoek: Ecumenical Institute for Namibia, University of Namibia, 1997.

Harrigan, A. *Defence Against Total Attack*. Cape Town: Nasionale Boekhandel, 1965.

Heitman, H-R. *South African War Machine*. Bramley: Galago, 1985.

_____. *War in Angola: The Final South African phase*. Gibraltar: Ashanti, 1990.

Herbstein, D. and Evenson, J. *The Devils are Among Us: The War for Namibia*. London: Zed, 1989.

Heywood, J. *The Cassinga Event: An Investigation of the Records*. Windhoek: National Archives, 1994.

Hooper, J. *Koevoet!* Johannesburg: Southern Book Publishers, 1988.

_____. *Beneath the Visiting Moon: Images of Combat in southern Africa*. Lexington, Mass.: Lexington Books, 1990.

International Defence and Aid Fund. *Fact Paper on southern Africa No. 8: The Apartheid War Machine*. London: IDAF, 1980.

_____. *Fact Paper on southern Africa No. 10: Apartheid's Army in Namibia — South Africa's Illegal Military Occupation*. London: IDAF, 1982.

Jaster, R. *The Defence of White Power: South African Foreign Policy under Pressure*. Basingstoke: Macmillan, 1988.

Johnson, P. and Martin, D., eds. *Destructive Engagement: southern Africa at War*. Harare: Zimbabwe Publishing House, 1986.

Katjavivi, P. *A History of Resistance in Namibia*. Paris: UNESCO, 1988.

König, B. *Namibia. The Ravages of War*. London: International Defence and Aid Fund for southern Africa, 1983.

Leys, C. and Saul, J. *Namibia's Liberation Struggle: The Two-Edged Sword*. London: James Currey, 1995.

Leonard, R. *South Africa at War: White Power and the Crisis in southern Africa*. Craighall: Ad. Donker, 1983.

Matloff, J. *Fragments of a Forgotten War*. Parktown: Penguin, 1997.

Mills, G. and Williams, D. *7 Battles That Shaped South Africa*. Cape Town: Tafelberg, 2006.

Minnaar, A., Liebenberg, I. and Schutte, C. *The Hidden Hand: Covert Operations in South Africa*. Pretoria: Human Sciences Research Council, 1994.

Minter, W. *Apartheid's Contras: An Inquiry into the roots of War in Angola and Mozambique*. Johannesburg: Witwatersrand University Press, 1994.

Moorcraft, P. *Africa's Superpower*. Johannesburg: Sygma/Collins, 1981.

___. *African Nemesis: War and Revolution in southern Africa 1945–2010*. London: Brassey's Ltd, 1990.

Namakalu, O. *Armed Liberation Struggle. Some Accounts of PLAN's Combat Operations*. Windhoek: Gamsberg Macmillan, 2004.

Nöthling, C. J. 'Military Chronicle of South West Africa (1915–1988)'. In *South African Defence Force Review 1989* edited by A. de la Rey. Durban: Walker-Remus, 1989.

Nortjie, P. *32 Battalion*. Cape Town: Zebra Press, 2004.

Pauw, J. *In the Heart of the Whore: the Story of Apartheid's Death Squads*. Halfway House: Southern Books, 1991.

_____. *Into the Heart of Darkness. Confessions of Apartheid's Assassins*. Johannesburg: Jonathan Ball, 1997.

Pfister, R. *Apartheid South Africa and African States: From Pariah to Middle Power, 1961–1994*. London: I. B. Tauris, 2005.

Phelan, J. *Apartheid Media: Disinformation and Dissent in South Africa*. Westport, Conn.: Lawrence Hill & Company, 1987.

Phillips, M. 'The End Conscription Campaign 1983-1988: A Study of White Extra-Parliamentary Opposition to Apartheid'. MA thesis, University of South Africa, 2002.

Pottinger, B. *The Imperial Presidency: P. W. Botha – The First Ten Years*. Johannesburg: Southern Book Publishers, 1988.

Rhoodie, E. *South West: The last frontier in Africa*. Johannesburg: Voortrekkerpers, 1967.

Saul, J. S. and Leys, C. 'Lubango and After: "Forgotten History" as Politics in Contemporary Namibia'. *Journal of Southern African Studies* 29(2) 2003:333–53.

Seegers, A. 'The military in South Africa: a comparison and critique'. *South African International*, 16 April 1986.

___. *The Military in the Making of Modern South Africa*. London: I. B. Tauris, 1996.

Seiler, J., ed. *southern Africa since the Portuguese Coup*. Boulder, Co.: Westview Press, 1980.

Snyman, P. H. R. *Beeld van SWA Gebiedsmag*. Pretoria: SADF Directorate of Public Relations, 1989.

Soggot, D. *Namibia: The Violent Heritage*. New York: St Martin's Press, 1986.

Sonderling, S. *Bushwar Namibia*. Windhoek: Eyes Publishing, 1980.

Spies, F. du Toit. *Operasie Savannah: Angola 1975-76*. Pretoria: SADF Directorate of Public Relations, 1989.

Steenkamp, W. *Borderstrike! South Africa into Angola*. Durban: Butterworths, 1983.

_____. *South Africa's Border War 1966–1989*. Gibraltar: Ashanti, 1989.

Stiff, P. *Nine Days of War*. Alberton: Lemur Books, 1991.

_____. *The Silent War: South African Recce Operations 1969–1994*. Alberton: Galago, 1999.

SWAPO Department of Information and Publicity. *To Be Born a Nation: The Liberation Struggle for Namibia*. London: Zed Press, 1990.

Toase, F. 'The South African Army: The Campaign in South West Africa/Namibia since 1966'. In *Armed Forces and Modern Counter-Insurgency*, edited by I. F. W. Beckett. London: Croom Helm, 1986.

Vale, P. ' "Whose World is it Anyway?" International Relations in South Africa'. In *The Study of International Relations: The State of the Art*, edited by H. C. Dyer and L. Mangasarian. London: Macmillan, 1989.

_____. *Security and Politics in South Africa: The Regional Dimension*. Boulder, Co.: Lynne Rienner, 2003.

Venter, A. J., ed. *Challenge: southern Africa within the African Revolutionary Context*. Gibraltar: Ashanti, 1989.

Visser, W. 'The Production of the Literature on the "Red Peril" and "Total Onslaught" in Twentieth Century South Africa'. http://academic.sun. ac.za/history/dokumente/literature_production. pdf

Warwick, R. 'The South African Military Under Verwoerd: SADF Popularization Amongst the White Community, 1960–66'. Paper presented to the South African Historical Society Conference, University of Cape Town, 2005.

Williams, R. 'The Other Armies: A Brief Historical Overview of Umkhonto We Sizwe (MK), 1961–1994'. *Military History Journal* 11 (5) June 2000. http://rapidttp.com/milhist/vol115rw. html

Windrich, E. 'South Africa's Propaganda War'. *Africa Today* 36 (1) 1989:51–60.

_____. 'The Laboratory of Hate: The Role of Clandestine Radio in the Angolan War'. *International Journal of Cultural Studies* 3 (2) 2000:206-18.

Weaver, T. 'Caught in the Crossfire: The War in Namibia'. *Work in Progress* 29 1983:4–10.

Wood, B. 'Preventing the Vacuum: Determinants of the Namibian Settlement'. *Journal of Southern African Studies* 17 (4) 1991:742–69.

Woods, D. *Apartheid – The Propaganda and the Reality*. London: Commonwealth Secretariat International Affairs Division, 1985.

Zartman, I. W. *Ripe for Resolution: Conflict and Intervention in Africa*. New York: Oxford University Press, 1989.

Militarisation and Gender

Cock, J. 'Conscription in South Africa: A Study in the Politics of Coercion'. *South African Sociological Review*, 2 (1) 1989:1–22.

_____. *Colonels and Cadres: War and Gender in South Africa*. Cape Town: Oxford University Press, 1991.

Cock, J. and Nathan, L., eds. *War and Society: The Militarisation of South Africa*. Cape Town and Johannesburg: David Philip, 1989. (Also published under the title *Society at War: The Militarisation of South Africa*. New York: St Martin's Press, 1989.)

Cohen, S. A., ed. *Democratic Societies and Their Armed Forces*. London: Frank Cass, 2000.

Cooke, M. and Wollacott, A. *Gendering War talk*. Princeton: Princeton University Press, 1993.

Conway, D. ' "In the Name of Humanity, Can You as a Woman, as a Mother Tolerate This?" Gender and Militarisation of South Africa'. MA thesis, University of Bristol, 2000.

Enloe, C. *Does Khaki Become You?: The Militarization of Women's Lives*. London: Pandorra, 1988.

_____. 'Beyond Steve Canyon and Rambo: Feminist Histories of Militarized Masculinity'. In *The Militarization of the Western World*, edited by J. Gills. New Brunswick: Rutgers University Press, 1989.

Gibson, J. 'American Paramilitary Culture and the Reconstitution of the Vietnam War'. In *Making War Making Peace: The Social Foundations of Violent Conflict*, edited by F. Cancian and J. Gibson. Belmont, CA: Wadsworth, 1990:86–99.

Hopkins, P. 'Gender Treachery: Homophobia, Masculinity and Threatened Identities'. In *Rethinking Masculinity*, edited by L. May and R. Strikwerda. Maryland: Littlefield Adams, 1992.

Jochelson, K. 'War, State and Society: Men, Masculinity and Militarism: Theorising Military Violence'. Unpublished paper, 1987.

Mann, M. 'The Roots and Contradictions of Modern Militarism'. *New Left Review* 162, 1987:35- 50.

Morrell, R., ed. *Changing men in southern Africa*. Pietermaritzburg: University of Natal Press, 2001.

Price, L. 'A Documentation of the Experiences of Military Conscripts in the South African Defence Force'. MA thesis, University of Natal, Durban, 1989.

Regan, P. *Organizing Societies for War: The Process and Consequences of Societal Militarization*. Wesport: Praeger, 1994.

Tomaselli, K. ' "Adapt or Die": Militarization and the South African Media 1976–1982'. *Reality* 16 (1) January 1984:8–13.

Tomaselli, K and Louw, E. 'Militarization, Hegemony and the South African Media, 1976–1986'. Paper presented at the 19th Annual ASSA Conference, University of Durban Westville, July 1988.

White, L. 'Civic Virtue, Young Men, and the Family: Conscription in Rhodesia', *International Journal of African Historical Studies* 37 (1) 2004:103–21.

Transition and the TRC

Abrahamsen, T. and van der Merwe, H. *Reconciliation Through Amnesty? Amnesty Applicants' Views of the South African Truth and Reconciliation Commission*. Braamfontein: Centre for the Study of Violence and Reconciliation (CSVR), 2005. http://www.csvr.org.za/papers/paptahv/.

Adam, H. and Moodley, K. *The Negotiated Revolution: Society and Politics in Post-Apartheid Society*. Johannesburg: Jonathan Ball, 1993.

African National Congress. First Submission to the Truth and Reconciliation Commission, 1996. http://www.truth.org.za/submit/anc.htm/.

Bell, T. and Ntsebeza, D. *Unfinished Business. South Africa, Apartheid and Truth*. Cape Town: Redworks, 2001.

Boraine, A. *A Country Unmasked*. Cape Town: Oxford University Press, 2000.

Christie, K. *The South African Truth Commission*. Basingstoke: Macmillan, 2000.

Cilliers, J. and Reichardt, M., eds. *About Turn: The Transformation of the South African Military and Intelligence*. Halfway House: Institute for Defence Policy, 1995.

Cock, J. 'Rethinking Militarism in Post-Apartheid South Africa'. Working paper series no. 1. London: Crisis States Programme, Development Research Centre, 2004.

Colletta, N., Kostner, M. and Wiederhofer, I. *The Transition from War to Peace in Sub-Saharan Africa*. Washington, DC: World Bank, 1996.

Dobell, L. 'Silence in Context: Truth and/or Reconciliation in Namibia'. Review of *Namibia: The Wall of Silence* by Siegfried Groth. *Journal of Southern African Studies* 23 (2) 1997:371–82.

Frankel, P. *Soldiers in a Storm: The Armed Forces in South Africa's Democratic Transition*. Boulder, Colo.: Westview Press, 2000.

Foster, D., Haupt, P. and de Beer, M. *The Theatre of Violence: Narratives of Protagonists in the South African Conflict*. Cape Town: Institute for Justice and Reconciliation, 2005.

Griffith, A. *Conflict and Resolution: Peace-building Through the Ballot Box in Zimbabwe, Namibia and Cambodia*. Oxford: New Cherwell Press, 1998.

Groth, S. *Namibia: The Wall of Silence: The Dark Days of the Liberation Struggle*. Wuppertal: Peter Hammer, 1996.

Hayner, P. *Unspeakable Truths: Confronting State Terror and Atrocity*. New York: Routledge, 2001.

Hearn, R. *UN Peacekeeping in Action: the Namibian Experience*. Commack, NY: Nova Science Publishers, 1999.

Howard, L. 'UN Peace Implementation in Namibia: The Causes of Success'. *International Peacekeeping* 9 (1) 2002:99–132.

Hunter, G. 'Die Politiek der Erinerung und des Vergessens in Namibia seit der Staatlichen Unabhängigkeit'. PhD thesis, Albert-Ludwigs-Universität, Freiburg L.Br., 2005.

James, W. and van der Vijver, L., eds. *After the TRC: Reflections on Truth and Reconciliation in South Africa*. Cape Town: David Philip, 2000.

Khoisan, Z. *Jakaranda Time: An Investigator's View of South Africa's Truth and Reconciliation Commission.* Observatory: Garib Communications, 2001.

Krog, A. *Country of My Skull.* 2nd ed. Johannesburg: Random House, 2002.

Leys, C. and Mamdani, M. *Crises and Reconstruction – African Perspectives.* Uppsala: Nordiska Afrikainstitutet, 1997.

Lush, D. *Last Steps to Uhuru.* Windhoek: New Namibia Books, 1993.

Melber, H., ed. *Re-examining Liberation in Namibia: Political Culture since Independence.* Uppsala: Nordiska Afrikainstitutet, 2003.

Meredith, M. *Coming to Terms: South Africa's Search for Truth.* New York: Public Affairs, 1999.

Posel, D. and Simpson, G., eds. *Commissioning the Past.* Johannesburg: Witwatersrand University Press, 2003.

Preston, R. 'Integrating Fighters after War: Reflections on the Namibian experience'. *Journal of Southern African Studies* 23 (3) 1997:453–72.

Ross, F. C. *Bearing Witness: Women and the Truth and Reconciliation Commission in South Africa.* London: Pluto Press, 2003.

Rotberg, R. and Thompson, D., eds. *Truth v. Justice: The Morality of Truth Commissions.* Princeton: Princeton University Press, 2000.

Shea, D. C. *The South African Truth Commission: the Politics of Reconciliation.* Washington: United States Institute of Peace, 2000.

Simpson, G. ' "A Snake Gives Birth to a Snake": Politics and Crime in the Transition to Democracy in South Africa'. In *Justice Gained? Crime and Crime Control in South Africa's Transition*, edited by B. Dixon and E. van der Spuy. Cape Town: University of Cape Town Press, 2004.

Slabbert, F. van Zyl. *The Other Side of History: An Anecdotal Reflection on Political Transition in South Africa.* Cape Town: Jonathan Ball, 2006.

Sparks, A. *Beyond the Miracle: Inside the New South Africa.* Johannesburg: Jonathan Ball, 2003.

Stanley, E. 'Evaluating the Truth and Reconciliation Commission'. *Journal of Modern African Studies* 39 (3) 2001:525–46.

Truth and Reconciliation Commission of South Africa Report. 7 Volumes. Cape Town: Juta and Co. 1998–2003.

Tutu, D. *No Future Without Forgiving.* London: Rider, 1999.

Villa-Vicencio, C. and Verwoerd, W., eds. *Looking Back, Reaching Forward: Reflections on the Truth and Reconciliation of South Africa.* Cape Town: University of Cape Town Press, 2000.

Wilson, K. *The Politics of Truth and Reconciliation in South Africa.* Cambridge: Cambridge University Press, 2001.

Demobilisation, Trauma and Memory

Bracken, P. and Petty, C., eds. *Rethinking the Trauma of War.* London: Free Association Books, 1998.

Caruth, C. *Unclaimed Experience: Trauma, Narrative, and History.* Baltimore: Johns Hopkins University Press, 1996.

Caruth, C., ed. *Trauma: Explorations in Memory.* Baltimore: Johns Hopkins University Press, 1995.

Colletta, N., Kostner M. and Wiederhofer, I. 'The Demobilization and Reintegration of Ex-combatants in Ethiopia, Namibia, and Uganda'. World Bank Discussion Paper No. 331, Africa Technical Department Series, Case Studies in War-to-Peace Transition. Washington DC: World Bank, 1996.

Colvin, C. J. 'Performing the Signs of Injury: Critical Perspectives on Traumatic Storytelling after Apartheid'. PhD thesis, University of Virginia, 2004.

De Jong, J. T. V. M. 'Public Mental Health, Traumatic Stress and Human Rights Violations in Low-Income Countries: A Culturally Appropriate Model in Times of Conflict, Disaster and Peace'. In *Trauma, War, and Violence: Public Mental Health in Socio-Cultural Context*, edited by J. T. V. M. de Jong. New York: Kluwer Academic/Plenum Publishers, 2002.

Draper, C. 'Psychological Experiences of Military Conscription in South Africa during the 1970s and 1980s'. Honours thesis, University of Cape Town, 1999.

Draper, C. 'The Border and Beyond: An Analysis of the Post-Border War Discourses of Families of Ex-SADF Soldiers'. MA thesis, University of Cape Town, 2001.

Eagle, G. 'The Political Conundrums of Post-Traumatic Stress Disorder'. In *Psychopathology and Social Prejudice*, edited by D. Hook and G. Eagle. University of Cape Town Press: Cape Town, 2002.

Edkins, J. *Trauma and the Memory of Politics*. Cambridge: Cambridge University Press, 2003.

Eisenhart, R. W. ' "You Can't Hack it Little Girl": A Discussion of the Covert Psychological Agenda of Modern Combat Training'. *Journal of Social Issues* 31 (4) 1975:13–23.

Garkawe, S. 'Modern Victimology: Its Importance, Scope and Relationship with Criminology'. *Acta Criminologica* 14 (2) 2001:90–99.

Gear, S. *Wishing Us Away: Challenges Facing Ex-combatants in the New South Africa.* Violence and Transition Series No 8. Braamfontein: CSVR, 2002. http://www.csvr.org.za/papers/papvtp8a.htm.

_____. *Now That the War Is Over: Ex-combatants, Transition and the Question of Violence. A Literature Review.* Violence and Transition Series No. 9. Braamfontein: CSVR, 2005.   http://www.wits.ac.za/csvr/papers/papvtp9.htm.

Grossman, D. *On Killing: The Psychological Cost of Learning to Kill in War and Society.* Boston: Little Brown, 1996.

Hamber, B. 'The Burdens of Truth: An Evaluation of the Psychological Support Services and Initiatives Undertaken by the South African Truth and Reconciliation Commission'. *American Imago* 55 (1) 1998:9–28.Herman, J. *Trauma and Recovery: The Aftermath of Violence.* New York: Basic Books, 2001.

Honwana, A. 'The Collective Body: Challenging western concepts of trauma and healing'. *Track Two* 8 (1) 1999:30–5.

Lamb, G. 'From Military to Civilian Life: The Case of Retired Special Forces Operators'. *Track Two* 2 (1 & 2) 2003:37–60.

LeBeau, D. *An Investigation Into Namibian Ex-fighters Fifteen Years After Independence.* Windhoek: Peace Centre, 2005. http://www.peace.org.na/PEACE_Full%20Research%20Report.

Mashike, L. and Mokalobe, M. 'Reintegration into Civilian Life: The Case of Former MK and APLA Combatants'. *Track Two* 12 (1&2) 2003:6–36.

Mokalobe, M. *Demobilisation and Re-integration of Ex-combatants in South Africa.* A Defence & Development Project Publication. Group for Environmental Monitoring (GEM), 1999.

Motumi, T. and McKenzie, P. 'After the War: Demobilisation in South Africa'. In *From Defence to Development: Redirecting Military Resources in South Africa*, edited by J. Cock and P. McKenzie. Cape Town: David Philip, 1998:194–202.

Nuttall, S. and Coetzee, C., eds. *Negotiating the Past: The Making of Memory in South Africa.* Oxford: Oxford University Press, 1998.

Phakathi, S. and van der Merwe, H. *Survivors' Perspective on the TRC Amnesty Process.* Braamfontein: CSVR, 2005.

Preston, R., Solomon, C., Gleichmann, C., Tamas, K., LeBeau, D. and Pendleton, W. *The Integration of Returned Exiles, Former Combatants and Other War-Affected Namibians.* NISER Research Report No. 9, Windhoek: NISER/UNAM, 1993.

Sandler, D. 'The Psychological Experiences of White Conscripts in the Black Townships. In *War and Society: The Militarisation of South Africa*, edited by J. Cock and L. Nathan. Cape Town and Johannesburg: David Philip, 1989.

Shay, J. *Achilles in Vietnam: Combat Trauma and the Undoing of Character.* New York: Simon and Schuster, 1995.

Shay, J. *Odysseus in America: Combat Trauma and the Trials of Homecoming.* New York: Scribner, 2002.

Shephard, B. 'Still in Shock: Treating the Aftermath of Trauma'. *Times Literary Supplement.* July 16, 1999.

Shephard, B. *A War of Nerves.* London: Jonathan Cape, 2000.

Solomon, Z. *Combat Stress Reaction: The Enduring Toll of War.* New York: Plenum Press, 1993.

Tham, M. 'What Happened to the Boys on the Border?'. *SA City Life* March 1999:24–9, 50. http://www.geocities.com/odjobman/citylife. htm.

Van der Merwe, C. and Wolfswinkel, R., eds. *Telling Wounds: Narrative, Trauma and Memory, Working Through the South African Armed Conflicts of the Twentieth Century.* Proceedings of a conference held at the University of Cape Town, 3–5 July 2002.

Van der Merwe, H. and Smith, R. 'Ex-combatants as Peacebuilders: Opportunities and Challenges'. In *Struggles in Peacetime.* Amsterdam: Netherlands Institute for southern Africa, 2006.

Willet, S. 'Demilitarisation, Disarmament and Development in southern Africa'. *Review of African Political Economy* 25 (77) 1998:409–30.

The World Bank. 'Demobilisation and Reintegration of Military Personnel in Africa: The Evidence from Seven Country Case Studies'. In *Dismissed: Demobilisation and Reintegration of Former Combatants in Africa,* edited by J. Cilliers. Halfway House: Institute for Defence Policy, 1996.

Young, A. *The Harmony of Illusion: The Invention of Post-Traumatic Stress Disorder.* Princeton: Princeton University Press, 1997.

Representations of the War

Baines, G. 'South Africa's Vietnam? Literary History and Cultural Memory of the Border War'. *South African Historical Journal* 49, 2003:172–92.

Batley, K. 'The Language of Landscape: The Border Terrain in the Writing of South African Troops'. *English Usage in southern Africa* 23. Pretoria: Unisa Press, 1992:14–27.

_____. 'Socialized Warriors, Not Heroes: Anti-Heroic Subversion in Writing by South African Soldiers in the Angolan and South West African Border War'. Unpublished paper, n.d.

Bernard, R. 'The Smell of Apples, Moby Dick, and Apartheid Ideology'. *Modern Fiction Studies* 46 (1) 2000:207–26.

Craig, D. 'The Viewer as Conscript: Dynamic Struggles for Ideological Supremacy in South African Border War Film, 1971–1988'. MA thesis, University of Cape Town, 2003.

_____. 'Screening the Border War, 1971–88'. *Kleio* 36 2004:28–46.

Cronje, J. C. 'Die Grens as Meerduidige Gewe in die Kontemporêre Afrikaanse Prosa'. PhD thesis, University of Pretoria, 1989.

Drewett, M. 'Battling Over Borders: Narratives of Resistance to the South African Border War Voiced Through Popular Music'. *Social Dynamics* 29 (1) 2003:78–97

Erichsen, C. W. 'Shoot to Kill: Photographic Images in the Namibian Liberation/Bush War'. *Kronos* 27 2001:158—82.

Gordon, R. J. 'Marginalia on *Grensliteratuur*: Or How/Why Is Terror Culturally Constructed in Northern Namibia'. *Critical Arts* 5 (3) 1991:79–93.

Haarhoff, D. 'From Awol to Apocalypse: Border Fiction and Frontier Epilogue'. In *The Wild South-West: Frontier Myths and Metaphors in Literature Set in Namibia, 1760–1988* Johannesburg: Witwatersrand University Press, 1991:193–223.

Hayes, P. 'Vision and Violence: Photographies of War in southern Africa and Northern Namibia'. *Kronos* 27 2001:133–57.

Heyns, M. 'Fathers and Sons: Structures of Erotic Patriarchy in Afrikaans Writing of the Emergency'. *Ariel* 27 (January) 1996:81–103.

_____. 'The Whole Country's Truth: Confessions and Narrative in Recent White South African Writing'. *Modern Fiction Studies* 46 (1) 2000:42–66.

Joubert, E. 'Afrikaanse "Grensliteratuur". Die Nuwe Afrikaanse Oorlogliteratuur'. *Die Suid-Afrikaan* Herfs (Autumn) 1985:46–8.

Koornhof, H. E. 'Works of Friction: Current South African War Literature'. In *Society at War: The Militarisation of South Africa*, edited by J. Cock and L. Nathan. New York: St Martin's Press, 1989.

Kriel, S. E. 'Vertellersmanipulasie in die Afrikaanse Grensliteratuur'. MA thesis, University of South Africa, 1989.

Maugham-Brown, D. 'Images of War: Popular Fiction in English and the War on South Africa's Border', *The English Academy Review* 4 1987:53–66.

Popescu, M. 'Translations: Lenin's Statues, Post-communism and Post-apartheid'. *Yale Journal of Criticism* 16 (2) 2003:406–23.

Roberts, S. 'The Invisible Enemy: South African Border War Narratives'. In *Readings in the Post-colonial Literatures in English*. Atlanta: Rodopi, 1993:89–98.

Rogez, M. 'Variations on a Frontier: J. M. Coetzee's Novel *Dusklands* in Context'. *Commonwealth, Essays and Studies* 28 (1) 2005:40–52.

Roos, H. 'Die Grens is Inderdaad bereik'. *De Kat* 1(5) 1985:90–2.

_____. 'Van Twee Debute uit Twee Wêrelde'. *Standpunte* 184, 39 (4) 1986:45–59.

_____. 'Perspektief op die Afrikaanse Prosa van die Twintigste Eeu'. In *Perspektief en Profiel. 'n Afrikaanse Literatuurgeskiedenis. Deel 1*, edited by H. P. van Coller. Pretoria: Van Schaik, 1998.

_____. 'Die Afrikaanse Prosa 1997–2002'. In *Perspektief en Profiel. 'n Afrikaanse Literatuurgeskiedenis. Deel 3*, edited by H. P. van Coller. Pretoria: Van Schaik, 2006.

Rossouw, M. ''n Vernuwende Blik op die Verlede: Afrikaanse Oorlogsliteratuur as (Alternatiewe) Bron van Geskiedskrywing oor die Indiwidu'. In *Vernuwing in die Afrikaanse Letterkunde*, edited by M. Hattingh and H. Willemse. Belville: UWC, 1994.

Salter, D. 'Exile, Return and the New South Africa – An Interview With Anthony Akerman'. *South African Theatre Journal* 18 2004: 257–6.

Strachan, A. 'Die Suid-Afrikaanse Prosa Vandag: Ingesteldheid in die Tagtigerjare'. *Tydskrif vir Letterkunde* 23 (4) 1985:79–81.

Tomaselli, K. 'The Border War: Cinematic Reflections'. *Reality* 11 (5) Sept. 1979:16–17.

_____. *The Cinema of Apartheid: Race and Class in South African Film*. London: Routledge, 1989.

Tomaselli, K. and Carlean, K. *Boetie Gaan Border Toe*. http://www.und.ac.za/und/ccms/publications/articles/boetie.htm

Tomaselli, K. and van Zyl, M. 'Themes, Myths and Cultural Indicators: the Restructuring of Popular Memories'. In *Movies – Moguls – Mavericks: South African Cinema 1979–1991*, edited by J. Blignaut and M. Botha. Cape Town: Showdata, 1992.

Van Coller, H. P. 'Border/Frontier Literature'. In *Space and Boundaries in Literature: Proceedings of the 12th Congress of the International Comparative Literature Association, Munich 22–29 August, 1988*, edited by R. Bauer, D. W. Fokkema and M. de Graat. Munich: Ludicium, 1990:254–9.

Van Coller, H. P. 'Afrikaanse literatuur oor die gewapende konflik in Suid-Afrika sedert 1963. 'n Voorlopige Verslag'. *Acta Academica* 22(4) 1990:74–91.

_____. ''n Eietydse Afrikaanse Prosaterugblik op die Grensoorlog (Deel 1)'. *Tydskrif vir Letterkunde* 37(2) 1999:31–9.

_____. ''n Eietydse Afrikaanse Prosaterugblik op die Grensoorlog (Deel 2)'. *Tydskrif vir Letterkunde* 37 (3/4) 1999:22–30.

Van Huyssteen, K. 'Populêre vs. Grensverhale: Twee beelde van die Angolese oorlog (1966–1989). MA thesis, University of Cape Town, 1998.

Viljoen, H. M. 'Borders and their Transgression in Recent South African Fiction'. In *Space and Boundaries in Literature: Proceedings of the 12th Congress of the International Comparative Literature Association, Munich 22–29 August, 1988. Volume 2*, edited by D. W. Fokkema and R. Bauer. Munich: Iodicium Verlag, 1990:118–23.

Autobiographies, life histories and memoirs

Andrew, R. *Buried in the Sky*. Johannesburg: Penguin, 2001.

Angula, H. K. *The Two Thousand Days of Haimbodi Ya Haufiku*. Windhoek: Gamsberg MacMillan, 1990.

Becker, H. 'Junge Frau im Exil: Ellen Ndeshi Namhila – eine Autobiographie'. *Periplus. Jahrbuch für Aussereuropäische Geschichte* 2002:60–73.

Bernard, E. and Twala, M. *Mbokodo: Inside MK: A Soldier's Story*. Johannesburg: Jonathan Ball, 1994.

Bopela, T. and Luthuli, D. *Umkhonto we Sizwe: Fighting for a Divided People*. Alberton: Galago, 2005.

Feinstein, A. *In Conflict*. Windhoek: New Namibia Books, 1998.

Fowler, B. *Grensvegter? South African Army Psychologist*. Halifax: Sentinel Projects, 1996.

Fowler, B., ed. *Pro Patria*. Halifax: Sentinel Projects. 1995.

Holt, C. *At Thy Call We Did Not Falter*. Cape Town: Zebra Press, 2005.

Leys, C. and Brown, S., eds. *Histories of Namibia: Living Through the Liberation Struggle – Life Histories Told to Colin Leys and Susan Brown*. London: The Merlin Press, 2005.

Geldenhuys, J. *A General's Story: From an Era of War and Peace*. Johannesburg: Jonathan Ball, 1995.

Hiyalwa, K. *Meekulu's Children*. Windhoek: New Namibia Books: 2000.

Kapuscinski, R. *Another Day of life*. London: Penguin, 2001 [1987].

Kasrils, R. *Armed and Dangerous: My Undercover Struggle Against Apartheid*. Oxford: Heinemann Educational, 1993.

Malan, M. *My Lewe saam met die SA Weermag*. Pretoria: Protea Boekhuis, 2006.

McAleese, P. *No Mean Soldier: The Story of the Ultimate Professional Soldier in the SAS and Other Forces*. London: Orion, 1993.

McCallion, H. *Killing Zone: A Life in the Paras, Recces, the SAS and RUC*. London: Bloomsbury, 1996.

Namhila, E. N. *The Price of Freedom*. Windhoek: New Namibia Books, 1997.

_____. *Kaxumba ka Ndola: Man and Myth: The Biography of a Barefoot Soldier*. Basel: Basler Afrika Bibliographien, 2006.

Nathanael, K. P. *A Journey to Exile: The Story of a Namibian Freedom Fighter*. Aberystwyth: Sosiumi Press, 2002.

Nujoma, S. *Where Others Wavered. The Autobiography of Sam Nujoma*. London: Panaf Books, 2001.

Orford, M. and Becker, H. 'Homes and Exiles: Owambo Women's Literature'. In *Contested Landscapes. Landscapes of Movement and Exile*, edited by B. Bender and M. Winer. Oxford: Berg, 2001.

Paul, M. *Parabat*. Weltevredenpark: Covos Day Books, 2001.

Sampson, L. 'A Time to Mourn'. In *Now You've Gone 'n Killed Me: True Stories of Crime, Passion and Ballroom Dancing*. Cape Town: Oshun Books, 2005.

Shityuwete, H. *Never Follow the Wolf: The Autobiography of a Namibian Freedom Fighter*. London: Kliptown Books, 1990.

Soule, A., Dixon, G. and Richards, R. *The Wynand du Toit Story*. Johannesburg: Hans Strydom Publishers, 1987.

Thompson, J. H. *An Unpopular War: Voices of South African National Servicemen*. Cape Town: Zebra Press, 2006.

Van Wyk, A. *Honoris Crux: Ons Dapperers II*. Cape Town: Saayman and Weber, 1985.

Ya-Otto, J. with O. Gjerstad and M. Mercer. *Battlefront Namibia: An Autobiography*. New York: Heinemann, 1982.

Imaginative Literature (drama, fiction/faction, poetry, etc.

Akerman, A. *Somewhere on the Border: A Play*. Amsterdam: Thekwini Theatre, 1983.

Badcock, P. *Images of War*. Durban: Graham Publishing, 1981.

Bakkes, C. J. *Die Lang Pad van Stoffel Mathysen*. Cape Town: Human and Rousseau, 1998.

_____. *Moer toe die Vreemde in*. Cape Town: Human and Rousseau, 2001.

Behr, M. *Die Reuk van Appels*. Cape Town: Queillerie, 1993. Translated as *The Smell of Apples*. 2nd ed. London: Abacus, 1998.

Clark, G. *The Small Bees' Honey: Stories*. Fredonia, NY: White Pine Press, 1997.

Coetzee, J. M. *Dusklands*. 3rd ed. London: Vintage, 1998 [1978].

_____. *Waiting for the Barbarians*. 2nd edition. New York: Penguin, 1982.

Coetzee, J. *Verby die Wit Brug: Kortverhale oor die Grens*. Cape Town: Human & Rousseau, 1978.

Eprile, T. *The Persistence of Memory*. Cape Town: Double Storey Books, 2004.

Essex, P. *The Exile*. London: Collins, 1984.

Du Plessis, H. *Grensgeval*. Cape Town: Human & Rousseau, 1985 [1972].

Du Plessis, M. *A State of Fear*. Cape Town: David Philip, 1983.

_____. *Longlive!* Cape Town: David Philip, 1989.

Ferreira, J. *Sitate om 'n Rewolusie*. Cape Town: Human & Rousseau, 1985.

Galgut, D. 'The Clay Ox'. In *Small Circle of Beings*. 2nd ed. London: Abacus, 1990.

_____. *The Beautiful Screaming of Pigs*. 2nd ed. London: Abacus, 1992.

_____. *The Good Doctor*. London: Atlantic Books, 2003.

Gordimer, N. *Jump and Other Stories*. Cape Town: David Philip, 1991.

Haasbroek, P.J. 'Anatomieles' and 'Aardrykskundeles'. In *Roofvis*. Cape Town: Human & Rousseau, 1975.

_____. 'Afskeid'. In *Verby die Vlakte*. Cape Town: Human & Rousseau, 1982.

Havemann, E. *Bloodsong and Other Stories of South Africa*. London: Hamish Hamilton, 1988.

Herzberg, P. *The Dead Wait*. London: Oberon Books, 2003.

Huismans, E. *Berigte van Weerstand*. Johannesburg: Taurus, 1990.

Joubert, E. *Melk*. Cape Town: Tafelberg, 1980.

_____. *Die Laaste Sondag*. Cape Town: Tafelberg, 1983.

Jürgens, R. *Many Houses of Exile*. Johannesburg: Ravan Press, 2000.

Kalmer, H. *Die Waarheid en Ander Stories*. Johannesburg: Taurus, 1989.

Kellerman, G. *Wie de Hel Het Jou Vertel*. Cape Town: Tafelberg, 1988.

Kotze, M. *Engele op Stelte*. Cape Town: Tafelberg, 1990.

Krüger, L. *'n Basis Oorkant die Grens*. Cape Town: Tafelberg, 1984.

LeToit, A. 'Grenssoldaat in die Suburbs'. In *My Nooi is 'n Tikmasjien*. Cape Town: Perskor, 1983.

Maartens, M. *Verste Grens*. Pretoria: Folio, 1986.

McCallaghan, A. *Jimmy Goes to the Border*. Translated as *Jampie Gaan Grens toe*. Pretoria: Daan Retief, 1983.

Odendaal, W. *Keerkring*. Johannesburg: Perskor, 1977.

Opperman, D. *Môre is 'n Lang Dag*. Cape Town: Tafelberg, 1986.

Philips, A. *Die Verdwaalde Land*. Cape Town: Queillerie, 1994.

Pienaar, H. *Die Lewe Ondergronds*. Johannesburg: Taurus, 1986.

Pieterse, H. *Omdat Ons Alles Is*. Cape Town: Tafelberg, 1998.

Pieterse, P. *Dag van die Reuse*. 1985. Translated as *Day of the Giants*. Pretoria: De Jager-HAUM, 1986.

Prinsloo, K. 'Fighting for Peace'. In *Jonkmanskas*. Cape Town: Tafelberg, 1982.

_____ . *Die Hemel Help Ons*. Johannesburg: Taurus, 1988.

Rall, H. *In die Tyd van die Uil*. Cape Town: Human & Rousseau, 1989.

Retief, B. *Tweede Prys is 'n Houtjas: Grensstories uit Wamboland*. Pretoria: Van Schaik, 1983.

_____ . *Half Boom, Half Mens en Ander Grensstories*. Pretoria: Van Schaik, 1986.

Roodt, D. *Sonneskyn en Chevrolet*. Johannesburg: Taurus, 1980.

Roodt, P. H. *Afrika is Blou soos 'n Lemoen*. Cape Town: Tafelberg, 1990.

Ryger, R. R. [pseudo. Michael Green]. *Beertjie en sy Boytjies*. Johannesburg: Taurus, 1991.

Serote, M. W. *Scatter the Ashes and Go*. Braamfontein: Ravan Press, 2002.

Steyn, J. C. *Op Pad na die Grens*. Cape Town: Tafelberg, 1976.

Strachan, A. *'n Wêreld Sonder Grense*. Cape Town: Tafelberg, 1983.

_____ . *Die Jakkalsjagter*. Cape Town: Tafelberg, 1990.

_____ . *Die Werfbobbejaan*. Cape Town: Tafelberg, 1994.

_____ . *Agter die Suikergordyn*. Cape Town: Human & Rousseau, 1997.

Trump, M., ed. *Armed Vision: Afrikaans Writers in English*. Craighall: Ad. Donker, 1987.

Van der Merwe, P. *Vir 'n Lewe*. Johannesburg: Perskor, 1974.

Van der Vyver, M. *Die Dinge van 'n Kind*. Cape Town: Tafelberg, 1994.

Van Heerden, E. *My Kubaan*. Cape Town: Tafelberg, 1983.

_____ . *Om te Awol: 'n Roman*. Cape Town: Tafelberg, 1984.

_____ . *Casspirs en Camparis*. Cape Town: Tafelberg, 1991.

_____ . *Mad Dog and Other Stories*, translated by Catherine Knox. Cape Town: Africa South Writing, David Philip, 1992.

Van Pletzen, J. *Liewe Ma: Briefe aan Kleinjan*. Pretoria: Van der Walt, 1980.

Van Zyl, D. *Slagoffers*. Cape Town: Tafelberg, 2001.

Various. *Forces' Favourites*. Johannesburg: Taurus, 1987.

Various. *Ses Wenverhale*. Pretoria: Human and Rousseau, 1988.

Venter, A, J. *Soldier of Fortune*. London: W. H. Allen, 1980.

Venter, E. 'Die Donner in Boetiefanie se Kop'. In *Witblitz*. Johannesburg: Taurus, 1986.

_____ . *Ek Stamel Ek Sterwe*. Cape Town: Queillerie, 1996.

Vermeulen, J. *Die Laaste Dans*. Cape Town: Queillerie, 1998.

Viljoen, L. *Klaaglied vir Koos*. Johannesburg: Taurus, 1984.

Weideman, G. 'Gelykenis' and 'Nagelaat'. In *Tuin van Klip en Vuur*. Cape Town: Tafelberg, 1983.

Wilhelm, P. *LM and Other Stories*. Johannesburg: Ravan Press, 1975.

_____ . *At the End of a War*. Johannesburg: Ravan Press, 1981.

_____ . *Some Place in Africa*. Craighall: Ad. Donker, 1987.

Index